SOCIAL TORTURE

Human Rights in Context

Research on human rights, or social and political issues closely related to human rights, is nowadays carried out in many academic departments, from law to anthropology, from sociology to philosophy. Yet, there is surprisingly little communication amongst scholars working in these different disciplines, and research that takes more than one perspective into account is seldom encouraged. This new series aims to bridge the divide between the social sciences and the law in human rights scholarship.

Books published in this series will be based on original empirical investigations, innovative theoretical analyses or multidisciplinary research. They will be of interest to all those scholars who seek an audience beyond the confines of their academic subjects.

SOCIAL TORTURE

The Case of Northern Uganda
1986–2006

Chris Dolan

Berghahn Books
NEW YORK • OXFORD

First published in 2009 by
Berghahn Books
www.berghahnbooks.com

Library of Congress Cataloging-in-Publication Data

Dolan, Chris, 1966-
    Social torture : the case of northern Uganda, 1986–2006 / Chris Dolan.
        p. cm.
    Includes bibliographical references and index.
    ISBN 978-1-84545-565-1 (hbk) -- ISBN 978-0-85745-291-7 (pbk)
    1. Uganda—History—1979– 2. Uganda—Social conditions—20th century.
3. Uganda—Social conditions—21st century. 4. Torture—Social aspects—
Uganda. 5. Violence—Uganda—Psychological aspects. 6. Human rights—
Uganda. 7. Uganda—Politics and government—1979– 8. Lord's Resistance
Army. 9. Humanitarian intervention—Uganda. 10. War and society—
Uganda. I. Title.

    DT433.285.D65 2009
    967.6104'4—dc22

                                                                        2008052522

British Library Cataloguing in Publication Data

A catalogue record for this book is available from the British Library

Printed in the United States on acid-free paper

ISBN 978-1-84545-565-1 (hardback)
ISBN 978-0-85745-291-7 (paperback)

CONTENTS

FIGURES

Maps

Diagrams

Tables

FOREWORD

How to address a war as destructive and long-running as that in northern Uganda?
Chris Dolan's startling and original answer begins with the observation that this
has not really been a war at all. Though typically portrayed as a military contest
between the rebel Lord's Resistance Army and the government (the parties that
signed a fragile cessation of hostilities in 2006), the conflict is better understood
– Dolan argues – as a form of 'social torture' that has maintained local populations in a position of 'subordinate inclusion'.

The key instrument here has been the camps or 'protected villages' into which
hundreds of thousands of people were concentrated, ostensibly (as the name implies) for their own protection. In this sense, humanitarian agencies have been
complicit in 'social torture'. Dolan notes that a great many Ugandans used the
word 'torture' to describe their own experience in the war. Then he shows how
'in the name of protection, the population experienced on a mass scale the key
elements of torture, most notably violation, debilitation and humiliation'. A
sense of uncertainty and lack of control were pervasive. This in turn fed into
other kinds of violence, for example when some of the encamped men, having
lost their ability to protect and provide for their families, embraced more violent
definitions of masculinity and various forms of domestic abuse. Indeed, the persistence of violence more generally reflects, in part, the process by which victims
have frequently become perpetrators. Meanwhile, blame has been internalised
by the victims, not least by the Acholi ethnic group that has born the brunt of
the violence. In these circumstances, using the label 'post-traumatic stress disorder' becomes inappropriate since the trauma is ongoing: in fact, the label becomes part of 'a structure of denial'.

Dolan emphasises that the rebels could have been overcome with a coherent
military strategy that did not alienate large numbers of civilians. Government
depredations have been much less publicised or criticised than those by the rebels, and this is in line with many other contemporary conflicts where govern-

ment actors have been given an easier ride than rebels. Significantly, when peace
has appeared possible, government actors have frequently sabotaged it.

The point of all this prolonged and intense suffering, Dolan emphasises, was
not so much to defeat the insurgency as to send a sharp message to the Acholi
people as a whole as well as to other potentially restive social groups in other
parts of the country. In this sense, the study resonates with other cases – including wars in Sierra Leone and Guatemala as well as the 'war on terror': the war
is not simply against the 'named enemy' and the imprecision of the response to
insurgency and terror, whilst alienating many people, serves a function in sending a message of intimidation to a much wider group.

This study is sure to provoke controversy, and never more so than when the
author says of many donors, NGOs, multilateral organisations and churches:
'… like doctors in a torture situation, they appear to be there to ease the suffering of victims, but in reality they enable the process to be prolonged by keeping
the victim alive for further abuse.' Dolan is not pulling any punches. He draws
on very detailed local knowledge. It is a beautifully written book, disturbing
and revealing. The analysis is clear and incisive. And crucially, Dolan gives a
voice to some of those who have been silenced by the common view that war
is simply a contest between one 'side' and the other. I believe this book will become a landmark in the study of aid and conflict.

– David Keen

ACKNOWLEDGEMENTS

There is no way to adequately acknowledge the multiple ways in which different people at different times have contributed to this work over its long gestation, and not all of them can or would wish to be named. This includes many people in the 'protected villages' who welcomed me with the words 'go and tell people out there what is happening to us here'.

I thank all my colleagues in ACORD, particularly Rosalba Oywa for her moral and practical support, Sunday Abwola for our work with the military, Andrew Olweny for guiding me around Kitgum district, Okello Vincent for looking after me when I was sick, and Christopher Ojera for enabling the whole process. The late Hon. Omwony Ojok, then Minister for Northern Uganda, deserves special mention for numerous conversations and for his commitment to getting key issues debated in public. For his medical intervention, I am forever grateful to the late Dr Matthew Lukwiya of Lacor Hospital.

For bringing their personal skills, analyses and suggestions to bear on the research I am indebted to: Latim William, David Okiya, David Okello, Anna Okwir, Stella Atim, Jude Ogik, Ongwech Otim Patrick, Kinyera Fred, Alice Jean Ochola, Oola Timothy, Oola Ben, Okwera Santo, Oringa Robert, Opio James, Obol Alex Okot, Oyera Martin Leko, the late Odoch Athii, and the late Odoko Amida Martin of Odek. Most particularly I am grateful to my colleague and friend, Komakech Charles Okot. For sharing his experiences in the LRA, I shall always remember and respect the late Yakobo Engena. To Father Carlos, who has the courage to speak out, my thanks also.

For back-stopping me in various phases of the development of this book, many thanks to Judy el Bushra, Niki Kandirikirira, Jeff Handmaker, Judith Large, Barbara Harrell-Bond, Effie Voutira, Faisa Loyaan, Ian Swartz, Shamani Shikwambi, Vanessa Farr and my brother Phil Dolan. All deserve special mention, as does Thi Minh Ngo for both moral and practical support. I owe special intellectual debts to David Keen and Tim Allen, both of whom stayed with this project for the long haul and encouraged me to publish, and to John Cameron and Tania Kaiser who engaged so rigorously and unstintingly with this work.

ABBREVIATIONS

ACF	Action Contre la Faim
AAH	Action Against Hunger
ARLPI	Acholi Religious Leaders Peace Initiative
AVSI	Associazione Volontari per il Servizio Internazionale
CDC	Centre for Disease Control
CO	Commanding Officer
CRS	Catholic Relief Services
DEO	District Education Office
EU	European Union
FEWS	Famine Early Warning System
GISO	Gombolola Internal Security Operative
GoS	Government of Sudan
GoU	Government of Uganda
HSM	Holy Spirit Movement
HURIFO	Human Rights Focus
HURIPEC	Human Rights and Peace Centre
ICRC	International Committee of the Red Cross
IGAD	Inter-Governmental Authority on Development
IGO	Inter-Governmental Organisation
IRIN	Integrated Regional Information Network
INGO	International Non-Governmental Organisation
KICWA	Kitgum Concerned Women's Association
LC	Local Council/Councillor

LRA	Lord's Resistance Army
LRM	Lord's Resistance Movement
MSF	Médecins Sans Frontières
MUAC	Middle Upper Arm Circumference
NGO	Non-Governmental Organisation
NRA	National Resistance Army
NRM	National Resistance Movement
NURP	Northern Uganda Reconstruction Programme
OPM	Office of the Prime Minister
PRO	Public Relations Officer (UPDF)
PRRO	Protracted Relief and Recovery Operation
PTSD	Post-Traumatic Stress Disorder
RPF	Rwandan Patriotic Front
SPLA	Sudanese People's Liberation Army
SPLM	Sudanese People's Liberation Movement
SCF	Save the Children Fund
UHRC	Ugandan Human Rights Commission
UNDP	United Nations Development Programme
UNDMT	United Nations Disaster Management Team
UNHCR	United Nations High Commissioner for Refugees
UNHCU	United Nations Humanitarian Co-ordination Unit
UNICEF	United Nations Children's Fund
UNLA	Uganda National Liberation Army
UNOCHA	United Nations Office for Co-ordination of Humanitarian Affairs
UPC	Uganda People's Congress
UPDA	Uganda People's Democratic Army
UPDF	Uganda People's Defence Force
USAID	United States Agency for International Development
WFP	World Food Program
WNBF	West Nile Bank Front

Map of 'Protected Villages' in which Fieldwork Was Conducted

Map showing Gulu, Kitgum, Nimule towns and the 'protected villages', in which the majority of fieldwork was conducted: Atiak Biabia, Acet, Anaka, Awer, Awere, Awac, Cwero, Odek, Pabo, Palaro.

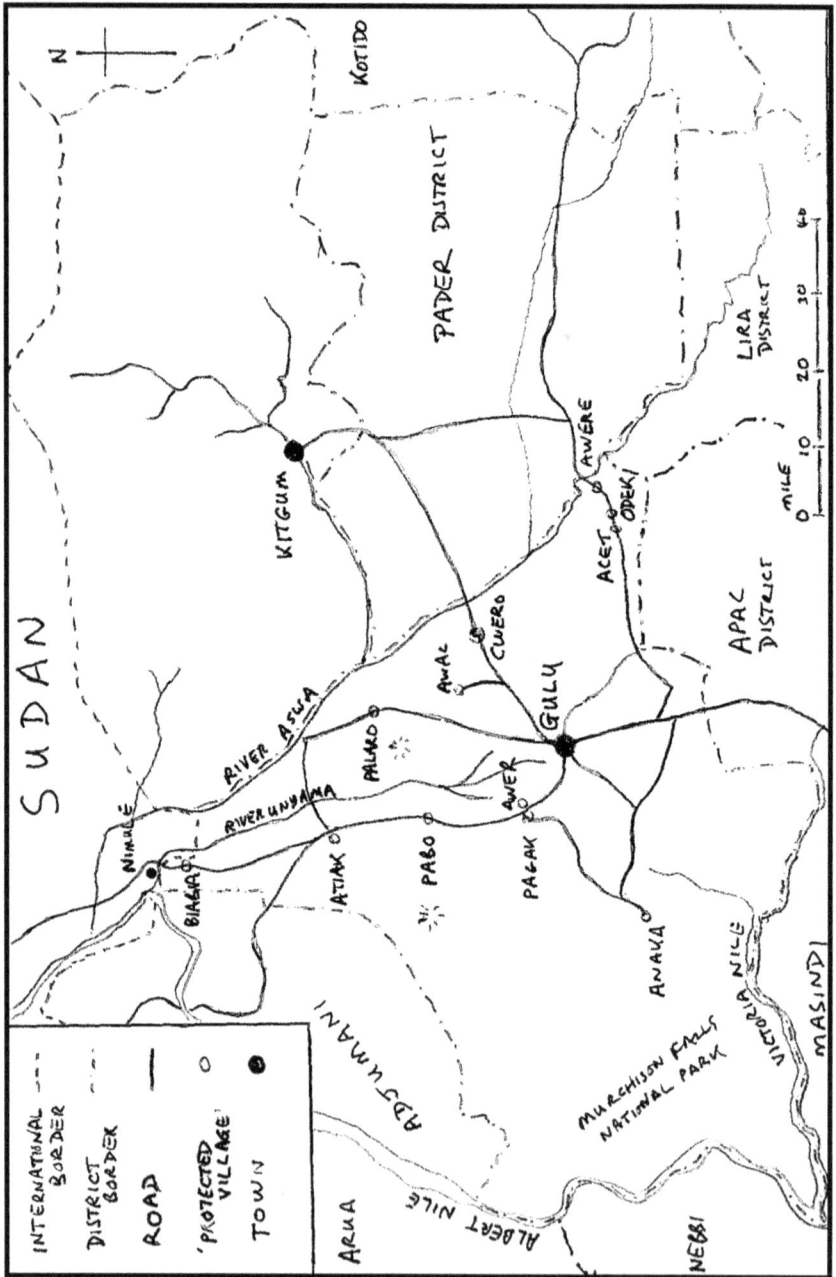

1

INTRODUCTION

Why, when almost every concerned party says they wish it would end, does a situation of suffering such as that in northern Uganda continue and indeed worsen? When I first went to northern Uganda in 1998 it was already a pertinent question; by 2006, with ninety per cent of the population internally displaced or in exile, further thousands raped, killed or forcibly abducted, and the economy in tatters, it was still more so. Even as the two ostensible parties to the conflict, the Lord's Resistance Army (LRA) and the Government of Uganda (GoU), stated their commitment to peace during two years of talks in the southern Sudanese town of Juba (2006–2008), the question and its answer remained fundamentally important. For the legacy of two decades of violence and violation in northern Uganda is well beyond the scope of any peace deal, not least because many of the actors are not even visible in the talks. Insofar as the situation in northern Uganda exemplifies the 'new wars' of the post-cold war era, the question and its answer should also have resonance in a number of other situations whose persistence taxes both the intellect and the imagination.

Contrary to popular presentations of the situation as being primarily an internal war between the LRA and the Government of Uganda, this book makes the case that it is instead a form of mass torture, whose principal victims are the population within the 'war zone', and whose ultimate function is the subordinate inclusion of the population in northern Uganda. The so-called 'protected villages' for the internally displaced are primary sites of this process, which I shall call Social Torture, as evidenced in widespread violation, dread, disorientation, dependency, debilitation and humiliation, all of which are tactics and symptoms typical of torture, but perpetrated on a mass rather than individual scale.

In this interpretation visible perpetrators include the Government and LRA, but a range of less visible actors are also involved, not least the donor governments, multi-lateral organisations, churches and NGOs. In many instances these can be regarded as complicit bystanders; like doctors in a torture situation, they appear to be there to ease the suffering of victims, but in reality they enable the process to be prolonged by keeping the victim alive for further abuse. Doing this serves a number of inter-linked economic, political and psychological functions for perpetrators and bystanders alike, and is underpinned by both psychological and discursive processes of justification, the most important of which is the idea that this situation is indeed a 'war' between the LRA and the Government. Furthermore, by virtue of the scale at which it operates, Social Torture becomes in several senses self-perpetuating and time-indifferent.

In short, whereas torture is generally seen as a tactic with which to prosecute war, in this situation war is being used as the guise under which to perpetrate social torture. Once this reversal of the relationship between means and end is clear it also becomes much clearer why the situation continues: steps to end the war focused on dealing with the LRA through negotiations or military means are necessary but not enough. What is also needed are interventions which address the multiple dimensions of social torture. These include addressing political and economic inequities, governmental impunity and harmful psycho-social dynamics. As those who in principle have the most power to make these changes are implicated in the social torture themselves, the focus has to shift from the intentions of visible perpetrators to the responsibilities of a far wider range of actors.

The Mainstream Discourse of Today's Wars

Arriving at this thesis was not a linear process. Rather it involved an iterative to- and fro- between review of academic literature, policy positions, media coverage, and field-work findings. In the course of this I came to see the literature in terms of two broad types; that which contributes to what I would characterise as the mainstream discourse of today's wars (which in turn informs the majority of policy and media coverage), and that which offers the building blocks of a counter-narrative. The mainstream discourse argues that post-Cold War conflicts are internal and bi-partisan in nature, as well as apolitical and at times irrational, and therefore posits them as detached from wider systemic dynamics at the international level.

An example from the 1990s of this preoccupation with the internal is Ramsbotham and Woodhouse's concept of 'International Social Conflicts' (ISCs), situations

> which are neither inter-state conflicts ... nor contained within the resources of domestic conflict management ... There are many other terms for this level of conflict, most commonly 'internal conflict' or 'civil war', but these do not capture the further twin characteristics of ISCs: a) that they are rooted in relations between communal groups within state borders (the 'social' component) and b) that they have broken out of the domestic arena and become a crisis for the state, thereby automatically involving the wider society of states (the 'international' component) (1996: 87).

The preoccupation with the internal also pervades the humanitarian sector, which objectifies such situations through terms such as 'complex emergencies', 'complex humanitarian emergencies' or even 'complex political emergencies' (CPEs). These are all terms which entered into humanitarian vocabulary following the creation of a safe haven with military peacekeepers in northern Iraq,[1] an event which marked a dramatic shift in the nature of UN interventions in a range of situations globally (Ramsbotham and Woodhouse 1996: 70).

Notwithstanding references to conflicts being rooted in 'relations between communal groups', the mainstream discourse simply adapts 'the Clausewitzian analysis of inter-state wars' (Keen 2005: 2) to an intra-state context, but sustains the same basic model of two-party wars which is so deeply embedded in the field of international relations and the related practical fields of mediation and conflict resolution (see, for example, Kelman 1992, Crocker 1999, 2001). In this model third parties are only written into the picture in a responsive capacity. Even in interventions based on a social-psychological perspective 'that sees conflict at least partly and at times predominantly as a subjective social process' (e.g. Fisher and Keashly 1996), the assumption prevails that third parties come in solely to help the conflicting parties sort out their internal muddle and play no generative role in creating that muddle.

The internal model of war is underpinned by two alternative explanations of what motivates the people who are visibly involved. Both of these largely exclude the possibility of political explanations. One is the substantial body of literature which regards such 'internal' conflicts as based on economic rationales. The perspective that simple 'greed' is what motivates people (more specifically, *rebels*), has tended to predominate, and is forcefully articulated by Collier (2000). A more nuanced economic perspective is provided by Stewart (2002), who explores the role of horizontal economic inequalities in creating a sense of grievance. Berdal and Malone (2000) argue that, although 'the presence of economic motives and commercial agendas in wars is not so much a new phenomenon as a familiar theme', the economic dimensions of civil conflict have not in fact been given sufficiently systematic attention; they therefore seek to explore how economic motivations, violence and destitution all reinforce one another and give rise to 'a particular dynamic of conflict' (Berdal and Malone, 2000; 1–2).

Another branch of the literature significantly discounts the existence of *any* rationale with which to engage, whether political or economic, and also presumes that today's conflicts are internal. This position has variously been termed the 'New Barbarism thesis' (Richards 1996: xiii) and the 'Coming Anarchy' school' (Keen 2005: 3). In his 1994 piece, *The Coming Anarchy*, Robert Kaplan manages to situate the problem of today's conflicts squarely within countries in which he sees a breakdown of the state monopoly of violence, the growth of informal and parallel economies and a thinning down of civil order, but also to suggest what the consequences would be for zones of order if such anarchy were to be allowed to spill over. Keegan, a military historian with a similarly high profile, also tends to present today's conflicts as internal, arising from 'tribal' enmities and irrational primitivism which had been long-suppressed during the Cold War. He argues that 'many of the newer states, particularly those brought into being by the dissolution of European empires, have been unable to liberate themselves from the grip of internal hostilities that pre-date colonisation ...' (1998, 66). The tactics of such internal wars are said to 'resemble those of the surviving Stone Age peoples of the world's remote regions, at their most savage' (idem, 68).

Although some have argued that such conflicts are best left to burn themselves out (e.g. Luttwak's provocative article *Give War a Chance* (1999)), the more usual view has been that solutions are to be found through third party interventions, such as those suggested by Keegan himself, namely 'progress in aid and development programmes allied to stronger alliances with other nations which strengthen the economic structures of such states and help to neutralise the political insecurities against which their governments constantly battle' (Keegan, 1998; 73). As such, fear of the spill-over of 'anarchy' is closely linked to a containment agenda.

As a whole, this body of literature presents war as a series of dichotomised possibilities; it is either externally or internally driven, it is either rational or irrational, and it is driven by either grievance or greed. When this lens is applied to today's wars it tends to find them as internal, irrational and driven primarily by greed – characteristics encapsulated in the 'New Barbarism' argument. These characteristics – or perhaps more accurately, characterisations – are visibly reflected in most presentations of the situation in northern Uganda. Often said to be a war of the LRA against its own people, and thus internal, fundamentally irrational, and without a cause beyond enjoying the fruits of its looting and pillaging, the situation is also presented as a two-party conflict, with the LRA and Government of Uganda as the key protagonists, and the Acholi people as the chief victim. LRA depredations receive considerably more attention than Government ones; indeed the Government is nearly always presented as intervening to protect its own citizens in response to these depredations. In this picture, NGOs, UN, donors, churches and media are all expressly viewed as external. They are presented (and view themselves), as responding to, rather than having any generative role in, the situation.

Building Blocks of a Counter-Narrative

Such interpretations of today's wars in general and of the situation in northern Uganda in particular, have a practical and political weight wholly disproportionate to their analytical and descriptive value. As Keen scathingly argues, chaos theories are the product of 'chaotic analysts', which unfortunately also serve the interests of 'international actors who might wish to justify parsimony and inaction' (Keen 2005: 4). In this respect, helpful parallels and connections can be drawn between the discourse on 'internal' wars outlined above, and Abrahamsen's analysis of discourses of development, and their role in sustaining particular external interests.

At the heart of Abrahamsen's argument lies the observation that the western discourse on good governance and democracy coincides with the end of the Cold War and the need to find alternative mechanisms and legitimations for implementing a neo-liberal economic agenda driven by the West (Abrahamsen

2000; 25–45). She notes that it constructs whole areas of the globe 'as objects to be reformed rather than as subjects with a history and with their own power to transform the world and react to changing circumstances' (idem 2000; 20). Effectively this discourse 'is implicated in power relationships and serves to perpetuate international relations of dominance and subordination' (idem, viii). Key to the discourses' success is that they do 'not take sufficient account of the interconnectedness of states and political forces in the global era, and that they maintain a strict internal/external dichotomy that is no longer an accurate or useful description of the world' (idem 2000: xi). In short, Abrahamsen identifies both the function (subordination) and the mechanism (partial representation and over-simplified dichotomies) of public discourses.

Many aspects of this analysis can also be applied to the literature on internal war outlined above. By asserting one primary motivation for war, the literature plays havoc with the subjectivities of people in war, indeed it silences them.[2] By focusing attention on some actors and diverting it from others it simultaneously discounts the importance of historical process and the possibility of 'external' involvement in and responsibility for the state of affairs in a given place. Its function is thus exculpatory (in that it casts silence on the sins of the past and present), justificatory (in that it justifies particular patterns of intervention), and politically oppressive (in that subjectivities are silenced, knowledge gaps created, and wars depoliticised). In short, the discourse on internal war (and the representations of northern Uganda which reflect it) has similar mechanisms and functions to those on good governance, democracy and development. Indeed it can be regarded as an extension of them.

To create a resilient counter-narrative to such mainstream discourses requires a firm empirical basis. This has been amply demonstrated by a number of fine-grained context-based analyses of particular conflict-related situations. The importance of external involvement in the dynamics of supposedly internal situations resonates throughout these readings, whether in the political economies of assistance (Harrell-Bond 1986, Keen 1994, De Waal 1997) and war (Berdal and Malone, 2000), or in the de facto cultural and political connections between very local dynamics and wider social and political processes (Girling 1960, Allen 1991, 1994, 1998, Richards 1996, Behrend 1999, Finnström 2003, Keen 2005). Work on the constructed nature of war and ethnicity (Jabri 1996, Turton 1997), as well as broader ranging political economy analyses linking 'new wars' with processes of globalisation (Kaldor, 2001) and global governance (Duffield, 2001) offer further support for such perspectives.

From a more psychological angle, Zur's work on Guatemala (1993, 1998), and Mamdani's work on the genocide in Rwanda in which he highlights the importance of understanding the complex interplay between a 'victim-consciousness' and a perpetrator role (1997b), offer important analyses of how ordinary people are drawn into and contribute to the dynamics of a conflict situation. Mamdani's work on the truth and reconciliation processes in South Africa also suggests the imperative of considering not just the visible perpetrators, but also the indirect beneficiaries of their acts (1997a, 1997b).

Gilligan, having spent twenty-five years working in and observing the American penal system, combines a psychoanalytical perspective with a public health agenda and a socio-political analysis to create an epidemiology of violence. He isolates humiliation and shame – notably in relation to men's sense of their masculinity – as the 'pathogens' causing violence. He suggests that perpetrators of violence have themselves generally been the victims of extreme forms of physical and psychological violence which weaken their self-worth and make them vulnerable to processes of shaming and humiliation. He argues that a penal system which punishes the violence born of humiliation by systematically ensuring the perpetrators are subjected to further humiliation and shame might appear self-defeating and counter-productive, but is in fact the result of deliberate choices made by the ruling classes. The latter wish to ensure that the lower classes (both black and white) turn the shame-induced violence of their social position against themselves and each other rather than against the ruling classes (Gilligan, 2000). While Gilligan's work is not directly addressed at the 'new wars', the importance of humiliation in the perpetuation of conflict – and linked to that, the withholding of dignity and recognition – is increasingly recognised (see, for example, Keen, 2005), though rarely addressed in policy or practice.

A reading of this more empirically based literature highlights the way in which reductive accounts draw attention away from the systemic dimensions and linkages of today's conflicts and violence, and the consequent involvement of multiple actors at all levels. It reinforces the importance of building a picture both of local involvement, and of the true extent of external involvement in supposedly internal dynamics. There is considerable power in the different ways in which Mamdani, Zur and Gilligan are all able to integrate historical, economic, political and socio-psychological factors into their analyses. These readings also underline the value of taking a 'bottom up' starting point which ensures that the subjectivities which are silenced by mainstream discourses are heard and inform the counter-narrative.

It was such 'bottom up' views which ultimately prompted me to explore the relationships between the situation in northern Uganda and the literature on torture. I was repeatedly struck while working there by how often people referred to what was happening to them as 'torture', and as a form of persecution. Many would describe the 'protected villages' as 'concentration camps', and even talk of a 'genocide'. Equally, it was very common for people to say 'we are all traumatised', and this language of 'trauma' had become common currency by the time I was in northern Uganda. UNOCHA, for example, argued that the LRA's practice of abduction had 'profoundly traumatized the entire population' (Weeks, 2002: 28), and a consultancy report for NURP II reported that:

> ... the districts of Gulu and Kitgum were found to be the most affected ... It was established that there was only a variation of intensity, otherwise in one way or the other, everybody was found to be traumatised (COWI, 1999; 68).

Initially I dismissed such usages, thinking they were due to English being a second language, or to rhetorical exaggeration in the interests of making a political point. After all, there is nothing unusual about the use of protected villages as a counter-insurgency strategy. Similar strategies were used by the Sandinistas in the mountains of northern Nicaragua, by FRELIMO in the fight against RE-NAMO in Mozambique, and perhaps most uncomfortably as a point of comparison, by Ian Smith in Rhodesia.[3] Moreover, when I asked what people meant by this use of 'torture', it turned out to refer to anything from various degrees of beating through being unlawfully detained under gruelling circumstances, to extreme violations such as the mutilations of the LRA. Effectively a whole range of abusive behaviours were being put under the rubric of torture. There seemed little connection between this broad picture of torture, much of which could be seen happening to the population at large in their daily lives, and the more conventional notions of torture as something which sets out to destroy targeted individuals in places well-hidden from the public gaze. And, given that there were instances of abuse which clearly did qualify as torture,[4] it seemed there was a danger of diluting the force of the term by seeking to apply it more broadly.

Article 1 of *The Convention against Torture and Other Cruel, Inhuman or Degrading Treatment or Punishment,* defines torture as

> any act by which severe pain or suffering, whether physical or mental, is intentionally inflicted on a person for such purposes as obtaining from him or a third person information or a confession, punishing him for an act he or a third person has committed or is suspected of having committed, or intimidating or coercing him or a third person, or for any reason based on discrimination of any kind, when such pain or suffering is inflicted by or at the instigation of or with the consent or acquiescence of a public official or other person acting in an official capacity.[5]

Although this definition puts an explicit emphasis on the intentionality of perpetrators, and appears to narrow the possible range of perpetrators to public officials or other persons acting in official capacity, it is in many other respects a broad and wide-reaching one. The phrase 'for such purposes as' suggests that while obtaining information, punishment, intimidation and coercion are major objectives of torture, they are not exclusive. The inclusion of suffering 'for any reason based on discrimination of any kind' makes the possibilities even broader. And while Article 1 talks of pain or suffering inflicted 'on a person' by 'a public official or other person acting in an official capacity', in other words implies a focus on individuals, Article 3 of the Convention, which prohibits the *refoulement* of an asylum seeker 'where there are substantial grounds for believing that he would be in danger of being subjected to torture', defines substantial grounds as including 'flagrant or *mass* violations of human rights' (emphasis added).

I therefore increasingly wondered if there were indeed parallels to be drawn between what happens to individuals in torture chambers and what was happening to the population living in the war zone, especially but not exclusively to those people living in the 'protected villages'. There is nothing in the convention definition which excludes the mass violations of human rights entailed in the forcible displacement of populations, or in the failure to provide physical security and access to basic education and health care, as described in Chapter 5. If these failings could potentially be considered a form of torture, this raised questions around who the actors might be, and how they could have organised and legitimised torture on such a grand scale. It also began to suggest that the protected villages, despite failing in the stated objectives of protection of civilians and counter-insurgency, might be serving a function after all.

When I then turned to the literature on torture I found analyses which, rather than privileging individual intention above all else, incorporated and integrated multiple elements, not least the impacts on victims but also the multiple actors and their roles, the benefits and functions of torture, and the mechanisms used to justify it. As such there were direct conceptual links to some of the 'building blocks' of a counter-narrative outlined above, indicating that a non-legal model of torture could and should incorporate elements from the existing literature on today's wars, not least considerations of political economy, social psychology, and discourse analysis.

In seeking to create a counter-narrative which would make explicit these linkages I initially focused on what the literature suggested about the following four elements: impacts of torture, actors, benefits and functions, and justificatory mechanisms.

Impacts

As Melamed et al. point out (1990), 'Torture is defined not only by the acts committed, but also by the individual's response to these acts'. In other words, it is not always necessary to know who the torturer was, how exactly they did it, or what their precise intentions were, in order to be able to diagnose a victim of torture. In asylum determination procedures, for example, medical examination to corroborate the claims of torture victims may count for more than the account of torture itself.

Diagram 1.1 Key Elements in Identifying Torture

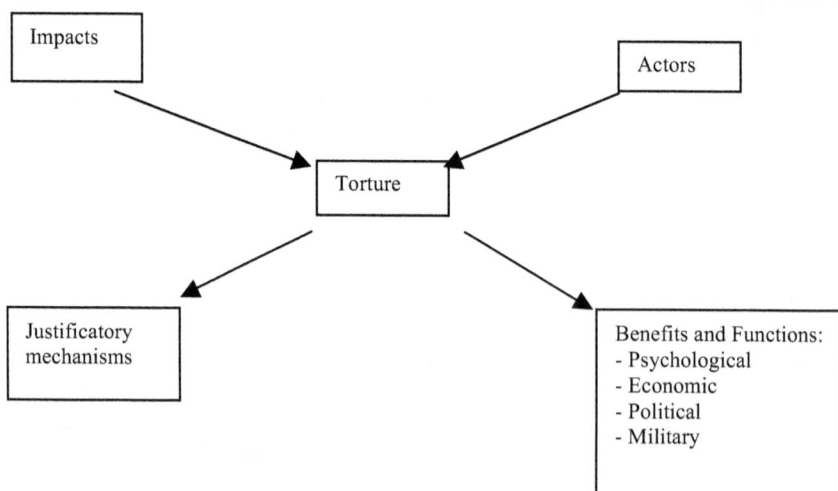

Some of the key states to be found in victims of torture, as summarised by Suedfeld (1990: 3), include debilitation, dependency, dread and disorientation.

Debilitation is the result of the captor deliberately inducing physical and mental weakness. The elements identified by Suedfeld as key to debilitating torture victims are 'Hunger, fatigue, lack of medical attention, lack of shelter from the elements, lack of sleep, beatings'. Linked to debilitation is a strong element of enforced dependency, both material and psychological. The former arises when victims are unable to meet their own needs, and Suedfeld describes how psychological dependency is created when 'friendships and lines of authority among prisoners are destroyed, and the prisoner is stripped of status and dignity'. Dread is described by Suedfeld as the state of mind induced in a victim who is kept 'in a constant state of fear and anxiety', and a key tactic in this is 'keeping the prisoner in doubt as to when if ever he or she will be released'. Disorientation is induced by removing the victim's sense of control by making events unpredictable and incomprehensible, a process which seriously hinders the victims' capacity to develop coping mechanisms (Suedfeld 1990, Melamed et al. 1990: 16). The main tactic to achieve this is to change the treatment of the victim 'in unpredictable fashion' (Suedfeld, 1990:3).

While debilitation, dependency, dread and disorientation are the states which torturers seek to induce, evidence of torture can also be found in symptoms which are less visibly linked to the act of torture itself. Thus victims may continue to exhibit symptoms related to their experiences long after the acts of torture are over. These would normally fall under the rubric of Post-Traumatic Stress Disorder (PTSD), defined as the development of 'characteristic symptoms following a psychologically traumatic event that is generally outside the range of usual human experience'.[6] Symptoms of PTSD which are particularly prevalent in torture victims include 'psychic numbing or emotional anaesthesia. There is loss of ability to feel close; frequently, intimacy and sexuality are not possible' (Melamed et al. 1990: 15). Studies such as those of Peterson and Seligman (1983) show that the 'uncontrollability of the onset and termination of victimization … best explains why some victims become numb and passive. They [Peterson and Seligman] believe that because the onset is unpredictable and the event inescapable, coping attempts are futile. Low self-esteem and self-blame are associated with this state' (Melamed et al. 1990: 15–16).

Along with victims of abuse and oppression more broadly, torture victims often get blamed by others for their own misfortunes, and tend to search for their own responsibility (i.e. blame themselves) for what happened to them.

Actors

Having once identified various physical and psychological states and behaviours as possible impacts of torture, it is necessary to read backwards to find the actors involved. Much of the literature on torture and genocide draws on a model of perpetrators, bystanders and victims. The term perpetrator, as used by Staub, encompasses not only 'the torturers themselves, but also those who are in charge of a system which perpetrates torture.' (Staub 1990:106).

The bystander group includes all those who either observe directly or at least are aware that torture is being committed, but take no action to prevent or stop it, despite having some potential to do so. This inaction may be because they are intimidated as a result of being aware of the torture of others, or because they share some of the perpetrator group's values (Staub 1990, 1995, Hilberg 1992). Staub distinguishes 'internal' bystanders who are individual 'members of society who are neither victims nor part of the perpetrator group', from 'external' bystanders whom he considers to be 'other nations' who fit into an international relations model of nations as metaphorical individuals in a community of states.

Closer scrutiny of the relationship between the actions of perpetrators and those of ostensibly passive bystanders suggests that over time the distinction between the two can break down. As Staub himself points out, using the example of the doctors who help to keep torture victims alive, it is disturbingly easy for actors to shift between bystander and perpetrator positions: 'although their participation may be seemingly humane, it usually serves the perpetrators not the victims – by helping to revive or keep alive victims for more torture or selecting methods of torture to minimize visible signs' (Staub 1990: 68).

Futhermore, there is reason to suppose that some victims become perpetrators themselves – possibly against a less powerful third party – as a means of dealing with their situation. Gilligan, for example, argues that 'The violent criminals I have known have been objects of violence from early childhood' (Gilligan, 2000: 45). As such, in analysing torture, it is necessary to hold two viewpoints simultaneously; on the one hand the snapshot or cross-sectional view, in which the perpetrator-bystander-victim distinctions are clear, on the other the filmed or longitudinal view over time, in which individuals shift between roles or indeed experience several roles simultaneously.

Benefits and Functions

Staub makes a convincing case that, alongside its overt functions of coercing direct victims into particular behaviours (e.g. yielding a confession, handing over information about 'rebel co-ordinators'), torture serves a psychological function for its perpetrators. He argues that rich and poor alike – when they experience 'difficult conditions of life' such as 'severe economic problems, persistent and intense political conflict, and rapid, substantial social change' – are liable to develop certain psychological needs. These include the need for a sense of security, a sense of 'positive identity' (both individual and group), 'a meaningful comprehension of reality, a sense of how the world is ordered and of one's place in it', and also a 'connection to others'. Turning against another group is one of a number of processes whereby groups will seek to meet these psychological needs rather than addressing the actual difficulties they face. Within this, scapegoating, victimisation, devaluation and dehumanisation of others all help people to recover a positive sense of self, and adherence to ideologies (whether religious or secular) helps to create a sense of how the world is ordered.

Devaluation and dehumanisation can be achieved in many ways. In Kelman's analysis, torturers label their victims as 'terrorists, insurgents, or dissidents who endanger the state' as a part of the dehumanisation process. To move from this kind of dehumanisation of a limited number of individuals to dehumanisation of an entire social group is relatively easy, as demonstrated by the post-September 11 2001 blurring of distinctions between the categories 'terrorists' and 'Muslims' by western governments and media. This is the more so if individuals behave in ways which appear to confirm the negative qualities already ascribed to the social group from which they stem. Once catalysed, the processes of devaluation and dehumanisation can quickly acquire their own momentum. As Staub points out, torture often renders victims 'bloody, dirty, undignified' such that 'they can easily be seen as less than human' – and as Gilligan establishes, when victims become perpetrators the fact they were once victims is forgotten, resulting in interventions focused on punishment rather than rehabilitation or reintegration.

Such processes for devaluing others and creating a sense of order are more easily catalysed where there is already a 'history of devaluation of a group of people', a 'monolithic rather than a pluralistic society', a cultural concept which has been frustrated, 'strong respect for and a tendency to obey authority', a history of aggression in which violence is normalised and made acceptable, and an 'ideology of antagonism' (Staub 1990, 1995: 101–103).

Alongside the military and psychological functions it is possible to identify political and economic ones. The links between the psychological and political ones are likely to be intimate in a situation such as Uganda; it seems probable that with the colonial legacy still within living memory, and with neo-colonial forms of control being exercised through concepts of 'modernisation', 'democracy', 'good governance' and 'structural adjustment', the psychological need for a strong sense of positive identity will be considerable. Achieving this is likely to entail, through devaluation, the subordination of minority groups, and, through the signals this sends, the control of the wider society as a whole.

The economic benefits arising from social torture scenarios, I would suggest, are likely to resemble those emerging in other situations of widespread suffering, as identified by Keen in *The Benefits of Famine* (1994); they could include the establishment of activities such as humanitarian relief interventions, the establishment of niche activities focused on identifiable 'victims' such as child soldiers, and the exploitation of captive markets by particular individuals and groups. The management of these in turn is liable to be linked to political functions, such as using economic rewards to buy off dissidents and potential critics.

Justifications

While the multiple possible functions of torture explain some of the incentives for keeping it going, it is also necessary to explain how the perpetrators and bystanders justify it.

In terms of justifying torture to themselves, the psychological processes adopted by perpetrators for immediate legitimation are similar to the mechanisms used to meet their underlying psychological needs discussed above. Staub summarises them as 'differentiation, devaluation, and moral exclusion' (1990: 52). Clearly the three are linked. Differentiation into an 'in' and an 'out-group' allows devaluation of the 'out-group'. Devaluation in turn makes the moral exclusion of the out-group more feasible, thereby enabling their torture. Kelman similarly describes 'dehumanization', along with 'routinization' and 'authorization', as what makes possible 'the exclusion of torture victims from the torturer's moral community' (1995: 31).

The psychological mechanisms employed by ostensible 'bystanders' to justify their apparent passivity share some characteristics with those used by the perpetrators. Staub points to their use of what he calls 'just world thinking', a process in which, 'Wanting to believe both in a just world and that they themselves will not become victims of random circumstances, people tend to view those who suffer as being responsible for and deserving of their fate because of their character or prior conduct' (1990: 56, 1995: 106). In other words, 'just world thinking' goes hand in hand with devaluation of the victims.

Elaborating a Model of Social Torture

In seeking to apply the above elements of the torture model to what I knew of northern Uganda I felt that while some of the impacts I observed closely resembled those commonly attributed to torture, the term torture as it stands within a particular strand of legal practice and the popular imagination, cannot do justice to processes and impacts on the scale I had observed. I also felt that the hidden processes behind the visible impacts were in some respects diametrically opposed to those we suppose to take place in individual torture. To capture this sense of both overlap and difference I arrived at the term social torture, a process which can be differentiated from individual torture around six key issues, as set out in Table 1.1 below.

Table 1.1 Key Differences between Individual and Social Torture

Individual torture	*Social Torture*
High Intensity	Low Intensity
Impact focused on individuals and their direct associates and family	Wide impact on society as a whole
Place and Time-bound	Geographically extensive and Time-indifferent
Dependent on small set of perpetrators with specific objectives	Involves multiple actors with broad set of needs, and is to a degree self-perpetuating
Perpetrators justify actions to themselves, using psychological mechanisms	Relies on justification to society as a whole, using public discourses
Interventions focus on individual justice and the identification of intention	Interventions need to focus on social systems and recognise that intentions are secondary to causal responsibilities

Low Intensity, Wide Impact

Whereas individual torture is conventionally thought of in terms of a highly intense and intrusive intervention, which impacts primarily on the individual victim and his or her immediate family, Social Torture can be characterised as 'low intensity' in that its methods and impacts are often not immediately visible but should be identifiable across society as a whole. In other words, while in individual torture only a minority are directly affected, in Social Torture only a minority will escape the impacts.

Low intensity goes hand in hand with a wide yet gradual impact. Its mechanisms are not always immediately identifiable for there is not always a simple one-to-one correlation between acts of torture and symptoms of such torture, particularly where the torturer is skilled in working so as to minimise visible damage. One symptom may arise from a number of discrete causes, or from a combination of them. For example, the literature suggests that the likelihood of PTSD among torture victims is increased if, amongst other things, the torture victim has already experienced 'the phenomenon of being forcibly uprooted from one's home', and if the victim is either very young or very old (Melamed et al. 1990: 20).[7] In short, it may be the cumulative impact of multiple violations which triggers a visible symptom, such that cause cannot be traced back to any one of those violations in particular. This suggests the need to look for impact over the medium rather than the short term, and to speak of causal contexts rather than single causal incidents.

Even when they are visible, impacts cannot always be traced back directly to a particular act. As studies of the families of Holocaust survivors and of the disappeared in Latin America have shown, the torture of individuals affects not just the immediate object of the torturer's attentions, but also those associated with that person in the form of symptoms such as withdrawal, depression, and intense generalised fear (Melamed et al. 1990: 25). It is thus possible for impacts to be transmitted across and down the generations without the continued need of a physical perpetrator. This distance between individual acts and overall impact contributes substantially to the gradual nature and low visibility of the phenomenon of social torture. As one MP in northern Uganda commented; 'This insecurity is a greater threat than the abductions. It is present every day but nobody sees it'.[8]

Geographic Extension and Time-Indifference

In the popular imagination torture takes place in very specific sites, generally away from the purview of the general public, at the hands of a very particular set of people, and over a delimited period of time determined by the limited capacity of the individual body and mind to resist torture. It has a beginning, when the victim is whisked away from their normal daily life, and it has an end, when the person, if still alive, may be returned to the 'outside' world, often with visible physical and psychological scars to deal with – in the midst of people the majority of whom have not undergone the same experience.

Social Torture, by contrast, rather than taking place in very restricted locations in short bursts, is both geographically extensive and time indifferent. The whole environment, in this case both the 'protected villages' and the war zone as a whole, are the site of torture – all the time. For most people, who have no resources with which to remove themselves from the war zone, there is no 'outside'. You are not whisked away from your daily life to be tortured; daily life is your torture. This is not helped if the 'outsiders', who in the individual model of torture give victims hope by creating political pressure on the victim's behalf, in this scenario are 'bystanders' whose inaction is itself a contribution to social torture.

If your whole world has become the torture chamber, then determining a clear beginning becomes hard. As I shall suggest in Chapter 3, it is never easy to know when a war truly begins. Nor is it easy to know when torture begins. If, as argued in Chapter 6, it is necessary to look at debilitation arising not just from discrete incidents but from the accumulation of such, then pin-pointing a particular incident as *the* torture becomes redundant. Forcible displacement prior to an act of individual torture does not just render the victim more susceptible to PTSD symptoms after such an act, it is a part of the torture process itself.

Just as the beginning is hard to pinpoint, so is the end. What people experience and the symptoms they exhibit can barely be described as post-traumatic, as for most people there is no end to the circumstances which caused the trauma. Whereas the aid workers in war zones are sent on R and R (Rest and Recuperation), there is no such respite for the population at large. From this point of view to use the term post-traumatic stress to describe what is happening inside the war zone can itself be seen as part of a structure of denial, or at least a refusal to acknowledge that there is no 'normal' or pre-traumatic situation to revert to. In short, the process of social torture is time indifferent, measured in years or decades rather than the days of torture to which the individual's body can be subjected.

Multiple Actors

Over time large sections of society (rather than a narrowly selected group of 'public officials') become involved in the process, and a synergy is established between the psychological needs and wants of some and the petty economic and political interests of others. These are needs which the various actors involved will deny, and interests which they will have no wish to see exposed. In drawing in multiple actors (particularly the so-called 'external' ones), social torture furthers underlying processes of social and political change over which individual actors have little direct control or influence, and, to the extent that their own interests are furthered by keeping quiet, little incentive to challenge. This integration of multiple actors into the dynamics of social torture challenges a key aspect of many existing models of conflict, namely the tendency to view conflict situations as somehow 'out there', completely other and detached from the contexts in which those doing the analyses are situated. If, as I shall argue, social torture has to be understood as a systemic process in which what is happening, for example, in Gulu, is influenced by and of import to those making decisions in Kampala, London, Brussels and Washington, then an 'internal' versus 'external' model will only hold insofar as it describes those who are physically inside the war zone and those who are outside it. It will not have any value in identifying causal responsibility for what is happening inside the war zone.

Self-Perpetuating

Once under way, social torture elicits from its victims states of physical and psychological debilitation, dependency, dread and disorientation and corresponding behavioural responses. These tend to mutually reinforce and deepen each other rather than resolving themselves, and thus contribute to perpetuating or escalating the situation.

For example, although torture is often visited upon the physical body in the first instance, it is at core an invasion of people's minds which is very difficult to reverse, such that methods and impacts ultimately become one and the same thing. As Primo Levi (1989) puts it, 'Anyone who has been tortured, remains tortured'. The mental state described as 'disorientation' is an outcome of torture, but being in that state is itself an additional form of torture.[9]

Even those who are being devalued may participate in their own devaluation, for discourses of devaluation catalysed by external actors (e.g. colonial notions of the 'native', or blaming the Acholi for what happened to them) are internalised by a particular population and quickly acquire a momentum which is independent of the actors who catalysed the discourse and continues long after they have left.

Not only is the invasion of the mind hard to reverse, it also finds expression in further physical debilitation. Both direct and indirect victims are subject to severe psychological stress, which is known to weaken the immune system.[10] This may increase morbidity, thereby accelerating physical debilitation and economic dependency, a state in which people are unable to fulfil or learn the roles which under normal circumstances would give them a sense of their adult identity (e.g. provision and protection). This in turn aggravates psychological debility.

Once physical dependency has been induced through lack of food and lack of sleep (which in turn is related to dread), people cannot afford to bite the hand that feeds them, and their time horizons become foreshortened by the realities of day-to-day survival in the war zone. Coping mechanisms adopted to ameliorate their personal situation in the short term often have the opposite effect in the long term. To eat today, for example, people resort to selling sex with its concomitant risk of HIV tomorrow (see Chapter 6).

In a sense torture becomes involuntarily self-administered, and, insofar as these behaviours are perceived and/or portrayed as self-inflicted, it also becomes possible to 'blame the victim' and thereby reinforce discourses of devaluation and dehumanisation. This diverts attention away from causes and directs it to symptoms, in a manner which is used to justify the action and inaction of those who in principle have the capacity to do differently. It becomes difficult for any of the multiple actors involved to step back and assess their true contribution to – or position in – the various intersecting cycles of violation and violence. Social Torture thus acquires a degree of momentum independent of the perpetrators' original actions or intentions.

Public Discourses

Because of the scale of social torture, and its potential visibility to the public eye, institutions such as governments, churches and NGOs need to convince their constituencies, congregations, and funding bases respectively, that institutional actions and inaction make sense and are legitimate. This is likely to be achieved through the manipulation of discourses and their accompanying silences. By focusing loudly on some elements of the situation, and keeping silent on others, these discourses serve to fragment and thus to divert attention from the bigger picture. Just as the individual perpetrator draws on a language of devaluation shared with other members of society to pre-empt any psychological discomfort with his own actions, so institutions and interest groups pre-empt the threat of their own failings being exposed by using discourses to externalise, make public and thereby involve their constituencies in processes of institutional self-justification.[11]

Overview of the Book

The book is structured in the following manner. Chapter 2 sets out the institutional framework within which the research for this book was conducted, and the key elements of the approach adopted in order to address the contextual and conceptual challenges arising from doing research both on and in a 'war zone'. To uncover the hidden rather than focus on the already visible, and to enable the emergence of a counter-narrative from those who are generally silenced by the mainstream discourses of the powerful, it was necessary to adopt an extremely open and non-prescriptive approach, in which the subjectivity of people living in that situation was given considerable scope and priority.

Chapter 3 serves a three-fold purpose. It begins with an objective history of major events occurring in northern Uganda over the period 1986 to 2006, including the various Governmental initiatives to deal with the LRA. It is 'objective' in the sense that few would dispute these happenings. This is then juxtaposed with peoples' subjective memories to illuminate the importance of bringing subjective accounts into 'objective' history, for when this is done it indicates that although there were undeniably elements of intra-ethnic violence, there were no obvious reasons for giving primacy to an intra-ethnic explanation as there were also inter-ethnic, nationalist, international and trans-national dimensions. Rather than being lead actor, the LRA appears to be one amongst many.

Chapter 4 therefore confronts directly the argument that this is primarily a war between LRA and Government of Uganda, first through a consideration of the nature of the LRA, then through a review of the gap between the Government's stated intentions and actions. The LRA is seen as having both a certain coherence and an identifiable cause – not least to confront the Museveni government, as part of a rejection of wider processes of social and political change. It is also shown to have been more of a force to be reckoned with than national and international propaganda generally allowed. However, it is also shown to have been inherently self-limiting by virtue of its rejection of 'modernity'. As an organisation it could in principle have been overcome by military means many years ago, and therefore does not offer a sufficient explanation for the continuation of the war. A review of the Government's approach to the 1994 Peace Talks – often cited as the closest they had come to a non-military solution prior to the peace talks which began in June 2006 – suggests that dealing conclusively with the LRA was never the aim of the Government and that its 'peace talks' were in fact a form of war-talk. Chapter 4 concludes that the main targets of Government policy and strategy were broader than the LRA and also extended to the Acholi population. The self-limiting nature of the LRA and the Government's lack of commitment to achieving peace allow the argument that this is primarily a Clausewitzian confrontation between two opposing groups to be substantially discounted, and suggest that the confrontation between LRA and Government, though real, is limited and is more important in its function as a disguise for a deeper process, namely social torture.

The following three chapters, which focus on the objective and subjective experiences of the bulk of the population in the war zone in Uganda, particularly in the protected villages, provide the evidence for this argument. They show how, in the name of protection, the population experienced on a mass scale, the key elements of torture, most notably violation (Chapter 5), debilitation (Chapter 6) and humiliation (Chapter 7).

Chapter 8, in reviewing this evidence, argues that in addition to those elements, dread, dependency and disorientation, are also evident throughout the war zone. In exploring these impacts it also becomes evident that while the LRA and Government were the two most visible parties to the situation, a multiplicity of other actors were also involved with differing levels of visibility and with different ways of making the situation function for them. Perpetrators, complicit bystanders and victims are all in place.

At the most mundane level the functions relate to the petty spoils of war-related corruption and the internal momentum of the 'aid industry'. At a more important level they relate to the shifting balance of economic and political power within and between states in the post-cold war era of globalisation. In this context social torture supports entire processes of social and political change, and here again analogies can be drawn between the functions of individual and social torture. When considering the Ugandan state's relative vulnerability vis-à-vis its own population and within the wider international community, the contribution of social torture can be seen as three-fold. While hard-won political independence demands that states control their own populations, it offers little in the way of economic power with which to exercise this control. Other means therefore have to be found: demonization of individuals and sub-groups, and militarization in the name of pacification, provide important opportunities. The political need of the Government is for a process of subordinate inclusion (rather than social exclusion) of the population in northern Uganda. Insofar as it breaks down social practices which distinguish the war zone from the wider state (e.g. cattle-based restorative justice mechanisms) and replaces them with alternatives (e.g. the Local Council system), it gradually establishes the inclusion of the targeted social group into the national structure but on a subordinate basis. Insofar as these processes are publicised at a national level (as Chapter 4 suggests they are), they serve as a warning to other social groups in other parts of the country.

The aid and development donors, while talking of good governance, are in fact complicit in this process, as it serves their own need to maintain the Government of Uganda in a subordinate position. By allowing the client state to break with international conventions, a series of latent conditionalities are created that enable these donor states to exercise leverage and control over the client. Yet insofar as the Government is able to implicate external actors, it limits to a certain extent the powers of intervention of those external actors and thereby increases the Government's room for manoeuvre.

To support the vested interests which develop, complex mechanisms are in place to legitimise the process, including the use of the mainstream discourse on war. This discourse, and the careful silences about the vested interests of those promoting it, justifies a whole range of interventions (with the stated intention of doing good and the observed impact of doing considerable harm), and obscures the need for alternative interventions. The discourse and its silences are thus shown to be a form of violence.

The low intensity and wide impact of social torture, its geographical extension and time-indifference, its involvement of multiple actors and the functions it has for each of them, and the way the dynamics of violation become to a degree self-perpetuating (particularly in the sense that some victims themselves become perpetrators) all offer explanations for why the situation in northern Uganda continues. Taking all these different elements into account, it is possible to see that the fundamental process is one of social torture, but that this is disguised by the appearance of it being a war.

Chapter 9 explores the implications of this analysis. As a counter-narrative to the mainstream discourse on today's 'wars' it highlights the limitations of models based on binary oppositions such as 'internal-external', 'greed-grievance' and 'rational-irrational'. It also highlights the practical limitations of legal approaches when it comes to dealing with multiple perpetrators, with the changing positions of perpetrators, bystanders and victims, and with the fact that people's behaviours are not reducible to the intentionality that lies at the heart of the *Convention Against Torture* definition. It suggests that the power of the concept of torture will be strengthened rather than weakened by broadening the lens from a primarily legal one to a more socio-economic, psychological and political one, particularly as such a lens suggests a correspondingly broader range of interventions to address human suffering in situations such as northern Uganda.

Notes

1. UN Security Council Resolution 688 of 5 April 1991.
2. In considering the political functions of silence it is useful to consider Kapucinski's observation that silence is 'a signal of unhappiness and, often, of crime. It is the same sort of political instrument as the clatter of weapons or a speech at a rally. Silence is necessary to tyrants and occupiers, who take actions to have their actions accompanied by quiet ...' (Kapuscinski 1998: 189).
3. As Lan records, 'During the last years of the war [in Rhodesia], the majority of the population had been forced into concentration camps, the so-called 'protected villages', in order to limit the amount of assistance they could give the guerrillas' (Lan, 1985: 230).
4. In 2002, for example, Amnesty was concerned that twenty prisoners illegally removed to a military detention facility in northern Uganda were at increased risk of torture or ill-treatment whilst they remained in UPDF custody (Public AI Index: AFR 59/004/2002).
5. *The Convention Against Torture and Other Cruel, Inhuman or Degrading Treatment or Punishment,* adopted and opened for signature, ratification and accession by General Assembly resolution 39/46 of 10 December 1984, entered into force on 26 June 1987.
6. The American Diagnostic and Statistical Manual.
7. Given what is known about the process of forcible displacement into the 'protected villages', this immediately makes a large proportion of the northern Uganda population, 90 per cent of which was displaced, increasingly susceptible to PTSD.
8. Then Minister for Northern Uganda Reconstruction, Hon. Owiny Dollo, *Bedo Piny Pi Kuc,* Gulu, 26 June 1998.
9. For an exploration of the difficulty/impossibility of erasing past experiences of war, see Bao Ninh, *The Sorrow of War:* 'Losses can be made good, damage can be repaired and wounds will heal in time. But the psychological scars of the war will remain forever' (Bao Ninh 1994: 180).
10. B.G.Melamed et al. in Suedfeld, 1990, p 16.
11. The term 'internalise', as used in psycho-analysis, 'means the process whereby inter-subjective relations are transformed into intra-subjective ones (internalization of a conflict, of a prohibition, etc.)'(Zur 1998: 189). By extension I shall use 'externalisation' to describe a process whereby intra-subjective relations (in this case the thought processes used by an individual to justify their non-intervention) are transformed into inter-subjective ones and given form through discourses.

2

THE RESEARCH PROCESS

The majority of fieldwork on which this book draws took place in Gulu and Kitgum districts from May 1998 to March 2000 as part of a wider DFID funded research Consortium on Political Emergencies (referred to in this text as COPE). At the time, I was working full-time for ACORD (an international Non-Governmental Organisation (NGO) with a long history of working in northern Uganda and other conflict-affected areas), and registered as a part-time PhD student. As the NGO member of COPE, ACORD had thematic responsibility for investigating the local impacts of complex emergencies and of interventions into them. Although it was initially proposed to do this in Rwanda, staff there expressed reservations about a large research project being carried out in their name, and Northern Uganda was suggested as an alternative. During my main period of fieldwork I was therefore based in Gulu town, with occasional trips to Kampala for administrative purposes. During this main research period I had a number of co-researchers, including ten fieldworkers, four part-time documentation assistants, and one full-time research assistant.

After my main period of fieldwork I made several further visits. One was in March 2000 when I returned to Gulu to co-facilitate a workshop on the implications of the research for ACORD's programming in northern Uganda. The second was from February – April 2002, just as Operation Iron Fist was getting underway. In January 2004 I visited again while conducting a Conflict Assessment for Christian Aid, and found that the humanitarian and military situation had escalated substantially (Dolan 2004). Subsequently I returned to northern Uganda during a national conflict analysis for SIDA (Dolan 2006), and for an assessment of humanitarian protection for the Overseas Development Institute (Dolan and Hovil 2006).

The approaches I adopted during the main research period were influenced by a number of factors. One was the simple fact of working within a development NGO and wishing to make the research as relevant as possible to the organisation's activities and to engage colleagues in the research process. Others were related to logistics, security and political sensitivities; rather than a post-conflict situation this was an ongoing 'war' with fluctuating levels of insecurity which cast a spell of uncertainty over everything and left the boundaries of what was possible or desirable distinctly unclear; in particular I did not know what my colleagues (particularly the fieldworkers based in the protected villages) would feel safe to ask or talk about.

At a much more conceptual level, I felt an urgent need to question the whole basis on which the COPE project had been structured, namely the belief that the local, national and international dimensions of conflict could be de-linked. The various fieldwork-based readings outlined in the introduction offered convincing evidence that careful attention to peoples' subjective experiences and interpretations at a local level offered greater insights into the linkages or systemic nature of a situation than the more 'theoretical' studies. This went hand in hand with a more political concern to give voice where it had been silenced. I thus needed an exploratory process which was both ethically and methodologically sound.

Institutional Setting

Whereas in all my previous research work I had been a member of academic institutions, here I was in a development NGO. Although it was fairly typical of development NGOs, in that research activities were very much the lesser partner in relationship to 'programme' activities, it had a commitment to research built into the name (Agency for Cooperation and Research in Development) and was open to being involved in a piece of work which went beyond more traditional needs assessments or monitoring and evaluation concerns.

In Gulu itself, ACORD had had a presence since the 1980s. Unlike the majority of other agencies it had never closed its office, even during the most difficult periods. It had a correspondingly strong reputation and profile, and when I went to do fieldwork people did not respond purely to my research activity, but also to their generally positive experiences of the agency I worked for. This also substantially eased the task of persuading the authorities of the legitimacy of the project. It also brought with it certain responsibilities vis-à-vis my colleagues; although I was there on a time-bound basis and with my own funding, I was expected to fit myself to a certain degree within the agency's existing practices. At a minimum this involved things such as participation in organisational meetings, and, more importantly, it meant I had to consider what impact my work would have on theirs and whether the two could be combined to mutual advantage. It also meant that I became a participant observer in the at times complex relationships between Government, humanitarian and aid actors. For example, in the three months following ACORD being kicked out of Kitgum district by an irate LCV chairman, I attended numerous meetings at local and national levels between the agencies, the LCVs and the office of the Minister for Northern Uganda Reconstruction.

Working in a 'War Zone'

As this example shows, even an established NGO such as ACORD faced challenges and a degree of vulnerability. The necessary authorisations were not always sufficient to gain access to individuals and places, or to address certain issues. Fluctuating security made travel outside the immediate vicinity of Gulu town unpredictable, and the context as a whole created high levels of suspicion, not just of me as an obvious foreigner, but also of colleagues whose personal political affiliations were not known but could put respondents at risk. Unlike an idealized Clausewitzian situation in which good and bad guys are clearly identifiable, here there was the official position on the 'bad guys' (the LRA), but no agreement on the 'good guys' – or if there even were any. Some people did not even see the LRA as primary protagonists, but rather as mere proxy fighters in a war between the Governments of Uganda and Sudan (see Chapter 4).

Possible respondents had many interpretations of our role as researchers, including that we were spies for foreign governments, or might feed our findings to the Ugandan government, or alternatively were rebel sympathisers ourselves. It was often extremely difficult to judge where a given respondent sat on the political spectrum, and how information flows worked. It was also the case that both respondents and co-researchers were likely to have occupied several different roles in their lives (e.g. civilian, soldier, rebel), each with different political overtones. And it was not uncommon for a person to have different close family members in several different political camps. They might have a brother in the bush, a sister in local government, an uncle in central government and cousins in London, Toronto or New York.

These high levels of ambiguity about identities, affiliations and political sympathies, created serious security/confidentiality concerns for researchers and respondents alike. This was particularly the case when researching the LRA, for even to ask a question about them in Gulu was liable to raise suspicion (or fear). Not only was documentation scarce, but to attempt to talk with the LRA could be viewed by the authorities as tantamount to collaboration – as *The Monitor* newspaper noted, 'When Presidential candidate Paul Ssemogerere told voters in 1996 that he would talk to Kony into abandoning the rebellion, he was branded a rebel himself'[1]. Even those who had been authorised to make contact with the LRA were at times arrested by the UPDF, as happened when three priests, carrying a letter from the Kitgum Resident District Commissioner, tried to meet with LRA Commander Toopaco on 28 August 2002.[2] Individuals offering to make contact with the LRA on my behalf often turned out to be linked with government security services. I could have interviewed returned child abductees in centres established for their rehabilitation, such as GUSCO, but I was reluctant to follow this well-trodden path. Just as Heike Behrend had observed that well before she wrote her own analysis of the Holy Spirit Movement, it 'had already been created by the mass media' (Behrend, 1999: 2), in the case of the LRA it was created not only by mass media but also by the UN and Non-Governmental Organisations using the testimonies of traumatised children who had escaped captivity and been processed through reception centres such as GUSCO and World Vision. While the testimonies seemed in many respects genuine, they provided a partial picture, as adult voices were largely absent. There were though few other obvious options. At the same time, the LRA were said to have eyes and ears everywhere – at any public meeting someone would comment to the effect that 'whatever we say here will be relayed to the LRA' – but nobody would go so far as to point out particular individuals. As a result one could never be sure who was who and had to regard everyone as a potential informer to Government or LRA – or to both.

The sense of being under surveillance was at times acute; it was not uncommon to meet a respondent for a meal or drink and then find somebody unknown sitting exceptionally close by, despite the availability of numerous empty tables further away. On one occasion in Kitgum, I spotted such a 'restaurant observer' at ten o'clock the following morning sitting 100 metres away from the ACORD office on a termite mound. From there he could observe our comings and goings while reading a book. Such scrutiny from security services meant that some respondents could also be at risk from being seen to talk with us, and raised serious concerns about the confidentiality of sources and security of data collected. Returning to my hotel room in Kitgum after a day's fieldwork to find that my laptop had been tampered with brought this home to me in a very direct fashion. Furthermore, for much of my fieldwork there were only a handful of telephones in Gulu town; any call from the post-office was bound to be listened to by the queue of other people waiting, and any fax received was likely to be perused by several people before reaching its intended recipient. This also led to a form of self-imposed censorship in discussing what was happening.

Conceptual Challenges

I felt I had to go well beyond simply documenting the impact of war and humanitarian interventions on people at a local level. I did not wish to simply repeat data collection that had already been done; some issues, such as LRA abductions and other atrocities already seemed relatively well documented – indeed they seemed amongst the few elements of the situation which did not require much research.

Furthermore, I felt that such documentation had a limited impact on the situation. From a humanitarian perspective, given the multiple indicators of suffering which already existed when I first went to Gulu in January 1998, northern Uganda should have been termed a complex emergency, yet it was not recognised as such, and the humanitarian imperative did not seem to be operating. Eventually – in November 2003 – it would come to be described by Jan Egeland, the UN's Under Secretary General for Humanitarian Affairs, as one of the worst humanitarian situations in the world[3] but in 1998, despite being already more than a decade old, the situation in northern Uganda had attracted relatively little international attention. From day one, therefore, I was confronted by questions about whether the label had any objective meaning (i.e. was linked to specific 'objective' indicators) or was purely politically contingent.

Horizontal Segmentation or Vertical Linkages?

I was also challenged by the way the larger COPE research project was effectively segmented horizontally: Officially I was supposed to focus at the local level, while others (in line with their academic disciplines – political science and international relations respectively) prioritised state and international dimensions of CPEs in their fieldwork. Although in principle each member was intended to also consider the questions identified by those working at the other two levels, in practice there was little space in this project structure for considering the linkages between levels. I found this limited and limiting, but reflected in the majority of NGO reports and policy documents; while the premise of internal wars had effectively penetrated this grey literature, the more subtle linkages between internal and external, such as are found in Kaldor and Duffield's discussions on new wars, generally had not. This suggested to me that a purely ethnographic approach to understanding the dynamics of war and its continuation would be irrelevant, and that even while conducting fieldwork at the 'local' level it was necessary to examine the connections between different parts of the conflict dynamic and different parts of the globe. To do this also indicated the need to go beyond the confines of traditional academic disciplines; to get away from the economist's preoccupation with economic rationality to look at more politically and psychologically complex models of behaviour and motivation; to discard international relation's fixation with two-party models of wars and their resolution and replace it with multi-actor models; and to take the anthropologist's concern with local level motivations and ideologies and integrate it with more systemic perspectives. Against the backdrop of these needs I felt that development studies, as an academic setting which embraces multi- or cross-disciplinary perspectives, was an appropriate 'home'.

I was encouraged in the pursuit of connections across levels (and disciplines) by Colson and Kottak's writings on linkages (1996). They observe that 'Contemporary anthropologists can no longer even hope to do ethnography among people isolated from world markets or unaffected by centers of political and economic power'. Furthermore, '... No matter what the subject or the research locale, we need to consider documents describing the interdependencies between local systems and larger economic and political networks' (Colson and Kottak, 1996: 107). They propose research focused on linkages, which they define as;

> ... a convenient term to encompass the multistranded involvement in the world system that ethnographers must now consider in conceptualizing the influences affecting values, categories, institutional arrangements, and other symbolic systems. The linkages perspective is the antithesis of traditional anthropological 'holism', which looked inward, assuming the existence of some entity, either a culture or a society, complete and autonomous. Linkages, crucial to social transformations, work to destabilize, rather than maintain, local systems over time. (ibid, 1996: 104)

Acknowledging Peoples' Agency

Furthermore, while some of the academic literature outlined above under 'building blocks' does explore how wars are experienced at a local level and how this feeds into the dynamics of war (and there is plenty in more theoretical models of 'grievance', 'particularism', 'identity politics' etc., which can be read as implying that these connections really matter), my sense at that time was that either there was something of a loud silence around this in the literature being drawn on by NGOs, or they themselves were selectively ignoring it. Much of the literature I read seemed to be peopled by concepts rather than real people, and, to the extent that people were brought into the picture, this was in terms of the impacts of war on them, rather than of their impact on war. In other words, the subjectivities and agency of those living in the most affected areas were often missing. From within the NGO sector it seemed clear to me that, as Zur commented in 1998, 'Despite recent interest in the anthropology of war there has been little documentation of how conflict is lived by the people caught in its midst or of how they themselves represent it' (Zur, 1998; 18).

Indeed, it could be argued that humanitarian and development agencies, by virtue of their specific mandates and the demands of funders for target groups and verifiable indicators, tend to turn people into passive victims whose objective needs can be addressed without enquiry into their subjective position or their own agency. Having just come from a year interviewing ex-combatants in Mozambique where I listened to their (extensive) grievances and wondered what this meant for the durability of the reintegration process there, and having joined an organisation with a commitment to working at the 'grass-roots', I felt that this silence about what motivates people living in such contexts, and about the extent to which they are actors in war despite living in difficult circumstances, needed to be both investigated and broken.

Ethical Considerations

This latter challenge was not just conceptual; I doubted that a study of this nature could be considered either methodologically or ethically sound if it failed to give space to the subjective voices of both respondents and co-researchers. My previous research experience with Mozambican refugees in South Africa (Dolan, 1996) and ex-combatants in Mozambique (Dolan, 1997), had made me sceptical about the value of adhering to a very tight and predefined set of methods, as these tend to block the unsuspected issues and angles emerging from the respondents' own analyses. This scepticism went hand in hand with my awareness that the thinking of everybody working in a research project is changed and deepened by the experience, and that there should be some scope for accommodating the ideas that result. In other words, in addition to reflecting the subjectivity of respondents in the research findings, enabling the subjectivity of my co-researchers within the research process was also an important consideration.

Another ethical concern was closely linked with security considerations; I did not wish to make decisions which put either my co-researchers or our respondents at risk of trouble from the authorities or other bodies (e.g. LRA, mob justice), nor did I wish to put people at risk by association with the project. My concern about safety, however, extended beyond what might be termed the political and physical safety of respondents, and into the question of psychological risk; although it was an area with very high levels of violence and violation and these were obviously issues of concern to the study, it seems to me that setting certain types of questions about deeply personal or sensitive experiences (e.g. 'how many people did you kill?' or 'how many times were you raped?') is ethically wrong if it puts the respondent under pressure to open wounds which the researcher has no way of dressing, let alone healing. Such questioning also, to my mind, implies that the questioner believes him or herself to occupy the moral high ground from which they can ask whatever they choose, because they have objectified the respondent to the point where his or her experience of being questioned ceases to matter. If, however, the respondent chooses to divulge deeply personal information, that is a different matter.

The fourth ethical consideration, and often the hardest to address, was to do as some of my respondents asked of me, namely to use what I learned to inform people outside. In other words I was explicitly asked to take seriously my responsibilities as a witness which putting myself in that environment had created.

Methods Adopted

Given all the above considerations, I wanted an approach which maximised respondent and researcher security, and which valued the subjectivity of co-researchers and respondents alike. It needed to be sufficiently structured to be practicable, yet remain sufficiently open to allow issues and methods that emerged to be followed up, while also incorporating joint exercises with my programme colleagues. In the end four broad strands emerged; ongoing work with and through fieldworkers in the protected villages, further key informant interviews and participant observation by myself, the collection of press clippings and various audio-visual data, and discrete research exercises with colleagues from the ACORD Gulu programme in which we primarily adopted focus group methodologies.

Composition of the Research Team

As the research progressed the team of people involved grew. After a few weeks in Gulu I met Komakech Charles Okot, who had already worked as a research assistant to Sverker Finnstrom, and we agreed to work together on a part-time basis. When I found myself stuck in Gulu with no certainty about how soon or how regularly I would be permitted by the authorities to travel to the protected villages, I had to find another way to do the fieldwork. In discussion with Komakech, we decided to seek people from a number of protected villages who could carry out fieldwork in an ongoing fashion by virtue of being resident there, could report to us on a regular basis, and could provide us with entry points when we were able to visit the villages ourselves.

We identified a number of potential fieldworkers from people whom Komakech knew as a result of working in the Uganda Red Cross. On the basis of our interviews with them, eight were chosen. As the work progressed, two additional fieldworkers joined us, one based in Gulu town, the other in Awer camp, such that we ended up with a group which was highly diverse in terms of backgrounds, experiences and political positions. It included individuals who had spent time in the bush, camp leaders, religious leaders, teachers, students, district councillors, and otherwise unemployed civilians. A major weakness, however, was the lack of women fieldworkers. The one woman who came for interview was not amongst those selected.

The names of the fieldworkers were registered with the authorities and each individual received a card and a letter of introduction to present on demand. Notwithstanding these administrative safeguards I still could not realistically pre-determine what it was or was not safe for the fieldworkers to investigate; while it was likely to be acceptable to document the visits of priests and politicians, I could not decide for them if it was safe to document an LRA raid or the Government's response to that. Just because fieldworker X could talk about an incident of rape I could not assume that fieldworker Y would feel able to do so, as each person had his own particular profile in his own camp, some of which offered more protection than others (e.g. teachers, camp officials), and some of which allowed access to otherwise little represented sections of the population (e.g. youth). I therefore consciously sought to create a situation in which such decisions were left to the fieldworkers' own judgement and individual sense of security.

In discussion with the fieldworkers we developed an approach centred around a report to be prepared and brought to Gulu for discussion on a monthly basis. This comprised several elements. The basic one was a standardised questionnaire, which covered relief deliveries (food, clothing, seeds and tools), health and sanitation services, education, sources of income, information flows (from LRA), visitors to the camp (e.g. politicians, religious leaders, journalists, cultural and recreational activities (in particular dances), deaths/burials/funerals. This was supplemented every three months with a price list of all items available in their local market. Information collected included cost of the item, and its origin, allowing us to demonstrate, for example; the sale of relief items, the importance of access to urban markets, and also the wide range of items produced, hunted or gathered locally, despite the ongoing insecurity.

To capture people's subjective experience and interpretation of the dynamics within the war zone, and for the fieldworkers to bring their own subjective view of what was significant to bear, they were given event and incident report sheets on which to write about any incident or event or issue they felt would be of interest to someone who knew nothing about life in the protected villages. This resulted in reports on a whole range of issues which it would have been impossible to specify in a pre-formulated questionnaire. In identifying incidents and events of interest, the fieldworkers became 'co-investigators' in the Freirean sense of taking an active attitude 'to the exploration of their thematics' (see Freire, 1996: 87). I subsequently clustered the reports as demonstrated in Table 2.1.

I have drawn heavily on these in providing qualitative evidence for the arguments made in the thesis. Wherever quotations have been used they seek to be as representative of the wider set of stories as possible. At the suggestion of one of the fieldworkers, these accounts were enhanced and supplemented through the use of cameras. Again, I did not specify what should be photographed, but requested that each photo be dated and given a brief explanation of what it depicted and where. In many cases the fieldworkers used such photographs to corroborate their written accounts and thus strengthened the quality of the incident and event data.

Over and above the monthly reports the fieldworkers also provided hand-drawn maps of their village, and on occasion filled in supplementary questionnaires related to the research, for example on HIV and conflict and on livelihoods. Each fieldworker also provided a history of the origins of his particular protected village. When the security situation allowed I would also visit their villages with Komakech. This allowed a degree of mentoring, corroboration of the findings they had already presented, and the development of relationships of

Table 2.1 Number of Reports by Subject Matter over the Six Months July–December 1999, from 10 Protected Villages in Gulu District

Type of incident	No.	Type of incident	No.	Type of incident	No.	Type of incident	No.
Raids and abduction	44	Religious activities	16	Theft	9	Weather	4
Health	42	Burning	13	Mob justice	7	Shooting	3
NGO activities	41	Poisoning	13	Music and dance	7	Cattle restocking	2
Education	38	Politicians	10	Adultery	5	Hunting	2
Actions by military	30	Rape	10	Land disputes	5	Population movements	2
Accidents	30	Home-guards and police	9	Lightning	5	Defilement	1
Government activities	22	Killings	9	Witchcraft	5	Corruption – clientelism	1
Domestic fighting	20	Local government	9	Administration – camps	4	Economy of war	1
Celebrations	19	Rebel movements	9	Ambushes	4	Combined Total	481
Traditional leaders	17	Suicides	9	Economy of camps	4		

trust with the fieldworkers, whom, in addition to their role as data gatherers, I also considered as among my key informants.

It is difficult to overstate the importance of developing such trust; I still remember the tension of the initial meetings, and how over the months this tension was replaced by what felt like a high degree of mutual confidence and trust. My sense was that the key elements in this evolution were regularity of contact, regularity of payment, confidence over time that their reports were not being shared with the authorities, and the visible influence of their opinions on both the content and methodology of the research. As this happened, so the nature of what they were prepared to document changed; reports became more critical and the material more sensitive. With a more rigid approach I would have expected the findings of the fieldworkers to become more homogeneous; with this very flexible approach each individual's reports became more rather than less distinctive as each individual felt more able to bring his subjective concerns to bear.

The diversity of the fieldworkers was also a major advantage in dealing with the political ambiguities of northern Uganda. Although it is impossible to verify, it is probable that by having this range of people involved, those parties with an interest in knowing exactly what was being done were in fact informed and updated by our own research staff. From a methodological point of view I was more interested in capturing a wide range of perspectives than in the consistency of data across villages, and again this was well met by the diversity of the team. In presenting data drawn from the fieldworkers' accounts, the village of the fieldworker and the date of the incident referred to are given in the endnotes.

In-Depth Key-Informant Interviews

In parallel to the ongoing monthly reports I also carried out numerous key informant interviews, generally together with Komakech, who would also translate when necessary. We began with interviews on the issue of refugees, the diaspora and remittances. These early interviews were the least successful, perhaps because they touched on too many sensitive questions, or because we were not familiar enough to ask them correctly, or because our identification of key informants was poor.[4] Later interviews, which in some cases involved interviewing the same person several times over, focused more on issues such as the peace process led by the then Minister for the North, Mrs Betty Bigombe, from 1993 to 1994, the creation of 'protected villages' from 1996 onwards, and the teaching and role of traditional dance.

The most in-depth key informant interview, which bears some discussion as I draw on it extensively in Chapter 4, was one conducted by myself over a ten days period with a returned LRA soldier. This was unplanned and resulted from our both attending a meeting in Kitgum in late March 2002. By this point, notwithstanding the problems of researching the LRA and the fact that documentation on LRA abductions and other atrocities already existed, I had realised that, given the central position accorded to the LRA in mainstream accounts, I would have to make my own assessment of its relative importance in the overall situation, and that this would require some insight into the LRA's internal dynamics and motivations. I therefore asked him if he would be prepared to tell me his story. Although he agreed to do so he then avoided me throughout the rest of the meeting and I assumed he did not really wish to. However, when I was subsequently in Kampala he telephoned to say he was coming to tell me the story there. In the event his story, from the day he was abducted in 1996 aged 19, to the day he returned to Uganda under the Amnesty in late 2001, took eight days to tell and a further two days to check through. Rather than taping it I typed it straight onto my laptop with him looking over my shoulder, and we ended up with a transcript of forty-four pages.

Against the backdrop of numerous accounts given by returned abducted children, this account is important because, at nineteen years of age, Jacob was already an adult when abducted, and he spent his six years mainly within the LRA's headquarters. His story confirms many of the elements of the feedback given by younger abductees, but adds a whole layer of information about the day-to-day running of the LRA and the gradual changes in political climate and their influence on the LRA – at least as he was able to perceive them. I have included the entire transcript as Annex A so that readers can assess the account for themselves.

For several reasons I did not prioritise key informant interviews with NGO or IGO staff. As an NGO staff member myself, I felt I would have numerous opportunities to engage in participant observation of NGO activities, such as weekly NGO security meetings. Most of the international and many local NGOs operating in Gulu district participated in the September 1999 conference,[5] and several international NGOs participated in meetings with the Government following the eviction of ACORD from Kitgum district. More importantly, I wanted to capture their role as institutions as perceived by their 'beneficiaries', rather than the opinions of individuals within them. As such I decided to rely to a large extent on the observations of their work as seen throughout the fieldwork, together with their own documentation and statements to the media. However, in the course of my eighteen months fieldwork and subsequent visits I had opportunity to have conversations with many aid workers and to get a sense of how they saw the problem and how they justified their approaches. I have tried to give an overview of those conversations, notably in Chapter 8.

Audio-Visual Data

Another major item, which informed my view of the LRA (and Government), was a video recording of the 1994 peace talks, which my research assistants transcribed and translated (see Annex B).

I felt that our findings would be stronger and more accessible if supported with visual documentation. In addition to photographs, a digital video camera was used to document a whole range of activities; food distributions, political occasions (e.g. NRM day), ceremonies (e.g. the installation of Archbishop John Baptist Odama, the anointment of a local chief), celebrations (e.g. World Women's Day, World AIDS day). These were dubbed onto standard VHS tapes and then edited. Again, while basic guidance was provided on how to use the digital camera, the decision about what to film in a given place or situation was generally left to whoever had the camera. Where it was not possible to use video recording, audio recordings of public functions and cultural activities were made. The team also taped radio broadcasts – covering occasions such as the District Council meetings and including the LRA's own 'Radio Voice of Free Uganda' for the few weeks that it succeeded in broadcasting to northern Uganda (see Chapter 4).

Media Monitoring

In the event I made relatively little use of the transcriptions of these recordings, and drew instead on newspaper clippings to give a sense of the kind of information circulating inside the 'war' zone. Newspapers were a constant feature of daily life in Gulu town. The two dailies, the *New Vision* and *The Monitor*, arrived with the first bus in the morning and by mid-morning were sold out. They were eagerly scanned and their contents fed into numerous discussions. On the one hand they were the only regular source of news, and provided some record of events as they occurred. On the other hand, they could not be consumed unquestioningly, the *New Vision* because it was Government controlled, *The Monitor* because it was subject to constant harassment by the Government. They also seemed inconsistent in the tone adopted, at times expressing a critical voice, at times simply reflecting official positions. The ambiguous space thus created contributed substantially to my own sense of being in a surreal environment in which nothing was quite as it seemed. To try and get an insight into this phenomenon I employed two part-time documentation assistants to go through these daily papers (including local language papers), clipping and filing those items of concern to the project (e.g. Sudan, LRA, Gulu and Kitgum districts, Diaspora, International NGOs, Human Rights, Gender, West Nile Bank Front, ADF).

Some of these (e.g. Sudan) were a useful source of information on 'linkages', others were more useful as a control of the quality of reporting as a whole (e.g. we could compare our own accounts of events in Gulu district with those given in the media). Analysing the discrepancies found through this juxtaposition of public information and our own primary data allowed some conclusions to be drawn regarding the manipulation of public information and thereby of public opinion (see Chapter 4).

Throughout the thesis I have quoted from these news clippings. In some instances I have used them as references for particular events, in others to demonstrate the biases in the opinions expressed in them, and in others to give readers a sense of the extent to which the media contributed to peoples' sense of disorientation and could thus be integral to the dynamics of situation.

Research Integrated with Programming – The Use of Focus Groups

To engage existing programme staff in the research process I was keen to establish joint research exercises with my colleagues in ACORD's Gulu office. These had to emerge during the course of the work rather than being cast in stone before I had even arrived. The opportunity to make a connection emerged around ACORD's involvement in a Belgian-funded project concerning traditional leadership, as it was agreed that some assessment of how this leadership was generally viewed should be carried out. From January 1999 we therefore embarked on research into the roles and responsibilities of traditional and modern leaders, as seen by the members of ten community-based organisations with whom ACORD had longstanding relationships. These included youth, subsistence farmers, women victims of conflict, and people living with HIV/AIDS (see Chapter 6). In each discussion we first drew up a timeline for the period 1986–1999 and asked people to remember one or two incidents which had happened in each year as a result of the war at national, district, community levels, and, finally, to them or their immediate family. It was a very simple but extraordinarily powerful method, which left the respondents to determine what to mention or to keep silent about. In each group, regardless of its composition, a litany of unceasing abuse and violation emerged. In addition to the better documented LRA abuses, this stage of the research revealed heavy levels of sexual abuse by the military, as well as rampant destruction of peoples' livelihoods by different forces at different points in the history of the conflict (see Chapter 3 for findings from one women's group). Had the exercise just been conducted with one group it might have appeared exceptional; when it became clear that such experience of violation was consistent across groups with very different profiles and in very different parts of the district, it was shockingly unanswerable.

These findings led us into a second phase of research with the ACORD programme on HIV and AIDS.[6] The main objective was to explore the perspectives of the military on issues of HIV and of sexual relations with civilians, again using focus group methods with groups of ordinary soldiers, officers, and military wives, both in Gulu barracks and in a number of rural detaches. Again, ACORD's existing relationships greatly facilitated this otherwise potentially problematic exercise. In most military sites where we carried out the research we were the first NGO to have visited. A third stage involved gathering data on livelihoods (see Chapter 5). Fieldworkers completed a questionnaire designed to supplement studies carried out previously by programme staff as part of their earlier work in this area (for discussion of findings see COPE Working Paper 32).

The work on traditional leaders involved all of us participating in and documenting numerous meetings in local communities, as well as the higher levels of local and central government policy-making. The latter also allowed close observation of some of the NGO/donor politics behind the stated aims of interventions related to the traditional leadership issue.

A further important source of data, which helped to shape the thinking of Chapter 7, was an in-house planning workshop conducted with all ACORD's staff from northern Uganda, including the COPE fieldworkers and documentation assistants. The proceedings of that workshop, conducted in early 2000, both corroborated and significantly added to my understanding of various forms of discrimination and humiliation. Indeed, it was an object lesson in how certain types of information (in this case the question of negative and derogatory racial and ethnic stereotyping) only emerge if the right questions are asked.

Dealing with Findings

Quite apart from the political challenges of conducting research in a politically charged environment and on potentially sensitive topics, there was also the problem of how to present the findings. The original proposal to DFID suggested that this be done in a small dissemination workshop at the end of the field-work period. There were a number of problems with putting this into operation; London was not an ideal venue since many people who could contribute to and draw from the discussions would have been excluded, and it risked accusations of 'extractive research' or worse; Kampala, given Uganda's north-south divide, presented similar problems, although access would have been easier.

At the suggestion of the ACORD Gulu co-ordinator, therefore, the workshop was held in Gulu, to allow much fuller participation by all those who had been involved in the research, and by people most directly affected by the situation. This demanded a certain level of commitment from the external participants who were willing to travel to and stay within what was still considered a high-risk area, but also gave them an opportunity to form their own impressions over and above what they heard in presentations and papers.

Rather than simply disseminating our own findings a wide range of organisations and individuals were invited to make presentations of their own experiences and research. By collaborating with the Acholi Religious Leaders Peace Initiative (a high-profile local initiative by the Muslim, Protestant and Catholic religious leaders working for peace in Acholi) and with last minute support from central government, we ended up, in September 1999, with an international conference with some 290 participants rather than the modest dissemination workshop originally planned.

Key issues from our own and other pieces of research were tabled and discussed for the first time, by actors ranging from village leaders right up to the Prime Minister of Uganda, and with inputs from a large number of international participants. These findings were juxtaposed with discussion of existing NGO activities and identification of gaps. Public discussion of the issues was thus dramatically broadened and this in turn contributed to the creation of a wider political space than had hitherto existed. Perhaps most importantly for the protection of researchers and respondents, the joint organisation contributed considerably to greater ownership of results, and demonstrated that the issues raised came not just from ACORD but from a wide range of research activities by a number of concerned individuals and organisations. As such it helped to put ACORD's research activities into a wider perspective, and contributed to raising awareness of a number of issues which had hitherto received little attention (such as investment in secondary and higher education, address-ing gender inequalities, promoting enterprise and employment, and investing in basic communications infrastructure). As the title of the conference suggests ('Peace Research and the Reconciliation Agenda'), it was an early attempt to go beyond a narrow focus on particular victim groups and to think through the broad range of issues which would need to be addressed if northern Uganda were ever to successfully recover from two decades of violation and violence.

The importance of individual profiles in this should not be discounted; it was in large part due to the intervention of two well-respected academics who had at one time taught President Museveni at the University of Dar-es-Salaam, that it was possible to broach the taboo topic of relations with Sudan. It became pos-sible for everybody to 'hide' behind somebody else, and get that person to safely make a contribution which they themselves would have been unable to make for reasons of their own sense of security. Equally it served to de-mystify research, as it became clear that everybody, from unemployed youth through to teach-ers and administrators, can contribute to a research process. The diversity and range of participants' profiles thus broke with traditional social and political stratifications and demonstrated the need and value of doing so. The combina-tion of Ugandan and non-Ugandan participation gave the meeting considerable power, as outsiders could ask questions which to an insider had either ceased to be points of discussion or had become 'taboo' topics. Outsiders also brought comparative examples from other places to bear on the discussion. Bringing together Ugandans from very diverse backgrounds was also useful: when a fun-damentalist preacher can challenge a minister, and an army commander can question the Prime Minister, progress has been made towards critical analysis which challenges existing frameworks rather than perpetuating them. Horizon-tal stratifications were simultaneously recognised and cut across. As one partici-pant subsequently noted, 'perhaps it is only across levels that the real questions which contextualise the experience of war may be asked, the questions normally voiced privately'.[7]

Other than a number of presentations of findings given mainly in London, my next attempt to put the findings into the public domain was through the pub-lication of an article under the title 'Which Children Count?'. In this I focused on the politics of humanitarianism as demonstrated through the question of abducted children (ACCORD, 2002). I was in northern Uganda at the time the publication was launched, and this coincided with a slightly shortened version being published in *The Monitor* as part of Charles Onyango-Obbo's regular opinion column. He subsequently reported that, rather than provoking his read-ers into writing in with their comments, it appeared to have shocked them into silence.

Within ACORD the research process informed and gave focus to the organ-isation's subsequent non-research activities, including a restructuring of activi-ties throughout northern Uganda. Our experiences fed into an ACORD-wide workshop on oral testimony and the development of guidelines for this, and it also influenced the agency's wider thinking about the role of research in programming. Perhaps the strangest, and ultimately most disappointing feedback process, was with our own funders. By the time we were asked to report back on this three years project, those who had originally commissioned the project were no longer around, and we were invited to present our findings during a DfID lunch-break, with ten minutes each for the three presenters.

Discussion and Conclusions

Overall the methods adopted, often as a result of discussions with my co-researchers, addressed the concerns I had; they allowed us to conduct field-work over nearly two years without any security incidents; they embraced and reflected the subjectivity of researchers and respondents alike and in the process took their viewpoints seriously rather than attempting to suppress the reality of their influence; instead of pre-imposing questions and analytical frameworks, which risked channelling rather than opening up thinking, they resulted in findings in which linkages were both implicit and explicit, and which took me beyond documentation and into the analysis of dynamics over time – informed by those most affected by the conflict.

Evidently these methods diverged considerably from more standard NGO-driven research, much of which focuses on very specific questions in order to inform what are generally pre-determined intervention agendas, which in turn have been determined by existing institutional niches and interests. There is little scope in the NGO world for 'blue-sky' research which seeks to take a fresh look at situations. As such I was fortunate in the space and time afforded me by my colleagues and the project as a whole. The methods adopted relied on the project being in place over a long period of time, and having the capacity to return several times to any one person or place. With the added advantage of a number of follow-up visits I was ultimately able to accompany the conflict for eight of its twenty years rather than creating a snapshot of one year. As such I did not just talk about fluctuations in security, I lived them. I had my own experiences of what it feels like to have the promise of peace held out (and all the curiously mixed emotions which that brings with it) only to see it dashed again. I observed the gradual development of external interest in the situation and the form that interventions took. This gave me far more confidence to talk about the dynamics of social torture over time. In this regard I was fortunate to be able to make several follow-up visits in the course of which I was able to verify certain impressions or explore issues further. This was particularly true of the question of suicide, a theme which had not struck me particularly in 1999, but which jumped out at me when I looked at the data in its entirety.

The methods adopted were also made possible by being based within an NGO. The integration of the COPE research with the research needs of existing ACORD programme activities provided a degree of security in that it allowed us to work with very diverse groups of people with whom the organisation already had a long relationship, to whom it had demonstrated commitment, and through whom it had created a constituency. The active involvement of long-standing ACORD staff in these activities added legitimacy, and gave access which would not have been possible if we had been perceived as doing 'research for research's sake'. Undoubtedly this way of working also influenced the methods adopted such that they diverged from a more purely academic model of research. In particular the need to identify and implement research activities in response to the agency's emerging programme meant that research instruments, rather than being pre-determined and piloted in advance, were developed on the spot.

On the other hand the experience highlighted some of the shortcomings of the agency when it came to dealing with a complex research process. While they provided support to the implementation of the research as outlined, they were less able to respond to the processes which the research triggered. In particular, the momentum and political support developed by the September 1999 conference was not capitalised on. More generally there was no institutional capacity to deal with key issues which such research can uncover; there was no specific budget for legal support, no staff to provide psycho-social support, and no capacity to provide the kind of national and international witness which both respondents and our findings demanded.

Evidently there were also certain limitations to the methods adopted. One of these has already been mentioned, namely the lack of women fieldworkers in the protected villages. The already considerable diversity within the types of information given by the male fieldworkers would undoubtedly have increased had women been represented as well. Certainly, were I to carry out another such project, I would insist on having a gender-balanced team. For while women's voices were heard in many of the reports, and women and men were were equally represented in all the focus group discussions, women's subjectivity was not brought to bear on field-work in the protected villages. Their involvement would have added an important further dimension to the findings.

A further limitation was that, while I developed an ear for quite a lot of Acholi, I did not learn to speak it properly and this meant that some of my discussions were mediated by the need for translation. Similarly, while all the fieldworkers wrote their reports in English, this was considerably more difficult for some than for others, and undoubtedly some details and nuances were lost. I felt, however, that because we were using several different methods of data collection, the short-comings in language in one area would be made up for in another. When it came to translating the transcript of the 1994 peace-talks video, for example, the final version was the result of several days' discussion involving the translator, a number of colleagues and myself. As we compared the translated transcript with the video almost sentence by sentence I became very aware of some of the ambiguities of language used, and also of the particular force with which language was used in that meeting.

From a personal point of view the research process had a high psychological impact; although at the time of collecting the data I felt well able to process it, I subsequently found, for more than a year after finishing the main period of field-work, that it was difficult if not impossible for me to work on the data. Even now, some years later, some of the data still has the power to disturb me. I was somewhat reassured to find that I was not alone in this, even though I had been given no warning it might happen. With the benefit of hindsight I feel that the standard model of PhD research, in which a year of field-work is followed immediately by a year of write-up, does not allow sufficient time for the individual to process the experiences and information that conflict zones provide.

Subjectivity and Objectivity

The question of subjectivity and objectivity is a vexed one. It could, for example, be argued that, because the nature of the information collected changed over the course of the field-work, it does not allow an objective analysis as the data collected at the end was not directly comparable to that collected at the beginning. There are several responses to this. First, certain questions were repeated throughout the fieldwork in the monthly questionnaire filled out by the fieldworkers. As such, some basic forms of data were collected in a consistent fashion throughout the research. Secondly, what would an objective account entail? It is clear when conducting field-work that nobody, whether 'insider' or 'outsider', has the only description, the whole picture or the only answer to a situation. The extent to which each of us saw the situation through very different eyes was perhaps most evident in the fieldworkers' photographs; the majority of photographs of one fieldworker, for example, were of group activities and official events, with most pictures featuring dozens of people against a wide backdrop. Those of another fieldworker were far more intimate in character, placing one or two individuals or objects right in the centre of the frame. This very diversity of viewpoints was proof – if proof were needed – of the dangers of assuming any homogeneity of perspective on many issues. The contradictions between different positions (insider, outsider, local, national, regional, international, diaspora, refugee, youth, women etc.) become a basis for dialogue within the team and with those beyond it. It is necessary on the one hand to be able to pin down some of 'what happened when', while still keeping multiple interpretations of these events in consideration.

A further question is whether quantity of data on a narrow question is better than quality of data on a diversity of issues. My own view is that, leaving co-researchers to determine the level of risk they were prepared to take was methodologically powerful in that it lead to findings on issues which could not have been pre-determined, such as suicide.

As fundamentally, the changing nature of the qualitative data over time was to me an indicator of the success rather than the failure of the methods, for I believed that recognition of the subjective and its influence was essential to an objective understanding. When, as time went by, the fieldworkers allowed their subjective voices to become more visible, it was for me a case of objectivity through subjectivity.[8]

In particular it alerted me to the complex interplay between trust, time, memory and disclosure; fundamentally research on sensitive issues requires relationships of trust between respondent and researcher over time. The fact that issues could emerge which would never have done so using a more rigid data collection strategy, must raise a considerable question-mark over the objectivity of any data collected without taking the time to build relations of trust and without the engagement of the researchers.

Notes

1. *The Monitor,* 16 May 1998, 'Let's Vote on Kony War'.
2. *Justice & Peace News,* August 2002, Vol. 2 – No. 5: p4.
3. IRIN, 28 January 2004, *The 18-Year Old War that Refuses To Go Away.*
4. Our starting point was for research staff to contact people known to them to have some family members living abroad.
5. ACORD, ACF, Amnesty International, AVSI, CRS, Christian Aid, Conciliation Resources, CPAR, DENIVA, IRC, Interpares, Life and Peace Institute, Mennonite Central Committee, NRC, Oxfam, Redd Barnet, SNV, Stromme Foundation, TPSO, ARLPI, ISIS, JYAK, Legal Aid Project, EPRC, Northern Uganda Media Forum, Peoples Voices for Peace, Gulu Development Association, Gulu Youth Peace Forum, GUSCO, Hunger Alert, Justice and Peace Commission, Kacokke Madit, KICWA, Dyere Tek.
6. See Chapter 6.
7. I am indebted for these observations to Judith Large.
8. I am indebted to Dr Thi Minh Ngo for this formulation.

3

AN OVERVIEW OF THE SITUATION IN NORTHERN UGANDA

Right now the people of Acholi are in a dilemma. They are neither pro-government nor pro-rebel, but they don't know how to go forward. Once we have clarity about which side will win, we can organise ... it is not possible for this war to end. It will cause a lot of division among the tribes of Uganda. When it started people saw it as just Acholi. Now they see Kony in Kasese, West Nile, Kampala ... (Elder, Gulu district, 1998)

Introduction

It is never easy to know when a war truly began (Azar, 1986; 36). Was it when deaths per year reached a certain level? Or the day the first shot was fired? Or before that, when conditions of structural violence (Galtung 1969) were created which would eventually lead to physical violence? Furthermore, what defines a particular period of violence as a war in its own right rather than simply one more in a succession of phases of violence? The so-called LRA war, after all, follows on from the violence of the Obote and Amin periods, violence during the establishment of colonial rule, and the depredations of the ivory and slave trade in the nineteenth century, to mention only the most obvious. When the explorer Samuel Baker described the Acholi area as he found it in January 1864, he drew a picture which was to be repeated over and over, not least in the years since 1986: 'For many miles circuit from Shooa, the blackened ruins of villages and deserted fields bore witness to the devastation committed; cattle that were formerly in thousands had been driven off, and the beautiful district that had once been most fertile was reduced to a wilderness' (16) (quoted in Gray, 1951: 125). When Girling conducted fieldwork in the area in 1951, he described it as a 'colonial society' and argued that 'it is long since the political organisation of the Acholi … was changed by the direct intervention of the British Administration' (1960: 84).

When a war truly begins is thus not an academic question. It lies at the heart of ambiguities about what it is that interventions such as conflict resolution, peace-building, truth and reconciliation and related transitional justice processes should actually be addressing. How far back do they need to go? Is it sufficient to address the most recent period only, particularly if that recent violence is a symptom of a failure to resolve grievances arising from earlier violence and violations?[1] Certainly many of the older people in northern Uganda made connections between the LRA war and injustices of both the colonial and postcolonial era; when I visited the remains of Baker's Patiko Fort in 1999, my guides could still show me the exact spot where the slavers kept their captives more than one hundred years earlier.[2]

Notwithstanding these substantive reservations about the way in which choosing a start-date risks pre-empting analysis of the current situation, 1986 offers a useful starting point, as the takeover by the NRM marked a dramatic shift in power – and the emergence of new non-state actors. Having recovered a degree of political strength under Obote II (1980 to 1986), the Acholi reverted to a position of relative weakness more akin to their experience during the Amin years (1971 to 1979). The national army, in which 30–40 per cent of troops had been northerners, was routed and replaced by what had been a rebel force dominated by people many regarded as foreigners at worst and southerners at best. Tutsis, who formerly had been their herds-boys, were suddenly the allies of the new regime, and the Karimojong, who traditionally had sheltered Acholi children in times of adversity, were now said to be rustling away Acholi cattle. People's sense of social and cultural cohesion and material security was severely threatened.[3] The decimation of cattle stocks in the early years of the war echoed the thefts by the slave- and ivory-raiders of the late 19th century, which had also resulted in 'The destruction of the once-large herds of Acholi cattle' (Girling 1960: 14). Willet Weeks gives a figure of 123,375 for 1983 dropping to 3000 in 2001 (Weeks 2002: 4). Gersony claims a drop from 285,000 for 1985 to 5,000 in 1997 (Gersony 1997: 27).[4] People's principal asset base was stripped away and, particularly post-1996, life in the protected villages further undermined peoples' subsistence strategies. The period 1986 to 2006 thus marked a dramatic reversal in fortunes for the majority of people in Gulu and Kitgum, a reversal within the lived experience of a significant proportion of the population.

This chapter begins with a brief note on the place of northern Uganda in national politics during the colonial and post-independence period, and then focuses on the period 1986–2006. After setting out the situation in seven distinct chronological phases, it presents the history of the period as remembered by the women of a self-help group, before closing by identifying some key issues and questions which lie at the heart of subsequent chapters. It is possible, as does Gersony (1997), to structure a post-1986 account in terms of the different movements (UPDA, HSM, Severino Lukoya, Early Kony, Current Kony), but this is problematic given that the movements did not constitute wholly distinct chronological phases. It also narrows the conceptual framework to one in which conflict between government and one insurgent grouping or another is the defining feature of the situation. To avoid these shortcomings, I have adopted a structure based on chronological phases of physical violence and relative calm.

Phase I: August 1986 to May 88
Phase II: June 1988 to March 1994
Phase III: April 1994 to early December 1999
Phase IV: Late December 1999 to March 2002
Phase V: April 2002 to November 2003
Phase VI: 2004 to 2006
Phase VII   June 2006 onwards

Each phase was characterised by a period of acute violence followed by lulls which ended when a failed 'solution' unleashed a new wave of ever more intensive violence. Phase I ended after a Peace Accord was signed with one of the main insurgent groups in northern Uganda, the UPDA. Phase II ended with the collapse of direct negotiations between Government and LRA in early 1994. Phase III came to an abrupt close following the signing of a peace accord between the Governments of Uganda and Sudan at the end of 1999, and Phase IV ended following the failure of a massive military operation code-named 'Iron Fist'. True to form the violence which this failed solution catalysed escalated the situation to previously unimagined levels of humanitarian need in Phase V. The overall trend, despite lulls, was one of escalation. It was only in Phase VI, following a damning and unprecedented critique of the situation by the UN, that there was a massive up-turn in external intervention and interest and a corresponding change in the pressures on the Government of Uganda. Phase VII was marked by the Government's decision to engage in peace talks with the LRA from June 2006 onwards, a move which generated some hopes of an eventual return home for the hundreds of thousands of IDPs in northern Uganda.

The Build-Up to War

Missionaries first arrived in the Buganda kingdom in the 1870s, and the area known as Uganda became a British protectorate in 1894. Under British rule development was driven by a divide-and-rule strategy whereby different ethnic groups and the regions they hailed from were favoured for different areas of activity – southerners (notably Baganda) for agriculture and the civil service, northerners (including the Acholi) for the security establishment.[5] As recalled by one Acholi elder (himself a former member of the King's African Rifles during World War II, and an elected chairman of a division in 1952 under British rule); 'The Acholi were promoted by the British Government to handle key administrative positions because of their tolerance and honesty. For example, the leaders of the police force and of the prison service were both Acholis. They would not steal anything and showed a great interest in their work'. When asked if this was a divide-and-rule strategy on the part of the British, his answer was that;

A father of many children will always develop a particular liking for one of them. The Acholi were the favoured child of the British. For example, British bosses would test their staff's honesty by leaving money and thing lying around to see if it would still be there. But to some extent divide and rule was manifested during the distribution of seeds to the different tribes. The Acholi were given cotton seeds, compared to the Baganda who were given coffee and tea which yielded a lot of money at that time. Even the bananas were different, the Acholi received Jamaica bananas, the Baganda received [a type called] Bayoya. This was a source of tension; when you went to Baganda you would find different seeds … The Acholi were told through agricultural policy that certain types of seed were unsuitable. [6]

As such no one group or sub-region enjoyed both military and economic power simultaneously, and discourses of ethnic difference were established which live on to this day. The promotion of Acholi to major positions in the security establishment for example, was, after independence, reframed as proving that they were militaristic, a notion which many Acholi themselves bought into.

Colonisation by the Catholic and Anglican churches added further complexities, with combinations of religious and ethnic divisions inexorably coming to underpin the political parties formed in the run-up to independence. The Uganda National Congress (UNC) formed in 1952 was predominantly Protestant, while the Democratic Party (DP) formed in 1956 was predominantly Catholic. The Uganda People's Congress (UPC) formed in 1960 opposed both the Catholic political movement and claims for an independent Buganda state, while the Kabaka Yekka (KY) party created in 1961 represented the predominantly Protestant Buganda kingdom's drive for autonomy. As such, by the time of independence in 1962, the organising principles of ethnicity, sub-region, religion and politics could only be extricated from one another with considerable difficulty,[7] but rather than creating a unified whole they had generated what – in a reference to Winston Churchill's description of Uganda as the 'Pearl of Africa' – has been described as a 'fragmented pearl' (O'Brien, 1997). Indeed, the independence constitution reflected a hierarchy of different ethnic groups, granting federal status to the kingdom of Buganda, semi-federal status to the kingdoms of Ankole, Bunyoro and Toro, and district status to Acholi, Bugisu, Bukedi, Karamoja, Kigezi, Lango, Madi, Sebei, Teso and West Nile (Mutibwa, 1992: 24). Following the coup by Obote, a northerner from Lango, in 1966, this independence constitution was suspended. The reformed constitution of 1967, which officially de-ethnicised the polity, angered those who had been at the top of it (in particular the Baganda), aggravating ethnic tensions and strengthening their importance as an axis of anti-government mobilisation. The whole question of the status of ethnic kingdoms and leadership remained live, resulting in concessions from the NRM Government such as the reinstatement of the *Kabaka* of Buganda in 1990, followed by the *Omukama* of the Banyoro, and the anointment of the *Rwot Moo* of the Acholi in 2000. However, these ethnic structures were weaker than in the past – not least because they could no longer collect taxes, this function having been taken over by county chiefs.

Ethnic/religious/sub-regional tensions increased incrementally over the following decades, and not just along north-south lines.[8] Examples often given in conversation include Idi Amin's use of soldiers from West Nile to persecute Acholi and Langi in the 1970s, the Karamajong's extension of cattle-raiding westwards to the Acholi sub-region in the early 1980s, and the involvement of Acholi soldiers in atrocities in the central Luwero triangle in the early 1980s.[9]

Phase I (1986 to 1988)

For people in northern Uganda, the period immediately after the capture of Kampala by Museveni's National Resistance Army in January 1986 was a strange time of holding one's breath while preparing for the worst. Someone who was fifteen at the time recalled how:

> When the news broke that the government ... was overthrown by Yoweri Kaguta Museveni ... there were repeated calls in the form of public addresses and rallies for [the] public to join the army of Tito Okello Lutwa to defend our land and properties from the invading Banyarwanda led by Museveni and others. The population were convinced beyond doubt by the army that no one would escape death if the NRA rebels captured Gulu district ...

> Day by day the numbers of UNLA soldiers who were coming from Kampala increased. Their arrival in town also meant increases in the numbers of vehicles as most of them were able to come back with vehicles and other looted items. One of my uncles came back with a lorry full of assorted looted items from Kampala.... There was no news of the NRA advance. In reality they were closing in from various fronts, but had not yet reached Karuma [where there is a key crossing over the river Nile].

He went on to describe how the UNLA soldiers forcibly rounded-up civilians, took them to the barracks and armed them with guns, pangas, spears, bows and arrows 'for confrontation with the NRA around Karuma bridge'.

By March 1986 the NRA had reached and taken Gulu town. A brief and deceptive lull soon gave way to extreme turmoil marked by the formation of a number of different insurgent groups. The Uganda People's Democratic Army (UPDA), known as 'Cilil', was made up of UNLA members who had fled northwards following the overthrow of Obote in July 1985 and Tito Okello in January 1986. Having passed through Gulu on their way north, they initially based themselves in southern Sudan, and made links with the Equatoria Defence Force (Allen, 2005b: 4) but, following problems with the Sudanese Peoples' Liberation Army (SPLA), came back to Gulu district and began attacks on the NRA.

> In 1987 they managed to surround Gulu town, and people were not able to go more than 1/2 kilometre from the centre of the town ... Life was so difficult in terms of food, feeding, recreation, education-wise and in all other aspects ... The government soldiers were so weak that the rebels could come to town and do what they wished to do without any resistance ... The rebels could go up to the barracks and exchange bullets with the government soldiers.

As well as the UPDA, a less conventional force, the prophetic Holy Spirit Movement (HSM), was built up under the leadership of a woman known as Alice Lakwena, who claimed to be possessed by a Christian spirit known as Lakwena ('Messenger'). The HSM's military wing, the Holy Spirit Mobile Forces, began operating in August 1986, only months after the NRA had established control over northern Uganda. This has been described in some depth by Heike Behrend (1999).

The NRA, after consolidating their position and reinforcing their numbers, responded to these various insurgencies with considerable force and brutality. As they moved outwards from Gulu town, their behaviour confirmed people's worst fears, as they 'started killing people, burning houses, looting food items and doing all other bad things to the local population' (see Tables 1–5 below for examples). By December 86 the NRA was seeking to capture '*Cilil*' and 'Lakwena' and their collaborators. One respondent, after hearing gun-shots, fled his home, but:

> All our family members who did not hear the gun shot were captured and died very terribly. The army moved into the whole area and captured every civilian within the surrounding area and assembled them within the Divisional Headquarters. At about 10.00 A.M. out of 33 people who were assembled 28 were killed and left at the Division along the road side ... From that day the Government army killed many people in various places within the Division. I slept in the bush for one and a half weeks and later on decided to move away to Kampala where I remained for three years up to 1989 November when I came back to Gulu.

Another respondent described how the army pursued them as they fled:

> Now when we saw the smoke of our burning houses, we decided to run and hide in a nearby stream called Lacwii. But as we were crossing ... it seemed the NRA realised [where] we were hiding ... because they started firing and bombing the Lacwii. This was a day I knew God protects and preserves. Bullets were pouring in our direction like drizzling rain, and their sounds were like popping simsim [sesame] ...

Although NRA features heavily in accounts of violence from that period, UPDA and HSM were also guilty of much looting, killing and burning (see Tables 1–5). There was also considerable destruction of infrastructure such as dispensaries and schools, and the beginnings of large-scale internal displacement.

Having reached Jinja in a circuitous march on Kampala, Lakwena's HSM was militarily defeated in October 1987. Lakwena fled to Kenya where she retained refugee status at the time of writing (2005). When a peace accord with the UPDA followed in May 1988, it seemed the worst might be over. However, it was an incomplete peace. Some remnants of both HSM and UPDA fed into the developing strength of the Lord's Army under Alice's father Severino Lukwoya, and the Lord's Resistance Army under Joseph Kony. Somewhat confusingly Kony's group began as the Holy Spirit Movement, changed its name briefly to United Democratic Christian Army, before eventually settling on the name Lord's Resistance Army (LRA). To add to the confusion, Kony also claimed to be possessed by the spirit of Lakwena.

Phase II (1988 to 1994)

By late 1988 it was clear that the war was far from over. In what Amnesty International describe as 'one of the most intense phases of the war, between October and December 1988 ... the NRA forcibly cleared approximately 100,000 people from their homes in and around Gulu town. Soldiers committed hundreds of extra-judicial executions as they forced people out of their homes, burning down homesteads and granaries' (Amnesty International, 1999: 11). Behrend describes how 'in November 1989, Gulu, the capital of Acholi District, was a city "occupied" by the NRA. Trucks carrying soldiers and weapons careered down the main street' (Behrend, 1999).

Many respondents recalled 1989 as the year in which

> The army's second division used to do this male rape, known as Tek Gungu, on any men who were arrested in the rural villages, over a period of six or seven months. Many of them subsequently committed suicide. To be victim of Tek Gungu was regarded as worse than being killed. There was a period when these events even entered into the songs people sang. Eventually local leaders protested and the whole unit was transferred.[10]

The toll on the economic and social fabric was beginning to be felt. Dowries were given in cash as cattle had been rustled, sexually transmitted diseases were perceived to be rising, the only large-scale industry in the area (the foam mattress factory in Gulu) relocated to Jinja, and there were repeated army 'operations' to identify rebel collaborators. Abuse of civilians remained the order of the day. One respondent who lost twenty-nine head of cattle in 1990 to soldiers, recalled being told that 'it was government policy to remove all the Acholi animals to be eaten by the army'.

1991 saw the beginning of LRA mutilations and maimings reminiscent of those of RENAMO in Mozambique, including the cutting of lips and noses and the use of padlocks on the mouths of people they thought might report them to the authorities. In April a major four-month Government anti-insurgency operation known as Operation North was launched under which travel was severely restricted and people were rounded up for screening. During this period 890 elders met in Viva Rest-house in Gulu (where they were fed courtesy of the 4th Division Commander) and passed a resolution that the population should be organised into 'bow-and-arrow defence units' to fight the rebels – a collaboration with the Government which did not escape the watchful eyes of the LRA (see Chapter 4).[11]

1992 saw the launch of the first Northern Uganda Reconstruction Program (NURP I), ostensibly 'an emergency operation aimed at restoring basic economic and social infrastructure as well as reviving economic activities in the northern region.' This targeted fourteen districts in total. While budgeted at U.S. $600 million in 1991, only $93.6 million would ultimately be disbursed (COWI 1999: 20–28).

The tit-for-tat relationship between Uganda and Sudan, which was to become more prominent in later years, was already visible at this point, with the bombing of Moyo by the Sudanese in 1990, and sightings in Gulu of the SPLA leader, John Garang, in 1991. International interest was demonstrated when Pope John Paul II visited Gulu in 1993 to pray for peace from a specially constructed podium which was still standing in the centre of Kaunda Ground six years later.[12]

In 1992 and 1993 violence abated, prompting several secondary schools displaced from 1988 onwards to return to their original sites.[13] Mrs Betty Bigombe, then Minister for Pacification of the North, led a series of face-to-face meetings between representatives of both Government and LRA in late 1993 and early 1994, raising hopes that peace was just around the corner (see Chapter 4). [14] Instead, an ultimatum from Museveni to the LRA in early February to come out of the bush within seven days or be killed, led to the collapse of talks and a dramatic resurgence of violence.

Phase III (1994 to 1999)

This third phase of the conflict took place against a changing national backdrop. Following the adoption of the 1995 Constitution, which limited the office of President to two five-year terms, Museveni was elected for a first term under the new constitution in May 1996 – effectively ignoring his previous ten years in power – and declared his intention to defeat the LRA militarily. The Local Government Act of 1997 devolved many functions and powers previously exercised by the Central Government, further deepening capacity problems in northern Uganda. Two years later a report for the second Northern Uganda Reconstruction Programme noted that 'under current decentralisation, districts have a tendency to compromise quality because of biases to recruit local ethnic personnel' (COWI 1999a: 21). A further development after the 1996 elections was the formation of the Acholi Parliamentary Group comprising all eleven elected Acholi MPs. This grouping would play some role in raising national awareness of the war, particularly in pushing a motion through Parliament calling for a national investigation into the situation.

Phase III was marked by ongoing LRA insurgency from rear bases in the Sudan, allegations of increased Sudanese support to the LRA, and a number of major atrocities which are generally attributed to the LRA. These included the Attiak massacre of 22 April 1995, the ambush of the Karuma/Pakwach convoy of 8 March 1996, the Acholpi refugee camp massacre of July 1996, St Mary's College abductions in October 1996 (the 'Aboke Girls'), and the Lokung/Palabek massacre of some 412 people in January 1997 (Gersony 1997: 38–44).

People began commuting into safer areas by night and returning to their homes during the day-time. Places such as Gulu town and Lacor hospital were overflowing with people sleeping in any available spot. One elder recalled;

> Before the protected villages in 1997 everybody was forced to come and stay in town. Some people sneaked back to the village because they had no money for food or rent. The churches were full, so was Kaunda Ground, Pece Stadium was full of tents, also Gulu medical [hospital]. Food was supplied by Red Cross, World Vision, Church of Uganda and Catholic Church. They [the displaced] were known as 'Oring Ayela', 'Those who have run from the problem.[15]

By late 1996 the Government began a strategy of 'protected villages'. Located in pre-existing hubs of local economic and administrative activity otherwise known as trading centres, these brought people from widely scattered small villages together into much larger aggregates ranging from a few thousands up to tens of thousands. They generally had a military presence (a 'detach') for the ostensible purposes of protection from the LRA. Although some people chose to move into such camps voluntarily, others were forced by the UPDF (see Chapter 5).

Together with LRA atrocities, the formation of the protected villages was the defining feature of phase III of the conflict, and in many respects remained so from that point forwards. From late 1996 there was a flurry of screening exercises known as *panda gari* (Swahili for 'climb into the truck'). Whereas the one in 1991 included women and children, most of the later ones focused on rounding up hundreds of men who were then obliged to identify themselves to the army – failure to do so could result in arrest on suspicion of being a rebel or a rebel collaborator.[16]

External factors were increasingly acknowledged. In 1997, for example, *The Monitor* reported that 'President Yoweri Museveni, after years of denials, has finally acknowledged United States assistance in its protracted northern war with Sudan-backed rebels'.[17] In June 1998, when the Uganda Young Democrats (with partial sponsorship from the British Labour party) organised a seminar on the theme 'Human Rights and Democracy', their Vice-President argued that 'This war is not ours. It is a war of imperialistic interests; a war of mineral wealth and oil in southern Sudan; it is a war of influence. That woman (Albright), who promised us nothing but guns to kill our own people and to protect American interests in this region, is bad'.[18] At the conference on 'Peace Research and the Reconciliation Agenda' held in Gulu in September 1999 the fact that the SPLA were hosted in northern Uganda was publicly acknowledged, and both the Local Council Chairman and the Resident District Commissioner argued that 'the major stumbling block is the problematic relationship with the Sudan'. An Acholi elder concurred: 'The war is not between Kony and the government – it is between the governments of Sudan and Uganda. The peace talks and conferences will not stop the war unless the Sudan and Uganda governments understand each other and Sudan stop support [to the] LRA and Uganda stop support [to the] SPLA'.[19] The MP for Gulu Municipality, while chairing a debate on the Sudan, asked the panellists to address a number of questions:

> 'What is Sudan's government stands towards neighbours and their intentions for the Region? What are the regime's chances of survival? I mean the Sudan regime, not any other regime.[20] What are the strength and the weakness of SPLA and the Northern opposition alliance? How are they affected by changes in tactics of those who back them in the region, and globally? What is the form and extent of greater power involvement? When we talk of the greater power, we mean those who have ever launched nuclear bombs.[21] And is the solution to the Sudan conflict a prerequisite for peace in Acholi Land and Northern Uganda?

At the end of the same conference the Minister of State for Northern Uganda noted participants' concerns that the Sudan could continue as 'the host and master of LRA and as the source of arms trafficking' unless diplomatic relations were regularised and 'we address issues about the role of SPLA and other rebel groups in the peace process in Northern Uganda'.[22] UNICEF gave a taste of interventions to come, when in June 1998 it called for LRA abductors to be tried at the International Criminal Court,[23] and a UPDF helicopter crash in July 1998 offered a further glimpse of international involvement, as the Russian-made Mi. 17, commonly known as *Sura Mbaya* (Swahili for 'Ugly Face'), had been piloted by an Ethiopian.[24] This prompted a statement from the LRM (Lord's Resistance Movement) that 'We are deeply sorry for the deaths of foreign nationals being killed in an internal war between Ugandans. We appeal to the Ethiopians to stop their nationals fighting us'.[25]

Three important civil society groupings emerged in this period, all calling for a negotiated solution; the diaspora grouping Kacokke Madit, the Acholi Religious Leaders Peace Initiative (ARLPI), and the revived Acholi 'traditional leaders'. With financial support from the British Government, the diaspora grouping, which described itself as 'a non-profit making forum dedicated to identifying and implementing practical initiatives to end the armed conflict in Northern Uganda by peaceful means', organised several big meetings (Kacokke Madit), the first two of which were held in London in 1997 and 1998 respectively. These were also attended by the Ugandan Government, Acholi Members of Parliament, religious leaders and district leaders. The third was convened in Nairobi in late 2000, but was terminated due to fears that delegates might be harbouring the Ebola virus wreaking havoc in Gulu at the time.

While the 1997 meeting was attended by LRA external coordinator, Dr James Obita, rumours put out by the New Vision that Kony would 'lead a delegation of his supporters'[26] to the 1998 one proved unfounded. One fieldworker reported that 'Last month [June 1998] they [the LRA] were telling people that they are not going to attend "Kacokke Madit" in London since it is a waste of money. They want the "Kacokke Madit" to take place either in northern Uganda or Kampala'.[27] The *New Vision* reported that in one preparatory meeting for Kacokke Madit 1998 Acholi exiles had 'criticised President Yoweri Museveni for 'not doing enough to protect and feed the people of Acholi particularly those in protected villages"'.[28] A few weeks later they reported the LRA's refusal to participate, apparently because they saw it as 'the brain child of President Museveni'.[29]

The formation of the Acholi Religious Leaders Peace Initiative (ARLPI) in May 1998 brought Catholics, Anglicans and Muslims from Gulu and Kitgum districts together under one umbrella. The inaugural meeting named *Bedo Piny pi Kuc* ('Let us sit down for peace'), signalled a commitment to a negotiated solution and was attended by, amongst others, the Resident Representatives of the World Bank and UNDP, the Minister of State for Northern Uganda, and the UPDF's 4th Division Commander. ARLPI's membership was subsequently expanded to include religious leaders from throughout northern Uganda, and over the following years they became increasingly critical players in the anti-war camp. These processes were given extra impetus by the installation of a new Anglican bishop of Gulu, Bishop Onono Onweng in May 1998, and a new Catholic Archbishop, John Baptist Odama, in early 1999. ARLPI was to become involved in trying to make links with the LRA, raising international awareness of the situation, and confronting Government misdemeanours.

The third civil society voice to emerge in this period was the revived 'traditional leadership'. Although widely welcomed at a local level, their restoration, far from being a purely local initiative, was in fact largely externally driven and enabled. The then Minister of State for Northern Uganda, himself an Acholi, promoted it inside Uganda with ideological support from a report written for a British NGO by a British Government Social Development Adviser. Funding came from the Belgian Government, and implementation capacity from the international NGO ACORD. The rationale was that if traditional leaders were reinstated they could do two things. Firstly, by virtue of their position they would be able to command the respect of the 'boys in the bush', who, it was asserted, would heed a call from the elders to lay down their weapons. Secondly, and also by virtue of their traditional roles, they would be able to effect cleansing ceremonies between returned rebels and their home communities, processes without which, it was said, reconciliation and therefore successful reintegration could not take place. Although there was no noticeable impact on levels of return from the LRA, the restoration did add another institutional voice in favour of negotiation to counter the Government's militaristic position.

There was thus increasing polarisation between the Government's preference for military solutions and civil society's favouring a negotiated one. In 1998 the Dutch chargé d'affaires reportedly said that the war in the north was affecting Uganda's image abroad and undermining its attractiveness to foreign investment. He also argued that 'the army is draining Uganda's sons in their prime who could otherwise use their talents to build up the country'.[30] Museveni remained adamant until mid-1999 that the situation demanded a 'military solution', ruling that negotiations with 'bandits' were out of the question. This was echoed by his brother, Salim Saleh, who said that 'the conflict will be solved by military means, not dialogue'.[31] When in 1997 the *Report of the Committee on Defence and Internal Affairs on the War in Northern Uganda* was published, it recommended pursuing the military option, obliging two Acholi members of the committee[32] to append a minority report urging a negotiated solution, as they felt this more accurately reflected the wishes of those consulted.[33] As such, dichotomised positions regarding a solution became an extension of the conflict itself.

Foreign governments offered some financial assistance, but generally made little (visible) strategic contribution to the debate at this stage. By 1997 the local organisation working with returned abducted children from the LRA, Gulu Support the Children Organisation (GUSCO), had established a reception centre with DANIDA funding.[34] Following a visit by the all-party International Development Committee of the British House of Commons, the British Government donated items valued at 44 million Shillings to GUSCO (approx. £14,000), and these 'included 80 mattresses, 40 double-bed-deckers, 15 sewing machines, a generator and computers'.[35] Only a few weeks later

Mrs Clinton also said her country through USAID will provide U.S. $500,000 directly to local groups including Concerned Parents Association and Gulu Save the Children Organisation to help them find abducted children and give them the medical care they need to heal. She also said they will provide another U.S. $2 million over the next three years for a new Northern Uganda Initiative that will help people plagued by rebel activities get jobs, rebuild schools, health clinics and their own communities.[36]

There was a gradual increase in interest from international organisations, with, for example, the establishment of a UN Disaster Management Team (UNDMT) charged with developing a Relief and Rehabilitation Programme for Displaced People in northern Uganda (WFP 1999: 20). In 1997, as well as Gersony's report on the war, UNICEF set up ACRIS – the Abducted Child Registration and Information System – to record both ongoing patterns of abduction and return, and to build a retrospective picture. Human Rights Watch and Amnesty International both produced reports detailing LRA atrocities (HRW, 1997, Mawson, 1997), followed by a further one from Amnesty International on Government abuses (Mawson, 1999). In 1998 the U.K.'s television Channel 4 screened a film ('The Mission') about the 1994 peace talks and the abduction of the Aboke girls in 1996. The Belgian organisation, *Pax Christi,* made a political decision when it decided to fund the travel expenses of the district chairmen of Gulu and Kitgum districts to go to Nairobi in 1998 'to meet a delegation of Lord's Resistance Movement/Army (LRM/A) in a bid to initiate peace talks'.[37]

From early 1999 there was a noticeable lull in LRA activity. Together with some changes in the political climate, notably President Museveni's agreement to allow people to talk with the LRA (though he himself refused to do so), this created hopes that peace was just around the corner. Several national and international NGOs moved into Gulu district, eager to revive 'traditional' leadership and reconciliation mechanisms, and to address the trauma of returned abducted children. The Belgian Government, in addition to the small yet politically significant amounts it invested in 'traditional leadership', put significant finance into upgrading the telephone system as part of NURP I, and, from 1999, USAID channelled large volumes of aid through an array of local and international NGOs, notably Red Barnet (Danish Save the Children).

The lull in LRA activity coincided with extensive UPDF activity in the neighbouring Democratic Republic of Congo. UPDF forces had been involved in various ways in the fighting in the DRC from 1997 (UN, 2001), and 1999 saw overt fighting there between UPDF and Rwandan Government forces. Despite the Lusaka peace accord of July 1999, fighting continued, some of it involving UPDF forces recruited from northern Uganda.[38]

District level consultations on NURP II ended with a national consensus workshop in Kampala in October 1999. The District Profile for Gulu and Kitgum, drawn up as part of this process, argued that

> The government must acknowledge the scale of trauma-related problems as underlying causes for conflict and underdevelopment. It is critical for all concerned parties involved in the war in the Northern region to develop the will to take the difficult political steps required to prevent further human rights abuses. The continued plight

of the lives of thousands of children and individuals who are helplessly affected by the effects of the war, calls for a strategy to resolve the war through peaceful means.

It also argued that, if peace were to be attained, the underlying causes of the conflict had to be addressed. It therefore stressed a need for 'trauma support systems' and a need to identify 'the interest groups causing insecurity', and thus added weight to calls for a non-military solution (COWI, 1999b; 21).

Perhaps as a political concession to these pressures, the Government signed a Carter Center-brokered 'peace agreement' with the Sudanese Government in Nairobi on 8 December 1999. The LRA had not been involved in direct negotiation, and within just two weeks of the peace agreement, the LRA re-entered Uganda from Sudan. Civilians who over the previous six months had begun tentatively leaving the 'protected villages' in order to return home, now found themselves being herded back by the army. Vehicles were ambushed and burnt on all roads out of Gulu except the Kampala highway, and rebels mounted attacks on Government targets in the heart of Gulu town. Phase IV had clearly begun.

Phase IV – Amnesty for 'Terrorists' (2000 to 2002)

In early January, people were again forced back into the protected villages in scenes reminiscent of the late 1980s and mid-1990s (see Chapter 5). On 17 January, having been pushed for primarily by those interested in seeing a non-violent solution to the LRA conflict, the long-awaited Amnesty Act was put in place. Many question-marks had hung over its development: Could it work without direct negotiations – peace talks – with the rebels? Would it be right to give unconditional amnesty, without ensuring that the culprits admitted and atoned for their crimes and some guarantee that they would not re-offend? What would be the implications for civil liability vis-à-vis Acholi who refused to recognise traditional inter-clan reconciliation mechanisms such as *mato oput* and compensation payments for damage done or lives taken (*culo kwor*)? How would it accommodate non-Acholi who might insist on enforcing their rights through civil courts? The timing and actual implementation of the Amnesty law were also concerns: should it begin before preparations to receive, demobilise and resettle returnees were completed?

As finally formulated, the Act offered amnesty for 'any Ugandan who has at any time since the 26th day of January, 1986 engaged in or is engaging in war or armed rebellion against the government of the Republic of Uganda'. Persons who voluntarily renounced such acts were to be pardoned and excused from criminal prosecution. To avoid the Commission having to deal with the large numbers abducted and returned within a matter of days or weeks it was only available for former LRA members who were above twelve years of age and who had stayed with the LRA for more than four months. In all other respects it was a 'blanket' amnesty, open to all members of rebel groups, including the leadership. It was initially to run for six months, with the possibility of extension by the Minister for Internal Affairs. Due both to lack of funding (the Government provided the Commission with just under U.S. $1 million annually for adminis-trative costs) and, some would argue, lack of political will, the amnesty process took some time to be put in place, with the Commission officially appointed in July 2000, and the Gulu and Kitgum offices opened in February and July 2001 respectively.

In parallel with these processes, a reasonable degree of security had been re-established relatively quickly in early 2000 following the LRA's angry outburst in late December 2001. By some accounts the LRA was under considerable pres-sure within Sudan in the wake of the Nairobi peace accord, and was seeking to make links with the Equatoria Defence Forces, a Sudanese rebel force operating in South Sudan. They finally met with the Carter Center in February 2000, and in July a ministerial meeting was hosted in Atlanta at which the Atlanta Joint Action Plan for the Implementation of the Nairobi Agreement was drawn up. A further meeting was convened in Khartoum in October 2000, and another in November, this time in Nairobi.

The UN Office for Co-ordination of Humanitarian Affairs (UNOCHA) re-ported that 'improved security and access in northern Uganda encouraged many relief agencies to establish semi-permanent offices in Acholiland. The number of agencies involved with relief assistance increased from five in mid-1996 to over 60 by end-2000' (UNOCHA 2001: 14). A severe outbreak of Ebola haemor-rhagic fever in Gulu district in late 2000 (thought by some to have been brought back from the DRC by a returning soldier) fuelled local and international calls for the dismantling of the protected villages.

On 3 June 2001 the Carter Center hosted a further implementation meeting in Nairobi. Gulu District's LCV Chairman met with the LRA on 4 June 2001, and the Government declared a demilitarized zone. In a further implementation meeting in Nairobi in November 2001, a letter was written to Kony asking him to participate in the dialogue, but to no avail. By late 2001, UNOCHA was re-porting increased movement between camps and home areas in both Gulu and Kitgum, and that 'Although District authorities have not directed 'decongestion' per se, there are numerous reports of people responding to new deployments by UPDF and creating settlements close to these. New smaller camps have been set up (from large camps) throughout the sub-county, especially around larger camps like Pabbo' (OCHA, December 2001, reported in Global IDP database).[39]

At a political level, 2000 saw a contentious referendum on the continued vi-ability of the 'Movement' political system, and 2001 saw President Museveni's re-election for a second term, though with virtually no support in the north-ern districts. Pader district was created out of the southern half of Kitgum dis-trict. During this period, the Amnesty Act although intended primarily for the LRA, in practice proved more popular with non-LRA insurgent groups. When the Gulu diocese Justice and Peace Commission investigated the fact that less than 400 LRA members had taken up amnesty by April 2002, they concluded that 'Groups in Acholi civil society have always held that a blanket amnesty is a crucial instrument in bringing a lasting peace to the troubled region. However, two and a half years after being passed by the Parliament of Uganda, the effects of the Amnesty Law in Acholi are not very much in evidence'.[40] Worse still, they found that over half of returnees were being pressurised to incorporate into the UPDF.

Throughout this phase, religious leaders made attempts to meet with LRA members, but these were generally disrupted by the UPDF. Meanwhile, pressure on the LRA from both inside and outside Uganda appeared to be increasing. The EU drew up a resolution in July 2000 calling 'on individual EU Member States to ban LRA operations and travelling of LRA representatives within the EU and between EU Member States and non-EU Nations' (2002, L12). In April 2001, the U.S.A.'s Department of State included the LRA on its 'B-list' of 'other terrorist organisations', and there was talk of using the Terrorism Act of January 2002 against LRA members in the U.K.[41] UNOCHA reported that 'With the development of the Uganda-Sudan relationship (by beginning of 2002), Kony has become increasingly isolated from external support and funding; especially as the U.K. has frozen bank accounts of known LRA and ADF collaborators as part of the crackdown on terrorism' (UNOCHA, 28 February 2002: 31–32).

In March 2002 Uganda passed its own Anti-Terrorism Act. This largely removed the space for senior people to return from the bush and engage in reconciliation processes. Conventional rules of legal construction stipulate that where two legal instruments are in conflict, the later instrument, in this case the Anti-Terrorism Act, takes precedence. Thus while the Amnesty Act granted amnesty for engagement in 'war or armed rebellion', the Anti-Terrorism Act rendered punishable acts carried out for purposes of 'influencing the government or influencing the public ... and for a political or religious ... or economic aim'.[42] It made no reference to the Amnesty Act, and designated the LRA/M as a terrorist organisation, membership of which was a punishable criminal offence. In principle therefore it effectively negated the Amnesty Act,[43] prompting one Amnesty Commission official to argue that 'the reason why top rebel commanders refuse to respond to the amnesty is because of the Anti-Terrorism Act'. It also put a serious damper on civilian attempts to make contacts with the LRA, as any dialogue with them could be interpreted as treason.

The discourse of a global 'war on terrorism' generated by the U.S.A. and its allies post-September 11 2001, translated into previously unthinkable anti-LRA actions on the ground. On 10 January 2002, Presidents Bashir and Museveni, together with then U.K. Secretary of State for Development, Clare Short, held bilateral talks while attending an Inter-Governmental Authority on Development (IGAD)[44] summit in Khartoum. They agreed on UPDF incursions into southern Sudan, with the stated aims of rescuing abducted children and capturing or killing Kony and his key commanders. In other words, an operation to deal with the LRA once and for all. UNOCHA reported widespread reservations about the operation's feasibility, its potential humanitarian impact and long-term political consequences, for it was seen as jeopardising 'long-term issues of reconciliation both within Acholi society and between Acholi and the rest of Ugandan society' (Weeks, 2002: 20–21). Religious leaders stated that 'it seems as if the hawks are flying higher and higher. Although the doves are not yet dead they are hardly heard'.[45] Nevertheless, troops began massing in the border areas known as Aswa Ranch from January 2002 onwards, where the U.S.A. sponsored 'routine training' for 6,000 of them.[46]

Phase V – Operation Iron Fist and its Aftermath (2002 to 2003)

Operation Iron Fist officially began on 8 March 2002, and a protocol was signed on 12 March with the Government of Sudan allowing the UPDF to attack Kony bases inside Sudan – with a deadline of 2 April. Although 10,000 Ugandan soldiers were deployed in south Sudan, and by the end of March claimed to have captured all four main rebel camps, this was at the cost of many UPDF soldiers' lives and an escalation of civilian suffering to new levels – seen from northern Uganda the primary indicator of military activity was trucks carrying live soldiers northwards and corpses southwards. At the first extension of the agreement in late May, the army spokesman reportedly said that 'this was "definitely the last phase" of the Ugandan army operation' and that 'Kony will either be killed or die of hunger, or surrender, within the next 45 days'.[47] There was, however, nothing to back up these claims, and by early June UNICEF pointed out that 'Only two infants – of some 3,000 LRA abductees whose return had been included in contingency plans prepared by humanitarian organisations – had been rescued by the UPDF'.[48]

Rather than capturing the LRA, Operation Iron Fist drove them into northern Uganda. By May 2002 insecurity was again severe, the operation was extended to 19 June and roads were built inside Sudan to facilitate the hunt for Kony, who, in a striking parallel with Osama Bin Laden, was allegedly hiding in the Imatong complex of hills. As UNOCHA reported on the IDP situation, established new offices in the north, and began working on a Government of Uganda policy on IDPs, UN involvement increased. The report was a first step in this process as it highlighted the many points of the UN's Guiding Principles on Internal Displacement which were not being addressed in northern Uganda (see Chapter 5).

In June 2002, the Government signed a formal ceasefire with UNRF II, a splinter group from the West Nile Bank Front formed in 1996. Some 2,500 fighters had taken up the offer of amnesty some months earlier, allegedly because of the pressure created by Operation Iron Fist.[49] At the same time, as the UPDF came under pressure, community leaders in Gulu and Kitgum were ordered to recruit at least five men each from their respective wards.[50] One extension of the agreement followed another, and by late August 2002 an estimated 30,000 UPDF forces were deployed in northern Uganda. Gulu alone was said to have contributed over six thousand Home-guards.[51] In September 2002 an agreement between President Museveni and President Kabila of the DRC committed Uganda to withdrawing its remaining troops from the neighbouring DRC, in return for action against Congo-based rebels hostile to the Ugandan government. By October, long after the 45 days promised back in May had passed, Museveni

announced 25 per cent cuts in social services budgets in order to fund the building of roads for the military in northern Uganda.[52] In November 2002, President
Museveni established a Presidential Peace Team (PPT)[53] comprising army officers, government ministers, and Acholi MPs, and he called on the LRA to assemble in designated areas, a call which was ignored. The pact with Sudan was
extended again in December, to last up to the end of January 2003. It covered
the same region as that covered by agreements on humanitarian access between
the Khartoum government and the United Nations.[54]

The PPT team was expanded in January 2003 to include representatives from
all districts of the Acholi sub-region. Led by Salim Saleh, it attempted unsuccessfully to meet the LRA in March 2003. The latter also rejected a second call from
Museveni to the LRA to assemble in designated 'safe-zones', and demanded
instead that a cease-fire be extended throughout the whole region. By April the
GoU's cease-fire offer had been withdrawn, and the PPT's efforts appeared to
come to a standstill. In May the chair of the PPT, Eriya Kategaya (formerly Minister for Internal Affairs), was dismissed from Government. In the same month
a 'Dialogue for Peace' workshop in Gulu resulted in the formation of another
peace team (*Uduru Kuc*), but this never made any serious intervention. According to one team member, this was because the LRA failed to name a corresponding team, but several individuals and organisations claimed to have made offers
to help link the PPT with the LRA, offers which were rejected.[55]

In 2003 the LRA took the war into eastern Uganda, reaching as far as Soroti
and Katakwi, as well as Lira district. As in the past, the LRA were not the only
source of violence, but they bore principal responsibility. Abductions increased
dramatically, with some estimates reaching as high as 5000 new abductions in the
period June 2002 – March 2003 alone (HRW 2003). Nightly commuting, which
had been one of the reasons for creating 'protected villages' in 1996, re-emerged
on a massive scale. It featured prominently in attempts to draw the attention of
the international community to the gravity of the situation, notably through
initiatives such as the 'Gulu Walk'. Less attention was given to an unprecedented
escalation in militarization. In response to the LRA's incursions, people in the
Teso sub-region formed an ethnic militia known as *Amuka,* a process speedily
brought under government control. The government itself then encouraged the
formation of a similar militia in the Lango sub-region (Rhino Boys) and ultimately in Kitgum district too (Frontier Guards), providing both arms and some
minimal training. By this process at least 25,000 men were brought under arms
in the space of little over six months, ostensibly to share the burden of protecting the civilian population and allow the army to intensify its pursuit of the
LRA (Dolan, 2004).

Phase VI – November 2003 to June 2006

The visit to northern Uganda by the UN Secretary General's Special Representative on Humanitarian Affairs, Jan Egeland, in November 2003, was one of
several crucial events that dramatically changed the whole situation. Against

a backdrop of internal displacement which by then affected 80–90 per cent of the population in the Acholi sub-region (by early 2004, the WFP were providing relief distributions to over 1.5 million internally displaced people in northern Uganda, including hundreds of thousands in Teso and Lango sub-regions), his observation that northern Uganda was one of the worst humanitarian crises in the world, sparked a significant increase in levels of external intervention over the next two years (notably from UNOCHA, UNICEF, OHCHR, UNHCR and its implementing partners). This had the advantage of drawing resources and attention to this hitherto seriously under-recognised situation, and the disadvantage of tending to depoliticise it by stressing its humanitarian dimensions. Whether there was benefit in the UN's decision to make northern Uganda one of the pilots for UNHCR's extension of activities to include IDPs, and for its controversial 'cluster approach', is not clear.

A second event, which further extended northern Uganda's role as guinea-pig for the international community, was President Museveni's decision in January 2004 to make a referral to the newly established International Criminal Court (ICC). His call for the Court to prosecute the LRA for war crimes was welcomed by the prosecutor, Luis Moreno-Ocampo, although most civil society organisations active in northern Uganda viewed it with considerable scepticism. They pointed out that it was at odds with the provisions of the Amnesty Act of 2000, an act which had only been passed after extended lobbying of a reluctant government, and which the LRA had only just begun to take up in significant numbers. As the first referral to the ICC it came to be seen as a test-case for the viability of the institution, and supporters of the ICC quickly polarised the debate by arguing that critics of the ICC were opponents of justice and proponents of impunity.

A third feature of this phase was the elections of February 2005, in which Museveni's NRM received virtually no votes across the conflict-affected regions of the country. As a local UN official commented, 'The north has always voted against Museveni's government, but this time it was clear. Now they [the government] have realised if they want to win the hearts and minds of the north, they have to do something.'[56] As part of the ongoing decentralisation process, Amuru district was created out of Gulu district during this period.[57] In addition to these internal changes, the installation of the Government of Southern Sudan following the Comprehensive Peace Accord in October 2005, and the holding of elections in the Democratic Republic of Congo (DRC) in 2006, both considerably affected the regional environment.

Phase VII – June 2006 Onwards

When peace-talks between the LRA and the Government of Uganda were announced in mid-2006, they took many by surprise and were greeted with considerable scepticism given the history of failed talks in the past. Nonetheless, the events of Phase VI provided some explanation for the Government's shift away from its hitherto rigid refusal to engage in talks. Additional motivating factors included the need to be seen to take action prior to the Commonwealth Heads of Government Meeting in November 2007 – and the (albeit remote) prospect of the ICC turning its attention to government actors. The signing of a Cessation of Hostilities agreement in Juba on 26 August 2006 (and its renewal some months later) did, however, create some hope that these talks were serious, as did the signing of protocols on comprehensive solutions, as well as accountability and reconciliation. While the same period saw relatively large numbers of the IDPs in Teso and Lango return home, the IDPs in the Acholi sub-region remained far more sceptical about the peace process. Thus although there was some movement into government organised 'decongestion sites', this was not the return home many were waiting for. Joseph Kony's failure to sign the final agreement in April 2008 inevitably created doubts about whether any of the potential of the protocols would be realised.

The War As People Remember it

The broad outline given above focuses on what are generally regarded as key players, events and processes. But within this there are numerous more personal histories which easily slip out of our consideration, when they should in fact be central to it. A sense of how the macro- and micro- pictures interact can be gained from the summarised findings of a discussion held with thirteen members of a women's self-help group at ACORD's offices in Gulu, 10 February 1999 (see Chapter 2 for discussion of methods). The results were shocking in the extreme.

The women's dominant memories were around physical harm, killing and abduction of relatives, and loss of properties. Telegraphic bullet points describe truly gruesome events, reducing a book's worth of personal tragedies to a page of code. People do not forget – even after thirteen years the memory of loss was acute and detailed, down to how many sacks of which type of grain were looted. And there was no closure – one woman whose son was abducted back in 1987 still talked of her son as being 'in captivity', as did the woman who lost two grandsons to rebel abduction in 1988. And while the multiplicity of perpetra-

Table 3.1 Incidents that Happened to Women and Their Immediate Families (Each Line Represents a Different Person's Memory)

Year	Incidents
1986	– 4 of my children were abducted by Lakwena. They returned after 4 months – 2 of my children died of a hand-grenade attack by the NRA – 2 brothers were killed by NRA (1 with a molten jerry-can, the other through beating)
1987	– My cattle (20 head) were taken, I was beaten and four girls were taken by Lakwena – Karimojong took 38 cattle belonging to my grandfather

(continued)

Table 3.1 (continued)

Year	Incidents
1987 (cont.)	– My husband was arrested by the NRA for 2 weeks, came back ill and died 3 years later
	– 2 of my brothers were killed by Lakwena
	– I was beaten, my son was abducted (returned after 1 year), and 5 goats were taken by Lakwena
	– My husband was killed, 28 cattle were taken, 4 huts and 6 granaries were burnt by NRA
	– My son, who was married with a daughter, was abducted and is still in captivity (LRA)
	– My brother drowned himself after NRA took 100 cattle
1988	– I was abducted and lived in captivity for 3 months. Some of my property was taken, others destroyed, one child taken who returned after 6 months
	– 3 of my brothers were killed by Lakwena and household property robbed
	– 10 goats robbed by Lakwena, 50 cattle by cattle rustlers
	– My husband was killed
	– 8 sons of my brothers were killed by NRA, who also took 30 head of cattle
	– UPDA burnt one hut, 2 sacks of millet, 8 sacks of sunflower, household properties, 2 granaries
	– 2 of my grandsons were abducted, one returned after 1.5 years, the other is still in captivity
	– My arm was shot by the NRA and had to be amputated
	– My brother was abducted by the UPDA
1989	– 4 of my brothers were burnt alive in their huts by the NRA who accused them of being collaborators
	– NRA burnt property including 4 huts, 3 granaries, 40 iron sheets, because the rebels had camped in the area
	– I was hit by a mine and my leg was amputated
	– My brother's son was killed by the LRA
1990	– 6 children killed by Lakwena (Bobi)
	– 1 man was killed by the NRA
1991	– My sister's daughter was abducted by LRA, and died in Agweng, Lira district
1992	– NRA took our maize mill
	– NRA took my brother's son's maize mill
	– NRA took my uncle's maize mill
	– My brother's house was used as an army office; to date there has been no rent payment made
1993	– LRA abducted my brother-in-law's son from Sir Samuel Baker School, he returned 1 year later
1996	– I was hit by an anti-personnel mine and lost my lower leg
1997	– I was hurt in the hip by a UPDF bomb
	– My brother-in-law's son was shot dead in the market place by the UPDF
1998	– LRA took 2 of my sons, they're still in captivity
	– LRA killed my father while he attended some funeral rights
1999	– LRA abducted seven children (1 girl, 6 boys), the girl returned after 2 weeks
	– LRA took 20 goats
	– UPDF burned 5 huts
	– LRA abducted 2 of my sister's children

tors was bewildering (NRA, Lakwena, UPDA, UPDF, LRA), the practices were consistent. Although in the overall picture, 1999 marked a lull in the violence, for the women in this group it was in many respects as dangerous as 1989.

When memories of things which happened in the respondents' home communities over the same period were added in, the picture became even more distressing (Table 3.2).

Table 3.2 Incidents within the Immediate Community

Year	Incidents
1987	– 9 women and children were killed by UPDA, left unburied and eaten by pigs – Children were massacred while dancing in Lawiyeadul village
1988	– NRA killed 8 men and dumped their bodies in a stream
1991	– LRA kill 6 – Serious NRA operation with people taken forcefully to various places for screening
1995	– Brutal killings (Atiak, Palaro, Alero, Pabo, Paicho, Patiko, Acoyo, Pawere, Awere)
1996	– 10 boys (10-12 years old) abducted by LRA, return after 2 weeks – 2 school girls abducted by LRA – 80 huts were burned by the LRA – Neighbour's shop was looted 3 times by LRA – 2 boys abducted but returned – Individuals were displaced in Gulu town
1997	– 9 children abducted (1 girl, eight boys: seven boys return, one killed) – 3 men killed by LRA – UPDF shoot dead a man when he failed to give the money they demanded
1998	– After the LRA had passed through the UPDF destroyed tobacco being fire-cured as well as other properties – 7 boys were abducted, 2 returned (LRA) – Dispensary looted (LRA) – 2 boys shot but survived in hospital (LRA) – 8 UPDF soldiers raped a woman in Laliya
1999	– February: 1 girl abducted and items looted by LRA – LRA shot dead a catechist and his wife

The women's own personal trauma was compounded by constant reminders of their extreme vulnerability in their immediate community. People were caught between army and rebels, with dozens abducted or killed by the LRA, and others rounded up and taken away as a result of the army's screening operations. Women were being gang-raped by their supposed protectors. It was a situation in which there was no one to turn to for safety (see Chapter 5).

This sense of vulnerability is deepened by an awareness of events in the wider war zone, and at national and even international level. From the collective memory of the thirteen women, five of whom had had no formal education at all, and only three of whom had completed secondary schooling, it was possible to construct a time line of many of the defining moments of the war at district and national level (Table 3.3).

Table 3.3 Incidents at District and National Level

Year	Incidents at a District Level	National Level
1986	– People forced by NRA from Olwiyo and Purongo to Karuma in Masindi district – HIV/AIDS in Gulu and Malnutrition	NRA/NRM took over power from the Government
1987	NRA shot at children during confrontation with UPDA; 6 girls die, as well as some boys	Holy Spirit Movement attempt to reach Kampala, stopped in Jinja
1988	NRA confiscated land without compensation (100 homesteads)	UPDA and NRA sign peace agreement
1989		Presidential amnesty to followers of rebels, not leaders
1990		NRA marched to attack Rwanda
1991	LRA maimings and mutilations	Acholi students at Makerere shot at by Uganda Police Force
1992	Landmines planted along roads	
1994	NRA attack community in Atiak market place	Peace talks led by Betty Bigombe flop because some people brainwashed Museveni and he gave a 7 day ultimatum
1995	– LRA massacre in Atiak – Meningitis outbreak – Massive planting of anti-personnel mines	
1996	– 80 huts burnt by LRA in Pece and Coyo – Jago of Anaka killed by LRA vehicle landmine – People forced into camps by UPDF – Scorched earth policy used by UPDF on people of Purongo – UPDF mobile raped women in market in Palaro sub-county – 2 elders killed by LRA (Okot Ogoni and Lagony) while pursuing dialogue for peace	Sudan Government said to be supporting the LRA rebels
1997	– 82 huts of IDPs burnt in Limo by LRA, 13 year old girl burnt and dies – 99 huts burnt in Go-down, Layibi by LRA – SPLA hosted and seen in Gulu town (Garang himself and various vehicles)	– Uganda accused by Sudan of hosting rebels – Discussions on blanket amnesty in parliament
1998	– UPDF shot people at funeral, 2 die, others wounded – Vehicle shot by LRA, medical staff die – Bishop of Moyo killed in ambush on Gulu-Adjumani road	Outbreak of cholera in most districts
1999	– Vehicle shot/ambushed by LRA in Wiayago river – Houses burnt: Pabbo 70, Anaka 50, Parabongo 6	

This group of women were very aware of what was happening elsewhere in the conflict zone – and often knew who the perpetrators were. Maimings and land-mines were attributed to the LRA, people being forced into camps to the UPDF. That the SPLA were 'hosted' and seen in Gulu town was noted, as were specific incidents such as the killing of the Bishop of Moyo. They knew of the major peace initiatives, and of the tensions with the Government of Sudan. The shoot-ing of Acholi students in Makerere University by Ugandan police force in 1991 was remembered, suggestive of the extent to which Acholi see themselves as a devalued minority group under attack in Uganda as a whole (see Chapter 7).

The exercise conducted with this group was repeated with nine other self-help groups of youth, farmers, and People Living with Aids (PLWA). A total of 171 people were involved (85 male, 86 female). Of the 136 who gave their educational status 10.2 per cent had no formal education, 46.7 per cent had 1–7 years of primary education, 25.5 per cent had reached GCE/GCSE'O' level, 3.6 per cent had GCE/GCSE'A' level, 6.6 per cent had further education, and 7.3 per cent had some tertiary education. Eighty-two per cent were married. Regard-less of gender, age, formal education level or occupation, similar patterns of traumatic experiences, together with similar levels of observation, well-guarded memory and sophisticated analysis would emerge. Adolescent youth recalled as many traumatic incidents as elderly farmers (see Chapter 7 for youth analysis of the actors in the war).

Out of the 171 people in the focus groups, eight (4.7 per cent) had themselves been beaten/tortured by government soldiers, twelve (7.0 per cent) by rebels. One had been imprisoned by government, fourteen (8.2 per cent) had been abducted by rebels. One had been raped by government soldiers, while six (3.5 per cent) had been shot and wounded (three by government, and three by rebels). When the number of instances was expanded to include close relatives, the extent to which the general population had experienced violation was clear (Table 3.4).

Table 3.4 Summary of Experiences of Individuals as Drawn from Timelines (1986–1999) Developed with 10 Self-Help Groups, Gulu District, February 1999

| | Perpetrators | | Combined | |
| | Government | Rebels | Total cases | % of all experiences |
Direct and Indirect Experience				
Beating/torture	10	16	26	12.8
Imprisonment	4	0	4	2.0
Abduction	3	70	73	36.0
Rape	4	1	5	2.5
Shooting	7	6	13	6.4
Killing of immediate relatives	29	48	77	37.9
Other psychological trauma	3	2	5	2.5
TOTAL	60	143	203	100%
As %	29.6%	70.4%	100%	

Whereas abduction was clearly a rebel preserve, killing was not. Twenty-nine out of seventy-seven killings were attributed to Government troops. Four out of five rape cases were also attributed to Government forces. Thus although overall the rebels were responsible for 70.4 per cent of major traumatic incidents to individual persons, the Government was responsible for nearly one third. When attributing responsibility for damages to personal properties, the picture was more or less 50:50 (Table 3.5).

Table 3.5 Attribution of Responsibility for 157 Instances of Damage to Personal Properties by 170 Participants in 10 Self-Help Groups, Gulu, February 1999

Action	Govt	Rebels	Total	as %
Burning	19	20	39	25
Looting	45	45	90	57
Confiscation	6	10	16	10
Bombing	1	0	1	1
Displacement	11	0	11	7
Total	82	75	157	100

If one puts all these figures together, remembering that they are drawn from a fairly representative sample of ordinary civilians in Gulu district, it becomes clear that the average civilian had, over the course of nearly two decades, experienced a relentless series of violations.

Discussion

When the outline of the major phases of the 'war' is juxtaposed with people's memories, it suggests that, from a longitudinal perspective, the LRA, rather than being the lead perpetrator, was one amongst many, including the UPDA, Karimojong, Lakwena, and NRA/UPDF. The levels of brutality, displacement and impoverishment, are extreme – and under-acknowledged. When Gersony argued that it was not possible to compare the violence in northern Uganda with the 'large-scale mass murder and brutality that characterized UNLA operations in the Luwero Triangle in 1983/4' (1997: 23), he seriously underplayed the devastation wrought on people in Gulu and Kitgum districts over nearly two decades (as compared with two years). Throughout my fieldwork I failed to encounter anybody who had not either experienced extreme abuse and atrocities first hand or witnessed them being exercised on immediate family members – often by government and rebels in quick succession.

Although the death rate and other impacts should have placed northern Uganda squarely on the lists of 'deadly conflicts' suggested by organisations such as the Carnegie Corporation in New York, it is not clear that the term 'war', as conventionally understood, adequately describes (let alone explains) what was happening. The fact that the elder quoted at the beginning of this chapter described people of Acholi as 'in a dilemma', a people who 'don't know how to go forward', is not surprising. The defining features were not the pitched battles between LRA and UPDF that conventional notions of war might suggest, but rather the phenomena of inexorably escalating displacement, dependency, debilitation, militarization, geographic reach and international involvement over time. Even humanitarians did not seem to grasp the extent of what was going on. It was only in November 2003, when the UN's Under Secretary General for Humanitarian Affairs saw fit to describe the situation as worse than that in Iraq,[58] that the gravity of the situation began to be acknowledged.

What the above account does demonstrate is that even by the late 1990s, President Museveni and his government, although in some respects exemplifying an 'African renaissance', in others remained in a weak position and faced a problem of control. Internal divisions juxtaposed with the fact that over 50 per cent of its budget came from external donors, made their hold on power considerably more provisional than was generally perceived. Nor could these internal and external pressures be dealt with discreetly, as they were closely related both historically and in the present.

Back in 1986, with the memory of how post-independence political parties had been overlaid with and become synonymous with ethnic, religious and political agendas, Museveni and the NRM made the achievement of national unity and the elimination of all forms of sectarianism point three of their ten-point programme. This goal underpinned the 'no-party' system and continued to inform the Government's doubts about the move to multi-party democracy being urged from both inside and outside the country,[59] a move which was eventually made in time for the 2005 elections.

Underlying the positive political project of national unity were very real military and political imperatives. If the rebel NRM was to achieve any kind of national and international credibility as the Government of a country – rather than merely being seen as the occupiers of a nominal capital city – then it had to establish control of the north. As described above, for some months following the taking of Kampala the NRA had no presence in – and therefore did not exercise control over – those parts of the country north of the Karuma Bridge (River Nile). Even once they did establish a military presence, they were regarded by many as an occupying force rather than as fellow Ugandans – not helped by the fact that many members of the NRA were Tutsis from Rwanda who would eventually return to Rwanda as part of the Rwandan Patriotic Front (RPF) in 1990.[60]

The real-politik objective of gaining control is suggested by Museveni's appointment of a Minister for *Pacification* of Northern Uganda (a term used by George Orwell to exemplify political euphemisms, words which serve 'to mask, sanitize and confer respectability' and to 'insulate their users and listeners from experiencing fully the meaning of what they are doing' (Cohen, 2001: 107)). Even with the amendment of this title to Minister for Reconstruction of Northern Uganda, the implementation of the Local Council system of non-party democracy, and the massive militarization of the north by the UPDF, the Government's authority was not fully established in 1999 and the relative importance of central and local government, members of parliament, religious and traditional leaders, remained in flux. While the interventions of national level church leaders, such as the call from the Archbishop of Kampala, Emmanuel Cardinal Wamala, to Kony, 'to stop fighting and accept dialogue with the Government',[61] posed no direct challenge to the Government, those of Acholi religious leaders did, for they 'appealed to the Government to declare Acholiland a disaster area and immediately enter into direct negotiations with Kony rebels. They have also demanded that Parliament revokes its recommendation for a military solution to the 12 year war which has devastated northern Uganda'.[62]

Amongst Government representatives in particular, decentralisation raised numerous questions about who had most power, despite the claimed complementarities of the centre and the districts.[63] These ambiguities further aggravated doubts about whether the Acholi had ever been truly 'pacified' and brought under political control, doubts which themselves were fed by the possibility that the LRA's apparent resilience was at least in part due to covert support from civilian Acholi. Furthermore, despite a project of national unity, colonial discourses based on notions of 'tribe' had been deeply internalised and remained an organising principle in many people's thinking. For example, one peace activist stated to me that his loyalties were, in order of priority, to himself, his family, his clan, his tribe, his country, and to the human race. Ethnicised thinking continued to pervade political organising and entered into the literature of international agencies,[64] creating an evident challenge for a Government aiming at national unity. At the peace meeting convened by religious leaders in 1998, for example, one Catholic priest held that:

> If the Acholis are united, who can come and separate us? If the Acholis are united, our voice shall be heard. Before the Movement system, how did the Acholi live? If they unite they will be like the Karimojong who responded to the raiders from Kenya by using students in Makerere to threaten secession and as a result were given weapons. Let the Acholi do the same.

He continued: 'People in Acholi come together to dig a garden and successfully finish it. If they are united they will be respected by other tribes. The tribe is something that comes from God. To be peaceful we should accept God into our lives'.[65] In one short speech he thus clarified that his vision of 'unity' was of the tribe not the nation, he also distanced the Acholi from the Movement, aligned them with the Karimojong and their approach to making demands on the state (including the threat of secession), conjured up the promise of tribal identity as the basis for respect, and brought God on side too. In doing so he exemplified a broader tendency to mythologize Acholi identity. This was further demonstrated in the religious leaders' appeal for Third Party Mediation published in the daily newspapers on 8 March 2004. This blended religious imagery with pan-African and ethnic rhetoric: 'We were moved by our moral and religious obligations as shepherds of God's people, especially of the weak and vulnerable. But we also found warrant for such solidarity in our noble African tradition best captured by the Lwo saying *oyoo opilo too ikom litinone* (The mother rat will die with her children)'.[66] The appeal describes how 'the Acholi traditional, social and moral fabric that once formed one of the most beautiful cultural tapestries in Africa is now in tatters'. It calls for mediation from internationally renowned Africans, with only the San Egidio community mentioned as possible non-African mediators.[67] Somewhat perversely, therefore, local 'peace activists' who claimed to be seeking a way out of the situation were doing so by appealing to the very factors used to divide and rule people in the first place.[68]

Ethnicised thinking was further evident in the call of the former Minister of State for Reconstruction of Northern Uganda for a conference which would 'include all the stakeholders in Acholiland and enable them to resolve the contradictions between them, before bringing in the international community'.[69] It was also reflected in formations such as the Acholi Parliamentary Group, and shaped donor and interventions such as the EU's 'Acholiland Programme'.

Alongside the conceptual climate created by discourses of 'tribe' was the concrete reality of a lack of military control. A WFP report of 1999 described how the organisation was adopting a partial approach and only assisting the population 'already under firm government control' (WFP 1999: 33), and one elder I interviewed argued that 'In the camps people are protecting government soldiers. People are failing to pay taxes as they have no source of income, therefore we can say they are under rebel control'.[70]

The sentiments of most Acholi towards the Government were clear, as they pointedly refused to vote for Museveni in presidential elections in 1996, 2001 and 2006, and, in opposition to the Government, called for a negotiated rather than a military solution to the conflict.[71] Equally in the Teso sub-region, the spontaneous formation of ethnic militias from late 2003 to early 2004, and the speed with which the UPDF moved to bring these under its own control (Dolan, 2004), was an indicator of how fragile the government felt the earlier pacification of the sub-region to have been.

The most pressing reality, though, was the glaring inequality between the north and south of the country, and the grievances this both reflected and gave rise to. As one *New Vision* commentator observed:

> Let us face it: life up there is what some defunct philosopher would call nasty, short and brutish. And it is being lived in the same country and under the same government with the rest whose most urgent problem is to cut down on the fats in their bodies ... Those fellows who did not know what their president looks like live in the same country with several thousand who surf the internet and communicate with friends all over the globe via email ...[72]

The degree of inequality was beyond ready redress. The task of holding together a country which did not fully feel it was a country was not made easier by being beholden to international donors for support. Paradoxically, Uganda's status as a success story and show-case for international policies was also an indicator of the extent to which its room for an independent development trajectory towards national unity had been compromised. When as a student at Dar-es-Salaam University in the late 1960s, Museveni wrote that he and his fellow students were 'probably reactionary puppets of neo-colonialism in the making' (Museveni 1970: 7), he was unnervingly close to predicting his own future.

Under structural adjustment policies, state services and large-scale infrastructural developments were cut back and the possibility of buying favour with the population at large was reduced. Restrictions on military expenditure and demands for demobilisation weakened the use of the military to keep a grip on power. Under an internationally driven agenda of multi-party democratisation, Museveni's 'no-party' system was coming under increasing challenge. And under de-centralisation policies, power at a local level was re-ethnicised and the whole concept of national cadres of civil servants was diluted. Indeed, even donor support for the re-anointment of traditional leaders could be seen as undermining a national project of anti-sectarianism. The development of a national IDP policy mentioned above involved developing institutional mechanisms to 'include direct participation of donors, UN agencies and NGOs in all IDP planning', and the early warning system was to involve an 'interagency Vulnerability and Assessment Mapping Group consisting of WFP, OPM [Office of the Prime Minister], SCF-U.K., FEWS [Famine Early Warning System] and IOM'. In short, the Government was becoming a minor player in its own major issues. The referral to the ICC which was made in 2004, and which was to become such a stumbling block to the peace talks in 2006, was in some respects an admission of loss of control, insofar as under the Rome Statute such referrals are only to be made where the state concerned is unwilling or unable to bring perpetrators to account.

That these frameworks imposed by the international donors were something of a straitjacket for the Government is evident from many defiant statements made by the President. An article in *The Monitor,* for example, went under the headline 'I will not kneel before donors, swears Museveni'.[73] At times donor-government tensions over issues such as levels of demobilisation, amnesty, and defence expenditure resulted in open wars of words between them. On 25 February 2004 MPs passed a resolution calling for the north to be declared a disaster zone. In March, following attacks on IDP camps in Lira district, tensions were such that the Donor Group on Northern Uganda, Amnesty and Recovery from Conflict[74] issued a statement in which they endorsed Parliament's February resolution and rejected 'the assertion that Donor's restrictions on Defence expenditure have impeded the UPDF's capacity to defend citizens from such attacks'. In May 2004 the donors rejected the proposed 2004/5 budget 'citing excessive public administration costs and unjustified increases in defence spending'.[75]

There were attempts to escape the straitjacket. The rapid subdivision of existing districts into smaller ones (e.g. Kitgum district became Kitgum and Pader districts) can be seen as a necessary 'divide and rule' tactic to counter the re-ethnicising influence of decentralisation – if ethnic identities could not be overcome through a super-ordinate national system then breaking them down into sub-ethnic groupings was an alternative.[76] Exercises such as *mchaka-mchaka* (political education – see Chapter 5) could be seen as an attempt at generating a national perspective; placing the President's brother Salim Saleh in charge of reserve forces could be interpreted as an evasion of the constraints of demobilisation. All these, however, might be termed political bricolage, making do with the little that is to hand.

The reality was that, with the de-fragmentation of the national pearl still unfinished business, with externally driven agendas threatening a degree of re-fragmentation, and lacking the resources to glue the ethnicised fragments together with large-scale economic development, the Government was left with relatively few options. While hard-won political independence demanded that the state control its own population, it offered little in the way of economic power with which to exercise this control.

Some Concluding Questions

The above narrative provokes numerous questions which are addressed in the following chapters. First, what can be said about the nature and motivations of the ostensible protagonists, the LRA and Government of Uganda, and indeed, are they the only actors who should be considered? Was the LRA much more successful than is generally allowed, or was it a less important player than it was usually made out to be? Given that it survived nearly two decades while numerous other rebel groups came and went, was this due to a particular resilience on its part – or was it *allowed* to survive? Equally, and related to this, was the Government serious in its stated intentions to find a solution to the war? Given that non-military solutions (Pece peace accord 1988, Bigombe peace talks 1994, Uganda-Sudan peace accord 1999, Amnesty Bill 2000) and military ones alike (Operation Iron Fist 2002, ethnic militias 2004) resoundingly failed to bring about any resolution to the situation and succeeded only in aggravating it, the integrity of purpose of those who designed and implemented such 'solutions' has to be open to scrutiny.

Particular questions also arise over the Government's integrity of purpose with regard to internal displacement. The increasingly destructive impact of living for extended periods in 'protected villages' led to growing calls for decongestion and resettlement but, until late 2006, virtually no steps were taken to do so. What then was the real function of a phenomenon which most people at least purported to regard as having negative consequences?

The escalation of non-military phenomena also prompts questions about the nature of the relationship between long-term and severe impact on civilians and the perpetuation of conflict. Did the inexorable escalation reflect self-perpetuating, indeed self-aggravating dimensions to the dynamics of the war? At times the conflict between the Government's stubborn adherence to seeking a military solution, and the equally strong resistance to this from an increasing range of civil society actors (Acholi MPs, religious leaders, traditional leaders, various UN bodies and NGOs), appeared to be as important as the conflict they all purported to be seeking a solution to. Indeed, at times even the civil society actors seemed to be fighting over who would be the one to bring peace. More importantly, perhaps, young men in their thousands were driven to join armed forces, whether the UPDF, the various militias set up in 2003, or indeed the LRA itself. What lay behind this phenomenon?

And what, given the evident involvement of international actors in various dimensions of the situation, are we to make of their relative importance in resolving or perpetuating the conflict? External involvement went beyond funding humanitarian or developmental schemes to include military training and other types of 'non-lethal assistance'. External support was also critical to what initially appears to be a very 'local' initiative, namely the revival of traditional leadership structures. This initiative was almost entirely driven by externally generated ideas and funding. Yet calls for an explicitly political intervention by the United Nations were ignored.[77] This prompts many to ask 'How bad does a situation have to get before action is taken?', beneath which lies a possibly more important question, namely what exactly is it that enables decision-makers to excuse their own 'inaction'? How was it that in an era of global communications, there was so little international outrage over this situation which, rather than being hidden away in torture chambers, could potentially be made visible to the public eye through various media, with the threat of at the least possible comparisons with the situation in southern Sudan, and at worst politically and economically damaging charges of complicity in abuses and atrocities? Where, in a world of 'human rights', 'democracy' and 'good governance', were those with the power to influence and intervene, and why were they not more active?

Notes

1. For an exploration of these tensions with regard to conflict in East Timor, see Dolan, 2004.
2. Samuel Baker built Patiko Fort in 1872 on the former site of an outpost for slavers.
3. This is not to mythologize the past; it is clear that subsistence in northern Uganda was always more difficult than in what is now southern Uganda. R. M. Bere, one of the first British administrators of the Acholi District, argued that 'A struggle for existence has governed much of the tribal history' (Bere, 1947: 5).
4. By January 2002, the District Veterinary Officer reported that Gulu had 6,800 head of cattle, 2010 of which came through the unpopular government programme of restocking, while others were bought from neighbouring districts (KM e-newsletter no 5, 15 February 2002).
5. For discussion on the extent to which considering the Acholi as purely a colonial construct may itself be a continuation of an 'imperial dialogue' which ignores pre and post-colonial identity formation processes, see Finnström, 2003; Chapter 2.
6. Gulu, 4 August 1998. He also reported that in World War II there were some 1,600 members of the King's African Rifles from Gulu and Kitgum (at that time all Gulu district), of whom about 800 were still alive and members of the King's African Rifles Association.
7. One explanation offered to me for why the Catholic Church in Gulu was slow to set up its Justice and Peace Commission (on 1 June 1998) was that 'the Gulu church is more DP sympathetic, while Kampala Peace and Justice is more NRM aligned' (discussion with Pax Christi representative, 5 June 1998).
8. For discussion of the ways in which anthropology was used to legitimise regional differences, see Finnström, 2003; Chapter 3.
9. Exactly who was actually involved in each of these examples is highly contested, in particular responsibility for atrocities in the Luwero triangle.

10. Gulu, 7 June 1998. When a local NGO, Peoples Voice for Peace, attempted to document the matter, they found it almost impossible to interview the victims themselves, and were obliged to interview women who were familiar with the cases instead (personal communication).
11. According to O'Kadameri these were actually started in 1992 by Betty Bigombe (2002: 36).
12. A wide open space near the middle of Gulu town, used for various public purposes.
13. Awere and Awac in 1993, Atiak in 1994 – all were displaced again (see Chapter 5).
14. The first major meeting was held on 25 November 1993 in Pagik parish, Aswa county, and a second followed on 10th January 1994. A third meeting was held at Atoo Hills on 22nd January, and a fourth on 2 February 1994.
15. Interview with elder, Gulu 8 August 1998.
16. Examples included 11 August 1996, 29 August 1996, 4 September 1997, 4 July 1998, 16 January 2000 (see also Finnström, 2003: 240).
17. *The Monitor,* 11 December 1997, 'Museveni Admits U.S. Help Against Sudan'.
18. *New Vision,* 8 June 1998, 'Kony: DP Attacks Albright'.
19. Gulu, 27 September 1999.
20. A tongue-in-cheek reference to the Museveni Government.
21. An allusion to the U.S.A.
22. The issue of the SPLA included their mobilisation within Uganda, with support from the Ugandan government (Professor Barbara Harrell-Bond, 30 September 1999).
23. *New Vision,* 26 June 1998 'UNICEF Condemns Kony'.
24. *New Vision,* 11 July 1998, 'Ethiopian Pilot Killed In Crash'.
25. *The Monitor,* 14 July 1998, 'LRA Claims It Shot Down Chopper'.
26. *New Vision,* 2 April 1998, 'Kony for London Acholi meeting'.
27. *Odek Pilot Report,* 21 July 1998.
28. *New Vision,* 11 June 1998, 'Acholi Exiles Criticise Museveni'.
29. *New Vision,* 18 July 1998, 'Kony Gives Conditions For Peace Negotiations'.
30. *New Vision,* 17 July 1998, 'War Damages Uganda's Image'.
31. *The Monitor,* 3 February 1998, 'Saleh Admits UPDF's Mistakes'.
32. Hon. Norbert Mao and Hon. Daniel Omara Atubo.
33. Parliamentary Buildings, Kampala, Uganda, January 1997.
34. The centre opened on 23 March 1997 with only 10 children. Designed to handle 75 children at a time, by January 1998, when I first visited, it had 263, of whom 32 were girls. The most recent arrivals said that once a girl has conceived she is taken to Sudan, from where it is more difficult to escape, hence the lower number of girl returnees. Since March they had reunited 306 boys and 60 girls with their families. Some children were directed to GUSCO by the RDC, most came from the military. GUSCO informed the army if they had any weapons on them. UNICEF had provided a lot of mattresses and nominated the centre for an award, WFP had given high protein biscuits, and the British High Commission had given 33 million Uganda shillings.
35. *New Vision,* 3 March 1998, 'Kony Victims to Get Sh 44m'.
36. *The Monitor,* 26 March 1998, 'Mrs Clinton Blasts Kony'.
37. *New Vision,* 4 July 1998, 'Acholi Leaders to Meet Kony Men'.
38. Correspondence on the diaspora listserve Acholinet estimated the figure at a questionable 25,000.
39. www.idpproject.org: Profile of Internal Displacement: Uganda, 11 October 2002, p 78.
40. Justice and Peace News (Gulu Diocese), Vol. 2 No 3, June 2002.
41. *New Vision,* 20 January 2002, 'Uganda Rebels Face U.K. Courts'.
42. Under Section 7 of the Anti-Terrorism Act, these include placing explosive or other lethal device in public places with intent to cause death or serious bodily injury, direct involvement or complicity in the murder, kidnapping or maiming or attack on a person or group of persons, and seizure or detention of hostages in order to compel a State, an international or inter-governmental organ, a person or group of persons, to do or abstain from

doing any act. Persons found guilty of these acts 'shall be sentenced to death if the offence directly results in death of any person or … in any other case, be liable to suffer death.'
43. Ibid, Section 10, as well as the Second Schedule thereto.
44. IGAD comprises Djibouti, Eritrea, Ethiopia, Kenya, Sudan, Somalia and Uganda.
45. *Justice and Peace News,* May 2002, Vol. 2 No. 2.
46. Announced on 22 January by Army Commander Kazini (KM e-newsletter no 6).
47. IRIN, 25 May 2002, UGANDA-SUDAN: No Rapid Solutions in Anti-LRA Campaign.
48. IRIN, 6 June 2002, *UGANDA: Little Acholi Gain from Anti-LRA Campaign.* See Also KM E-Newsletter No 10.
49. IRIN, 19 June 2002, UGANDA: Government in Peace Deal With UNRF-II Rebels.
50. IRIN, 6 June 2002, *UGANDA: Little Acholi Gain from Anti-LRA Campaign.* See also KM E-newsletter No 10.
51. *The Monitor,* 24 August 2002, Army Deploys '30,000' Troops Against Kony.
52. IRIN, 21 October 2002, Budget Cuts Aimed At Boosting War Against Rebels.
53. IRIN, 6 November 2002, President Sets Up Team For Talks With Rebels.
54. IRIN, 3 December 2002, *Anti-LRA Pact Extended.*
55. Gulu, 19 January 2004.
56. Interview with UN official, Kitgum, 16/8/06.
57. Decentralisation, advocated by the World Bank, took on its own peculiarly politicised momentum in Uganda. From 1999 to 2006 the number of districts virtually doubled from 43 to 81, at times leading to increased ethnic tensions and even splits within ethnic groups. Yet at the same time, there was a re-centralisation of certain key powers. Thus the appointment of the Chief Administrative Officer was taken away from District level and centralised. Equally, the removal of graduated tax, which had been collected by District authorities, decreased local control of the tax base.
58. IRIN, 28 January 2004, The 18-Year Old War That Refuses To Go Away.
59. As pressure grows for multi-party democracy in Uganda, Museveni continued to warn 'against pluralism based on ethnicity, religion and other divisive factors' (*New Vision,* 9 June 2004, 'Museveni Advises on Multipartyism').
60. This was also true of the NRA in Teso sub-region according to one respondent who had been tortured there in the late 1980s: 'Each of us was caned 12 strokes on the buttocks and then told to lie facing the sun for the entire day. We had to keep turning so that we really faced the sun. Every two hours we were asked [various questions].… At that time all the NRA commanders were Rwandese, and they were the torturers' (Gulu, 7 June 1998).
61. *New Vision,* 9 April 1998, 'Accept talks, Cardinal tells Kony'.
62. *New Vision,* 20 January 1999, 'Acholi Want Disaster Zone'.
63. In late 1999, for example, the LCV Chairman of Kitgum district, without consulting the District Council, closed down the ACORD programme in the district. The then Minister for the North was unable to call this self-styled district 'President' to order.
64. E.g. UNICEF, 2001: 3–13
65. Bedo Piny pi Kuc, 27 June 1998.
66. *The Monitor,* 8 March 2004.
67. For full text see KM E-newsletter No 47, 7 April 2004 (www.km-net.org) .
68. This exemplifies the (unconscious) collaboration of the oppressed with the agents of oppression and domination discussed in Finnström (2003: 68), but contradicts his view that 'secession of the north has never been an issue' (2003: 148, 160).
69. Hon. Owiny Dollo MP, Gulu conference, 29 September 1999.
70. Interview, Gulu, 4 August 1998.
71 Perhaps this prompted the resolution passed at a meeting in Kitgum district 'that if you want to bring a solution, you have to accept that you are both an Acholi and a Ugandan' (comment by participant at *Bedo Piny pi Kuc* meeting, Gulu, 26 June 1998).
72. *New Vision,* 22 March 1998, 'Fats kill in Kampala as Kony kills Acholis'.
73. *The Monitor,* 17 May 2004.

74. This comprised the head of delegation from the European Commission, the ambassadors of Austria, Belgium, Denmark, France, Germany, Ireland, Italy, The Netherlands, Sweden, United Kingdom, Norway, U.S.A., Japan, as well as representatives from UNDP, World Bank and USAID.
75. IRIN, 14 May 2004, Donors Reject Proposed Budget on Grounds of Defence Spending.
76. The relationship between what Girling terms 'domains' within Acholi is a historically complex one, with the western domains (effectively Gulu district) more closely linked to the Bunyoro kingdom than the eastern ones (Kitgum/Pader), and quicker to make alliances with the British (Girling 1960). The reality of divisions within the Acholi was apparent in the run up to the Betty Bigombe peace talks when elders from Kitgum were pitted against those from Gulu (see Chapter 4).
77. This was in contrast to the steps taken with regard to the Darfur situation in Western Sudan from 2003 onwards.

4

RECONSIDERING THE
LRA–GOVERNMENT DYNAMIC

'People say that Kony is uneducated, but the uneducated man has killed people for the last fifteen years; what have the educated done to solve the problem of war in Acholi land?'[1]

Introduction

The situation in Northern Uganda is generally presented as a war between two actors, the LRA and the Government of Uganda. There is, though, little consensus on the nature of the two parties, particularly the LRA, or the reasons for their involvement. Under the various labels of 'madmen', 'religious fundamentalists', 'messengers of God', 'criminals', 'bandits', 'terrorists' and 'dogs of war', at least four characterisations of the LRA are discernible; the LRA as a an irrational organisation without political purpose (e.g. Bramucci, 2001: ii, Weeks, 2002: 9), the LRA as seeking to install a Christian fundamentalist government in Uganda (e.g. USDS, 2002: 124, IRIN, 12 September 2002), the LRA as a personality cult (e.g. Vlassenroot and Doom, 1999: 19–22), and the LRA as proxy warriors for the Sudanese Government and thus as legitimate targets in the wider 'war on terror' (e.g. Vlassenroot and Doom, idem, *New Vision,* 7 February 1998, *The Monitor,* 11 December 1997). What links these otherwise conflicting representations is an implicit model of the LRA as the aggressor and of the GoU as reacting to aggression, active in the search for solutions, and focused on the protection of its citizens.

Looked at in quantitative terms alone, the UPDF should have been easily capable of dealing with the LRA and protecting civilians. Compared with the LRA's guessed size of 1,000–5,000, it numbered at least 50,000–60,000 troops (excluding ethnic militias), of whom at least 20,000 were deployed in the north. It had its own track record as a rebel group to inform its understanding of the LRA, and it had military successes against other insurgent groups, most pertinently the ADF in western Uganda in the late 1990s. At various times it had collaborative support for military activity inside Sudan from both the SPLA[2] and the Government of Sudan. And it had 'non-lethal' support from the U.S., including military training and information, as well as the room for manoeuvre created by Uganda's international reputation and the global 'war on terrorism'.

Notwithstanding all these advantages, it did not provide adequate protection to its civilian population in the north, let alone root out the LRA. Museveni himself, on a visit to Amuru protected village in 1998, reportedly said 'I am very sorry to find you in such a situation. I am sorry to find you not in your homes. The fact that you are still suffering is the fault of the army and government'.[3]

Explanations for such failures centred on a lack of resources (e.g. *The Monitor*, 3 February 1998, 'UPDF weak to fight rebels – Minister', see also Weeks, 2001: 32), to which could be added context-related question-marks over the UPDF's capacities, including the effects of HIV/AIDS on troops, donor pressure to reduce defence expenditure, and low morale reflected in what the UPDF refers to as 'individual indiscipline' and numerous instances of drunken incompetence (see Chapter 5). Many saw the problem as one of vested interests, 'another case of the phenomenon identified by David Keen in the "Benefits of Famine" – enough people do well out of the war that it continues until there is nothing left'.[4] As early as 1994, Betty Bigombe, in negotiations with the LRA, warned that 'There are many who do not want peace to prevail. There are those people who are benefiting from the war. There are others who think that if this thing ends, they will have nothing to lean on'. (See Annex B.)

Gersony argued in 1997 that 'Corruption at officer levels has also limited the army's commitment and morale and has filtered down to the enlisted ranks' (1997; 35).[5] Behrend felt that, for Government and rebel soldiers alike, the war had become a mode of production 'which was more profitable than peace' (1998; 116), and even NRM members made allegations 'that the commanders who are sent to the regions are only interested in doing business and not defending the people from Joseph Kony's brutality'.[6] The national papers also reported on specific instances of corruption. These included embezzlement of monies intended for fuel 'for military operations against Joseph Kony rebels',[7] the diversion of supplies (including medicines) from the UPDF to the LRA,[8] and the payment of salaries to 'ghost soldiers'.

These various constraints on the UPDF's capacity, however, could not explain why the UPDF was only selectively unsuccessful; why did they manage to deal with groups such as the ADF, but not the LRA? For many people, Museveni's apologies rang hollow and the real question was not the Government's military capacity to solve the situation in the north, but its political will. In short, as the quotation with which I open this chapter implies, the reality of a war in which the uneducated survive well beyond expectations and the educated perform seriously below expectations, demands that the standard presentation of the LRA-GoU war needs revisiting, starting with the nature and motivation of the two parties concerned.

This chapter therefore first assesses the considerable ambiguities about the LRA's composition, numbers and civilian support base, and then look at its modus operandi. Survival strategies, internal organisation, and political messages are scrutinised, and the 1994 Peace Talks between the two parties are examined (drawing on an account developed from two primary sources (see Annex B)), for further evidence of the LRA's political position. The Peace Talks also exemplify the position of the Government, which is further considered through a scrutiny of subsequent initiatives to deal with the LRA, including the 1999 Nairobi Peace Accord, the 2000 Amnesty Act, Operation Iron Fist and the 2004 referral to the International Criminal Court.

The findings suggest that the LRA did present a military challenge, indeed was more organised than derogatory terms such as 'rag-tag army' would imply, but was a self-limiting force which it should have been possible for the Government to deal with decisively; it was resilient but not invincible. The 1994 talks demonstrate a power-play between Government and LRA in which the LRA attempts to maximise the recognition and validation given it, the Government makes strenuous efforts to minimise these by seeking to humiliate and belittle the LRA instead, and the LRA eventually resorts to violence. As such, the talks were an instance of 'war-talk' rather than peace talks, and set a precedent for subsequent initiatives and dynamics that, under the same guise of a wish for peace, in essence created the space for further militarism and the dynamics of social torture.

The LRA's Ambiguities

Anyone attempting to assess the role of the LRA in northern Uganda is faced with a number of ambiguities, particularly concerning its composition and the extent of civilian support and links with the LRM. They are also faced with a media which fuels rather than resolves these ambiguities.

Composition

Estimates of LRA numbers fluctuated considerably, from a high of 3,000–4,000 (Gersony, 1997: 35), through the U.S. Department of State's figure of 2,000 (USDS, 2002: 124), to a low of 1,000–1,100 (OHCHR, 19 April 2001). A year after the latter figure appeared, UNOCHA doubled the figure again, to some 2,000–3000 fighters, accompanied by a further 2,000 wives and children (Weeks, 2002: 8). Within the question of numbers there was additional ambiguity about what proportion of LRA fighters were children. The precise number of abductees and returnees was not known, but there was a widespread belief that the LRA was largely composed of abducted children. A BBC report that 'More than 14,000 children are estimated to have been abducted ... since 1986 ... and taken to southern Sudan to fight or serve as sex slaves' was typical in purveying and perpetuating such beliefs, as were its estimates that 'nearly 90% of LRA fighters are enslaved children – nearly 6,000 are still missing and it is not known whether they are dead or alive'.[9]

The fieldworkers' accounts suggested that more than half of abductees were adults, and thus did not confirm the image of an organisation which focused primarily on abducting children. When UNICEF published its findings in 2001 they indicated that the 20,000 adults abducted, up to that point, represented two-thirds of overall abductions. They also showed that 77.7 per cent of the 10,000 abducted children returned within a year and a further 15.9 per cent the following year (UNICEF, 2001: 7), significantly weakening the possibility that 90 per cent of the LRA's fighters were enslaved children. When I compared the numbers known to have been abducted, and the numbers GUSCO, World Vision and Kitgum Concerned Women's Association (KICWA) claimed to have reintegrated, the results suggested that the number of children left in captivity was in the hundreds rather than the thousands (Dolan, 2002).[10]

The vision of an organisation built on abduction of children was linked to notions of its irrationality and lack of education. Yet some members at the LRA's core had received training in locations as diverse as Israel, America and Germany before ever joining the LRA. Brigadier Kenneth Banya ('Mzee Banya' in the Organisational Chart, Annex A section 9), captured by the UPDF in July 2004, had studied industrial chemistry followed by seven years training in the U.S.S.R. – in flying MIG-21 fighter planes and MI-17 helicopters.[11] And, for a minority of LRA recruits, the Government of Sudan provided training opportunities ranging from security issues (Annex A, section 3.9), to the politics of 'globalisation, unity and diversity, achievements of the freedom fighters, the role of African countries to the international community, Sudanese assistance to freedom fighters in Africa' (Annex A, section 3.11). The majority of recruits though were trained simply in how to 'dismantle and reassemble guns' as well as target practice, and 'field-craft' training, such as how to parade, take cover, and assault the enemy.

The Extent of Civilian Support

One of the biggest ambiguities related to the LRA was the extent of civilian support for the organisation. While international observers tended to argue that there was no longer any support base (Gersony 1997: 35, Global IDP database, Westbrook 2000: section VI), within Uganda the issue was not seen in such a clear-cut fashion (see also Finnström, 2003: 144). Some agreed with the respondent who argued that while there had initially been sympathy between rebels and population, 'the relationship … has been torn apart since the LRA changed its approach in around 1990'.[12] But Government and non-Acholi more generally harboured doubts about the extent of Acholi sympathies with the LRA, fearing that an evident dislike of the Government, as expressed in voting patterns, equated either to passive sympathy for the LRA, or, worse, to pockets of active support. One commentator argued that 'The solution [to the conflict] lies with transforming the attitude of the Acholi populace from saying "Pa Ngeyo" (I don't know) to any inquiry about the whereabouts of rebels to "Angeyo" (I know)' (Asowa-Okwe, 1996: 26). The Government made its suspicions evident by staging various screening exercises known as *panda gari* from 1991 onwards (Chapter 3), as well as through the whole policy of 'protected villages' (See Chapter 5.1). Indeed, those who tried to resist going to the protected villages were warned that they would be treated as rebel collaborators if they did not move.

The possibility of some civilian support should not be wholly discounted. In the 1994 Peace Talks, one of the elders in the Government delegation was a known 'co-ordinator' whose house was used by the LRA to store goods which were then taken to Kitgum and sold for cash (see Annex B). LRA co-ordinators within the civilian population are known to have at times provided shelter (Annex A section 1), carried goods between LRA and UPDF (Annex A, section 3.17), and supported the LRA in sick bays located throughout the Acholi sub-region (Annex A, section 8). Furthermore, there were widespread grievances and desperate circumstances, leading Norbert Mao, MP for Gulu Municipality, to point out that,

> Unless the government can persuade the Acholi people that they are part of the new Uganda that's being built, and that they are not just being left to suffer as a punishment for their past allegiances, something bad could happen.[13]

And for increasing numbers of orphans, the LRA might appear a survival route when all other options seemed closed. As one person commented in a discussion about AIDS orphans; 'Some of these children when abducted don't come back, others join the rebels due to poor care for them, some join the Home guard'.[14] While some were willing helpers, it is undoubtedly the case that others, as Human Rights Watch argue, 'collaborated' out of fear and the absence of any feasible alternative (1997; 36). Clearly there was no easy way in which to respond to prohibitions and injunctions such as those outlined above. People were intimidated and did not know what to do next. To disobey the LRA was risky, but so was leaving the camps against Government orders. Many found themselves in an invidious and unenviable position, not just caught between two forces, but in a very real sense 'of' them too, with numerous households having had some members abducted by the LRA and others recruited into the Home guard or UPDF. As such, the question of civilian support remained open.

Links with the Lord's Resistance Movement

A related ambiguity was around the nature of the relationship between the LRA in Sudan and those claiming to be members of the Lord's Resistance Movement (LRM), or the political wing of the LRA. Some people in Gulu certainly believed the links to be close. One elder argued that, as some members of the diaspora had fled in fear of their lives, they would want 'to do something to reverse that situation', such as 'giving direct support to rebels or lobbying arms suppliers for arms and funds. Or by giving encouragement or morale'. In his opinion 'Divisions in the LRA/M are government propaganda. Those in exile will try to get back to [be] the Government ... How did illiterates manage to persuade a country like Sudan [to support them]? The political wing plays a very important role[15] (see also Finnström, 2003: 161–172). The media also at times suggested a strong connection between the LRM and Joseph Kony (e.g. *New Vision*, 18 July 1998, 'Kony gives conditions for peace negotiations', *The Monitor*, 28 April 1999 'Kony shuffles top officers'). Certainly materials emanating from Acholi claiming to be members of the LRM were highly politicised, antigovernment and anti-UN and anti-NGO intervention. They showed a strong awareness of the need to establish political credibility, returning repeatedly to five major issues; that they were not Christian fundamentalists, that they had a political agenda, that there were many government abuses which were being covered up, that western organisations were hypocritical and had vested interests in war, and that the media, in particular the western media, were responsible for anti-LRA propaganda.

However, there were some fundamental ambiguities about the extent to which the LRM actually linked with or influenced the LRA. In January 1998, for example, Dr. James Obita, a London-based Acholi claiming to be the LRM's spokesman for Kony, was reported as having been admitted to Juba hospital while waiting to meet with Kony: 'The security source said Kony's reluctance to meet Obita indicates that Kony owes his allegiance to the Sudanese government, and not to people in Nairobi and London who claim to be members of his external political wing'.[16] While this may be an example of anti-LRM propaganda as suggested by Finnström and others, my interview with Jacob raised further questions: his account locates the LRM secretariat not in London but in Khartoum and Juba, and he narrates the development of the LRA's political side as happening inside Sudan, with considerable Sudanese support – which might explain why people going to Nairobi to deal with the LRM generally came away disappointed. This is perhaps why, when the Chairman of the Parliamentary Committee on Defence and Internal Affairs was mandated in 1996 to 'inquire into all aspects of the war currently going on in northern Uganda with the aim of bringing it to a speedy end', he wrote directly to 'Mr. Joseph Kony, Lord's Resistance Army' rather than the LRM.[17] Similar doubts were carried into the 2006 peace talks, with sceptics arguing that the LRA team negotiating in Juba were not the 'real thing', as Joseph Kony and Vincent Otti resolutely kept away from the talks themselves.

The Role of the Media in Creating Ambiguity

Day-to-day national media coverage, replete with seemingly contradictory information about the LRA, fuelled a sense of ambiguity. On many occasions the headline in one paper (e.g. 'UPDF traps Soroti rebels')[18] would be flatly contradicted a few days later by those of its competitor ('Kony has 800 men, beats

UPDF trap').[19] At times the same paper would appear to contradict itself in the same edition. Following LRA attacks on three protected villages in May 1998, for example, *The Sunday Monitor* reported a UPDF statement 'that the LRA is now so incapacitated that they can no longer raid UPDF positions',[20] and in the same issue detailed a deadly attack on a bus on May 6th in which

> ... the bullets came in furious bursts as the rebels advanced shouting in crazed voices: 'Nek gino weng, nek gino weng (Kill them all, kill them all)'. They were many and in UPDF uniform.[21]

The paper may have juxtaposed the two stories as a way of signalling its reservations about the UPDF position, but such reporting was disorienting. Its speculative nature compounded the multiple ambiguities of day-to-day life in the war zone, creating – or at least exacerbating – the LRA's elusive quality, its apparent capacity to be both everywhere when it came to explaining atrocities, yet nowhere when it came to the UPDF dealing with them once and for all. It left civilians – whose major source of information was the two daily newspapers – in constant doubt and uncertainty as to what was actually going on, and wondering what, if anything, to believe. As one observer in the *New Vision* wrote: 'Joseph Kony and his ragtag Lord's Resistance Army have been disturbing Gulu and Kitgum districts for 11 years now, claiming to be waging a war. But, like Hamlet's ghost, "tis here! 'tis there! 'tis gone!": Where is Kony's war?'.[22] In the surreal ambience thus created the questions sometimes went further; Gulu's Resident District Commissioner commented at a meeting in February 1998 that 'This war cannot be ended by guns alone. Dialogue will help, but whom do we talk to? I appreciate all attempts to reach Kony. Who knows whether Kony exists? Maybe it is a mystery'. It was to be another eight years before Joseph Kony was finally interviewed by the BBC and thus had his existence confirmed.[23]

The LRA's Modus Operandi

Notwithstanding the above ambiguities, there is considerable consistency of findings about the LRA's modus operandi, in particular its human rights violations. NGOs,[24] UN organisations,[25] and international media alike,[26] have catalogued killings, maimings, rapes, theft and looting, burning of homes, destruction of crops and, most notoriously, the abduction of civilians, including children. Asked to describe LRA raids, one fieldworker simply said 'RAMPANT'.[27] The two hundred plus accounts I received from the fieldworkers in the protected villages for the period September 1998 to March 2000, as well as from various key informant interviews and focus group discussions, confirmed this overall picture (see Chapters 3, 5–7) and also indicated that raids were carried out in Sudan on both civilian and SPLA targets (Annex A, section 3.2 and 3.17).

The picture of abduction was mixed: those taken to serve as temporary porters for looted goods were at times released within a matter of hours or days. When twenty schoolboys were taken in a raid on Awer in June 1998, for example, fifteen

... came straight back because most of them lasted [i.e. stayed with the LRA] for between three days and one week, so they didn't pass through World Vision or GUSCO.
They were welcomed with a lot of sympathy, but they have now gone to stay in town
for security.

Of eight people abducted from one fieldworker's home in Odek in June 1998,
five had returned by late July. At other times though, very few returned. Of the
eight people taken in two separate raids on Palaro in June 1998, only one, a boy
of fourteen had returned one month later.[28] Those taken for induction into the
LRA faced a brutal process: abductees could be chained together, forced to carry
heavy loads, beaten, and made to march for miles (Annex A, section 1). They
frequently came under attack from UPDF air and ground forces, and large numbers died of thirst or were killed, either because they could not sustain the pace
or because they were seen to be breaking various rules. 'Blocking forces' would
follow groups of captives and kill off any stragglers (idem, section 5).

The LRA was also notorious for mutilations. One nun from northern Uganda
testified that 'If any of the children try to escape and are caught, the rebels make
examples of them to discourage and prevent further escape attempts. These examples include the mutilation of ears, noses, arms, legs, and even lips, or brutal
killings while their peers are forced to watch'.[29] Most reports suggest such mutilations were done to civilians as an example to other civilians, rather than to
abductees as an example to other abductees. They also suggest that, unlike abductions, which continued throughout the entire war, mutilations were not a constant, with 1991 and 1996 standing out as years in which such atrocities took place
in large numbers. By contrast with raids and abduction, there were no reports of
mutilation during my fieldwork, although the memory of earlier ones was very
live. There were renewed reports in 2005 in the wake of failed peace talks.

Administration and Control

Inside the LRA the exercise of control began with the initiation of recruits,
and this is prominent in Jacob's account. Repeated brutal (and at times lethal)
beatings, both following abduction and upon arrival in the camps in Sudan (Annex A, section 2.1), were a part of this, followed by more ritual processes, akin
in some respects to age-group initiation ceremonies, in which new abductees
were 'smeared with Ashes, shea nut oil, and sprinkled with First Water' and instructed on LRA regulations (idem section 13). Given that there were numerous
non-Acholi in the LRA (such as the LRA's spokesman at the 1994 peace talks,
Kony's Holy Spirit Secretary, and the WNBF members who joined on 17 March
1996 – idem, section 3.3) these processes, which echo the incorporation of non-
Acholi into farm work groups known as *Komponis* in the Sudanese Acholi area
in the 1970s and 1980s (Allen, 1987), were no doubt intended to help incorporate
non-Acholi into the 'New Acholi' identity Kony sought to build in the LRA. As
Jacob describes it, 'All the tribes who joined the LRA were termed to be the new
Acholi community, 'Acholi Manyen' (Annex A, section 2.3). However, it is clear
that these attempts were only partially successful. Nine non-Acholi command-

ers who escaped to Juba and Khartoum in 2000 left due to feeling marginalised as non-Acholi (idem, section 4.1).[30]

Control was further exercised through administrative mechanisms, religious ritual, and various prohibitions, particularly relating to gender relations. The administrative structure merged military and non-military models (see Annex A, section 9 for organisational chart). Although the overall leader was referred to as the 'chairman', he had under him four brigades (each with several battalions), a political wing, and 'Control Altar' which included administrative functions along with signals, air defence, logistics and medical matters, religious matters and an intelligence department.

Details of all new arrivals were recorded and used for daily 'Parade State' or Roll Call. At these information about 'sickness, deaths, births, absence without leave, duties, loss of weapons, food distribution would all be noted', processed through first Brigade and then overall Headquarters, to reach Joseph Kony by 10.00 A.M.. Information was thus consistently channelled from the bottom of the organisation to the very top. There was also radio communication between forces inside Uganda and headquarters in Sudan; they were not operating independently as self-contained 'bandits', but were closely monitored and controlled. This could not all have been sustained by one man. When the Government delegation in the second talks of 1994 complained that Kony's absence showed a lack of commitment, his representative countered that the LRA was more than just Kony:

> ... you should note that if we (the officers) were not there or the young soldiers were not there, or if the officers who have come were not there, Kony would not be in the bush.

Notwithstanding these structures and mechanisms of control, however, the fact that 93.6 per cent of recorded child abductees managed to escape within two years of capture, indicates that internal surveillance was less than successful (or that other LRA members were turning a blind eye more often than the choice of testimonies published by child agencies would have us believe).

The LRA model diverges from more conventional command structures in placing the spirits at the top of the organisational chart (see Annex A section 9). Jacob's account identifies only four spirits (Juma Oris, Silindy Makay, Who are You?, Divo), compared with the eight identified by Allen (1991: 374), but both agree that Juma Oris was the principal one. These spirits were said to advise on a range of matters, including health, military decisions, and ritual processes, and to communicate through the medium of Joseph Kony, who is sometimes referred to as Laor (the messenger).[31] The spirits could visit at any time and send Kony into a trance, during which everything he said would be recorded by his secretary and later used as the basis for decision making (Annex A, section 10).

Spirit possession was integrated into and supported by a wider religious framework, centred around the Yards, circular open-air spaces 'with an altar in the middle and a thatched hut where clean water and shea nut oil is kept for anointing people'. These were maintained by 'controllers' concerned both with preparing people for marriage and the like, but also with influencing the course of battles (Annex A, section 11). On Fridays, the Yards would be used for prayers lasting the whole morning, and also as an occasion for Kony to 'comment on the issues that have been happening during the week' and 'tell people some of the messages revealed to him by the Holy Spirit'.

Various prohibitions were laid out in Kony's regulations, and resembled but were more specific than those disseminated to civilians (see above). They included a ban on alcohol, smoking and marijuana (see Annex A, section 3.4), and various foods such as 'mango, oranges, lemon, edible rats, pork, honey,[32] sheep, duck, eggs … and so on' (idem section 2.3). They also extended into the area of gender relations.

Most descriptions of the LRA argue that abducted girls and women were then further coerced into becoming 'sex slaves'.[33] Raids at times involved incidents of sexual violence, and both the children that abducted women and girls brought back, and their own medical needs, confirmed that they had indeed become 'wives' to the soldiers. Allen argued that while Kony's followers were meant to keep to similar prohibitions to those of Alice (i.e. not to have intercourse), in practice they did not (1999; 379), and Behrend also attributed large-scale abduction to the removal by the spirit Silly Silindi of the interdiction on men and women having sex.

However, the image of a free-for-all does not hold up. As in the broader society, gender relations were used as a key instrument of control over both men and women. Male-female relations were the primary concern in four out of the thirteen regulations on which Kony lectured the newly arrived abductees. Relationships had to be 'authorised by the military council' (Annex A, section 2.3), and in point of fact 'It is the chairman who decides if you are ready for a woman; even if you don't want you are given' (idem, section 6). Marriages with foreign women were not allowed (idem, section 2.3), ordinary soldiers could not talk to 'any woman belonging to a commander unless authorised to do so', and women were obliged to 'all go to collect water and firewood together. They would also garden together.'

Men who were allocated women were then expected to perform sexually, and given medical treatment if their women complained that they failed to do so. Interestingly, 'Cases of bwoc (impotence) included both people who were already bwoc at home, and others who became bwoc after abduction' (idem, section 6. See section 8 for herbs used for impotence).[34] Women whose husbands were killed would, after a certain period during which rituals were performed, be allocated to another man. The importance attributed to fertility is demonstrated in pregnant women being placed in sick bays away from military activity (idem, section 7), and the intricate linkages between questions of fertility and the purity of the 'New Acholi' (idem, section 2.3).[35]

Measures were taken to prevent 'prostitution', and homosexuality was punished with execution (Annex A, section 6). In the 1994 Peace Talks, the LRA brought forward for punishment one of their members who was caught defiling a young girl (Annex B). Gender-specific prohibitions to maintain 'purity' were visible in the structure and operations of the Yard, with the sitting area divided into four discrete sections for officers, men, young men and boys, and women and children respectively. Furthermore, 'a menstruating woman can never enter the Yard' (Annex A, section 12), and the jerry cans in which blessed water was stored, 'are not touched by any women' (idem, section 13). 'Controllers' were men only, and they were also the only ones wearing dreadlocks. The exception to this gender order is that Silindy Makay, one of the four holy spirits said to guide Joseph Kony, was a woman.

Once these internal prohibitions are understood, it becomes more comprehensible why, by contrast with other insurgent groups, LRA abductions of women were low. From 1986 to 2001 women and girls represented 20.8 per cent of those abducted in Kitgum district, and 16.7 per cent in Gulu (UNICEF, 2001: 7).[36] This was approximately half the level of female abductions by the ADF in Kabarole and Kasese (42.9 per cent and 38.5 per cent respectively).[37]

Survival and Proxy Warfare

A consideration of the LRA's survival mechanisms, and the role which its relationship with the Government of Sudan played in these, shows that while they clearly stole to exist, they did not simply 'exist to steal'. Although the looting of civilians was important (and there were reports from returnees that they enjoyed better food while staying in the bush than when living in the protected villages), the pickings inside Uganda became ever poorer over time, and the amounts that could be carried on foot back to Sudan were self-limiting. No amount of abduction could overcome this – the more abducted, the more to be carried. The other two key elements of the LRA's survival strategy were a combination of self-reliance and external assistance from the Sudanese government. Self-reliance included food production in and around camps in Sudan, and the use of herbal/traditional remedies in sick-bays maintained throughout Kitgum and Gulu districts. For Jacob, this indicated the extent to which the LRA had become 'blocked', as 'people were now returning to village life although we were in military combat'. In the sick bays, looted medicines were combined with remedies made from roots, fungi, specific ashes, animal furs, skins etc. (Annex A, section 8). They could not address all medical needs – many returnees required treatments, and there were reports of cholera outbreaks resulting from serious food and water shortages (idem, section 3 for example)[38] – but they do nuance the picture of gratuitous looting. Reports of medical supplies being diverted from the UPDF to the LRA add a further twist.[39]

The characterisation of the LRA as a proxy force is supported to an extent by the many forms of assistance provided by the Sudanese Government. When Jacob and other abductees arrived in Issac they were collected in Government of Sudan trucks (Annex A, section 1.3). When there were acute food shortages Government lorries brought 'food and other assistance to the LRA camp in Aru' (idem, section 3.1). When combined NRA/SPLA forces attacked the LRA, Sudanese reinforcements were sent to Jebeleen (idem, section 3.5). They built a new camp there and remained for the next three years, during which time, Sudan took a lot of interest in LRA, giving LRA the opportunity of making a lot of ambushes and burning most of the SPLA vehicles which were supplying food and arms brought from Uganda' (idem, section 3.6). Sudanese officials informed the LRA about the imminent arrival of a delegation in Uganda looking for the Aboke girls (idem, section 3.8). Even when, in the wake of the Nairobi peace accord in 1999, relations with the Government of Sudan soured and food supplies dried up, local links were maintained with some Sudanese army commanders who exchanged LRA produce for 'essential commodities like sugar, salt, drugs, clothing and fuel for their vehicles.'

However, the LRA were not entirely beholden. The relationship began to break down when the Government developed doubts about the LRA's use of donated materials (Annex A, section 3.10), and when the LRA attacked Sudanese civilians in the vicinity of their camp. These incidents, coinciding with the Carter Center negotiations in late 1999, led the Government of Sudan to give them just five days to shift camp from Jebeleen to Nisitu. Although Government of Sudan representatives met with Carter Center representatives and Kony in Nisitu in 2000, when proposals to relocate the LRA 1,000km northwards were broached, the contact broke down; Kony lost trust and 'decided to stop receiving supplies of food, arms and uniforms from Juba', arguing that 'any food being brought by Arabs must not be accepted because they may be poisoned'. At this time the LRA began making overtures to the Equatoria Defence Force to establish alternative alliances (idem, section 3.18). Evidently it did not see itself as a collection of 'proxy warriors' dependent exclusively on the Government of Sudan.

LRA Motivations and Politics

The political views of the LRA are at least partially discernible from its attempts to communicate with the civilian population, and its internal workings as described by key informants, particularly the focus on cleansing and purity along ethnic lines. To communicate verbally with the civilian population the LRA would occasionally gather people together in a particular village and conduct a meeting.[40] More usual methods included dropping letters on roads and paths, or nailing them to trees. At times messages, which included prohibitions, commands, comments on political developments, warnings of imminent attacks and taunts to the military to follow them, would be given to people found outside the camps, or to released abductees, sometimes with precise instructions about whom to give the information to (e.g. security personnel).

Prohibitions designed to protect the LRA included telling people not to run or raise the alarm if they see the LRA, as the LRA would otherwise attack that village, not to go and hunt as they might come across the LRA's hiding places, and not to ride bicycles as these were a way of taking information to the government – the LRA could force you to dismantle your bicycle or break your calves by hammering on them. Other prohibitions appeared aimed at undermining the Government. In February 1996, for example, they 'issued an edict banning settlement within four kilometres of roads and prohibiting the use of bicycles. Their intention was the tight control of a population inaccessible to government troops which would provide cover and supplies for the rebels'.[41] They also told people not to stay near government soldiers or follow their rules, and not to travel in vehicles – those doing so were said to be carrying produce which would better be given to the rebels. A further set of prohibitions related to religious beliefs, and included telling people not to work/dig on Fridays or Sundays, not to keep pigs,[42] and not to slaughter white chickens, which were regarded as something holy.[43]

Sometimes people were told to leave the camps and go home to dig, partly to undermine the 'Government's administrative policies', and partly to ensure they would not get caught in the cross-fire (on the other hand people in one village were told to stop gathering food from their abandoned lands). In some cases, the message was one of blackmail: one returned abductee in Anaka had been told to tell people that, should the LRA come to the village and find no food items, they would react by planting landmines such that the fields would be 'locked by landmines'.[44]

Comments passed to civilians about the political situation in mid-1998 included that they would soon oust the NRM government, that their rebellion should be seen as a national struggle, and that they 'don't want killing of the local population for the Holy Spirit has forbidden massacre'. There was also a message to 'let all capable boys and girls join the LRA so that they remove Museveni from the chair of Uganda'. In some messages, they described themselves as messengers of God and stated that the ideology of the LRA was based on the Ten Commandments of God. They also they let it be known that they were not going to attend the *Kacokke Madit* (Big Meeting) in London, organised by members of the diaspora, since they viewed it as a waste of money, and that they wanted it to take place either in northern Uganda or Kampala. They accused the Government of 'selling the land of Acholi using the land-bill', and said that 'The poisoning of WFP relief supplies is proof that the government wants to kill the Acholi'.[45]

For a few weeks in early 1999, before the signal was blocked, the LRA broadcast daily from 5–6 P.M. on 31 MB/SW, a station they called 'Radio Free Uganda'. One fieldworker described it as propagating 'all kinds of aggressive languages … against the government in Kampala.' Another reported that 'This campaign is causing fear. Because in their broadcast they [LRA] talk of war. Yet people thought that normal life was coming in place'.[46] When a fieldworker raised the issue of the radio with some soldiers he was drinking with, he was asked why he was listening to rebel radio – was he a rebel collaborator? The broadcasts, some of which were in English, included news, music and 'commentaries'. On 3rd May 1999, for example, a commentary entitled 'Dictator Museveni is in problems', accused the president of 'over-staying' in power, and argued that Museveni's Government was coming under pressure for misuse of funds. It demonstrated familiarity with a wide range of political and economic actors such as the IMF, and with debates about the referendum and the Government's overrun on military expenditures. Other rebel groups, including the ADF, a rebel movement fighting in western Uganda at the time, the West Nile Bank Front, the National Freedom Army and the National Rescue Front, were referred to as the 'Patriotic Forces'. The Government was accused of laying 5,000 landmines on the Uganda-Sudan border, and Museveni of 'violating the bogus 1995 Constitution' by sending troops into Sudan without the approval of parliament for a 'suicidal attack' under the pretence of 'containing the Karimojong warriors'. The broadcaster likened 'Museveni's efforts' to those of a 'dying bull', claiming that 'new soldiers and the local defence soldiers which have been amassed at the Sudan border are running away because they fear to face battle that will cost them their dear lives'. Some attention was also given to problems with Uganda's judiciary.

On 6th May Radio Free Uganda criticised the 'NRM regime' for 'encouraging mob justice in Uganda' and argued that 'Museveni's regime can never stop inventing stupid propaganda stories and lies to punish the image of the patriotic forces in its endless attempts to undermine the popular armed struggle of Uganda'. In particular the commentator denied stories that rebels were resorting to cannibalism as a result of hunger, and that the LRA was 'involved in the slave trade in Sudan'. He gave examples of where Government 'propaganda' did not correspond to reality, in particular how government claims to have wiped out the rebels were untrue: 'no sooner had they said such lies than the rebels appeared again with the more devastating firepower to destroy government forces'.

These broadcasts belie the claim that the LRA lacked any political position and had no interest in communicating with the civilian population – clearly they wished to, but were suppressed at the first sign of success. This pattern was repeated with Radio Mega FM, a community radio station established in Gulu with a turn-key grant from DFID and a commitment to peace-building. Having first gone on air in October 2002, it soon boasted 51 per cent of the radio listeners in the northern region,[47] but, following a call-in from Joseph Kony and Vincent Otti during a live broadcast in December 2002, the station was prohibited by Central Government and local UPDF from broadcasting further LRA contributions and warned not to discuss 'contentious or "emotional"' issues (Dolan, 2004: 13).

Politics of Rejection

Although the LRA did not eschew the use of modern technology, its political agenda did not always fit readily into the conceptual frameworks of the institutions observing it – for it was fundamentally rooted in rejection of those institutions and the 'modernisation'/'westernisation' they represented. To the extent that it emphasised ethnic power transcending existing state boundaries, for example, the LRA in south Sudan, particularly in areas occupied by Sudanese Acholi, would not necessarily see itself as being outside its ethnic 'home'. In 1960 Girling wrote that 'they [Acholi in Sudan and Uganda] are still one people and any change in the present situation might lead to a demand for them all to be united under one political authority' (1960: 1). Writing in 1991, Allen argued that Kony was fighting for 'judgement', and that like Alice, he felt he was 'saving the Acholi "tribe"' by cleansing it of bad people (1991: 379). Both he and Behrend comment on Alice and Kony's attempts to cleanse their Movements and the Acholi people as a whole of witches, witchcraft and pagan spirit mediums (*ajwakas*).

Commitment to 'cleansing' the old is evident in Kony's speech to the newly arrived abductees. In this he places emphasis on saving people from the evils of contemporary life and from the Government's 'agenda'. He also portrays the LRA as 'the only chosen people of God who are fighting using the assistance from the Holy Spirit', and as one of the two elephants under whose feet the 'elites of the Acholi tribe' will be crushed if they don't stop supporting Museveni. As Jacob noted in an aside,

> issues which made Kony unhappy with the Museveni government included the sale of land, privatisation of industries, and the 'spread of the Tutsi empire' (especially the way in which Acholi was being diluted by outsiders being brought in and marrying Acholis ...).[48]

The emphasis on purification is also captured in reports that they describe themselves as 'God's messengers',[49] and in the creation of a whole cadre of 'controllers', '"clean" people who don't quarrel' and who 'are ready to teach other people who fell into mistakes' (Annex A, section 11). When military activities are curtailed by the breakdown in the relationship with the Government of Sudan in 2000, 'they started traditional teachings about village life in Uganda and differences in how people are undertaking culture these days' (idem, section 3.18).

The attempt to build something new is evident in the integration of elements of Islam, such as Friday being a day of prayer and rest, and the prohibition on eating pork, as well as in the way aspects of the LRA's own experience are formalised into annual celebrations, such as Juma Oris Day on 7 April, and Whistle Day on 1 December.[50] As described above, new recruits were anointed (Annex A, section 13), and in the process recruits who were not themselves of Acholi origin were said to become 'New Acholi', even if this was little more than a rhetorical acceptance. The emphasis on addressing male impotence and female infertility can be seen as reflecting the desire to build up the New Acholi, as can the apparent care to ensure that pregnant women were not exposed to warfare. The 'New Acholi' could thus be described as a mythologized 'Old' Acholi, cleansed of the corruption of westernising influences, though building on Christian messages about creating a new society.

The 1994 Peace Talks

The 1994 talks, often regarded as the closest the GoU came to seeking peace with the LRA prior to the Juba talks of 2006–2008, established the template for subsequent GoU-LRA interactions, in that the LRA sought recognition and control, while the GoU sought to humiliate and belittle the LRA. Key Government negotiators included Mrs Betty Bigombe (then Minister for Pacification of Northern Uganda), Colonel Wasswa (4th Division Commander) and Colonel Tolit. On the LRA side the main speakers were Kony himself, and Commanders Omona and Odego.

The LRA sought recognition through many sources; physical control over events (the structuring of the meetings, the capacity to kill or not to kill, to eat or not to eat, etc.), but also in the terrain of tradition (who has a better grasp of it?), religion (who can use the Bible to greater effect?), and ethnicity (who is a real Acholi?). The choice of the Atoo Hills as a venue was possibly for symbolic reasons as it was the former base of Kilama, a UPDA commander who died shortly after coming out of the bush in the 1988 peace talks, and was widely believed to have been killed by the NRA. In refusing to allow the Government delegation to proceed unless they left their weapons behind, in imposing multiple roadblocks and inspections, and in 'cleansing' the Government delegation with holy water, the LRA exercised further control. In multiple ways they also determined the parameters of the discussions. They set the Government delegation two key questions – which Kony himself then said he knew they were not in a position to answer. They also drew heavily on discourses of Christianity, tradition, ethnicity and race to argue their legitimacy.

Kony's speech makes it clear that he saw the traditional leaders as corrupted and therefore neither legitimate nor credible negotiating partners: not only had they blessed the rebels one moment and cursed them the next, but they failed subsequently to carry out traditional cleansing ceremonies after cursing them. The elders were also reminded that they had supported government-organised bow and arrow brigades, and that, by entering the battle zone for the peace talks, they had broken with Acholi tradition in which elders do not engage in the battle zone at all. The fear that these comments, together with the LRA's refusal to eat the food offered by Bigombe, provoked in the elders, is suggested by the diarrhoea attacks some of them reportedly succumbed to.

The emphasis on ethnicity, which is consistent with a concern for Acholi purity as described above, is evident throughout the transcript of the meeting: the fact that Odego, the LRA spokesman, was a Lugbara rather than an Acholi was emphasised, as was the fact that Colonel Wasswa (the UPDF 4th Division Commander) was a Muganda. In both cases their otherness was used to reinforce the centrality of Acholi identity – Odego pointed out that he was convinced that the elders accompanying Bigombe were 'true Acholis because otherwise they would fear being killed'. Kony reminded the elders that they had said in 1986 that a Munyankole cannot lead the Acholi, and Tolit made much of the fact that he was himself an Acholi and that this gave him the license to speak in the negotiations. This was not missed by Odego in his response to Tolit ('Son of Acholi and my brother, let me respond …').

Race was also used to determine belonging and exclusion: 'The white man' was a subtle presence at several points. At the second meeting Odego (LRA) suggests that they should work towards a written agreement, a suggestion which Tolit (GoU) questions on the grounds that they have successfully used verbal agreements up to that point and that if they were to 'take it the white man's way (munnu-munnu) ... then we must know and see what you have written down. We have to look at it very carefully, because if ceasefire is done the white man's way then there are usually very many conditions!' As such, the white man became a metaphor for non-traditional approaches and for a failure of trust. By wanting something in writing, it was implied, the LRA were not just questioning the integrity of the GOU, they were showing their own lack of integrity – and a failure of Acholi authenticity. At a later stage Bigombe, in trying to smooth over a difficult moment in the talks, said

> we have not come here for a post-mortem, to dig for what has brought us problems, but we have come to heal it. This is why I want us to start looking forward. The White Man would say 'we should start focussing on the future'.

She thus used the idea of the white 'other' as a mask behind which she could create a shift in the dynamics, a task which would have been more difficult for her to do as an Acholi woman, especially given that Kony regarded her as a mother who should be looking after her children at home.

Both sides, in different ways, used an appeal to religion to justify not explaining themselves: the LRA said they were guided by the Holy Spirit and therefore beyond question; the GOU said they were guided by the Bible verse which indicates that Government authority is God-given – and that the LRA should therefore not question them. The language of cleansing was used by the Reverend in the Government delegation, but actualised when the LRA sprinkled 'holy water' over the Government delegation before permitting them to sit down for discussions.[51]

The use of discourses to mark belonging and exclusion was a central feature of the LRA's demands for recognition and validation – and of the Government's refusal to give it. In the second meeting, for example, the LRA opened proceedings by calling for the national anthem to be sung, a call which would usually be the prerogative of a government official (and from the video it appears that Bigombe chose not to participate in singing the anthem). But it is the bitter exchange between Tolit on the Government side, and Omona on the LRA side, over the use of the term 'local' to describe the peace negotiations, which brings this struggle into focus most clearly.

The term 'local' is heavily loaded in the context of severe under-development which characterises northern Uganda. It is generally used to describe an object or process used by people who have the aspirations but not the resources to be 'up-to-date'. A 'local' car-wash, for example, is not an automatic machine with high pressure water jets and soft brushes which pass over your vehicle while you sit inside it, but a team of men with buckets and cloths who clean cars next to a pond or stream. 'Local' can also describe an arrangement beyond official purview. The following is a pertinent example:

> If a rebel reports to the barracks and says he wants to be a Home guard there is a local arrangement with the Intelligence Officer and Commanding Officer that they receive the salaries of other soldiers who have been killed but are still on the payroll.[52]

In other words something 'local' is perceived as a second rate or unofficial substitute for 'the real thing'. Tolit's description of the peace talks as 'local' suggested that it was not necessary for the Government to invest serious resources into the process, and seemed calculated to belittle the importance of the LRA. His subsequent stress on how important the process was to Uganda as a whole, not just to the Acholi, is correspondingly questionable.

Omona vehemently rejected any suggestion that the LRA had been defeated and wanted recognition of the fact that these were negotiations, not surrender by the LRA. The whole discussion about who was present and who was absent is evidence of the importance of receiving and withholding recognition; Museveni never attended, and Kony on the second occasion sent Omona as a representative, and both sides were suspicious of the sincerity of the others as a result.[53] O'Kadameri's account suggests that the LRA had reason to be suspicious:

> It is imperative to note the ad hoc nature of this process. At no time were the top army leadership including the President willing to tell Bigombe unambiguously that she was doing the right thing and had their full support (2002: 38)

There was also a thinly veiled sense of superiority in some of the Government statements, as when Tolit used Paul's letter to the Romans to support the argument that at the end of the day the Government knew what was best. The LRA reacted by pointing out the Government's attitude (for example, Omona said 'let us stop despising one another'), and by the use of irony. There was something of the velvet-gloved fist in Kony's comment that from the SPLA-GOU relationship the LRA had learned the value of friendship, and thinly veiled sarcasm in Odego's reminder of the Acholi proverb that 'doing things in a hurry gave the hyena its spots – like an army uniform'.[54]

Whether or not Tolit's personal animus against the LRA was allowed to prevail over the government position is debatable. While the LRA played on Tolit in an attempt to create divisions within the Government delegation, O'Kadameri's account suggests that Tolit did represent the more hard-line position in Government and that Bigombe and Wasswa were more or less on their own. This view is supported by Museveni's repeated statements that he would never negotiate with the LRA.

Discussion

Overall the findings indicate that the LRA–GoU war was a real part of the situation in northern Uganda, and they confirm some elements of popular characterisations of what the LRA *did*. However, they also suggest that the reality of what the LRA *was* in some respects diverged considerably from the stereotypes, and that, beneath the appearance of taking steps to end the war, the Government was pursuing the opposite course. These divergences indicate a need to reassess the nature of the war.

Thus the LRA's raids and abductions are confirmedly brutal, with no mercy shown for those who could not sustain the pace, and killings a part of a process of deliberate intimidation of survivors, as well as a security measure. However, child abduction, while a reality, is shown to be the lesser part of a far larger pattern of adult abduction and a degree of voluntary recruitment. As for what the LRA was, it appears that, rather than a somewhat chaotic and poorly organised bunch of bandits carrying out these acts without any purpose other than their immediate survival, it was relatively organised, rational and motivated. Though it did engage in heavy looting from civilians, this was a means to an end rather than an end in itself, and as such does not support the implications of terms such as 'bandits', nor of statements such as 'They are not intent on fighting Ugandan government soldiers, they have come to steal'.[55] Although the reliance on brutality and the centrality of Kony and the Spirits to the organisation encouraged some observers to dismiss the LRA's motivations as 'vague', 'ill-defined', and essentially unimportant, it was perhaps the juxtaposition of these behaviours, and the incorporation of spiritual, religious and political agendas – in disregard of somewhat euro-centric concerns with categorisation – which lay at the heart of the LRA's resilience. By playing them off against each other at different times and for different purposes, Kony was able, in his capacity as a spirit medium, to maintain a tight grip and a degree of independence for himself.

The spiritual element is clear in the four controlling spirits for whom Kony is a medium, and also in the use of non-conventional 'weapons' such as 'first water' and 'white stones'. Whether he was a true medium for the spirits, or he used the spirits as a medium through which to channel his own wishes, is impossible to ascertain. It appears that, whichever is the case, many of his members had great belief in his predictive powers, and this allowed him to command considerable respect. The fact that the soldiers who had begun to dialogue with Government inside Uganda in 2001 went back when called by Kony, despite having been loaned equipment and granted safe passage, is some indicator of the hold he exercised over them. Unlike the HSM, though, some of whose soldiers stormed forward armed only with rocks and water, the LRA was further armed with hi-tech equipment such as Geographical Positioning Systems, radios and satellite telephones, as well as weapons captured during clashes with the UPDF and SPLA.

The religious elements are to be found in Kony's description of the LRA as a Godly organisation on a mission to bring the Ten Commandments to Uganda, and in the existence of a whole cadre of 'controllers' whose functions in all aspects of the organisation are akin to those of priests. As indicated by the day of prayer being Friday rather than Sunday, this was more than Christian fundamentalism, it also accommodated elements of Islam.

The political element, as evidenced in the wish to overthrow the Museveni government (and the 'Tutsi Empire'), was also unequivocal – as was the wish to deal with the 'corruption' of the present day. The LRA clearly attempted to communicate a political agenda to the civilian population, unattractive though it was to the Government, state-centric UN organisations, and NGOs embedded in western models of political systems. There was thus no choice to be made between the LRA being a political, religious or indeed animist organisation, for it contained elements of all three under a military umbrella, and its members were both volunteers and conscripts, with correspondingly heterogeneous motivations and grievances. In its somewhat millenarian claim to be a war against evil and its ambition to create a 'new Acholi' (*Acholi manyen*), carried over from the earlier Holy Spirit Movement, the LRA to an extent integrated the three elements, and can be seen offering at least the appearance of an opportunity to pursue one or other of them. This probably enlarged the pool of external actors who saw in the LRA a possible vehicle for their own agendas – thus the Sudanese support for political training for LRA members, the attempt by the WNBF to join forces in 1997, and the EDF's openness to overtures in 2000. That the organisation was seen as a potential political threat by the Government is suggested by the rapidity with which the latter shut down at least two of the LRA's avenues for communicating its political agenda to civilians. This was perhaps also in recognition of the fact that key LRA members at times enjoyed substantial inputs in the form of training, both in military technology and of a more political nature, part of a complex relationship between the LRA and the Government of Sudan, which reveals neither complete dependence nor a position as 'dogs of war'.

Within the organisation the three-in-one formula had its uses for both leaders and followers. Leaders never needed to explain any action entirely in terms of one or the other of the three components. Decisions did not have to conform to the internal logic of any one of the three strands, and ultimate explanations could always be attributed elsewhere. But it was not just the leaders who could benefit from this fluidity of emphasis. Although the psychology of LRA members is generally discussed in terms of end-states such as 'brutalised', 'traumatised' and 'fearful', something rather more complex probably happened over time, a necessary adjustment by abductees to their new situation, however unwillingly they were drawn into it. Yes, they were exposed to and forced to participate in brutal activities – but it is not clear that this turned them all into brutes.[56] Alongside the brutality there was an eclectic mixture of Christianity, spiritualism, and politics to choose from when it came to explaining to themselves why they were there. Abductees therefore probably reached a compromise with the reality they found themselves in and 'bought into' at least one of the elements of the LRA's discourse (especially if their escape options were limited), pretending to believe in the others as and when necessary for their survival.

Indeed, people would not necessarily see any tensions or contradictions between these elements, for they are all to be found within civil society. It is notable that in the speeches of Kony and Omona they make no attempt to explain them away. It is only in materials of the London-based LRM, targeted at a western audience whose politics have been largely secularised, that we find the need to explain away the religious overtones in the name Lord's Resistance Army, and the vehement denial of a Christian fundamentalist component.

Successfully containing such potentially contradictory elements within one body appears to have contributed to the LRA's resilience, given that the organisation survived far longer than any other Ugandan rebel group since 1986. But the very complexity of the LRA's discourses and agenda was at times also a weakness. They enabled a rather heterogeneous set of people to be accommodated within one organisation, but they could not create a homogeneous understanding of what they were fighting for, either within the organisation or outside it. In addition, even where one or other element of the agenda made sense, the ugliness of the LRA's military tactics were an obstacle to popular support. New recruits were told that 'LRA as a rebel movement has no room to spare for our enemies because whenever we go for battle we kill, we murder, we rob and loot without being sympathetic to our enemies'. In other words, a virtue was made out of the very feature of the LRA which most detracted from the possibility of winning wider support.

A related weakness is that while all three elements of the LRA agenda coexisted, they were not equal. The spirits appeared to be the core of Kony's power base, and individuals who attempted to 'modernise' the LRA through emphasising more recognisably 'western' approaches did not fare well. Any 'moderniser' in the LRA was confronted with the fact that Kony had made the creation of a 'New Acholi' the centrepiece of the LRA's vision, and was thus unable to climb outside an ethnic framework. Although he tried to overcome this by declaring all newcomers as 'New Acholi', in practice he failed, and non-Acholi who saw in the LRA a potential vehicle for their political agendas, were frustrated by the ethnicised nature of the command structures. Furthermore, the refusal of various political representatives to return from Khartoum to the camps when called, can be read as indicators of a loss of control by Kony.

Given that many abductees were Acholi in origin, this might not have been a major problem, but it is unclear whether the impact of decades of displacement on Acholi culture (see Chapters 5–7), would increase or decrease the resonance of an appeal to a mythologized past Acholi way of life – the more so when the LRA's actions had contributed to inducing dread, debilitation and disorientation in the population in general. Furthermore, internal grievances were created by the extreme degree of control exercised over people. Even volunteer members could not always abide the many regulations. People thus decided to appear to conform but were often just biding their time.[57] The fact that Kony became involved in micro-managing processes such as the selection of women for individual soldiers, when combined with its importance as a form of regulation, strongly suggests that the LRA could never grow beyond a certain size.

Further Nuances and Characterisations – Local Context

It is important in this discussion to also stress that, while the LRA may have been 'among the most brutal [rebels] in Africa'[58] they were by no means unique, whether in their methods, world-view, or political agenda. There are clear historical precedents both in northern Uganda and elsewhere, all of which allow its excesses and apparently unique practices to be put in comparative perspective. In northern Uganda points of comparison are to be found with the 'Nubis' of the turn of the century and the Holy Spirit Movement of the 1980s. The former, a group of just one hundred mutineers, kept the whole Acholi area in a state of unrest and turmoil, and were regarded by the incoming British administrator, Delmé-Radcliffe, as the principal obstacle to stability there. When he launched a campaign against them in April 1901, the Nubis, as the LRA were to do nearly a century later, divided into smaller groups and proved extremely difficult to track down, not least because they intimidated the local population into keeping their location secret.

The worldview of the LRA, generally dismissed as obscure and irrational, is closely related to that of the HSM. These include the centrality of spirits in decision-making processes, complex initiation and cleansing rituals, various prohibitions, and the Holy Spirit Tactics, which Behrend describes 'as a way of combining modern Western military techniques with ritual practices' (Behrend 1998: 115). Although they differ in some details, the prohibitions documented here resemble those documented by Allen more than ten years earlier (Allen 1991: 377). The admixture of mystical (e.g. if you eat certain foods you are more vulnerable in battle) and obviously pragmatic (e.g. no drinking or smoking), is strongly reminiscent of the HSM's prohibitions. Similarly, the way military success and failure alike confirmed Kony's predictions (if you fail it is because you have not obeyed the spirits or you are unclean) is identical to the controlling behaviour of Alice Lakwena and guilt-making processes found in the HSM (Behrend 1999: 45). The prohibitions of the LRA are also similar to those described by Lan (1985) for ZANLA in Zimbabwe.

Practices of anointment, as well as resembling the HSM's 'Holy Spirit Tactics', are also to be found in earlier history. Anywar (1948: 75), for example, records how Nubis stationed in present day Gulu in 1889, fled when they learned that Arabs were coming from the Sudan, because they had heard rumours 'that they [the Arabs] anointed themselves with a preparation which rendered them immune from attack, even from gunshot'. There is nothing new, then, in the idea that either the HSM or the LRA could protect themselves from being shot by anointing themselves before battle. The ceremonies in the yard for new abductees echo earlier Acholi ones for captives taken from other clans during slave raids, wherein a captive would be taken to his captor's ancestor shrine, where 'one of the old women sprinkled on him a mixture of flour and water' after which he would be fed special foods for several days, have his head shaved and his clothes changed (Girling, 1960: 108–109).

The use of gender as an internal control mechanism was derived directly from the broader society. Although there were women soldiers, and although there was no differentiation between men and women when it came to making them kill, or be killed (Annex A, section 1.1–1.2), gender roles inside the LRA conformed closely to very stereotypical 'masculine' and 'feminine' ones held in northern Uganda more generally (see Chapter 7). This is evident from the moment Jacob is abducted; boys were chained together, girls were not, being made instead to carry looted goods (Annex A, section 1). Women were regarded as the property of men. Indeed, Kony's attempts to intervene in relations between men and women, an attempt to realise his commitment to establishing a purity he felt had been lost in modern-day Uganda, would have considerable resonance with Acholi traditionalists. His statement to Bigombe, during the peace talks of 1994, that she has 'a good feeling for a mother who should be looking after her children at home' (see below), makes his position clear. Somewhat ironically therefore, he voiced the very concerns expressed by many Acholi about social breakdown and the loss of their value system – concerns which have 'uncontrolled' (i.e. not controlled by elders) sexual relations at their very heart.

The belief that it is possible (and important) to communicate with the spirits of 'dead' persons, and that they have a major responsibility for what befalls the living, is in no way peculiar to the LRA, and would make sense to many Acholi, such beliefs having been well documented amongst both Ugandan and Sudanese Acholi. Ogot (1961) describes how 'there is no direct personal relationship between God and man; and therefore the only means of reaching God is through the prophets or ancestors'. He argues that only those souls who are unable to communicate with the living are 'completely dead'; 'The other departed souls, that is, those who are only 'dead', are as much part of the society as living members. They are 'fed', appealed to during hard times, and at funerals, greetings are sent to them by the living relatives' (Ogot 1961: 128).

More than a decade later, a Norwegian Church Aid report considering the culture of Sudanese Acholi similarly describes how 'The spirit of the dead is believed to take a profound interest in the activities of their descendants, and for being responsible for most of the good – and much of the evil too – that befalls them' (Storas, 1975: 7–8). Twenty years after this, at a meeting in 1998, the Koch Clan was described to me by one pastor as having a spirit medium who was 'like a radio receiver' with 'no memory of the messages she transmits. ... The problem was to inform the medium when she was not in a trance of the things she had said when she was in the trance'.[59] Although not all people shared such belief systems, nobody would find them unusual; just as there was nothing unusual about Alice Lakwena being a spirit medium (Allen 1991), so Joseph Kony was unexceptional.

Such comparisons suggest that the LRA's politics are situated in and shaped by reactions to far broader processes of social and political change, as were the HSM's, and should be understood in terms of their societal logic rather than the logic of the individuals involved. Allen's exploration of the response to outbreaks of sorcery and witchcraft in the Madi area of northern Uganda in the 1980s is useful in this regard. He argues that these outbreaks, which themselves were in response to socio-political changes and stresses, were dealt with by female diviners and healers who cut across the authority of (male) ritual elders. Paradoxically, therefore, their attempts to restore order did not reverse social change; they established a new order which confirmed some of the underlying social changes which gave rise to disorder in the first place. The new was legitimated by integrating it with practices from the past, albeit somewhat re-framed (Allen 1991; 385). In Madi the language of Christianity enabled the practice of spirit possession to be re-legitimated under the new order; spirit mediums claimed to be 'prophets' rather than 'ajwaka', they communicated not with 'jok' but with 'tipu', and (with the encouragement and collaboration of Resistance Council leaders (and indeed the knowledge of the Church)) sought to cleanse 'their neigh-bourhood of lajok, "witches", and lawol, "sorcerers", some of whom might well be their own competitors,' thereby helping to establish 'viable communities' (Allen 1991, 1995). In conclusion, Allen says; 'We begin to see why Alice Lakwena and Joseph Kony were not just dismissed as lunatics, and how resonant their ideas were when linked with long-term local historical and cultural processes' (Allen, 1991; 393).

Refining the Characterisations – Comparative Experiences

The LRA can be contextualised not just within northern Uganda, but within comparative experiences of rebel movements elsewhere. As Kaldor notes in her discussion of 'new wars', the fusion of guerrilla tactics of evading direct confrontation with counterinsurgency tactics of promoting 'fear and hatred' rather than winning 'hearts and minds', were a characteristic of war in the 1990s. Most rebel groups enjoy various forms of support from external sources, including taking refuge in rear bases in neighbouring countries – indeed, the presence of the SPLA in Gulu and Kitgum districts was testimony to this. The use of children is also widespread, and assertions that 'almost uniquely to this rebel group, [they, the LRA] abduct children to join their forces'[60] were patently untrue. Use of child soldiers was unusual neither in Uganda nor in many other armies on the continent. The NRA itself was famous for its *kadogos* in the 1980s, and in the 1990s UPDF instructors provided three to six months infantry and weapons training for children recruited into rebel forces in the DRC.[61] Rebel forces such as the Revolutionary United Front (RUF) in Sierra Leone are well known for having under-age youth under arms. Even the use of mutilation is not uncommon, with clear parallels between the LRA's methods, those of RENAMO in Mozambique in the 1980s (HRW, 1992: 43), and of the RUF in Sierra Leone in the 1990s (Richards, 1996: 6). And Girling describes how, historically, 'the solitary killing from ambush of women and even children of another domain' was one means whereby an Acholi man could acquire the *nying moi*, or 'killer name', the third of the three names he would acquire in his lifetime (1960: 102).

When coming to the supposedly bizarre behaviours of Kony, close parallels can also be drawn with the role of spirits in the guerilla movements in Shonaland, Zimbabwe, as described by Lan (1985). He argues that the guerrillas gained legitimacy through associating with spirit mediums whose own source of political credibility with the peasantry was their rejection of colonial norms and structures. In particular, because under British rule the chiefs 'had become minor civil servants with the power of constables' (1985: 137), the peasants were keen to shift allegiances to the dead (i.e. pre-colonial) chiefs (*Mhondoro*) whose spirits they communicated with through the mediums. The guerrillas thus succeeded because of their capacity to be seen by the peasantry as aligned with pre-colonial history and power structures.

In similar vein, Kony offered himself as a medium to spiritual authorities outside unpopular terrestrial structures, authorities who, furthermore, as in 'traditional' Acholi beliefs, were intermediaries between human beings and God/*Jok*. Kony's Holy Spirits correspond broadly with the *mhondoro*, though while the LRA spirits are eclectic in their origins, the *mhondoro* were specifically the spirits of chiefs of the past. Joseph Kony and the Holy Spirit secretary correspond closely to the spirit mediums and their assistants, the *mutapi*: 'The medium requires the *mutapi* because he needs help when he is possessed, and also because he is a stranger within the province of his spirit, whereas the *mutapi* is familiar with the area' (Lan 1985: 61)[62]

In this system, even if the medium is making conscious decisions under the guise of being possessed, this cannot be acknowledged. Lan argues that the source of the energy of the spirit/medium system lies in the 'creativity of the medium', but that this has to be 'successfully (though unconsciously) concealed and denied' ... 'consensus and innovation must be delicately balanced if the medium is to survive. A successful medium must develop great skills in leading simultaneously from the front and from behind' (Lan 1985: 67). It appears that Joseph Kony generally succeeded in establishing and maintaining this balance. Having to refer all major decisions to Spirits was of course a useful mechanism for making unaccountable decisions and thus made it difficult for others to engage with. Allen notes that, during the peace talks with the UPDA in 1988, attempts to negotiate with Kony's group 'proved impossible, since so many issues had to be referred back to the spirits (Allen 1991: 374)'.

In sum, the LRA should not be considered as in any significant sense exceptional, and interpretations of it which suggest that it is should be regarded with a degree of scepticism. To the extent that it succeeded in accommodating multiple agendas, the LRA acquired a certain resilience. It could both take passengers on board, such as the WNBF soldiers, and it could itself become a passenger, as when it received support from the Government of Sudan. This might explain the paradox that it failed to have a decisive impact on the political landscape of Uganda on the one hand, yet obstinately refused to go away on the other. It was thus both better organised and, in a sense, more motivated, than it was generally made out to be.

However, it was also intrinsically self-limiting. When it failed to integrate its non-Acholi passengers as full 'members' in its vision of a pre-modern Acholi future, they fell away. Although tens of thousands of abductees passed through the hands of the LRA over the years, the majority escaped, and many others were killed. The core was therefore necessarily small, though not without skills. And to the extent that Kony insisted on micro-management, it had to remain that way.

When this fact is placed alongside the scale of the UPDF, particularly when operating jointly with the SPLA and with 'non-lethal' support from the U.S.A., it seems improbable that the LRA could have survived for so long had the UPDF really wished to deal with them. If Delmé-Radcliffe could track down the Nubis at the turn of the twentieth century, why could the Ugandan Government not do the same with the LRA? When reviewing the Government's various military and non-military initiatives to deal with the LRA, it is difficult to escape the conclusion that while they all bolstered an appearance of doing the right thing, there was little political will behind these exercises in image management, whether to bring closure to the situation or to generate support from civil society in northern Uganda.

An Appraisal of the Government's Initiatives

Although there were always individuals with good intentions, most strikingly Bigombe, they worked without substantive support from their leaders. Contrary to the view that the 1994 peace talks were a moment of real opportunity, they effectively heralded a dramatic escalation of the scale of war, and are more aptly described as 'war-talk' than 'peace talks'. Colonel Tolit's provocations and President Museveni's ultimatum can be read as a microcosm of and contribution to a wider attempt by the Government to humiliate and discount the rebels. This only served to entrench them in an oppositional mode, and created the space for further militarism on the part of the Government. The humiliation must have been the more keenly felt as, contrary to portrayals of it as irrational, the LRA clearly had leadership elements who could engage in intellectual sparring on equal terms with the Government representatives.

The pattern of provocative belittling and humiliation by the Government, followed by increased violence by those humiliated, appears to be a key dynamic in this war; it seemed that the Government was bent on goading the LRA back to violence whenever they were quiet for too long. The signing of a Carter Center mediated peace accord between the GoU and GoS on 8 December 1999 was another clear instance. The failure to incorporate the LRA, reinforced the message that the LRA was not of central importance and triggered a resumption of violence by the LRA. Only in February 2000 did Carter Center representatives somewhat belatedly meet Kony and other LRA leaders in Nsitu, Sudan.

Attempts to belittle the LRA were evident not just at these key events; they were ongoing and integral to the Government's dominant mind-set. Although in 1998 the then Minister of State for Northern Uganda, Owiny Dollo, obtained financial support from the Belgian government 'to help him pursue peace talks' along with other non-military initiatives such as 'granting amnesty to rebels and persuading the Sudanese government to stop backing Kony',[63] the Government's more usual position was that 'There is no compromise with these terrorists and criminals',[64] and that there was nothing to negotiate with, 'because their struggle is aimless'.[65] This position went hand-in-hand with what Gersony described as 'the NRA's excessive confidence in its ability to launch heroic efforts to quickly defeat its enemy'. In March 1998, for example, during the same visit to Amuru camp in which he apologised for the army's failings, Museveni also

> ... gave fresh ultimatum to the LRA rebels whom he refers to as 'bandits'. 'Either the rebels come out of the bush and live with you or we shall exterminate them', he said. He said he is in Gulu to see to it that complete security is restored in Gulu and people return to their homes in a few months.[66]

A few months later, when the LRA carried out raids in Teso, the UPDF claimed to have 'trapped' them (see Chapter 3). Major General Salim Saleh, Overseer in the Ministry of Defence (and the President's half-brother) reportedly regarded the LRA's move into Lira and Teso as 'a golden chance for the army to wipe them [the LRA] out ... He said the rebels have now been blocked from retreating into Sudan and will soon be wiped out from inside Uganda'.[67] In the event – as on so many prior and subsequent occasions – the LRA readily evaded attempts to surround them.

The Government's habit of talking peace while making war shaped its responses to repeated calls for non-military solutions to be pursued. In March 1996 a group of Acholi elders met with President Museveni and called for a non-military solution. In January 1997 Acholi MPs on the Parliamentary Sessional Committee on Defence and Foreign Affairs appended a minority report challenging the Committee's recommendation of the continued pursuit of a military solution. In April 1997, at Kacokke Madit's first meeting, the Government was urged to pursue a non-military solution. In early 1998 the British NGO International Alert called on the GoU, Acholi elders and LRA 'to give dialogue another chance in order to end insurgency in the north'.[68] Numerous newspaper articles pointed out the hollowness of Museveni's military promises and urged him to engage in talks (e.g. *East African Impact:* week ending 15 March 1998; *The Monitor,* 18 March 1998 'Offer Kony's men a deal', *The East African* 18–24 May 1998 'Gov't Should Talk to Rebels')

The Government responded to such calls by adopting a compromise position in which it pursued the military option while appearing to allow non-military alternatives to be pursued in parallel by civil society actors. This position was captured in the *New Vision* of 19 June 1998 when two articles were printed side by side on the front page. One, under the title 'Talk Peace, Commission Pleads', reported the Uganda Human Rights Commission's appeal to the Government to hold peace talks. The other, under the title 'No Kony Talks, Museveni Insists', reported that 'President Yoweri Museveni has vowed not to talk to the rebels. However, he said he had no objection to other people trying to negotiate with them'.[69] He thereby not only ignored an important civil society voice, he also demonstrated the blurring of the line between his personal animus against the LRA and the Government's official position, a blurring which remained a constant throughout the war.

What this meant in practice was soon found out by the Acholi Religious Leaders Peace Initiative. Since its founding 1998, ARLPI had had some success in establishing dialogue with the LRA. Its later meetings with the LRA, however, were disrupted by UPDF attacks, as happened in Pajule on 26 April 2001 (ARLPI, 2002b). Such attacks were explained away as being due to a 'lack of co-ordination' between the GoU's interlocutors and the UPDF, but dealt a severe dent to talks. The situation was further aggravated when the Government banned all contact between the ARLPI and the LRA for some time. This consistent undermining of the religious leaders' attempts to act as go-betweens suggests that they represented something of a threat to the state's agenda, which increasingly appeared to be to ensure that any non-military solutions would fail.

It was not just religious leaders who were undermined. Over the years the pool of people in a position to enter into dialogue with the LRA was progressively reduced, with many key individuals coming under attack as 'collaborators' for their efforts to support meetings. Yusuf Adek, the key link person for the Bigombe peace talks in 1993/4, was arrested and charged with treason in 2001 and detained for over a year. By 2004 he was, unsurprisingly, no longer prepared to act as a link person, despite approaches from a range of interested parties. Offers to initiate contact made by various other groups who felt they had some link with the LRA, appear to have been turned down. For example, one fieldworker in Odek, himself an Internal Security Operative, claimed that on 20th March 1999 a group of elders, local government officials and relatives of Kony from Odek sub-county, went to Kampala but were unsuccessful in seeing the President 'just because their movement from Gulu to Kampala was not known to any of the top government leaders in Gulu District like the R.D.C., LCV Chairman, DISO'.[70] I was also told in January 2004 that offers by Concerned Parents Association to make contacts with the LRA were ignored. For civil society in northern Uganda the Government's refusal to engage with these alternative proposals was alienating and also suggestive of more than a lack of political will on the part of the Government.

The same reluctance to engage seriously with non-military solutions was manifest in the Amnesty Act of 2000. The development of the Act, while it to an important extent captured civilian aspirations for a peaceful and non-retributive solution, again failed to include the LRA, and was entered into and extended with visible reluctance on the part of the President, who made repeated statements that it should not apply to the LRA's leadership. Its implementation with regard to the LRA was at best lethargic, particularly when contrasted with how it was used with UNRFII in West Nile. It was also a further instance of unilateral decision making by the Government, with wording designed to make very clear who the winners and losers were.[71] Put in place in January 2000, the initial period of six months was extended repeatedly. Prior to its extension on 17 January 2004, the Government announced plans to amend it to exclude the top leadership of the LRA, despite the fact that members of the Amnesty Commission, as well as civil society, remained keen for it to apply to all members of the LRA.[72] The extension was eventually made under duress, as the World Bank threatened to withhold U.S. $3.2 million for a Special Project for 15,300 irregular forces in Uganda if there were no extension. Having begrudgingly extended it by six months, the Government subsequently announced that the extension would in fact only hold for three months.[73] Just prior to its expiry, the British Minister for International Development, Hilary Benn, encouraged the GoU to extend it further.[74]

The Amnesty process was never adequately resourced, and there were some doubts about differential distributions of funding to different returnee groups.[75]

In theory persons granted amnesty were to be offered a resettlement package including non-food items and a cash payment of 243,000 Uganda shillings (approx £80).[76] In practice, of the 2,600 reporters (term used to describe persons applying for the amnesty) registered in Gulu as of 20th January 2004, only a small number had received kits.[77] Similarly, of the 1780 registered reporters in Kitgum district (1392 male, 388 female), 991 had received their amnesty certificates, but only 222 had received their resettlement packages.[78] This lack of resettlement packages may have hampered the utility of the amnesty for LRA returnees.[79] It is also likely that news filtered back to the potential amnesty seekers both of reporters being killed by the LRA and of the UPDF coercing reporters into joining them rather than allowing them to reintegrate into civilian life (the LRA member whose account I present in Annex A, refused and is known to have been killed as a result).

For higher-ranking members of the LRA – and those seeking to engage in dialogue with them – the Amnesty Act was further undermined by the Anti-Terrorism Act of 2002[80] and Operation Iron Fist which began at the same time (see Chapter 3). Yet more evidence of the Government's lack of commitment to non-violent solutions was furnished by Museveni's decision to refer Kony to the newly established International Criminal Court for investigation. In making the referral in January 2004 he had a televised meeting with the Chief Prosecutor of the ICC, creating the impression that the ICC was already working hand in hand with the government before the decision to investigate had even been taken.[81]

For those working at the ICC this was a public relations blunder which they would struggle to recover from. Although at a memorial service in Barlonyo IDP camp following a massacre there in February, Museveni, said (in typically hectoring style) that, 'You [LRA] still have a chance to come out ... [under amnesty] But if you do not, you die',[82] the referral flew in the face of the principles of blanket forgiveness built into the Amnesty Act, provoking considerable concern in civil society circles. In the view of the Chairman of the Amnesty Commission a reconciliation process would have been preferable,[83] and Acholi politicians warned that prosecution of Kony before the ICC 'is not healthy as it could scare Kony into killing more people'.[84] Religious leaders saw it as making dialogue even more difficult, and children's rights organisations, such as Concerned Parents Association, meeting with the ICC Prosecutor, expressed concerns it would bring down even harsher punishments on abducted children who might have witnessed atrocities. It also wrong-footed the U.S. Administration, who had begun calling for the GoU to negotiate with Kony and were even beginning to fund their own 'Northern Uganda Peace Initiative'.

Effectively, by making the referral to the ICC, the GoU had once again undermined civil society calls for reconciliation, and directed the spotlight at the LRA as the cause of all the problems. By accepting the referral with alacrity, the ICC played into this – thereby reducing people's confidence in the ICC as an impartial institution. These dynamics prompted a public statement from Amnesty International, which welcomed the ICC Prosecutor's announcement, but stressed that any investigation 'must be part of a comprehensive plan to end impunity for all such crimes, regardless of which side committed them and of the level of the perpetrator'.[85]

When Operation Iron Fist is added to this picture, the Government's lack of commitment to a solution seems further demonstrated. For at the time when the Operation was launched , both the Nairobi Accord and the Amnesty (notwith-standing their serious weaknesses) were beginning to show some beneficial con-sequences for northern Uganda in the form of slowly rising numbers of returnees and tentative steps towards contacts mediated through the religious leaders. Operation Iron Fist, rather than crushing the LRA, crushed these signs of hope. It aggravated the military and humanitarian situation beyond anybody's worst fears, bringing it to a point which justified unprecedented levels of militarization but still failed to bring a definitive solution. Furthermore, by obstinately declar-ing its preference for a military option, despite the majority of actors calling for the opposite, the Government showed a serious disregard for popular opinion in the north, thereby guaranteeing the continued alienation of the civilian popula-tion whose support it could have been wooing.

One interpretation, as already referred to above, is that there were vested eco-nomic interests involved. But by contrast with a situation such as DRC, where the economic gains to be made were truly substantial, in northern Uganda they are better regarded as the opportunistic exploitation of opportunities created by the Government's (non-economic) motivations for wishing the conflict to con-tinue. As such, the vested economic interests cannot offer a full explanation for the war's continuation.

Another interpretation is that the Government's behaviour was not so much a matter of political will as of political immaturity; key government members were simply unable to rise above their personal animus against the LRA and respond to the LRA's demand for recognition. The LRA's demands were after all fairly evident: Many of its actions, including the killing of one of their own members in front of the peace delegation in order to show 'that we still have power', the violence following Museveni's ultimatum in 1994, the violence following the 1999 peace accord in which the LRA had no say and in which it felt betrayed by the Sudanese government, and the poor take-up of the Amnesty Act of 2000, can be interpreted as reactions to this combination of Governmental hubris and LRA humiliation. They all demonstrated that even if the Government refused to take the LRA seriously in talks, it would have to take them seriously militarily. They constituted a clear demand for recognition and acknowledgement; from a psychological perspective alone, it is clear why the LRA insisted so emphatically that 'we are not surrendering'.

Instead of finding a way to give such recognition, the Government's actions seemed shaped by a determination to humiliate the LRA.[86] Its appointment of a woman as chief negotiator may have been interpreted as a calculated insult to the LRA's masculinity, and certainly some Government representatives (notably Col. Tolit) used the peace talks of 1994 as an opportunity to seek to humiliate and belittle the LRA's representatives, thereby consolidating the LRA's sense of grievance against the Government (see also Finnström, 2003: 300–303). This dynamic of treating them as marginal – or 'local' – was perpetuated in the build-up to the Nairobi accord of 1999, and the attempt to belittle them verbally was kept alive not just by the Government of Uganda, but by comments such as that of Hilary Clinton that 'The LRA call themselves soldiers but they are cowards'. [87]

Many people believed that, had it wished to, the Government could have pursued a negotiated settlement. It had done so with the UPDA in 1988, with the Teso insurgency in the early 1990s, and with the UNRFII in the late 1990s (African Rights, 2002: 9). Museveni himself was personally involved in mediating the Somali peace talks in Kenya at which he reportedly 'deployed the rhetoric of black African nationalism to call for an end to what he termed the 'slow genocide' in Somalia'. [88] He was also praised by the Nobel Peace Prize Committee 'for his efforts in helping resolve regional conflicts and combating the spread of HIV/AIDS', [89] acclamation which for those familiar with northern Uganda seemed perverse in the extreme. [90] The glaring divergence between the Government's failures to achieve a solution for northern Uganda and these apparent successes elsewhere, combined with a lack of consultation, a failure to involve key players, a disregard of the wishes of the civilian population, and an obtuse refusal to engage in a peace-oriented manner with the psychology of the LRA, were a continuous reminder that, as the late Dr Lukwiya (Superintendent of Lacor Hospital) put it, 'The government is not very concerned about Acholis, is not concerned about the words of Acholi, has no respect for them'. [91] It seemed improbable that a consummate politician such as Museveni was unaware of what he was doing. Although Gersony sought to argue that Museveni dealt as he did in northern Uganda because he was ill advised by his senior advisers (Gersony, 1997: 35), he spent enough time with the UPDF in northern Uganda that he could hardly fail to be aware of the impact of his policies.

Conclusions

The LRA was more motivated and organised than it was made out, and the GoU less committed to finding a solution than concepts of wars as something you fight to win would have us believe. Indeed, for the GoU winning seemed to lie in keeping the opponent alive for as long as possible, in particular by using humiliation tactics to provoke him into reacting whenever the situation became calm for too long. In this interpretation the Government's behaviours, whether in military or non-military interventions, were not driven by political immaturity, but rather aimed to achieve the opposite of what was stated – namely to bring the situation back to the boil rather than to find a solution.

This could be seen as simply a military tactic, for although its 'peace initiatives' lacked integrity, the Government could claim that it had tried just about all non-military approaches to bringing the war to an end, and that because they did not work it was justified in pursuing a military solution. The subsequent military initiatives appear to have been more useful for deepening the militarization of society than for bringing an end to violence (see Chapter 3).

However, the LRA-GoU dynamic is more than merely military, for it contains many elements which are compatible with the model of social torture. The abuses of the LRA towards its abductees are those used by torturers to create dependency in their victims. Its modus operandi during raids contribute to a sense of dread in the population, especially as the extent of the threat, rather than being pinned down by careful analysis, is shrouded in ambiguities created and perpetuated by Government, NGOs and the daily media. The mixed messages sent by the GoU (it says it is seeking a solution and is open to a 'dual approach', but this is contradicted by all its actions prior to 2006) create a sense of disorientation in civil society. Its attitude towards the LRA is one of devaluation and dehumanisation, and its wilful disregard of civil society is further evidence of this. Indeed it could be argued that it was seeking to create disaffection and the resultant ambiguities about levels of civilian support for the LRA, such that at a national and international level it was not just the LRA but also the Acholi who were seen as a dehumanised threat of indefinable dimensions.

For most people living inside the war zone, the failure of the various 'solutions' in the face of the hopes invested in them, and the message of lack of political commitment which these failures conveyed, were nothing new, they merely aggravated a conviction that the Government was against them. They had, after all, first hand experience of a lack of government commitment to them, particularly in the form of the so-called 'protected villages' and all that they entailed.

Notes

1. *IOM Needs Assessment,* 2001; section 2.1.8.3. Men, Wira-Awora.
2. For an account of incursions into south Sudan in 1996 in collaboration with the SPLA see Annex A, Section 3.5.
3. *The Monitor,* 18 March 1998, 'UPDF Occupy Hills at Sudan Border'.
4. ODI HPN Report, November 1997 http://www.odihpn.org/report.asp?ReportID=1686
5. My own fieldwork suggests that the lower ranks profited very little from being in the war zone and often went hungry, knowing full well that some of their officers were building luxury houses for themselves in Kampala using profits derived from the war.
6. *The Monitor,* 18 July 1998, 'Army Abandons War for Riches'.
7. *New Vision,* 6 April 1998,' UPDF Officer Charged'.
8. *New Vision,* 11 April 1998 'Two Kony Bodyguards Held in Kampala'.
9. BBC News Online, 'Appeal for Uganda's Abducted Children', 8 December 2000.
10. Since Operation Iron Fist began in early 2002 the rate of abduction sky-rocketed, but it remains the case that insufficient effort is made to maintain a balance sheet of abductions and returns.
11. IRIN, 15 July 04, *Senior LRA Commander Captured by the Army.*
12. Awer, June 1998.
13. BBC News, 2 November 2000, 'Uganda's Rebel War'.
14. Atiak, August 1998.
15. Elder, Gulu, August 1998.
16. *New Vision,* 5 January 1998.
17. His letter of 21 November 1996 received a reply from Otii Lagony on 14 January 1997.
18. *New Vision,* 27 May 1998.
19. *The Monitor,* 29 May 1998.

20. *The Sunday Monitor,* 17 May 1998, 'LRA Raid Three 'Protected' Camps During Carey's Visit'.
21. Ibid, *'Fire and Death on Black Wednesday'.*
22. *New Vision,* 3 June 1998.
23. BBC, 28 June 2006, 'Uganda Rebel Leader Breaks Silence'. (http://news.bbc.co.uk/go/em/fr/-/2/hi/programmes/newsnight/5124762.stm)
24. E.g. AVSI's report by Bramucci, 2001: ii. (USAID funded), HRW (1997, 2003), Amnesty International (1997).
25. E.g. UNOCHA's report by Weeks, 2002: 9.
26. E.g. BBC News – *Crossing Continents,* 2 November 2000, 'Uganda's Rebel War'.
27. Odek pilot, 21 July 1998.
28. Palaro pilot, 30 July 1998.
29. Testimony of Sister Mary Rose Atuu of the Catholic Religious Congregation called Little Sisters of Mary Immaculate of Gulu, Northern Uganda, before the Joint Hearings of the House Subcommittee on Africa and the Subcommittee on International Operations and Human Rights, on the subject of Sudan and Northern Uganda, July 29, 1998.
30. They were apparently all described as criminal/fraudulent Ugandans by Museveni in a paper sent to Khartoum when they applied for amnesty in July 2001. The Carter Center described them as 'hardliners' because they were suspicious of the amnesty. Seven of the nine eventually came to Gulu in January 2002 under the Amnesty Act.
31. The term used by Betty Bigombe in the 1994 talks.
32. Notwithstanding this, Jacob's also recalls stealing honey during a raid on a village inside Sudan.
33. E.g. BBC News Online, 'Appeal for Uganda's Abducted Children', 8 December 2000. IRIN, 24 May 2004.
34. Male impotence in the war zone is discussed further in Chapter 7. The term *bwoc* seems related to the myth of the Pabwoc lineage as told by Girling: 'Bwoc their ancestor was being pursued by enemies when he came to a deep river. A tree growing beside the bank bent horizontally to allow him to cross and stood erect again when his enemies tried to follow him' (Girling 1960: 78).
35. Note also that when the children from the LRA and Government of Sudan camps mingled too much, this was one ground for shifting camp.
36. This amounted to 2,619 in total in Kitgum, or 175 per year over the same period, and 1,971 in Gulu, or 131 per year. Of these 66 per cent of those abducted from Kitgum returned, and 45 per cent of those from Gulu, suggesting that over fifteen years a total of 2,250 women were kept in the LRA.
37. International agencies also treated returnees in a highly gendered fashion. While waiting in Juba to be transferred to Khartoum, the escapees were shown 'films of how a woman can stay with a man and again may decide to refuse a man' (section 4.2), but once they reached Khartoum, this choice was made for them by the international agencies: 'Children and women were handed over to the organisation called Save the Children while men were to be kept by the International Organisation for Migration' (section 4.3). Jacob's account suggests that the possibility that any affective ties could have been established while living in the LRA was discounted without consultation.
38. *New Vision,* 20 June 1998, 'Cholera Hits Kony Camps'. This report also talks of Jabulein camp at thirty-nine miles from Juba, which ties in with Jacob's account.
39. *New Vision,* 11 April 1998, 'Two Kony Bodyguards Held in Kampala'.
40. E.g. 19th –20th July 2002 at Okungu-Gedi camp, Amuru division (KM E-newsletter no 22, 8 August 2002).
41. Jon Bennet, in *Forced Migration Review,* 7 April 2000 – http://www.fmreview.org/fmr078.htm.
42. In July 1998 people in Palaro slaughtered and ate their pigs because of this order. In one instance in 1996 the LRA forced a family to kill a pig and eat it raw. In others the threat

was that if found the number of people killed would correspond to the number of pigs found.

43. One respondent reported that on many occasions Kony's army have been seen carrying a white sheep, apparently because it would repel the Government soldiers. White stones, white ashes, white chickens etc. all seemed to be attributed particular symbolism and powers.

44. Anaka, 28 January 2000.

45. Camp pilot reports, June 1998.

46. Palaro, 1 April 1999.

47. It broadcasts to Gulu, Kitgum, Lira, Moyo, Adjumani, Yumbe, as well as parts of southern Sudan. Programmes are also available to the diaspora on the internet at www.km.net .org.

48. The presence of large numbers of Rwandan Tutsi refugees in the NRM in the late 1980s (some of them sent to Northern Uganda as part of the pacification process), and the support given by the Museveni Government to the Rwandan Patriotic Front in its return to Rwanda are no doubt part of this charge.

49. For example, *Sunday Vision,* 7 June 1998, 'The Day Kony Rebels Eluded Salim Saleh inside Teso Bush'.

50. This commemorated a time when the LRA were being pursued inside Uganda and could only communicate with each other using whistles. In December 1998 Joseph Kony reportedly used Whistle Day to reshuffle his command structure.

51. This is the 'First water' (*Pi Kot Maleng*) described in Annex A, section 13.

52. Awere pilot, 29 July 1998.

53. The absence of both Joseph Kony and President Museveni throughout the Juba peace talks in 2006–2008 similarly undermined their validity.

54. This presumably alludes to the use of camouflaged uniform.

55. BBC News – *Crossing Continents,* 2 November 2000, 'Uganda's Rebel War'.

56. There are several indicators that elements of solidarity survived the 'brutalisation'; new abductees were warned by old hands to hide their feelings and intention, Jacob let his friends know his intentions to leave, and the feelings described when they are leaving Khartoum for Uganda seem very normal. Furthermore, people established families which, as Jacob's account suggests, at times attempted to stay together even when no longer under the compulsion of the LRA.

57. The Nairobi agreement in December 1999 created an avenue for escape, in that prior to that an escapee could expect little sympathy if they headed north to Juba – indeed, even in early 2001, Jacob and his colleague feared they might be sent back to the LRA by the Sudanese intelligence. Equally, to head south was to face severe obstacles.

58. *New Vision,* 18 November 1998, *Rebels Pose as Saints on Internet.*

59. Discussion at *Bedo Piny pi Kuc,* 26 June 1998.

60. BBC News – *Crossing Continents,* 2 November 2000, *Uganda's Rebel War.*

61. Amnesty International (Campaign against Child Soldiers), April 2001.

62. Paul Okodi, the Holy Spirit Secretary, was in the HSM under Alice Lakwena.

63. *New Vision,* 25 June 1998, 'Kony Peace Talks: Belgium to Help'.

64. *New Vision,* 20 June 1998, 'Museveni Rejects Rebel Compromise'.

65. *The Monitor,* 23 February 1998, 'UPDF Boss Says No Peace-Talks'.

66. *The Monitor,* 18 March 1998, 'UPDF Occupy Hills at Sudan Border'.

67. *Sunday Vision,* 24 May 1998, 'Saleh Blocks Rebel Retreat'.

68. *New Vision,* 10 February 1998, 'U.K. Group Calls for Dialogue on War'.

69. *New Vision,* 19 June 1998.

70. Odek report, 4 April 1999.

71. In the event it proved of greater benefit in resolving other insurgencies than in helping to address the war in the north. LRA reporters in the first three years accounted for only 39.6 per cent or two-fifths of all reporters, with the UNRFII and West Nile Bank Front

accounting for the majority of the rest (29.86 per cent and 20.48 per cent respectively). (*Amnesty Commission Report 2000–2003,* Table 3: Reporters by Former/Fighting Rebel Groups, p 17).

72. IRIN, 16 December 2003, *New Amnesty Law to Exclude Top LRA Leaders.* BBC interview with Museveni, 25th December 2003, reproduced in *The Monitor* newspaper 27th December 2003, p 4. See also 'Uganda to Step Up War Against Rebels' in *The East African* 12–18 January 2004, p 5.
73. IRIN, 23 January 2004, *Government Curtails Amnesty Extension.*
74. IRIN, 7 April 2004, *Extend Amnesty for Northern Rebels, U.K. Minister Tells Government.*
75. Main funding sources were EU, DANIDA, and Irish Government. According to one Amnesty Commission official, the U.S.A. did not give much because 'they prefer the military side of the story'.
76. Payments were not standard. One group of 403 former WNBF members received Ush 500,000 each (*The Sunday Monitor,* 18 January 2004 'Homecoming after 23 years').
77. Amnesty Commission, Kitgum 21st January 2004.
78. Amnesty Commission, Kitgum DRT office, January 20th, 2004, 'Projected Activities for the Kitgum DRT Office', January to June 2004.
79. On 3 January 2002 one of Museveni's advisors, Kakooza Mutale, declared that returning rebels had no right to receive resettlement packages from Government – ARLPI Chronology 2002.
80. Act number 14 of 2002.
81. For the ICC's public position see www.icc-cpi.int.
82. IRIN, 29 March 2004, *Mixed Reactions to Barlonyo Service.*
83. *The East African,* 16–22 February 2004, pp 1 and 16.
84. Ibid, p 16.
85. *AI Index:* AFR 59/001/2004 (Public).
86. In a *New Vision* article of 5 February 1998, it was reported that handwritten leaflets were distributed in Kalongo (Kitgum district) stating that 'Civilians, the Army and Police Seem To Be Big-Headed' (*Kony Wants Talks*).
87. *The Monitor,* 26 March 1998, 'Mrs Clinton Blasts Kony'.
88. *The East African,* January 12–18, 2004.
89. *New Vision,* 29 May 2004, 'Museveni Possible Nobel Candidate'.
90. It was only one in a whole series of accolades for Museveni: in June 2004, for example, he was awarded the 'Golden Plate Award' by the Washington DC-based Academy of Achievement Foundation, 'for his illustrious stewardship of the country' (*New Vision,* 14 June 2004, 'Museveni Receives Award').
91. *Bedo Piny Pi Kuc,* 26 June 1998.

5

PROTECTION AS VIOLATION

The overwhelming protection problem remains the horrible health and social conditions in camps causing high mortality and morbidity rates well above emergency
levels and rampant exploitation of a desperate population by UPDF and others in
positions of power. (*UNHCR Assessment of IDP Movement/Return and Protection
Concerns*, December 2006)

Introduction

Faced with a considerable gap between the Government's stated intentions and
its actual achievements in pursuing solutions to the situation in the north, many
people sought to read its underlying agenda from its actions rather than its
words. The most telling action was the Government's 'calculated enforcement
of displacement' (WFP 1999: 6) into internally displaced camps described as
'protected villages'.[1] This began in October 1996, the same month as the LRA's
notorious abduction of 125 school-girls from Aboke School in Lira district.

The exact number of camps which had a military presence and were therefore considered 'protected' fluctuated, as did the populations within them. The
overall trend though, throughout the period 1996 to 2006, was for numbers of
displaced persons to increase. The first WFP food relief was delivered under an
emergency operation to 20 protected villages in Gulu in January 1997. It aimed
to feed 110,000 people. Within a year this had been revised upwards to 257,000,
and by May 1999 upwards again to 325,000. To this were added 81,000 people
in five villages in Kitgum. As such, by 1999, they formed the vast majority of the
585,000 people at risk in Uganda as a whole, a figure that placed Uganda tenth
in the world in terms of 'areas with the most people in need of assistance' (Jefferys, 2002: 5).[2] By July 2000 the figure for northern Uganda was 472,000,[3] and
by mid-2002 WFP's working figure was 522,000. Of these the 372,000 located in
Gulu District comprised approximately 74 per cent of the district's population,

and the 150,000 in Kitgum and Pader Districts represented 28 per cent of their total populations.[4][5] At this point WFP extended its relief operations by another three years, to last until 2005.[6]

By March 2003, following large-scale incursions of LRA forces into northern Uganda as a result of Operation Iron Fist, the number displaced had escalated still further, to over 800,000 people, or more than 80 per cent of the total population of the affected districts.[7] Numbers had leapt in Pader district, from 17,000 people in one camp in 2002, to over 240,000 people in 13 'major camps', all in need of food relief from WFP.[8] The largest camp in Gulu district, Pabo, whose population was well over 40,000 at the time of my fieldwork in 1999, by 2004 was closer to 65,000.[9]

The objectives were ambiguous. One camp leader, who witnessed his camp being set up, remembered them as being; 'To avoid abduction; to save the properties of the innocent; to save the lives of people; to cut communication between the masses and the rebels'.[10] This juxtaposition of a concern with protecting peoples' physical security and a suspicion that these very same people might be supporting the rebels – and therefore in need of containment – reflected fundamental ambiguities in the relationship between people in northern Uganda and the southern-dominated Government. For many people, the formation of the camps reinforced the impression gained at the hands of Government forces from 1986 onwards (see Chapter 2), that they were believed to be rebel collaborators. As one critic wrote:

> One measure adopted by the government is particularly resented by the population of Gulu and Kitgum: the institution of 'protected camps'. These are camps where

Diagram 5.1 Escalation in Numbers of Internally Displaced People in Gulu/Kitgum/Pader, 1997–2003

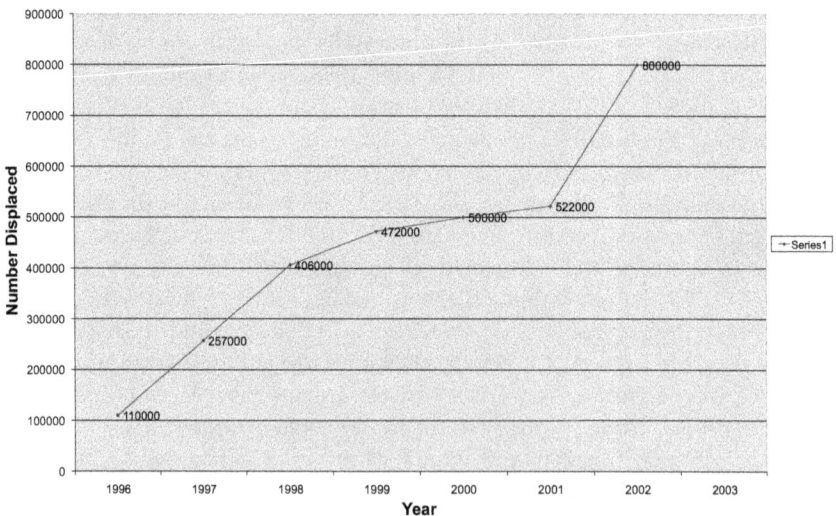

the civil population is gathered 'to be protected against the attacks of the rebels'. In reality, the camps aim at preventing the population to give any kind of support to the LRA. The fact is that, while staying, as prisoners, in the 'protected camps', people cannot cultivate, cannot produce, become totally dependent on aid.

He voiced further suspicions that, over and above a simple counter-insurgency strategy, the camps were a form of comprehensive retribution for atrocities the Acholi were alleged to have carried out in the early 1980s, particularly in the Luwero triangle. For him the protected villages were 'not very different from 'concentration camps'', and he believed that 'Many Ugandans, especially in the south, dismiss this tragedy, just saying that 'they are having what they deserve. It's their turn now. When they have enough ... they'll stop'' (Murru, 1998: 11).

Even from a less subjective perspective, the camps were shocking. Looked at historically, the camps were a gross disruption of previous settlement patterns. Girling identified 950 villages in Acholi District during his research in 1951, at a time when the total population numbered only 215,000. Middleton, in his research amongst the Lugbara at the same period, specifically contrasted their dense settlement patterns with the more spread out ones of the Acholi (1970: 7). To put the majority of a population now numbering over 1 million into less than fifty settlements was therefore a radical measure, with radical consequences. At a rally in Gulu market in January 1999, the MP for Gulu municipality reportedly described camp life as

> ... just like living in hell which is full of rape, torture, and other forms of mistreatment. He also observed that staying in the camp is causing poverty since people have no space for cultivation. [He said] there is even no protection from the government as instead civilians are used as human shield by the army. He said the camp life is violating human rights which are too numerous to mention.[11]

For a long time though, despite attempts by Ugandans to draw attention to the situation, the international community was silent. While the Aboke abductions gained global attention and condemnation and became synonymous with LRA brutality,[12] the extreme deprivation and multiple forms of violence inherent in the camps, and the mass social dysfunction which they generated, drew remarkably little international reaction. Even when it eventually did, such as in a 2002 report by UNOCHA, direct criticism of rights abuses by the Government were avoided, and the villages were instead imagined as opportunities for the Government to consolidate its international image:

> ... if the perpetrators of terrorist acts are allowed to keep a society paralysed, the society loses and the terrorists 'win'. The protected village system has contributed mightily to putting the Acholi in the losing position. It is time for Ugandan society and its political leadership, which in this generation have shown themselves to be so creative and resourceful, to find ways of restoring the proper balance. (Weeks 2002: 5)

By this point though, as numbers had continued to escalate, the protected villages were no longer just a feature of the war zone: for the majority of the population, they were the war zone. Both the policy of internal displacement into 'protected villages', and the manner in which it was implemented, had come to be seen as an unambiguous signal about how the Government felt towards them. For as this chapter documents, the camps were indeed sites of violation of rights 'too numerous to mention', sites of what Finnström describes as 'enforced domination' (2003: 197). Part I considers the formation of the camps, Parts II to IV the violation of people's rights to livelihoods, health and education services respectively, and Part V the violation of the right to protection of physical security. These violations were fundamentally important to processes of physical, psychological and cultural debilitation (Chapter 6), as well as humiliation (Chapter 7), and form the foundations for the argument that this was a situation whose primary function was social torture rather than war.

Part I – Formation and Organisation

From the very beginning there were reports of the use of force to get people to move, and all the villages in which we worked had had some experience of this.[13] In Awere, for example, only a few hours after giving people four days notice to move to the camp, the UPDF began shelling areas they wanted cleared.[14] Similarly, in nearby Odek, people were given 'a four day ultimatum for people to leave the northern side of the main road. The same evening at about 5 to 6 P.M. they [UPDF] started bombing the area, up to midnight, using Mambas.[15] Nobody was killed, but property was destroyed and nobody was compensated. People fear to raise the issue'.[16] In Cwero 'it was by military authority that the exercise was carried out, following some atrocities carried out by rebels. The military personnel ordered everyone in the village to come to the [trading] centre where the camp was established. Many people did not obey the order but later were forced to come to the camp'.[17] In Atiak a first influx in 1996 of Resistance Councillors, teachers, parish chiefs and pupils from surrounding areas, was followed in 1997 'when the UPDF started forcing people from village to camp near the barrack. Thereafter, those who refused to come or follow their orders had their houses burned'.[18] For many, therefore, it was hardly a voluntary movement. As one elder observed, once the army started firing artillery and using helicopter gunships against those who refused to move, 'It was worse than being in the protected camps'.[19]

In Anaka the camp was first set up in December 1996 and people were told to settle within a designated area of 5km by 5km. The call was renewed in September 1997, but an LRA attack on the camp on 9 October prompted people to return to their homes. A few months later, in December 1997, 'soldiers were scattered in all villages to go and tell everybody to come and settle in Anaka, and [to tell them that] the move was to take only three days'.[20] In Awer similarly:

> The first [phase] was when people were brought from all around. It was soon very overcrowded and a lot of people started to go back to their villages. There was then a second phase of people being rounded up, but this time they were put into a number of new camps, namely Pagak, Parabongo, Kaladima, Olwal and Guruguru.[21]

As this shows, on occasion people became so overcrowded that they re-dispersed even if this meant not receiving assistance. Other fluctuations in population and physical size were the result of army orders. In October 1998, for example, following numerous rebel disturbances, people living on the outskirts of Awer camp were compelled by army and camp commanders to move closer to the centre, causing

> ... tremendous loss in terms of properties, transportation, destruction of the huts built and additional expenditure to erect new shelters in a squeezed place. There is serious fear of death in case of an outbreak of diseases among the people – which may be worse than the rebels' atrocities.[22]

In Odek (which was neither protected by military forces nor provided with food relief by WFP), people trying to minimise exposure to rebels and maximise access to food aid and their own land, oscillated between their home areas and the camp in neighbouring Acet. As a result 'it looks as if all the camp population in both Acet, Odek and Awere have huts in the camps and in their original home village to enable them to shift according to situations and circumstances'.[23] When, on 20 November, the LRA resumed operations in Odek sub-county, 'some of these displaced people who went back to their villages are again coming back to where they were camping to reconstruct their temporary structures'. By 14 December,

> Despite the presence of some pockets of rebels roaming around the villages no serious atrocities have so far been committed on the people staying in the camp. However, 33 households have resumed staying in the camp out of those who had left for their home villages'.[24]

Similar oscillations happened again in December 1999 following the Nairobi Peace Accord between Sudan and Uganda and the LRA's return to Gulu district. In Palaro, people preparing large-scale Christmas celebrations in thanks for the prevailing peace were suddenly ordered to hold them indoors with no noise. Anybody going to repair their original homes outside the camp was ordered to return, only to find that their home in the camp no longer fell within the reduced perimeters of the camp.[25] One woman and her child who were found outside the camp limits were shot by UPDF on 26 December 1999.[26]

In Pagak a meeting was called by the UPDF and camp leaders on 28 December 1999, urging anybody who had left the camp to return, and requesting the community

> ... to reduce the rate of drunkenness so that at night they [the UPDF] can be able to detect what is taking place easily. He also requested members in the camp to reduce making high noise [levels] which can obstruct the army from detecting things which can disturb the peace of people in the camp ... [and] to stop moving at night after 7.30 P.M. This is to enable the security personnel to monitor the movement of foreign bodies in the camp. Lastly, he instructed children from 7 years–13 year old to be protected by their parents because these are the age range of children required by the LRA because training them is simple and when taken far away they can forget about their parents and home and may not be in a position to trace the whereabouts of their home.[27]

Physical Layout and Shelter

To make guarding the settlements with limited numbers of soldiers more feasible, people were settled in very restricted spaces. Multiple villages were squeezed together, generally on either side of a main road and with a pre-war trading and administrative centre at their heart. Frequently the military detach was located very near the centre of the camp, surrounded on all sides by civilians, prompting one respondent to note that:

> They started the camp to be the 'protected camp' – but this camp should be called Protected Barracks because they want people to build their homes/houses one square mile around the barracks ... The barracks has no free side without the civilians surrounding it [i.e. it is not exposed at all].[28]

Following multiple raids in October/November 1998, Awer camp, with a population of 3733,[29] was reduced to 2 square km. In Pabbo there were over 42,000 people from over 120 villages, settled into eight zones of 2 square km; each was divided into sub-zones. Huts were tightly packed, often with little more than one metre between each, unlike a traditional homestead where huts would be widely spaced, traditionally around a central fireplace, the *wang-o*.[30] As the overwhelming majority of roofs were thatched, fires could consume dozens or even hundreds of huts in one go. In February 1999, for example, 51 huts were burned in one blaze in Anaka. In March 2000, 728 huts in Pabbo's Zone C were burnt down in a single incident, leaving approximately 4000 people without shelter.[31] A fire in June 2004 left at least 6,000 homeless.[32] While such fires were generally attributed to accidents with cooking fires, or to small children playing with fire while their parents were away digging, the congestion also made the camps vulnerable to deliberate arson; in March 2000, a rebel attack on Padibe camp, which at the time hosted 30,000 IDPs, left between 400 and 800 huts burned.[33]

There were virtually no sanitation facilities. In June 1998 Pabbo had one pit latrine for every 168 people. Of the total of 250 pits, 150 were built with slabs and roofing provided by World Vision, but by the time they were finished half were already full. Cwero had one for every 260 people. Odek, population 8,000, had only 3 pit latrines. In several villages fines of around Ush (Uganda shillings) 3,000 could be imposed on people who refused to build pit latrines, and in Anaka it was reported that the Local Councillors appointed youths who could 'with the permission of the LC1, put you in a house called a "tank" [if you refused to dig a pit]. You sleep there for one or two nights. Then you go and do what you were refusing to do before'. The lack of functional pit latrines led to several displaced schools being closed for weeks at a time while facilities were being built.

Administration

With populations numbering in the thousands rather than the hundreds who would be found in a village under more normal circumstances, the administration of camps was complicated by multiple and overlapping authority systems. Cwero, whose population fluctuated between 3500 and 4700, had people from

34 different villages and at least 15 clans. Awach, population 10,300, had four parishes and 52 villages represented. In the case of the much larger Pabbo, 9 parishes, 121 villages, and 28 clans were represented.[34]

There was a correspondingly complex and disorienting web of overlapping civilian authority structures, involving the ones which people brought with them from their original villages (elders, *Rwodi Kweri*),[35] the local council of the place they moved to, and those elected to administer the camps (camp leaders). At times it appeared that everything was everybody's business, as all could attend Local Council meetings. There was no standard procedure for these structures. In Anaka the Local Council met twice weekly, in Pabbo twice monthly, and in Cwero only once monthly.[36] There was, though, a hierarchy. The Local Council had more authority than the camp and zonal leaders/Rwodi Kweri, who had an advisory capacity and were responsible for disseminating resolutions of the Council. In Atiak the 8 camp elders (one from each parish) were chosen by the camp population and met twice per month to discuss issues such as the relationships between the people in the camp, the need for group farming to address the lack of food relief, and the protection of 'young ones from being abducted by rebels'.[37] To clarify the roles of local councils from LC1 up to LCIII the Deputy Speaker of Gulu District Council conducted a seminar in Pabbo Camp. He informed participants that the LCs:

> hold the right to make by-laws, including fixing rates for bride-price, taxation policies, and initiation of development projects. They should avoid themselves implementing decisions; this is the role of civil servants such as parish chiefs at Parish level and sub-county chiefs at division level. The LC also holds the right to monitor non-governmental activities in their area, and should ensure that corruption and bribery do not exist in their mode of operation.[38]

Inevitably disputes would arise between the different types of administration, as in a case from Pabo, where the Local Council

> ... accused the Camp Commandant of frustrating policy on development of the sub-county and of being disrespectful towards the council, including refusal to attend council deliberations whenever summoned and arresting people without the authority of the council.

Although 'The District Speaker and the District Secretary for Education intervened over the matter' and the commandant was suspended,[39] a further meeting was necessary in March 2000. This time the Local Council Chairman came under attack for having a vested interest in 'subduing the power of the camp commandant'. When those running the meeting

> gave guidelines to the masses to talk they criticised L.C. III administration for wanting the post of camp administration to go to his campaign manager. They wanted a vote of no confidence on the division council but we advised them to be patient. Then camp commandant Otim Thomas was reinstated after three months without operation.[40]

The confused relationship between Local Council and camp leaders led the District Authorities to appeal to all NGOs, IOs and donors to respect the legal basis of Local Council Government when working in or visiting camps and always approach them first. In the past many visitors go straight to introduce themselves to the camp leaders, which [behaviour] over time has proven to undermine the position of the LC leaders. The camp leaders have no formal power. Most of them were elected on an ad-hoc basis when the camps were first established, but there is no system of rotation in place.... The general view expressed by the District Authorities and partners on this issue is that there is need for sensitisation of both camp leaders and of the international community on the informal character of – and limitations in – the Camp leaders' mandate.[41]

The military also became involved in camp administration. Sometimes they ordered people to move closer together so they could be more easily protected. This extended to appeals for co-operation and co-ordination between civilians and UPDF 'in order as to ease their work and for the sake of better survival in the camp', and warnings to people to consider environmental hygiene to prevent the outbreak of disease.[42] In Awer in November 1999, the military became involved in a dispute over the chieftaincy:

> Very early in the morning Home-guards set up road blocks on every path to stop anyone going in the field. People were forced to attend the meeting whether they liked it or not – even some school children were forced by the Home-guards to go and attend the meeting instead of going to school. Many people were beaten by the Home-guards on that day irrespective of size and age and the nature of work one does.

> In this meeting the camp officials and the LCs settled quarrels among certain people who were rivalling to be elected as Parabongo clan chief [It was eventually settled on the basis of heredity. The man 'elected' was the son of a previous chief].[43]

Diagram 5.2 Organigram Showing Approximate Positions of Government and 'Traditional' Authorities

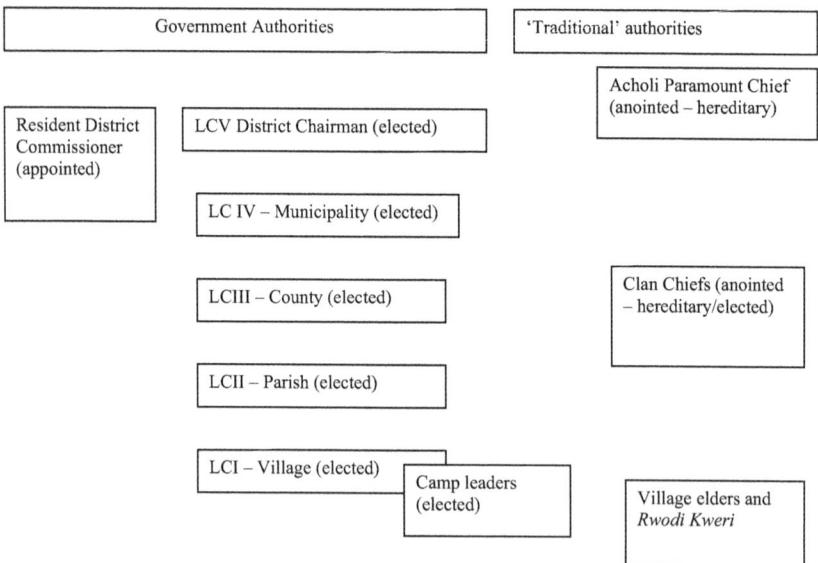

Government Authorities	'Traditional' authorities

Resident District Commissioner (appointed)	LCV District Chairman (elected)	Acholi Paramount Chief (anointed – hereditary)
	LC IV – Municipality (elected)	
	LCIII – County (elected)	Clan Chiefs (anointed – hereditary/elected)
	LCII – Parish (elected)	
	LCI – Village (elected) / Camp leaders (elected)	Village elders and *Rwodi Kweri*

A further, but central, complication in the administration of camps arose from the range of relief organisations, each with their own preferred manner of working and choice of which of the multiple authority structures to work through. In Atiak-Biabia, for example, the World Food Program, ICRC and World Vision, adopted three completely different beneficiary registration procedures. WFP used camp leaders and *Rwodi Kweri* to conduct door-to-door counts, which were then compiled and sent to the WFP for endorsement before registration took place. As the fieldworker noted, 'it was not effectively done, many people missed out'. ICRC, by contrast, used its own fieldworkers to carry out registration, numbering each house and then moving door-to-door to register inhabitants. Each household was subsequently given a card, and the distributions did not cause much complaint, although in at least one case a distribution had to be cancelled when it was found that the cards had been issued in a corrupt fashion. World Vision, which was targeting malnourished children aged 6 months to 5 years, trained parish councillors in measurement of Middle-Upper-Arm-Circumference (MUAC) and weight-height ratios.[44]

Mchaka-Mchaka

Overlaid onto this complex aggregation of disparate forms of authority, were political training courses, commonly known as *mchaka-mchaka*. These were organised by the NRM and held throughout Uganda, and in this regard northern Uganda was no exception. Described by Human Rights Watch as serving 'to rationalize the NRM's denial of political rights of freedom of expression, association and assembly',[45] attendance at such training was said by many to be a pre-requisite for those who wished to attend university, or work in Government service. A teacher from Gulu High School who had attended a training held at Gulu airfield in 1994 described how

> The instructors spoke in Swahili. If you spoke in English you got beaten. They would start very early in the morning with military drilling, followed by politicisation (role of army, history of Uganda). After lunch there would be further drilling and politicisation. This lasted for one month. They were also trained to handle an AK47. At the end they were given certificates.

Asked what he had gained from it, he answered:

> how to dismantle an AK47. I didn't learn anything new about the history of Uganda. It was a de-mystification of the gun and the creation of defence capacity'.[46]

The *Mchaka-mchaka* held in Pabo camp in early 1999 (24 January to 5 February), under the title 'The Struggle for Peace and Development', had a comprehensive agenda over and above the morning drills and training in 'military awareness' and 'personal administration'. The historical element encompassed Uganda's pre-colonial history, political and economic geography, colonialism, backwardness and underdevelopment. It then moved into post-independence politics, democratic process and constitutionalism in Uganda, as well as decentralisation. Broad themes included Human Rights 'with emphasis on the civil, political, economic and cultural life of women', 'regional cooperation and integration (Gov't Policies towards its neighbours)', 'building an integrated self-sustaining economy, Privatisation and liberalisation'. There was also a 'Review of the Security situation and Methods of conflict resolution', 'Roles of Security Organs (UPDF, ESO, ISO, Police)', 'Protection of National Independence and National Unity'. Economic issues included the 'Modernisation of agriculture', the 'Attention of Investors and good Economic policies', 'Poverty Eradication and household role in it'. Social issues ranged from the 'Government's Programme towards the provision of social services, improvement of the health sector' through the implementation of the Universal Primary Education scheme, the development and improvement of infrastructure in Gulu district, and the inclusion of marginalised groups in politics for development e.g. Youth, Women etc. Corruption and misuse of office, the land reform programme, the role of district councils in Development (Local Government Act), the roles of NGOs were also worked on, together with a discussion about the 'importance and need for a referendum'.

The passing out of 305 cadres on 14 February 1999 was attended by, amongst others, the National Director of the Movement Secretariat, the Director of Mass Mobilisation and Education in the NRM Secretariat, and various district officials. An army band led the parade, followed by cadres dressed in white T-shirts bearing the slogan 'Pabbo Peace and Development'. In response to resolutions drawn up during the course and read out by a Local Councillor (which touched amongst other things on the security situation, social services, problems of 'congestion and attitude of redundancy'), the Movement's Director responded 'by saying that government will use every avenue possible to solve these problems. People should have faith in the government and abide by the constitution of Uganda'. The passing out ceremony, which ended at 1.30 P.M., then turned into a big party: 'Disco dance were conducted transnight whereby the cadres really enjoyed themselves very much. Local brews were drunk as well as beers and soda. Pabbo trading centre ran short of brewerages that day'. [47]

The modernising thrust of *mchaka-mchaka* in 1999 went beyond the simple 'creation of defence capacity'; it also had a more concrete agenda, namely to determine who was inside the national system, and who would stay outside. In this regard the symbolic importance of having national-level directors attending the passing out ceremony is considerable.

Part II – Subsistence in the Camps

Notwithstanding the two body-blows dealt by the loss of cattle and forcible displacement, there was an appearance of considerable economic activity, even when insecurity levels were high. Many of the vegetables, grains, and fruits were either grown within the vicinity of the camp, or harvested from the home area (at considerable risk), or gathered in the bush (again at considerable risk). There was also a degree of commerce with neighbouring districts.

Furthermore, some surpluses were still being grown, even once the majority of the population were in camps, and were at times sufficient to merit transporting to Kampala. In June 1999, for example, farmers from Cwero took twenty-eight bags of sorghum to Kampala where they sold it at Ush 125 per kg. The more intrepid businesses/business people at times also risked travelling to the protected villages to buy up surplus produce. In March 2000, for example, Nile Breweries went to Cwero camp to purchase sorghum.[48] Generally, though, surplus produce was bought by small-scale women traders known as *awaro*. They would travel by *boda-boda* (bicycle) from Gulu town to the nearer villages such as Awer and purchase by the mug or the kilogramme. Crops purchased and sold in this way included groundnuts, beans, simsim (sesame), maize, cassava, tomatoes, sorghum and millet. They would then return to Gulu town to sell at a mark-up. Some larger-scale business people would use an *awaro* as a purchasing agent – once she had paid for the produce, the buyer would collect it with his truck.[49] Individuals with sufficient produce to merit the trip would take their own produce to town for sale for the same price as that given by the *awaro* [i.e. without the mark-up the *awaro* would put on].

Trade flourished during Christmas periods. In late 1998, despite the relative unrest, there was substantial commerce between Kampala and Gulu in the run-up to Christmas, with up to fifteen trucks per day arriving laden with consumer goods and departing again laden with produce for sale in the capital. At the same time

> people from the village stepped-up the rate of bringing in their produce for sale in the town and in turn purchased those items not found in the village such as executives (expensive) clothes, shoes, Radio cassettes, tapes, fish, Bags, etc. All the vehicles coming to the town or going outside to the villages or other neighbouring districts would be overloaded with luggages of people. This caused a lot of accidents with reported cases of overturning whilst on the road.[50]

For those with the necessary capital to invest in renting, clearing and ploughing land and buying seeds, returns for some crops could be significant.

Table 5.1 Crop Prices during Fieldwork Period, 1999 to 2000

Crop	100kg Sacks/Acre	Price obtainable per bag (Ush)[51]	Value of harvest from one acre[52]
Rice	25–30	25,000–30,000	625,000–900,000
Maize	25	12,000–18000	300,000–450,000
g-nuts (shelled)	7.5	18,000–30,000	135,000–225,000
Simsim	2–3	36,000–60,000	72,000–180,000
Sorghum	5–6	12,000–12,800	60,000–76,800
Millet	2–3	18,000–24000	36,000–72,000

Rice was easily the most profitable, followed by maize and groundnuts. By far the least profitable was millet, a staple of the Acholi diet. Prices varied widely between places and from season to season. A sack of groundnuts which cost Ush

18,000 in Awer in August 1999 cost Ush 30,000 in Pabo in November of the same year. Equally, a sack of maize, which cost Ush 20,000 in Pabo in October 1998 (a period of high insecurity), cost just 12,000 in Cwero a year later (low insecurity). Even within the same village, prices fluctuated dramatically over time: whereas a sack of simsim cost Ush 60,000 in Cwero in March 1999, by March 2000 it had sunk to Ush 36,000.

Those with sufficient capital, storage space and connections, would buy crops when they were readily available and then re-sell at a later date. For example, in April 1999 'a businessman from Atiak ... transported to Gulu town 12 sacks of green beans which he had hoarded in his store at the camp after purchase between January–February'. Another businessman from Atiak bought up peas in early 1999 and stored them for some months, before transporting them to Gulu in May that year[53] – using a District Water Development pick-up which had gone to repair boreholes in Atiak.

Some goods, such as shea nut oil, were processed in the camps, with a 300ml bottle (old Fanta bottle) selling at Ush 500 in Atiak (August 1998).[54] Yeast used in brewing alcohol was made by taking raw millet (bought by the mugful) which, once germinated, would be dried, ground and mixed with flour. Items such as beef, pork, chicken and fresh fish, which in peacetime would have been locally produced, generally had to be imported. Domestic produce and imports from other parts of Uganda were supplemented with relief goods, such as cowpeas or maize. Often these were sold by individuals in small amounts to meet a very specific need for cash, but there also appeared to be organised scams going on. In some places it was possible to buy relief goods originally intended for Sudan: a 20 litre drum of American cooking oil from Operation Lifeline Sudan could be bought in Atiak for Ush 25,000 (Dec 1999) and re-sold in 1/2 litre units for almost double the money.

Access to Land

Although the situation created opportunities for those with sufficient capital, for the majority such activities were completely out of reach, and while there was a lot of activity in the market, most of it was of a very marginal nature. This is suggested by the very small scale of most transactions (basics such as maize and cassava flour, beans, tomatoes, onions were sold in units of between Ush 50 to 500, equivalent to between £0.03 and £0.30). Relative to this other items were very costly, e.g. a second-hand pair of trousers (Ush 5,000 upwards (£2.27), or a trip to Kampala (+/- Ush 25,000 (£11.36). Even where people had sufficient surplus crops to make it worthwhile taking them to Gulu to sell, they sold by the kilo, whereas business-people bought by the sack. For example, in March 1999, the fieldworker noted three crops being taken from Odek to Gulu: rice (Ush 620 per kg), simsim (Ush 400 per kg), and tomatoes (Ush 25,000/box). This suggests that people were not really selling a surplus, but rather in order to meet very specific expenditures requiring cash, e.g. medications, school fees or dowries.[55]

When land usage is considered, the very marginal nature of agricultural activity is confirmed. Figures for 1991 show that subsistence farming accounted for 77 per cent of economic activity and employed about 95 per cent of the population (COWI, 1999b: 50).[56] By 1999, although 'Arable land is very fertile and makes up 87.4 per cent of the total land area', less than 10 per cent of land was being utilised yearly.[57] The issue was not lack of land, but access to it, due to the effects of displacement and the protected villages policy. Writing in 1999, WFP evaluators argued that

> The issue of land allocation for resettled and temporarily encamped IDPs is still little understood, particularly in the north. Large areas of Acholi clan-held land lie fallow, but its allocation to IDPs has not always been possible, leaving the displaced dependent on international assistance beyond the acute emergency phase. WFP needs to investigate the political and cultural roots of this anomaly. (WFP, 1999: 31).

The reasons for lack of access to land were various. Although land is communally owned in the sense that outside urban areas people do not hold individual land-titles, it is nonetheless managed and used such that newcomers do not have automatic access to their own plot, particularly in those areas closest to settlements. Whereas in their home villages people were within easy distance of their land (referred to as 'gardens'), in the camps they were often very far removed from it. In many camps curfews were imposed, limiting movement to daylight hours and making it difficult for people to move back to their home areas to dig their land, or even forbidding such movement altogether. Following the re-entry of rebels into Gulu district in November 1998, the commander of the northern reserve forces, Colonel Oketta, issued an order that no civilian should move more than 1km outside the camps. Compounding the army-imposed curfews, the LRA had also issued prohibitions on working on Fridays and Sundays as

> Those two days are days of worships for Muslims and Christians respectively, and the LRA has informed the population that if they work on those days they will be killed. People go out to dig in the morning at about 7.00 A.M. and come back home between 10 A.M. and 12 noon.[58]

Newcomers therefore were often reduced to farming any small plot they could gain access to, including hiring land from an existing owner. In 1999 the cost ranged from Ush 20,000 to 40,000 per acre per growing season, changing little by 2001.[59] Often the owners would rent out a piece of land for one season to get it cleared of shrubs and trees, and then, the hard labour having been done, would use it themselves the following season. On top of rental costs, ploughing ranged from Ush 20,000–40,000 per acre using oxen, and similar amounts using a tractor. Since cattle stocks had been almost wiped out, there were very few oxen available. Pabo, with its population of 42,000+, had only one pair of oxen available for ploughing in 1999. Other villages had none.

Given unreliable and inadequate food rations, and notwithstanding UPDF and LRA prohibitions, people continued to try and return to their land to cultivate. In December 2001 (before Operation Iron Fist), UNOCHA estimated that

25 per cent of the IDP camp population were accessing their gardens.[60] It was always high-risk. Having been given pangas and hoes by ICRC, for example,

> those who went back home for cultivation at Pakwong Parish were disturbed by remnants of rebels who demanded for their pangas and collected them on the 2/5/99 night (the same night the items had been distributed). This incident forced the cultivators back to camp because they feared mutilation using the pangas collected from them.[61]

There was some danger of landmines planted by both UPDF and LRA. Lacor Hospital had its first 26 landmine victims in 1995. In 1996 they accounted for 126 out of 515 war-related injuries, dropping down to 19 out of 318 in 1997.[62] Of the 560 war-related amputations dealt with in the AVSI centre for disability and rehabilitation in Gulu Hospital, 53 per cent were caused by landmines, 33 per cent by gunshot, 7.7 per cent by mutilation (e.g. with a panga), and 6.3 per cent by bomb-blasts.[63]

While 53 per cent indicates the importance of land-mine injuries relative to other forms of injury, it does not reflect the full scale of the issue – in many cases victims either died on the spot or from shock and bleeding before reaching medical care. A conservative estimate would be at least 100 victims annually or two every week. Extrapolated backwards to the beginnings of the war in 1986, this suggests a figure of at least 1,500.[64] To this must be added the fact that such incidents almost always affect not just the blast victim, but also their immediate dependants, as in the case of a woman who stepped on a mine and whose child of six months subsequently died

> … because there was nobody to breast-feed it and there was no money for milk and posho. Opio went to World Vision for assistance but by the time he got back the child was dead. The woman had walked over the place twice while going to her plot to collect food.[65]

Quite apart from the danger of landmines, people were liable to be abducted by the LRA or arrested/attacked as rebel collaborators by the UPDF. In February 2000, for example, five people were shot at by a UPDF helicopter while attempting to collect foodstuffs from their home village. One was killed, the others taken to Kitgum hospital.[66] Further risks stemmed from leaving children unattended in the camps, with many stories of children burning down huts by accident.

Asked to describe people's cultivation, the fieldworker in Biabia noted:

> They go outside [the protected village] starting from 7.00 A.M. and come back between 5 and 6 P.M. (after which there is a curfew). Problems include starvation, rain, distance, running the risk of meeting LRA, beating by government soldiers in other places where they go to collect food stuff etc. Some are ploughing on land from local institutions and relatives, others own their own land. The children above 5 years old are sent to school and those below are left starving.[67]

Reductions in Hunting

Hunting had always been a component of livelihoods, used to enrich the diet of the hunter's household, as a source of cash, and as proof of masculinity.[68] Hunters would go deep into the bush and stay there for a number of days or weeks, accompanied by their dogs, and curing the meat they killed before returning to the camps. It was inherently risky, with reports of hunters being attacked by pythons and gored to death by buffalo.[69] It had always been controlled (in the precolonial era designation of hunting grounds was a major source of inter-village conflicts, and in the colonial period the authorities restricted communal hunts 'in order to preserve some of the game from too rapid extinction' (Girling, 1960; 16)). As a result of war, wider processes of 'modernisation', and the constraints of life in the protected villages, however, the parameters of risk appeared to have expanded.

In western Gulu district, near the Murchison Falls National Park, many people would leave the camps to hunt (see also Finnström, 2003: 211–212). Sometimes, such as in late February 1999, following encroachment of buffalo from the park, this was authorised and no participants came to harm. More often, gun-ownership and hunting were banned, with severe consequences for those caught. From Anaka it was reported that two men caught in the park with guns and 'eight pieces of smoked hippo meat' were beaten by the UPDF after one of them confessed that 'he had only wanted a balanced diet'.[70] They were lucky, for those who ventured into the park itself were liable to be shot at by game rangers and/or UPDF when caught hunting. After one sixteen-year-old who borrowed a gun from a Home guard stationed in Anaka went hunting in the park, 'Some people heard of the sound of gun shots ringing from the park on Wednesday 21/4/99 at about 10.00 A.M. – and that was it – the game rangers were busy with the poachers. Up to now his dead body is not seen'.[71] My respondent concluded, however, that such incidents would not serve as a deterrent and that although 'many villagers lost their lives in the National Park poaching, more people will still go to hunt'.

In Awac, soldiers arrested a group of about forty men who had gone hunting for meat for the Christmas celebrations. They were taken to Awac detach where they were

> tortured seriously and all their meat was removed. This left the families of the hunters to celebrate Christmas with Beans and greens as their Meal for that day. And it was only the dogs that were left untortured by the soldiers. Otherwise with the beatings some were not able to sit upright.[72]

One group of hunters from Pabbo, having built a camp and put some of their catch to cook, went to check other traps, before returning to find themselves under fire from

> … rebels who took position before they arrived on the site [and] shot a lot of bullets on these hunters. They all dropped away the meat and took off for their safety. Fortunate enough no bullets hit any of the hunters. It was believed that these rebels were 19 in numbers … [73]

Road-blocks set up to catch hunters selling meat on the black market, did not always catch just hunters:

> A staff member of Anaka hospital hired a Boda-Boda to transport a basin full of drugs/capsules and thermometers to a destination I do not know. The drugs were the

property of the hospital here. The consignments were intercepted at Aparanga military check point (the road block was set up in a wise way to screen out smoked meat transported by hunters to black markets). The *Boda-Boda* on reaching the check point was stopped and when his luggage was checked he revealed that it was the property of a staff member of Anaka hospital. Some UPDF were sent to arrest him, and he was sent to Gulu for further questioning. LCs here complained that UPDF should have informed the office of the LCs before taking the offender to Gulu.[74]

Other Alternatives to Agriculture

For those without access to land, other activities had to be found. As the camps became ever more entrenched, an uneven and shifting mixture of coping and survival strategies emerged. For some, camp life created opportunities for a quantum and permanent shift in their economic activities. UNDMT, for example, argued that, even if free to do so, 28 per cent of those residing in the protected villages would not return to their home villages because 'Many have resided in trading centres for six years and have adopted new skills or occupations that are more lucrative than agriculture'.[75]

Youth frequently set up very small shops with investment support from those already earning an income: 'Some lock-up shops have flourished quite remarkably by some youths in the camp. Income from LDU and teachers' salaries are major contributions of the investments'.[76] Another option open to physically fit male youth was to set up as a *boda-boda* (bicycle taxi). This involved either owning a bicycle or moped, or paying a part of the daily takings to the owner of such a vehicle. For those with pedal cycles it was taxing work – some were cycling up to 90 kilometres per day carrying both people and their goods.

Not surprisingly there were always people on the look out for a fast buck. During the time I was in Gulu, my research assistants were on several occasions approached by people wanting to sell me items ranging from leopard skins, which it was illegal to hunt, to a drug known as *Katube-Katube,* which appeared to be a 'local' Viagra. One fieldworker reported how during traditional dances boys would trick girls by mixing *Katube-Katube* with a sweet called 'Bingo', another how it 'could turn you into a rapist – you'll want to fuck anywhere where there is a hole'. There were also reports of members of the diaspora obtaining free drugs from the National Health Service in the U.K. and sending them to relatives in Gulu to sell.

For most people, however, the only way to access cash was through various forms of casual labour known as *leja-leja.* These included digging a strip of land known as *katala* or *okori* (the exact size and payment varied according to location), digging a pit latrine (Ush 10,000 per pit), cutting the grass in someone's compound (Ush 500). Those ferrying water got paid Ush 100 per 20 litre jerry can (this could sometimes be as low as Ush 50 per 20 litre jerry can carried for a distance of 1 mile[77]). Those making bricks received Ush 50 per brick, while those transporting them received Ush 100 per 10 bricks (Awere). Collecting firewood (high-risk due to insecurity) brought Ush 600 per bundle. Some people found employment maintaining the roads for the government, or during feeder road rehabilitation.[78] For slashing grass and hoeing, and filling in small pot-holes they received about Ush 15,000 fortnightly. A few found work on agricultural projects – the maize plantation at Patiko prison paid people Ush 500 per 3 lines of maize weeded. Others cut poles at Ush 400 each (Awere), and others wove mats. To make one mat, which could be sold at Ush 4,000, took about one week. Some young men would try to earn money procuring women for soldiers, and in Gulu town there were certain places where women could earn money 'exposing their private parts'.

Often the socio-economic differentiation in a camp was insufficient to generate many opportunities for casual labourers. In Awach it was said that 'there is no leja-leja in the camp, except teachers [who] can pay people to dig and heap potatoes'.[79] And not everybody paid in cash. People digging in the expectation of being paid cash could find themselves given items such as soap, sugar, salt, or clothes instead.

When they were paid, the purchasing power of the amounts paid was marginal. Ush 100 bought one aspirin, Ush 500 one 350ml bottle of Coca-Cola. When contrasted with the cost of health care, it is even starker: Ush 15,000 to be admitted to Lacor hospital, and considerably more for some traditional healers. The inability of people to find the kind of sums needed to rent a piece of land (at least Ush 20,000 per acre) and plough it (another Ush 20,000 or more) becomes evident. To earn Ush 20,000 would take 40 days at least – assuming you could get 40 days consecutive work and that you did not have to spend any of the money as you went along.

Some people resorted to petty theft, and this became an agenda item in camp meetings, as in Awere where 'The chairman said he had got many cases of stealing in the camp ... mainly goats, foodstuff, clothes, money, etc.'.[80] For many women, however, the complex and labour intensive process of brewing alcohol was a very real option.[81] A still could in principle yield about twenty 750 ml bottles per day, but supply was at times greater than demand: 'Many women are brewing booze daily; however there is little market for the product. The price being charged is 300 shillings for a certain bottle which is slightly less than one litre and 200 shillings for a half a litre'.[82] One form of alcahol required no distillation; maize or millet flour was simply mixed with yeast and left to ferment for 1–2 days before being filtered. This was not just done inside the camps – business people would also bring it by bicycle and convoy from Adjumani and sell it at Ush 400 per jug.[83]

Group Formation

Some people addressed their individual lack of capital by forming into groups, of which there was a startling diversity, especially amongst women and youth. In Atiak, for example, the Catholic Women's Group had forty-five members engaged in 'promotion of agriculture, running a grinding mill, and protection of orphans as a result of instability from 1986'. They had received external support from a local politician who donated a grinding mill. Opit Kic Women's

Association, with fifty members, had similar objectives but had received no external support. A further group, the Mother's Union Pupwonya Association, worked on promotion of agriculture, as well as cultural dances like *Apiti,* and health education through drama. Some groups of this nature received training in management and book-keeping from agencies such as ACORD, and this was intended to 'increase their bargaining power in case of loans advanced to benefit the rural women or groups'.[84] As such they were often associated with a modernising agenda and were reportedly 'very organised in their structure of management'.[85] As an interface between ordinary peasant farmers and various external actors, such as NGOs and Government, they provided a degree of protection to their members and for the external actors they were easier to work through.

Food Aid

As access to land became ever more problematic, so people became increasingly dependent on food aid, despite their best efforts to find alternative sources of income. WFP's original Emergency Operation (EMOP 5816.02), which began in late 1996 when the camps were established, was replaced in April 2000 by the Protracted Relief and Recovery Operation (PRRO 6176). This benefited 340,420 IDPs in Gulu district, and 2,270 beneficiaries of micro-projects in different categories of vulnerable groups (malnourished children, pregnant and lactating mothers, TB patients, orphans, formerly abducted children). It went beyond simple food relief to also include 'general food distribution, school feeding of primary school pupils; food for work/assets; food for training projects; supplementary and therapeutic feeding of moderately and severely malnourished children respectively; and provision of food to other vulnerable groups' (WFP, 12 March 2002). Under Food For Assets (FFA), WFP claimed for the period 2000–2002 '2.8km of community roads constructed by 6,820 beneficiaries, three-quarters of them women; 137,000 bricks for school construction in Awer, Bardege and Atiak, so far 4 blocks with a total of 19 classrooms have been constructed. Other projects included fish farming and afforestation; women groups in Anaka have planted about 15,000 trees. 50 groups trained in fish farming techniques' (WFP, 12 March 2002).

The WFP School Feeding Programme provided one cooked meal per day to 94 schools in 46 centres, reaching 27,626 boys and 21,306 girls. Plans to expand to a further 32,000 children were to be supported by resources from the U.S.A. under the USDA Global Food for Education Initiative. The PRRO 'anticipated a gradual return of IDPs to their original homes by the years 2000 to 2002 and therefore a phase-down of relief activities matched with an increase in school feeding and FFA', but as displacement continued apace the majority of programme resources remained focused on relief activity. In 2001 more than half its total expenditure of $36 million was in the Northern Region. PRRO 6176, which ended on 31 March 2002, was replaced with PRRO 10121.0, under the title 'Targeted Food Assistance and Recovery of Refugees, Displaced Persons and Vulnerable Groups in Uganda'. By this point the total population of Gulu was estimated at 469,700, of which an estimated 79 per cent were in 33 IDP camps. 67 per cent in 20 camps were being assisted with WFP's General Food Distribution (GFD). The distribution of cereals, pulses and vegetable oil was supposed to meet 'about a quarter of the daily kilocalorie requirements of the IDPs, and is distributed on a one and a half month cycle, with NRC the WFP's implementing partner' (see Chapter 6 for case study). The new PRRO envisaged 'an increase in self-sufficiency of substantial numbers of IDPs over a three-year period as they return to their original neglected home areas', reducing the load from 400,000 in Gulu and Kitgum to 115,000 in the third year (WFP, 12 March 2002), though no explanation was given as to why this should occur.

Problems with Distribution

For the first two years food distributions assumed five people per household 'irrespective of the actual number per household'. This improved following a re-registration process in May 1999, but rations were still not proportional to the number of people in a household, and were thus still perceived as unfair:

> The W.F.P. found that a household with few people should get less food than a household with many people. That could have been alright – but look … A family with two people received 10kg of maize, 2kg of cowpeas, and 0.5kg of oil, [while] a household with six people should have got more than that – say three times the item – but it was 20kg of maize, 3kg cowpeas, and 1kg of oil.[86]

Complaints from Palaro were similar.

> Here I would like to put some hints on the ways food is distributed by this World Agency to the needy people. Firstly, the relief food is distributed on a household basis. This is very much unfair since the ratio given doesn't tally with the number of people in that household. For example, a woman with eleven children and a husband is given 25kg posho, 3.7 kg beans or cowpeas and two litres of cooking oil. Similar to a woman of one child and a husband. Which means the number of hungry mouths is not being considered.
>
> Secondly, the WFP workers are very unkind and untransparent when dealing with the people. At times some households are not given their share because they fail to identify their husband's name or the number of children they have as some women get confused having seen food-stuffs. Lastly, the last food distributed (30/06/98) was posho which was rotten and not fit for human consumption.[87]

Some technical problems were relatively minor, such as asking several households to share the contents of one 5 litre can of oil when supplies were running low.[88] Others were more serious, such as WFP setting quotas for how many people it would register in a particular place,[89] and the influence of the District Disaster Committee in deciding which camps would receive food relief. In Awere, for example, people felt they were being discriminated against because Kony originated from that area.[90]

The difficulties of maintaining an accurate register when the security situation and related population movements were in constant flux, must have been considerable. In the 1999 lull, for example, people returning from other districts and from the towns used the camps as staging posts but were not registered: 'WFP had fixed numbers: 2643. Anyone above that got nothing'.[91] At times rations would be reduced to make sure everybody got something. In Atiak on 8 December 1998, for example, 'People were combined into three households for 50 kgs of posho in some parishes, mostly the last villages' [i.e. under 17kg per household rather than the 25kg standard ration].[92] At other times the correct ration was distributed until supplies ran out, leaving those at the end of the list empty-handed.[93]

Registration problems were compounded by the range of household arrangements, including polygamous families in which each wife had responsibility for herself and her children, but not for those of co-wives. Even where registration was reasonably accurate 'Some of the beneficiaries missed out – especially women – because of looting of food by youths and men'.[94] It was not uncommon for distributions to cause fighting. As one respondent noted,

> In a society (community) – there are the privileged and the unprivileged – so unless managers (WFP) can identify the two, there will be chaos ... Names of beneficiaries should be revised, so as to alleviate the abundant cry. If the names of the beneficiaries correspond uniformly with the items to be distributed, and the staff are also polished [i.e. trained], I hope the humanitarian support will endeavour to support those victimised but not the opportunists ...[95]

There were also confirmed instances of petty corruption by those responsible for distributions. In Palaro 'Business-men follow the convoy and buy from NRC staff at 18,000 shillings for a bag of soya beans',[96] and in Pabbo 'There was mild selling of cooking oil by the representative of World Food Program to business people'.[97] At times camp leaders succumbed to temptation, as in the case where, following an ICRC distribution, the 'Palaro camp leader had 100 hoes, 40 pangas, 40 axes and untold number of bars of soap. Local councillors investigated and many others including the Movement Chairman were implicated in the fraud'. Following a public meeting the corrupted camp leader was voted out and 'a good number of parish representatives' were sacked.[98]

When the commander of Acet camp unsuccessfully campaigned to be elected as LCIII chairperson of Odek sub-county, he took his revenge on the voters:

> Those who did not vote for him in the LC 3 election do not get registered and missed the items. Parishes of Palaro and Lamola are the most affected people for meeting the wrath of the commander in not voting him into the office'.

Several other problems were noted:

> The WFP maize flour distributed in the camp in most cases are expired so women are using them to make local brew, this further causing the rate of drunkenness to rise up in the camp.

> The dispensary men have turned the food meant for the malnourished children to be their own. They are now refusing to register other malnourished children as beneficiaries.

> The relief items given by the NGOs to the camps, particularly the ICRC, is inadequate, thus causing divisions between those who missed and those who benefited.[99]

Apart from food relief, ICRC played a major role with occasional distributions of seeds and tools, as well as household items such as blankets, soap and jerry cans.[100] Matching supplies to demand was easier for these. To ensure an up-to-date registration, they would visit the camps about a month prior to the distribution: 'households were grouped in three classes A B C that is group A [1–4 people] 1 Blanket 3 bars of soaps 1 small jerry can. Group B [5–7 people] 3 blankets 4 bars of soap 1 big jerry can. Group C [8 or more] 4 Blankets 5 bars of soap 1 big jerry can and 1 small jerry can'.[101] The same groupings were used for distributions of seeds (e.g. beans, maize, millet, cassava, tomatoes, egg-plant, cabbages, onions, rice, soy-gum, okra, groundnuts, capsicum) accompanied by planting advice and a warning that 'the seeds are dusted with poison therefore it should not be eaten'.[102] Many of these crops were grown in the camps and were to be found on sale in the camp markets, suggesting that they were a useful intervention in terms of increasing the range of foods available and also as a source of cash income.

In addition to the distribution of seeds by humanitarian organisations, there were some smaller commercially driven initiatives. For example, in March 1999 the Agricultural Extension Department gave 2 mugs of sunflower seeds per household in Atiak, promising to later buy the produce for oil.[103] On 30 April CRS also gave 5kg/acre/person of sunflower seeds: 'The seed was distributed free of charge, but on condition that after the harvest the outcome of it should be sold to them, i.e. to CRS Uganda'.[104] Western Acholi Cooperative Union gave out 10kg cotton seeds per person, Odek camp, 31 May 1999, also in the expectation of buying the crop.[105] International NGOs occasionally made once-off distributions, such as when World Vision gave school uniforms and blankets to orphans in Awer,[106] and at times benevolent individuals made generous donations, such as in Palaro where someone distributed 24 hoes each to the six *Lukeme* groups in the camp.[107]

Demonstration Sites

One of the more paradoxical NGO interventions into livelihoods – given that camp dwellers clearly knew what to do when given seeds and tools – was to initiate so-called 'demonstration' plots such as the World Vision-USAID Food Security Project demonstration site in Pabo, where people were to be taught improved agricultural techniques. In practice these became integrated into the relief economy. When the World Vision programme in Gulu and Kitgum produced 500Mt of beans and 37Mt of maize these were sold to WFP for distribution to Sudanese refugees. In their press release of 7 May 1999, announcing the first deliveries of food from World Vision to WFP, they claimed that 'through this scheme and procurement, WFP and World Vision were able to inject 140,000,000 Ush [shillings] into the rural economy of Gulu district'. They went on to say

> WFP and World Vision would like to … encourage the people of Gulu and Kitgum to follow this example that will lead to self-sustainability. WFP and World Vision will continue supporting efforts of the Acholi people to develop Gulu and Kitgum

districts. Development that will help building peace and understanding in the north and in Uganda.

The implicit message was clear; people's impoverishment is their own fault – if only they knew how to farm properly they would be self-reliant. The perversity of making people in camps, who were themselves recipients of food aid, and whose problem was lack of access to land rather than lack of agricultural skills, produce food for donation to people in refugee camps elsewhere, was not alluded to. The wilful blindness of such initiatives to the fact that, as UNOCHA described, this was a population 'accustomed over generations to a situation of relative self-reliance and even prosperity' (Weeks, 2002; 5), was striking.

Calls To Allow People To Return Home

Research findings consistently indicated that although people in principle wished to return home there would be no immediate exodus from the camps whatever changes occurred in the policy context. IOM found that 55.3 per cent of respondents felt that insecurity was 'too high to allow for a safe return'.[108] ARLPI found that although 'the overwhelming majority of the people ... declared their wish to return back home as soon as possible', it was necessary to distinguish 'those who would only go back after they are assured of a minimum of protection and security at their villages, and a good number of people who would be ready to go immediately at their own risk, whether or not the rebels are still around'.[109] UNDMT's technical group noted in late 2001 that 'the Government has publicly declared its intention of seeing IDPs return home as early as March 2002', but argued that only about 72 per cent of the populations of protected villages would return to their original homes should the situation improve sufficiently to enable them to do so.[110] In early 2002, UNOCHA found an overwhelming desire to be allowed to return home, but that if allowed to happen according to peoples' wishes and the guiding principles on internal displacement, this would be a gradual rather than one-off process (Weeks, 2002: 33).

Despite the consistency of opinion of both local and internationally contracted researchers that people would return home gradually if allowed to do so, the Government of Uganda did not give the green light for dismantling the camp system fully, though from November 2000, prompted in part by the outbreak of Ebola haemorrhagic fever in Gulu district in September 2000 and fears that this could wreak havoc in the congested camps, the 4th Division Commander began to talk of a 'decongestion' plan. Under this, people would be moved back to a specific area within their parish of origin (but not necessarily to their place of origin), with some military protection provided (as well as the promise of eventual electrification). As such, people would be 'resettled' into smaller versions of the existing camps, not into their original homes.

The proposal was viewed with scepticism, as it did not offer a return to peoples' original homes, and the most fundamental premise of a successful resettlement, peace with the LRA, had yet to be achieved. In February 2001, ACORD researchers reported that most individuals ... looked at this [decongestion policy] as a political move to win votes since government and army officers strongly advocated for it. Many also believed this policy was due to the responsibility they [the government] felt they owed the people after bringing 'Ebola' from Congo into the district ...[111] Concerns were expressed that 'When permanent resettlements are built and in future peace returns to Acholi, who will own the area? How about those that own the land that people are resettled on, where will they go?'

The researchers concluded that 'With such perceptive questions and many more that continue to mingle in the back of our minds, there is a need to see that this [decongestion] could be another major source of 'war' and conflict after the current insurgency ends' (ACORD February 2001: 8–9). Furthermore, as UNOCHA argued, 'the proposals for so-called 'decongestion' ... would do nothing to remedy the loss of economic autonomy and personal autonomy that is at the heart of the problem' (Weeks 2002: 26).

In the event, although some people were moved from Pabo to a number of smaller camps in Kilak County, decongestion was never fully adopted as a policy, and those who did move also maintained their homes in the original camps. The likelihood of return diminished further on 1 December 2001, when President Museveni announced in a meeting with the Sudanese chargé d'affaires in Uganda that unless the Government of Khartoum relocated Kony to the north of Sudan, the displaced could not go home.[112] With the beginning of Operation Iron Fist in February 2002, all early moves towards informal 'decongestion' came to a definitive end.

By 2006 'Considering the need to urgently decongest those IDP camps which, because of their structure and overcrowding, pose a serious threat to the life, human rights and dignity of the displaced population'[113] the term decongestion was back in circulation; although by this time there were many more humanitarian actors questioning the extent to which decongestion represented an effective resolution of the IDP situation, humanitarian actors worked hand in hand with governmental authorities to identify decongestion sites.[114] District Camp Decongestion Working Groups were established, and 'Standard Operating Procedures for IDP Camp Decongestion' were issued. From late 2006 onwards UN-HCR advocated strongly for 'Freedom of Movement' for IDPs. The considerable potential for this position to undermine the 'protected villages' policy was lost as UNHCR failed to link its position with a strong critique of decongestion sites, preferring to see moves to such sites as proof of freedom of movement, and arguing in its December 2006 report that:

Freedom of Movement (FoM) does not necessarily imply return at this stage, unless IDPs choose to return. It does imply allowing IDPs greater freedom to make their own choices and to become more self sufficient at their own pace, if and when the security situation allows. More importantly, it implies that we work with the UPDF in new ways to encourage them to provide security to areas, rather than only to camps and cordons.

As such, from late 2006 onwards there was a proliferation of such sites but little return to places of origin (this was by stark contrast with Teso and Lango sub-regions, where IDPs returned home in large numbers in 2006). UNHCR's December 2006 Report went on to note that:

> IDPs are waiting for a clear statement from the Government and UPDF that specifically states IDPs can move from the camps. This is an important aspect of FOM. After many years of being forced to remain in camps with enforced curfews with the fear of being beaten, detained or shot if they violated the movement restrictions or curfews, IDPs need assurances from the security forces that they can move without harm.[115]

Block Farming

Ambiguities about 'decongestion' and its relationship to return home contributed to camp dwellers' fears that in their absence their lands would be taken over by other people. While this did not appear to have happened on any large scale over the period covered by this research, there were, besides the talk of building 'permanent resettlements', several initiatives which fuelled such fears.

In March 1999, attempts were made in several villages to establish 'block farming', schemes whereby groups of villagers would return to their home areas (but not to their own land) to clear the land and farm on a commercial scale, with special protection afforded by the army. Various elements of the army, including the President's brother and the commander of the northern reserve forces, were centrally involved in these schemes, at times in collaboration with international NGOs.[116]

In Atiak, for example, the commander of the reserve forces came personally to encourage people to form into groups of ten for the purposes of block farming in an area at Adar, where they would reside with soldiers deployed to protect them. They were told

> They should aim for 40x60 metres for each person and place the plots together. This is called block farming ... Furthermore, each group of ten should have production, finance, mobilisation and public relations committees.[117]

He was accompanied by a Gulu-based and university trained representative from Catholic Relief Services (CRS) who said CRS would provide seeds and food for those who registered in groups of ten.

Another example was the Kilak Foundation for Rural Development. Set up in March 1999, with founder members including military personnel (including the Commander of Reserve Forces),[118] councillors from Kilak county, sub-county chiefs, Movement chairmen, LC III chairmen, as well as youth and women leaders,[119] its members were called to a security meeting in Pabbo Court Hall on 17 May 1999:

> The purpose was to resettle people to Apar which is 30 kilometres away from Pabbo camp on the west. The groups of 35 vigilantes ... agreed to take off for Apar on Monday 24/5/99. The purpose is to resettle displaced persons in their original homesteads and increase production. The UPDF gave them guns for their movement. They were warned by LCs not to misuse the guns given to them for their own protection ... [and that if they did] the court of law will take action immediately.... By 30th May they had not yet gone because they were waiting for food supplies from Col. Oketta.[120]

When in March 2002 I asked what had happened to the Block Farming initiative, respondents in Pabo told me:

> At the beginning it looked successful because World Vision also used it for the promotion of food security (they had a big plot on the Gulu-Kitgum road). But mostly people have come back to the camp. It became a scheme to eat government money; The Vice President [Specioza Kazibwe] built a big hostel for students at Makerere [the most important university in Uganda] out of some of that money …

Another block farm was started near Palaro in the grounds of Patiko prison farm. In Awere Kal 150 Home-guards set up a plot to grow rice. Hunger Alert – a local NGO of which Janet Museveni, the First Lady, was a patron – encouraged a block farm in National Teachers College Unyama in March 1999, another in Lamogi Division in April 1999, and one in Pabbo Palwong in June 1998.[121]

Fears that 'protected villages' had an ulterior motive were given sharp focus by the publication in May 2003 of Salim Saleh's proposals for a Security and Production Programme (SPP).[122] Although the scheme was not official government policy, the fact that it came from the President's brother inevitably raised fears. The more so as it envisaged incorporating all 800,000 people displaced in the Acholi Sub-region into 45 highly militarised production units, each containing 17,500 people, of whom 736 per unit would be involved in civil defence. The Salim Saleh Foundation for Humanity described the SPP as

> a strategic plan for solving the insecurity in Acholi region. It will work through beefing up local defence using community youth volunteers who are recruited and trained specifically to secure the production areas in which they live. They will train under the UPDF and be supervised by the local Uganda Police, under the community-policing programme.

In what can be read as a criticism of Acholi failure to defend themselves it argued that this would encourage the Acholi to become more pro-active in their self-defence:

> The stakes of defence are even higher if the population is defending production. For instance, the Kibbutzim system in Israel combined defence and production …

Some respondents believed that the SPP was in fact a ploy to take away land from the Acholi and give it to western companies. Many believed that British-American Tobacco was involved in the 'land grab', as they were already operational in the West Nile region and had a site in Gulu town.

Part III – Access to Education

The disruption of education began long before the policy of protected villages was put in place, and its consequences were already foreseen by Colonel Tolit in the 1994 peace talks, when he warned that

> … in 3 or 4 years time … even if Government said they wanted a son of Acholi to become a doctor, there will be no suitable people because people are no longer going to school.[123]

When teachers found themselves a target of LRA killings and abductions, some took refuge in towns. In 1998 thirteen of Awach's seventy teachers rode to Awach daily by bicycle: 'They leave Gulu at about 5.30 A.M., reach at 8.00. The parents [of the pupils] cook some food for them, with support from UPE funds'.[124] For most, this was not an option. By August 1999, the District Education Officer reported that 115 out of 176 primary schools in Gulu district were displaced. There were 137,000 pupils enrolled under UPE, and 1,800 teachers, of whom 500 were untrained.[125]

In the small camp of Attiak-Biabia on the border with Sudan there was one primary school with 239 pupils, one qualified and seven unqualified teachers. Awach, with its population of 10,300, had 8 primary schools with 3,311 pupils. There were 62 classrooms and 70 teachers, of whom 60 were qualified.[126]

In Pabbo approximately half the teachers were qualified; the rest had completed secondary schooling. Eight of the ten primary schools were housed in temporary structures and giving classes outside under trees.

Table 5.2 Primary Schooling in Pabbo Camp, 1998

Name of School	Pupils	Teachers	Pupil: Teacher ratio
Labala	544	9	60
Pabbo	1580	23	69
Pogo Okuture	187	4	47
Pawel Langeta	576	7	82
Lalem	506	6	84
Abera	668	4	167
Olinga	223	3	74
Mpala	196	3	65
Otong	156	5	31
Palwong Jengari	163	3	54
TOTAL	4799	67	72

Cwero's one primary school had 411 pupils in four classes. One of the five teachers was qualified. A further 11 teachers had moved to Gulu.[127]

In many places, such as Awer[128] and Pagak,[129] schools would be aggregated, with one headmaster elected as the overall administrator, the other as deputy. Finances were kept separate, in order to avoid problems in allocating materials if the situation normalised and schools went back to their original sites.[130]

Much school building was done by parents. Red Barnet (Save the Children Denmark) insisted that beneficiary parents mobilise local resources by making bricks, and bringing river sand (for cement) and stone aggregates.[131] The agencies provided items such as cement, roof beams, roofing materials and window frames. In Awere P7, after the chairman of the school management and PTA received a letter from Red Barnet about building classrooms, the parents of 1,700 pupils came under pressure to make and lay bricks. They even made a by-law 'that if there is anybody who will refuse to work, then the office of Jago must come in together with the office of LCIII Odek'.[132] In a meeting of the PTA for Abaka Primary School (Palaro) the 93 parents present were asked to contribute 1,000 blocks each for the construction of the school,[133] a considerable in-kind contribution given that casual labourers were being paid Ush 50 per brick and that they had already cleared the site and started work on collecting the materials.

The shortage of structures and basic furniture such as chairs and desks was demonstrated when pupils returned to school in January 1999. They found that they could not re-start because both the buildings and the equipment were being used for the *mchaka-mchaka* (political education – see Part I). The closure of schools due to lack of sanitation has already been mentioned, and there were occasional closures due to insecurity.

Universal Primary Education (UPE)

Universal Primary Education, which in principle gave four children per household access to free primary education, was not as unqualified a success as was often claimed. In 2002 the Gulu District Education Officer noted that it had resulted in a doubling of class sizes from 50 to 100, and of overall enrolment from 70,000 to 140,000, with resultant shortfalls in classrooms (500 still needed), pit latrines, and teachers' housing, shortfalls which could only be met with donor support.[134]

Most fieldworkers felt that UPE had undermined Parent-Teacher-Associations' role of 'catering for the welfare of the students and teachers, promoting education, supporting cultural activities etc. which are at a minimum today because of poor co-ordination right from the grassroots'.[135] Parents were also said not to want to buy school uniforms, 'maybe [because] they think it should come from UPE. [In Odek] Only 3 out of 57 pupils paid for their mock exams (they cost Ush 1500 for four papers)'.[136]

Asked how Universal Primary Education (UPE) was being implemented, the fieldworker in Awach replied 'It is being implemented well. Many pupils joined school. Parents send pupils to school due to good cooperation with teachers through the organization from Uganda Government and materials for school reach for pupils'. However, 'the problem is the teachers; many are 'ghost' teachers. If you go, you find only 25–32 [out of 70 on the books] actually teaching'.[137] By March 2000 various schools were receiving Classroom Completion Grants intended to meet some of the deficit in classrooms resulting from increased enrolment.

UPE appeared unable though to address the issue of orphans whose parents died due to war or HIV/AIDS. Most camps had no clear figures. As one camp leader commented;

> It is difficult to tell the number of AIDS orphans as there is no programme for them here. Also people are very reluctant to admit to having AIDS, you can only guess due to slimness ... If at all they are there then the AIDS orphans are being looked after by

their relatives and kind friends as their guardians. To make the decision about who looks after which children, family members gather to discuss. Those with least children take more, and there might also be an attempt to address gender balance ... It is as well difficult to assess the number of orphan children with the case of their parents killed in the war. They are actually many in number.[138]

When taken into other households (generally of extended family), such children often fell outside the UPE's quota of four children per household. The Social Services and Economic Development Department of the Diocese of Gulu and Kitgum sponsored a small number of primary students,[139] but this was an under-researched area. The scope for organisations concerned with children's rights should have been considerable if the following description from Atiak is any indication:

> Some of these children when abducted don't come back, others join the rebels due to poor care for them, some join the Home guard. Some of these children suffer a lot because they hold their own house and when registration for food is done they are not registered. However, three households of such kids were registered for WFP.[140]

All the above suggests that UNOCHA's assertion that 'Access to universal free primary education has been one of the brightest successes of this period of displacement among the Acholi' (Weeks, 2002; 29), should be qualified, particularly when primary school drop-outs and teacher de-motivation are considered.

Drop-outs

The 4,799 enrolled in Pabo's displaced primary schools in 1998 represented approximately 25 per cent of 5–14-year-olds, even worse than WFP's 1999 report that less than 30 per cent of that age group were enrolled in full-time schooling (1999: 18). It was not just a question of enrolment, but also of how many dropped out (see Table 5.4.).

This shows, firstly, the falling off in enrolment in higher grades. In Palaro, first year primary students accounted for around 40 per cent of total enrolment, while those reaching P7 accounted for 4.5 per cent. In Odek the reduction is less extreme, but follows the same pattern – of 65 enrolled in P7 in March 1999, only 23 sat for Primary Leaving Exams on 2 November the same year. Secondly, it shows the male-female imbalance, with male students predominating in all years above P2.[142]

These snapshot figures are born out by the findings of a large scale quantitative survey conducted in 2001 by the International Organisation for Migration (IOM). This showed that primary completion rates were lower than the already low enrolment rates. Of 813 men and 677 women surveyed, IOM found that only 17.86 per cent of men and 16.14 per cent of women had completed primary school. 1.74 per cent of men and 0.68 of women had completed secondary. 0.38 per cent of men had achieved GCE/GCSE A-level, 0.13 per cent of women. No women had attended university, and only three of the 813 men.[143]

Of those taking Primary Leaving Exams in 1997, only 48 pupils achieved Division 1, a figure which declined to 26 in 1998.[144] In short, lack of access to edu-

Table 5.3 Primary School Enrolments in Palaro, Abaka, and Odek P7 Schools

	M	F	TOTAL	Year as % of total enrolment	Male as % of total by year
Palaro P7 School					
P1	119	157	276	42.7	43
P2	43	48	91	14.1	47
P3	47	31	78	12.1	60
P4	37	25	62	9.6	60
P5	35	24	59	9.1	59
P6	46	6	52	8.0	88
P7	25	4	29	4.5	86
	352	295	647	100	54
Abaka P7 School					
P1	68	40	108	39.3	63
P2	24	18	42	15.3	57
P3	30	15	45	16.4	67
P4	18	9	27	9.8	67
P5	14	13	27	9.8	52
P6	9	7	16	5.8	56
P7	10	0	10	3.6	100
	173	102	275	100	63
Odek P7 School					
P1	106	96	202	23.3	52
P2	77	88	165	19.1	47
P3	60	52	112	12.9	54
P4	60	60	120	13.9	50
P5	72	35	107	12.4	67
P6	58	37	95	11.0	61
P7	37	28	65	7.5	57
Total	407[141]	396	866	100	51

cation was perpetuating disadvantage across the board, as well as perpetuating gender inequalities. One fieldworker described the apathy of his three brothers aged under eighteen, all of whom had left school:

> They have lost interest completely. One was sent but left after one year, saying he would be late to marry (tradition is on his side as parents would want you to marry as many wives as possible).[145]

Teacher Motivation

In January 1999, following the Christmas vacations, the majority of Cwero's teachers failed to return to school, prompting the school management committee and parents to complain to the Chairman LCIII. He forwarded their message to the District Education Officer, who then threatened the errant teachers with dismissal unless they returned by 19 April (i.e. after missing a term).[146] Problems of teacher motivation were not unique to Cwero. In Odek the inspectors found teachers:

very reluctant in making schemes of work and lesson plans and many of them miss coming to school including the head-teacher of Odek P7 school. They then concluded by giving serious warning to teachers to improve on their duties for the well being of the pupils and they said they will frequent their inspection to schools this year.[147]

In a visit to Awere, the Minister for Education and Sport reportedly accused some headmasters of misusing UPE funds for drinking, and threatened that

> any Head teacher who will be caught misusing the UPE will be arrested and sued to Court. He advised the teachers to work very hard so that the standard of education must up-lift.[148]

Secondary Schooling

Whereas in each camp primary school students numbered in their hundreds if not thousands, secondary students were counted in dozens. In 1998 in Atiak there were 15 secondary school students, of whom 10 were studying in the adjacent districts of Adjumani and Moyo. Cwero had only 13 secondary school students, of whom eight were actually studying at the time of the report.[149] 30 of the 50 secondary level students from Awach were said to be studying.[150] By 2002 the Gulu District Education Officer estimated the overall enrolment in secondary schools (public and private) at about 5,000, compared to about 140,000 in primary schools.[151]

This was due in part to high drop out rates at primary level, but also to a dearth of opportunities for secondary studies in the rural areas. At one point or another, as a result of the conflict, and without direct orders from the district education office, all of the district's village secondary schools had been displaced into Gulu town.[152] For most this first happened in the late 1980s,[153] well before the establishment of the IDP camps. Some schools had suffered multiple displacements. Awach Senior Secondary School, for example, had moved site six times between 1988 and 2002. By 2002, only two secondary schools operated outside Gulu town. One was Pabo Secondary School (SS), which had re-opened in the protected village in 1998 and had 150 attending students (less than half of those enrolled were in a position to study, due to financial problems), the other was Keyo SS, which had re-opened in 2001 and had 23 students attending. All other secondary students wishing to study in Gulu district had to go to Gulu town. There they could join either the displaced state-controlled secondary schools, or, money permitting, one of twelve private secondary schools. These provided stiff competition for the state-run schools. As one headmaster of a private school said 'Obviously we play a very big role in the district. Without them the government headed schools cannot accommodate all of them. There is no expansion in their infrastructure'. This included establishing a 'school dependents' scheme, open to disadvantaged students from S1–S6. During their free time they do some work at the school, e.g. helping as worker's porters on construction during the vacations. In the headmaster's opinion 'This also sends a message that the school minds about children'.[154]

Conditions in boarding schools were basic. As one headmaster exclaimed; 'hostel? More like a real camp. Students carry foodstuffs from home, they pay money for grinding [of grains], cooking, firewood etc. There are currently 69 in the camp, all boys'.[155] In Awac Senior Secondary School, where over 50 per cent of the students (i.e. approx 100) came from Awac, the hostel for boys could accommodate 40. There was no provision for girls because 'there was no adult to look after them'. Pabo SS, with students from Pabo, Atiak and Lalogi, had no hostels. Most students stayed with relatives or in rented huts – often up to four sharing one hut.

In terms of feeding, the headmaster of Awac explained that the students normally brought 38kg of maize per term and 25kg of beans, and contributed Ush 11,000 to pay the attendant who cooked for them, as well as the cost of salt, onions, and firewood, noting that 'The fees are low because most of the parents are displaced'. In the case of neighbouring Lukome school, they had tried to provide feeding once, but most parents couldn't pay the extra Ush 30,000, so no food was being provided at the time of the research. As Pabo's headmaster noted, WFP had turned down requests to supply food for lunches in secondary schools. The students at St Joseph's Layibi were quite fortunate therefore:

> I wouldn't say it [the diet] is good, but we follow government recommendations, basically posho and beans. We give them meat twice weekly on Wednesday and Sunday, we give rice on Fridays. During harvesting time we add potatoes and cassava, some vegetables. Breakfast is maize porridge.[156]

In early 2002, as Operation Iron Fist was about to get under way, most displaced secondary schools were in the early stages of re-establishing a presence on their original sites. In some cases this involved re-building infrastructure prior to moving any students back: Atiak had been putting up a classroom block and workshop, but still had no windows, doors or floor. Awac SSS was constructing classrooms and latrines on its original site and in 2001 had put up two classroom blocks with help from GUSCO. Awere SS, along with Opit SS, Omoro Memorial SS and St Thomas SS benefited from a fund-raising event held on 27 November 1999 in Opit P7 School, organised by the Omoro County Development Association. The objectives of this were to raise funds for building eight science laboratory rooms, buying apparatus for the laboratories and thereby 'uplift the standard of practical science education in these 4 schools'. All people of Omoro County and other donors were expected to contribute, the head-teachers of the 56 primary schools in Omoro County were summoned to pay Ush 5,000 each. An estimated 2,500 people attended (including twenty-one MPs). Although certain key people such as the Resident District Commissioner were notable by their absence (this was taken as an indication that they viewed the event as multi-party rather than Movement), Ush 15-20 million was raised. By January 2000 rebuilding was well underway, with parents collecting building materials and preparing bricks.[157]

Koch Goma SS had also been re-constructing back in the village, again with

... the parents doing the construction. They have roofed, floored and plastered. We now need 3 more classes and one office to be roofed. We had planned to do S1 there this year but now it is impossible. The preparation was too delayed and there is renewed insecurity. We found it would be difficult for teachers and students to stay there'. Similarly, on 1 March 2002 the Lukome PTA chairman and his vice proposed that they go back to site, but the headmaster told them that it was still too risky.

It was not a decision to be taken lightly. Apart from refurbishment and re-building, the issue of security was far from resolved. Furthermore, the composition of the student body in each school had changed over the years, such that many students in a given school no longer originated from the home area of that school, and so would be unlikely to wish to move to that village should the school return. Similarly the teachers – in Lukome SS for example, only two of the thirteen teachers were from Lukome. As such it was logical to move back in stages, setting up a first year class only to begin with, while keeping their more senior classes in Gulu town.[158]

The problems facing schools which returned were significant. Pabo SS, with a catchment extending from Atiak to Lalogi and an enrolment of over 300 students, was located 2 miles from the centre. It lacked water (students brought it from over one mile away), classrooms, accommodation, and protection:

The soldiers promised protection and they are there at the site the whole day. However on 24 February rebels crossed the Gulu-Atiak road and fired some shots to scare the soldiers away. We have now sent a request to the 4th Division requesting for a small detach to be located there permanently.[159]

Keyo enrolled 20 students in 2001 and ended up with 15. In 2002 they had 10 pupils aged 14–18 in S1 (they had given admission letters to 16), and 13 aged 15–18 in S2 who were continuing from the previous year. There was only 1 girl in S1 and two in S2. As the headmaster explained, poverty was the major obstacle:

We have some very bright students but we are unable to push ahead. At times schools try to assist such students but they cannot go far. Sometimes they pay ½ fees, some-times they are given manual labour – for example two students built a kitchen and will not pay fees for one term.[160] There was also a suggestion made in a meeting of the PTA that if students could lay bricks they should be allowed to do so; none has responded so far. Students are also able to pay by instalments. A good number have paid a first instalment of Ush 35,000 plus the Ush 10,000 for feeding (normally the food is beans and posho).[161]

To stay in school required considerable levels of commitment. When we interviewed the 23 students of Keyo SS, they told us that they came to the Keyo site because it was near to their homes, allowing them to do domestic and agricultural work before school – 17 of the 23 had been digging earlier that morning. They also chose it for its relatively low fees of Ush 61,000. That said, only 2 of the 23 had paid the full amount, eight were paying by instalment. 13 of the 23 were raising their own school fees through planting rice and groundnuts, and quarrying stones. Five were paid for by parents/guardians. Four were not taking any lunch in order to save Ush 10,000 per term (approx £4.00 at that time).

The headmaster of St Joseph's College Layibi noted a marked shift in the composition of the student body: 'The problem now which needs research is that the majority of Acholi are from Kitgum and Pader, not Gulu. It has been the same for the last 2–3 years, possibly due to higher levels of displacement in Gulu. Also there are more functioning primary schools in Kitgum and Pader …'[162] The problem of girls dropping out of secondary school was dramatically illustrated in Pabo, where girls entered with worse scores than boys, before allegedly eloping with 'businessmen whom they don't end up marrying. So we get 30 girls entering S1 but only 5 finishing S4'.[163] All these factors suggest that displacement in the name of 'protection', which was far higher in Gulu than in Kitgum or Pader, was directly correlated with a violation of the right to education.

Part IV – Access to Health Care

Health service provision varied. In several camps some form of clinic was available (whether government-run dispensaries or NGO and church-supported clinics). Some had community based health workers, and in most there was a range of small 'drug shops' and traditional healers. One Community Health Worker I interviewed was selling Panado, Junior and Real Aspirin, disinfectant, Chloroquine injections for Malaria and Pneumonia (she could not afford to buy Quinine), Vermox and Mebendazole for intestinal parasites, Gentian Violet for fire burns, Metronizadole for diarrhoea, and Penicillin for chest pains. After her original stocks from the Ministry of Health were raided by the LRA the Ministry refused to replace them and she had to buy her own using money from her husband. She had very tiny amounts of each medicine.[164]

Awach with its population of over 10,000, had little more than an empty shell of a building with a couple of iron bed-frames in it (personal observation). Anaka had two clinics run by the Church of Uganda and the Catholic mission respectively, and numerous traditional healers. It also had a hospital boasting one resident doctor and a number of medical assistants in 1998. The hospital was in principle free of charge, though in some instances, for example the removal of a foetus from the womb of a woman who had committed suicide (see Chapter 6), they demanded exorbitant payment. Dental and sight problems were addressed through occasional visits by doctors from Gulu hospital. Pabbo, population of 42,000 plus, had one health centre providing drugs on an irregular basis, and five privately owned drug shops. Awer had an emergency dispensary established by the government. Awere had no clinic; immunisations by visiting health teams were the only health service provision.[165]

Those with acute conditions would, security situation and finances allowing, seek attention in the nearest hospitals. For some (e.g. Atiak) this meant travel to Adjumani, but for the majority it involved travel to Gulu – often strapped into a wicker chair tied to the back of a bicycle, or, if money allowed, by paying a passing vehicle to carry the sick person.

Standards of treatment varied dramatically between the 'free' government hospital in Gulu, and the mission-based St Mary's Hospital Lacor. The former was a run-down institution with poor facilities and staff seeking to supplement their salaries elsewhere. Doctors opened privately owned clinics in town, while nurses would siphon off some of the limited medical supplies for sale in the 'drug shops' in the villages. Lacor hospital, by contrast, had a very high standing nationally. After the conflict began in 1986 the hospital found difficulty keeping staff: by mid-1987 it had lost its senior staff and was left with the Superintendent, one other doctor and the founding couple. Most nursing staff had also left. They had since been able to recruit new doctors and nurses, but their average stay was just 1.5 years, making the development of services problematic. Nonetheless, by 1998 Lacor had 23 doctors and 460 beds, still insufficient for in-patients numbering around 650, with extra patients generally on mattresses on the floor. The hospital compound was full of relatives providing care and attention to in-patients. Further thousands slept in the compound every night in search of shelter from the LRA, on average some 4,000 'commuters' per night, along with about 3,000 permanently displaced who had established themselves in one corner of the compound following the Atiak massacre in 1995. The rebels entered the hospital quite frequently, with the Superintendent himself abducted for a week in 1989.[166]

For most people Lacor Hospital was expensive (though cheap relative to 'traditional healers'). Outpatient treatment for malaria cost Ush 500 for a child for the whole treatment, and at least Ush 2,000 for an adult. For those admitted as in-patients there was a standard bed-fee of around Ush 15,000, which covered bed and medical care.[167] The church-run clinics in Anaka charged Ush 200 for children and Ush 500 for adults, while in Awer the cost of treatments varied depending on the type of disease. The flat rate in Pabbo's clinics and drug shops for consultation and treatment was Ush 800 per head. In the drug shops an aspirin tablet cost Ush 10 per tablet and chloroquine cost Ush 20 per tablet. An injection in a drug shop for children cost Ush 250, but for an adult it cost Ush 500. For those going to Adjumani hospital a blood test cost Ush 500, stool test Ush 700, and x-ray Ush 5000.[168]

People obtained the necessary funds in a number of ways. In Pabbo 'people obtained [money] by selling firewood, wild okra, and hiring out their labour' (see Part II above for examples of casual labour), while in Awer it was said that 'Some sell foodstuffs given them by the World Food Program, others engage in local trading, i.e. buying essential commodities from town and taking it to the village. Others sell crops produced in their small plots within the camps'.

In addition to curative services, some camps had Community Based Health Workers trained by the District Medical Office in Gulu. Their primary roles included immunisation, education on issues of personal hygiene and environmental cleanliness, midwifery, and the sale of medications. In some places women were trained as Traditional Birth Attendants by the District Medical Office, with funding from UNICEF,[169] and in one instance the Family Planning Unit of Gulu Hospital ran a three weeks training for eight people (seven men, one woman) to distribute medication (the Pill) 'and to teach people the importance of family planning to make them not to run into problems of feeding and medical care'.[170]

Perhaps the most concrete preventive health interventions were the National Immunisation Days. For example, on 7 to 8 August 1999 and 25 to 26 September 1999, 5,700 children under the age of five were vaccinated for polio at seven centres in Anaka sub-county.[171] In Acet 2,048 were immunised, with the LC1 chairpersons responsible for the mobilisation of parents.

In late June 1999, when there was an outbreak of cholera in Biabia Elegu parish during which three people died, staff from the District Medical Office went to Atiak for two weeks starting on 24 June 1999. They closed down the school, brought tablets for treating drinking water (ten tablets to each household), and took specimens for laboratory analysis.[172]

Other problems such as river blindness were addressed through occasional visits from the District Medical Office and Ministry of Health officials.[173] There were also various public health 'education' or 'sensitisation' initiatives, such as the celebration of World AIDS Day in Anaka on 1 December in 1999, which involved some 3,500 people. Such events focused on the biological aspects of HIV transmission, rather than sociological and economic factors. Other health education initiatives bordered on the surreal: at a nutrition sensitisation workshop held on 30 November 1999 by Ministry of Health Nutrition Unit, and headed by a doctor from Entebbe, fifty-four community leaders from the six parishes in Pabo were told that kwashiorkor in children was a symptom of too much carbohydrate and too little protein. The message was that 'the target now is to feed our children on protein food and the diet must be well balanced. Child spacing was very much emphasised in the workshop since Pabbo is noted for early marriage which might lead to defilement and early breakage of marriage'. In light of most camp dwellers' economic circumstances and the clear relationship between camp life and malnutrition, this message seems particularly inappropriate. When combined with the message about child-spacing, it exemplified a wider tendency to blame the victims.

Infestations were dealt with in various ways. In early 1999 free-roaming pigs and goats were held responsible for an infestation of jiggers in Anaka. The fieldworker described the solution;

> On Saturday 24/4/1999 at about 1:34 P.M., I witnessed one mother pig hit with spears to death and her pork divided between north, east, south and west – to the loss of the owner of the pig who got no share at all. The pig had six youngsters in the womb. It had nearly harrowed off the germinating ground-nuts in the field of one hospital nurse here ... With such a tight rule on pigs and goats the camp looks clean. So you see that the authorities are fighting for health and sanitation.

In some places NGOs became involved in the delivery of basic services. World Vision, for example, delivered medicines to Acet village on a bi-monthly basis, but also worked on '(i) sanitation (ii) drug distribution to other dispensaries (iii) malnutrition cases (iv) latrine work shop and water quality protection'. Health messages and instructions were delivered in collaboration with local councillors. At a meeting called by World Vision, for example, the women's councillor for

Odek 'said if there is no latrine in the trading centre Acet, then the centre is going to be closed; even in the market places there must be latrine of nearly eight
doors. She added that government policy states that in the trading centres there
must be one latrine for each shop'.[174]

Abortion, which remains illegal in Uganda, was nonetheless a major health
issue. In September 1998, there were at least four attempts at abortion in Anaka.
One fifteen-year-old succeeded by taking 'a mug full of crushed cassava root
juice'. Another aborted after washing pesticide-treated bean seeds and drinking
the water. A third took over twenty chloroquine tablets; 'She aborted but she
almost lost her life. She was taken to Lacor hospital for treatment. On learning
that she had made an abortion, the doctors in Lacor fined her thirty thousand
shillings for attempting to lose her life and in addition she paid fifteen thousand
shillings for bed fee'. Another fifteen-year-old was not so lucky, and died after
an overdose of chloroquine.[175]

HIV/AIDS was addressed in diverse ways. Some urged the use of condoms.
The Officer in Charge of Awer detach, for example, used the opportunity of a
meeting about reducing the size of the camp 'to appeal to the parents to sensi-
tize their children on Aids awareness. He added that boys and girls should use
Life Guard or Protector [brand-names for condoms], should they have need for
sex with their opposite partner'. He appeared unaware that condoms were not
available in the camp, whether in the shops or clinic.[176] UNICEF sponsored a
programme of HIV/AIDS awareness raising known as PEARL (Programmes to
Enhance Adolescents' Reproductive Life), and ACORD was involved in distributing an HIV awareness publication 'Straight Talk' and the co-ordination of
HIV testing in Gulu district. The churches, by contrast, condemned the use of
condoms.

Most military wives we interviewed had very little education and awareness-
raising on HIV/AIDS – and even if they did, it did not help them much. Asked
whether they had ever been given any training about AIDS, they answered that
'No, only the soldiers were sensitised – and they don't pass on the information
to their women … If you as a wife insist on talking about HIV and AIDS, the
soldiers become angry and threaten to beat you up on account that they say you
are stopping them from loving your co-wife'. They also reported considerable
problems accessing medical treatment; particularly in the more remote rural detaches. Asked if they ever got blood tests, one woman in Gwengdia answered;
'Recently my husband told me that he was going for a blood test in town, but
ended up spending two nights with prostitutes in Kasubi – is that what is called
blood testing?'

The vacuum created by weak health services was partially filled by traditional
healers, who were popular but not legally recognised. As a result 'Their numbers
are not well established. They do not usually accept to be counted for fear of
being prosecuted'.[177] They used herbal remedies for physical symptoms such as
snake and scorpion bite, Buruli ulcer,[178] wounds, tetanus, dental diseases, nasal
bleeding, diarrhoea, headache, cough etc. They also addressed a major gap in
the 'modern' services;

They actually treat people affected with devil spirits, casting them off. They also treat barren ladies to bear children, [and do the] same to boys who fail in playing sex. If a boy is impotent he tells his parents (there is a belief that if a mother touches her new born son's private parts before he is more than three days old he will be impotent).[179]

In August 1998 Awere and Palaro had women healers only, Atiak had five women and three men, Cwero had eight women and only three men. Some felt this was changing, arguing that 'They used to be largely women, but with increasing poverty men are joining in'.[180] Certainly relative to the 'western' medical services the traditional healers could be very expensive – in 1998 the average cost in Anaka and Pabbo was from Ush 5,000 upwards. People found this money from a variety of sources, including 'selling the property they own, selling foodstuffs, chickens, and other produce from their fields. Some treatment hangs on credit ... hiring labour, selling firewood to the employees (teachers etc.) in the camp, and selling wild okra and spinach'.[181] Alternatively they paid in kind, as in Biabia and Atiak where payments ranged from '1 chicken to 1 cow'. Payment 'Depends on type of diseases. For example for dental cases you pay one chicken or Ush 1,500 , while Ghost cases are Ush 20,000–50,000'.[182]

In Awer, where there were about eight traditional healers, the cost was even higher:

Minimum cost is 15,000 Ush up to 50,000 Ush or even 100,000 USh. People pay this in terms of domestic animals like goats, sheep, pigs and chickens. Sometimes family members contribute the money from the various activities they do like farming, working for leja-leja for rich people. At times the people may fail to pay the amount demanded and for that reason may be detained at the traditional healer's place until the cost is met – or else they make you die.[183] Some people get money by making local beer.[184]

An important element of traditional medicine was that 'It is relatives who decide whether to take someone to the witchdoctor'. However, some clearly regarded 'witch doctors' as a major problem. Following the death of seven children under the age of ten in the Bibia Barracks, the Political Commissar [– liaising between UPDF and community] asked an ACORD fieldworker to sensitise the community on the need to take children to hospital rather than the witchdoctors in order to reduce child mortality.[185] Some Christians regarded the traditional healers as 'witchdoctors' (the LRA also had a prohibition against the use of witchdoctors), or accused them of being quacks, as suggested in the report of a healer in Gulu town 'who used even to say he had a cure for AIDS; you had to buy jerry cans full of a liquid he prepared. Of course if you died he said you hadn't been following his instructions correctly'.[186]

This brief overview of health-related activities indicates the paucity of free provision, the way this strengthened the market for traditional healers, and the accusatory tone of much of the public health education; minimalist assistance (e.g. provision of vent pipes for latrines) went hand in hand with implicit criticism. People with no access to resources were told that they were having sexual relations too young, not feeding their children a balanced diet, not planning their families well and having too many children they could not feed properly as a result. They were also told they should be building latrines immediately otherwise the government would close down their market place. Problems which were essentially related to a situation over which people had little control, were portrayed as issues of personal moral responsibility. Once again it seemed to be a case of blame the victim.

Part V – Access to Protection

The failings of the 'protected villages' in protecting people's access to subsistence opportunities, education and health services, might have been more excusable had their stated purpose, the physical protection of their inhabitants, been assured. But it was not. Rather than protecting people from physical violence the villages contributed to its generation, and, as the quotation from UNHCR's December 2006 protection report suggests, the supposed protectors were themselves often the violators. This paradox began with the phenomenon of 'protected barracks', in which the soldiers' quarters were often at the centre, surrounded on all sides by civilian huts. In Pabo, with a population of 42,000 plus, there was at one time a 'detach' of 1,500 soldiers. Gwengdia detach near Awac (population 13,613 in early 1998[187]) had at least 800 soldiers. In many camps, though, the numbers were far smaller, with Home-guards and Local Defence Units providing reinforcement.

In Awere there were some 120 Home-guards:

> About 15 of them are known to be former rebels. They are good fighters. If a rebel reports to the barracks and says he wants to be a Home guard, there is a local arrangement with the Intelligence Officer and Commanding Officer that they receive the salaries of other soldiers who have been killed but are still on the payroll'.[188]

As such some people were being simultaneously being demonised as perpetrators of atrocities and being made responsible for providing protection from such atrocities.

Although there were reports of truck-loads of youth arriving from Adjumani district too,[189] the majority of Home-guards were local youth, recruited both voluntarily and by force. In Awer in September 1998, people were first requested to join the Home guard. 'Later on, the message was left with the LCs to recruit people forcefully into Home-guards so that they could be trained to become soldiers … Some boys on seeing that they were being pressurised, decided to join the Home-guards voluntarily …'[190]

From Atiak it was reported how

> … at first the Government said they needed 10-20 people from each parish to be Home-guards. They worked for 1–2 years then were changed to Local Defence Units. From LDUs they were changed to UPDF. This month they are training more Home-guards as old ones are now UPDF/LDU. They want 80 from each sub-county, aged 18–30. To get these they divide by the number of parishes. In Atiak there are eight parishes, therefore each should give 10 people. The recent recruitment drive asked for those who were willing. The previous time you were forcibly collected and then screened. This time you register with the LC1, get sent to the LC3, then go for training. Payment

for food allowance is 35,000 every two weeks, i.e. 70,000/month, but it is not regular, that is why they sometimes misbehave.[191]

In Palaro the UPDF were stationed some 4km away, and in the camp there was a group of about one hundred Home-guards who had been recruited in the area:

This started in 1989 with forcible recruitment. These Home-guards stay in their barracks during the day and sometimes guard the inlet roads at night. When LRA movement is reported, they go to the area and sometimes follow them. But in many cases if the rebels raided villages for food and so on at night, the people of the village have to persevere or are on their own until morning when the government come in. These soldiers get very little posho after many months. Mainly they rely on their salaries/wages which are not punctual. As they are children of the area they also get relief supplies from WFP, and the camp leader collects food for them. I have also seen plots around their barracks; it seems they have started self-help projects to generate food. These soldiers have not been trained (they get two weeks training). As such their mood or characters change with the situation. Sometimes they are not appealing, sometimes they co-operate with the people.[192]

Given divided loyalties, forcible recruitment, and poor levels of training and equipment, the Home-guards' unwillingness to put themselves at risk was understandable. There were consistent reports of the UPDF and Home-guards/LDUs failing to respond to LRA raids. It was common practice for the UPDF to respond only hours after first being alerted to the presence of the LRA, by which time they were long gone. Following an LRA attack on the edge of Gulu town on 8 August 1998, for example, LCs who went to alert the UPDF soldiers stationed a few hundred metres away were threatened with being beaten up if they did not go away. The soldiers eventually arrived some four hours after the rebels had already left. UNOCHA similarly reported that 'Residents consistently complain that when they are under attack, the military detachments in the adjacent barracks fail to respond effectively or in a timely manner, and that these units (many of which are in fact under-paid and under-trained Local Defence Units, not regular UPDF troops) are in fact themselves often the source of violence and criminality' (Weeks, 2002: 18).

Response depended on the nature of the military forces; mobile forces were thought better: 'those who are stationed in the barracks they just say they are waiting from their side only'.[193] When the threat level to soldiers was low, as when a lone rebel called Lutip was discovered trying to visit his mother in Acet camp, the response was robust: He had already looted one goat and obliged someone to cook it for him, when

… one of the villagers who knows him very well rushed to the camp and tipped off the army at the detach. The army rushed to the place and found him seated outside waiting for the food to get ready. Sensing danger he fled away into the bush, all attempts to shoot him by the army were fruitless. Instead only the chair on which he was sitting was destroyed by the bullets. The army did not disturb the person in whose home the food was being cooked.[194]

Often there were simply inadequate numbers, obliging the UPDF to ask people to move closer and closer together, as noted above. The LRA made a point of highlighting the lack of UPDF reaction to them. On 1 January 2000 they invaded

Awer and let villagers know 'that Awer is a good place because it did not give them any difficulty. There are no soldiers who could chase them away for that reason they will come back for a second time'.[195]

These failures of military protection had high costs for civilians. Gersony was certain that 'the LRA has shot, knifed, hacked and bludgeoned to death thousands of unarmed Acholi civilians during the past two years in the absence of armed persons, opposition or challenge of any kind' (Gersony, 1997: 44). In Atiak in mid-1998 the LRA were said to 'raid people mostly three or four times a week. It depends on the insecurity of the week.' Raids often followed directly on the delivery of food relief by WFP, but could also involve far more than looting of foodstuffs. At midnight on the 14 February 2000, for example, 'L.R.A really attacked Pabbo camp ... whereby six innocent people were killed, including one soldier. One soldier was abducted alive and was still in captivity. 41 huts were burnt leaving 210 people homeless'.[196]

Constant pleadings of insufficient manpower were difficult to understand in the face of evident militarization, forcible recruitment of Home-guards, and military adventures in the DRC. It was also frustrating for civilians to feel that they were supporting a force that did not do its job. When the LRA infiltrated Otuke county, Lira district, 'The unhappy people complained to the *Sunday Monitor* that on several occasions they have alerted the UPDF of rebel presence but have instead been rewarded by a slow reaction. "They wait until the rebels have gone then they go and eat our chicken", they said'.[197]

The petty spoils of war extended beyond livestock:

> ... undiscriminating cutting down of mature trees by the UPDF/Home-guards had arose bitter feelings on the camp population since they were doing it without even consulting the landlords [with whom] ownership of those trees rested. Secondly, the forest department in town were not aware business of timber is being carried out by the army. But then there was also fear on the Camp population to come openly and criticise the behaviour of the army.[198]

There were also reports that UPDF soldiers in Gulu had earned money hiring out guns to thugs to rob civilians with.[199] To add insult to injury, civilians were often the victims of UPDF violence, making them feel caught between Government and LRA. When one 29-year-old man went 4km outside Palaro camp to collect materials for his hut, Government soldiers mistook him for a rebel: 'They fired at him causing serious injuries on his left hand. He has been taken to Gulu hospital. People are now in a fearful state about any encounter with both UPDF and rebel soldiers'.[200] People travelling by road were often stopped by UPDF soldiers and forced to conduct manual labour along the roadside, clearing high grass and cutting down trees, sometimes several times on one journey.[201]

There were innumerable accounts of rape by soldiers. In Awach in July 1998, for example, after three women were raped

> The first culprit was sent to Gulu police but they dropped the case. In the second case the soldier grabbed the woman while she was making beer at night. The soldier was collected by the mobile unit. He has not been seen again, though the case was sent to their boss. The third case was a 45–50 year old woman, living alone. The soldier came,

arrested her and raped her in her room. She made an alarm, but the soldier escaped without identification.

The respondent argued that

This issue [of rape] will not finish in our area because of women selling beers to soldiers at their times, not following home regulations. In addition to that we have young boys who have interest to drink, but no money. Soldiers give them money to look for a girl for them. Failing to do this he [the boy] is just appointed a woman immediately [i.e. the boy is used for sexual purposes]. Un-understandable.[202]

Often action was only taken when it became clear that important people were giving attention to the case. In the case of a girl aged twelve, who was raped at night by a Home guard and managed to pick him out in an identity parade the next day, the soldier concerned was stripped of his uniform and gun and detained for a day. It was only when a councillor arrived from town to conduct some training and took up the case that the man was taken to the police and charged.[203]

Some individual commanders evidently terrorised the local community. At one point in Palaro, 'the commander of the local defence unit ... widely known as Lotoo-Ngang ('Many Deaths'), had been pursuing his duties all along his days. Unfortunately, what he was doing was contrary to the authority conferred to him'. His actions included taking the salaries of Home Guard deserters and leaving them only with a token amount, using re-captured deserters to work the ten-acre farm he established near the barracks, and authorising individual civilians 'to kill domestic animals which went [strayed] into his farm – a source of meat for him. I was told he killed more than 70 head of sheep, cattle, etc.' Eventually 'All these evidents and many others including rape and defilements were cases reported against him and some of his juniors. Now he has been transferred with his best supporter'.[204] Transferring soldiers away from the scene of their crimes rather than any kind of judicial process seemed to be the army's way of dealing with such cases.

When Was the LRA the UPDF?

Against this back-drop of UPDF violence, it was not always clear that the LRA really was the chief protagonist in any given incident. It was not uncommon for people in protected villages to claim that they were raided by Government soldiers in rebel disguise. This was already a problem in the late 1980s. Behrend writes how in 1989, 'Especially at night, 'rebels', militiamen, and government soldiers moved about in small groups plundering farms. Since they all wore the same uniforms, one could never be sure who the plunderers were' (Behrend, 1999: 7).

In one account of the 1995 Atiak massacre, an incident in which a minimum of 200 people were killed, the leader, a former NRA soldier who had been retrenched in 1992:

joined the Home Guard but collaborating with his brother who was in the LRA. They agreed to kill the commander of the Home Guard, who used to be his friend but had become more successful career-wise. At five A.M., when the rebels came to attack

Atiak, he went to meet them. Before that he told his other brother (who was also a Home guard) to leave the barracks.[205]

In another incident a Home guard from Odek detach took his gun and returned home

> where he joined up with Okot to rob people. Okot had been an LRA but escaped and returned to their home and didn't report to World Vision trauma centre. So the habit of robbery still sounded nice for him as he used to do that under the leadership of L.R.A. Commanders.

This pair proceeded to rob clothes and money, to rape a woman who had given birth two weeks earlier, and shot one man in his left upper arm, breaking the bone.[206]

The blurring of identities was often down to individual initiative: 'On the 12/07/98 at Awer camp in the night at around 11.30 a government army soldier came and entered the camp in the name of the LRA, well armed, demanding for money from those he found'.[207]

The government position, as stated by the Minister for Northern Uganda at the ACORD peace conference, was that;

> It has never been government policy to harass civilians – any cases have been due to the indiscipline of individuals and should always be reported to the authorities. The military and security forces must stay within the law and observe human rights. The government is striving to improve, (it should be recognised that we started from a position of complete chaos) and we commit ourselves to ensuring that the changes will be real.[208]

In one incident where soldiers had beaten up villagers and burned down sixteen houses after one of their colleagues was killed in a bar brawl, the Fourth Division Commander offered himself to be beaten by the affected villagers, saying: "What I want you to understand and accept is that the acts of the soldiers was on their individual capacities but not that it is a UPDF policy to cause destruction to civilian property".[209] Somewhat paradoxically, by offering himself to be beaten, he was in a sense accepting responsibility for what had happened – and almost certainly relying on the fact that nobody would dare to beat him for fear of subsequent retributions.

It was not always a matter of individual responsibility. Often commanders themselves appeared to be involved in passing their troops off as LRA rebels. One respondent described how people were disturbed by 'poor administration of UPDF commanders who use the soldiers to behave as LRA'. He went on to specify that this included 'beating people' and 'robbing food stuff during the night and day time. For example on 24/07/98 they came to Pupwonya side of the camp and looted hens, ducks, goats and posho given by WFP, plates, saucepans for cooking, raping girls etc. This was under the command of Captain O. from Palukere Barracks (Home-guards)'. In this particular instance action was taken and 'He was sued in LC3 court. He had no clear explanation, but people attributed it to irregular salaries. Their detach was very small and far from Atiak trading centre. His rank was stripped, he was transferred to Patiko, also obliged to pay back to those he stole from'. Further problems included 'road-blocks on the road, taking civilian bicycles for their own moving, without compensation for the bicycle. When you try to resist you will either be beaten seriously or given gun fire around you.' The respondent noted that 'All these problems were forwarded for consultation in the LCIII office. When he called for the army official to come for security meeting, [he] refused to meet the civilian population'.[210]

When civilians in Awer questioned the order to move their houses closer to the detach, the Officer in Charge warned them that 'people must know that they [the UPDF] can change themselves under the umbrella of the rebels and then kill the civilians and no-one will be in a position to distinguish whether that act was done by the government soldiers or the rebels'. His intimidation worked: 'From that time many more people are being displaced. People have started erecting shelters for themselves in the new marked areas'.[211]

Accusations that some attacks which were blamed on the LRA were in fact perpetrated by the UPDF occasionally received press coverage. On 28 February 1998, *The Monitor* ran an article under the title 'UPDF, Not LRA Rebels Ambushed Gulu Bus.' This was later refuted by the UPDF Public Relations Officer, prompting an editorial comment that

> the fact that the ambush took place only 300 meters from a major UPDF detach doesn't help the army's case. This is not the first time the army has been blamed for attacks on civilians in the North, where it is supposed to be battling rebel Joseph Kony's Lord's Resistance Army (LRA) and protecting the people. Numerous times, the UPDF and its officers have been accused of carrying out acts of retaliation against suspected rebel accomplices, and for attacking civilian settlements.[212]

An opinion piece the following day argued that 'it will remain very hard to deny the possibility that disgruntled elements in uniform are engaged in crimes against humanity up north ...'[213]

With soldiers both failing to provide protection and involved in much of the day-to-day violence themselves, there was constant tension between civilians and military. When a soldier in a local disco in Awer was hit by a stone he shot his gun in the air and the disco was closed down.[214] When Home-guards shot their guns into the air to scare the birds from their newly sown seeds 'people again imagined rebel invasions'.[215] When a house was burgled in Paromo village and residents argued that boot-prints found in the compound indicated that soldiers might have been responsible 'the soldiers rejected completely these claims and warned the civilians never to continue with making those statements otherwise the end result would be worse. This gave a lot of fear to both civilians and the Local Councillor making everything come to a stop'.[216]

At times tensions exploded:

> On the 9 October 1999 at Olwal [located 22 km northwest of Gulu Town] five people died and eight others were injured ... when a Home guard sprayed bullets when the youth were for Aguma dance celebrating Uganda's independence anniversary day ... The Home Guard who sprayed the bullets was not found. He escaped and up to date nobody knows where he is. He is a man from Atiak. The reason [he] sprayed bullets at people was that he quarrelled with one civilian – a resident of the camp ... because

he wanted the wife of that civilian man. After he was fought, he ran to the barracks and collected a gun.

As the profile of the northern Uganda situation increased, so too did steps to be seen to be doing something about failures of protection. In June 2004 two detach commanders in Apac and Kitgum districts faced court martial 'for failing to protect the lives of civilians in displaced people's camps'.[217] In many respects, however, such steps were too little too late.

People's Responses

One response to the lack of protection was to obey the commands to move closer to the military.[218] Another was to sleep in the bush surrounding the camps in temporary hideouts known as *alup*. Each household kept the locations of its *alups* secret and alternated between them frequently. When I began fieldwork in mid-1998, most of the fieldworkers were sleeping in the bush with varying degrees of frequency. The fieldworker in Atiak reported:

> I slept in the bush three times in July when the rebels came and abducted some people to carry some food stuff. I did not leave any person [of my family] sleeping [in our house] ... When it is insecure every time/day you have to sleep in the bush. It is agreed by the camp residents that whenever you hear about rebels you have to notify others even during night-time, this process continues all through the camp. We use a different route to our shelters every time. They are very small. Some people just have polythene sheets.[219]

In Odek it was worse; the fieldworker had slept in the bush 'throughout last month [July], leaving nobody sleeping in the camp. We shift every two days. Only the family knows where the place is. We go about 10 P.M., all at once, taking only a bed sheet and papyrus mat'.[220] This movement did not reflect unreasonable paranoia – the fieldworker's four brothers, two sisters and two nephews had all been abducted in June that year (see Chapter 2). In neighbouring Awere the fieldworker had slept in the bush twenty nights of the month preceding his report. It was not, however, without risks: 'because when you are got [i.e. if you are found] either you are abducted, beaten or killed'.[221] In Palaro 'The camp residents normally prefer sleeping away from the camp for fear of being attacked or abducted by rebels'.

It was not just the threat of abduction by the LRA: 'boys in the camp have resorted to sleeping in the bush at night in order as to avoid the forceful recruitment in to Home-guards by the UPDF. Thus both government and the rebels are now a threat to the camp population particularly the youth'.[222]

People's responses to ongoing violation did not generally include any form of organised protest, a point which is returned to in Chapter 6.

Discussion and Conclusions

Regardless of who did what in the mid-1980s, and of whether the Government had a retributive ethos, the objective and sustained reality of life in the camps appeared to many a clear indicator of the Government's present and ongoing lack of commitment to protecting the rights and interests of the civilian population. For from the day they were initiated in the name of protecting the civilian population, these villages instead became sites of their abuse, and this did not change over the course of the following ten years.

The process of forming the protected villages through the fusion of dozens of villages into single units, reversed the fundamental principle of Acholi settlement patterns described by Girling (1960: 56–57), namely that of fission, the splitting off of sub-units from a village to go and establish new ones as a means of dealing with 'a fundamental tendency for a state of imbalance to be set up in the village' (e.g. resulting from population growth or competition over resources). When people's subsequent lack of access to livelihoods, education and health services is considered, it is clear that their enjoyment of rights in all these areas was severely curtailed. This could not be excused on the basis that the camps did at least guarantee physical security, because they did not do that either, at least not to any meaningful or consistent degree. All domains of peoples' lives were characterised by an extreme lack of certainty. Food aid was sporadic and the amounts given fluctuated, schools came and went. Messages from Government were inconsistent, and authority structures were multiple, such that lines of authority and accountability were unclear. Instances of this included parallel justice systems and different relief service providers using completely different registration mechanisms.

In fact, the 'protected villages' violated all major categories of rights, and just about all the UN's 'Guiding Principles on Internal Displacement'. UNOCHA argued that they were established without due consultation with the people affected (which violated Guiding Principle 7.3), lasted longer than required (Principle 6), failed to recognise peoples' dependency on their land (9), failed to achieve basic standards of living in terms of shelter, water, food, sanitation, clothing, medical care (18, 19), and infringed on the right 'to move freely in and out of camps or other settlements' (14). Furthermore, people had not been protected against 'rape, mutilation, torture, inhuman or degrading treatment or punishment and other outrages upon personal dignity, such as acts of gender-specific violence, forced prostitution or any form of indecent assault' (11), their properties had largely been destroyed or looted (21), and they remained liable to attack by the UPDF under suspicion of being LRA (10.2) (Weeks, 2002: 22–25).

This policy which failed to protect, and which was implemented by representatives of the state who were themselves active perpetrators – the picture, in short, of protection as violation – escaped close international scrutiny. Veiled by pressing humanitarian needs and the more self-evident atrocities attributed to the LRA, it was possible for the political nature of the almost total disregard of people's rights as citizens, and the insidious consequences of this disregard, to be consistently downplayed in national and international coverage of the situation. Yet once 'protection' is recognised as violation, this fundamentally alters the parameters within which to analyse the situation in northern Uganda. From one in which LRA atrocities are taken as the beginning and end of the problem, the

Government's violations move to centre stage. Not only did people live with fear of abduction from the LRA, but they lived with fear of the lack of a future.

It is not a simple matter of comparing like with like, of arguing that looked at quantitatively the picture of violations is far less one-sided than it is generally presented. It is even more serious than that. The violations perpetrated by the civilians' supposed protectors are double violations, insofar as the act of violation, when perpetrated by a supposed protector, is also a violation of the duty to protect. In some important senses these double violations are liable to have even more disastrous social and psychological impact than the ones perpetrated by a clearly identified enemy, for they breach a relationship of trust which is cardinal to a healthy society. In abusing persons who, by the very nature of the contract between state and civilian, have subordinated themselves to the power of the state for the purposes of physical security, the impact of the abuse is multiplied, particularly as the victims are generally silenced as a result of their powerlessness. To the extent that the perpetrators are drawn from the local population (as were members of the Home-guards, Local Defence Units and some UPDF) it becomes a triple-violation in that people are turned against their own.

. In this respect, violations perpetrated by the state are akin to those perpetrated within a family. When rape is incestuous it can be more damaging to the victim than rape by a stranger, as the perpetrator is the very person whom the victim would usually turn to for support and solace. In incest there is no-one left to turn to. The victim is often dependent on the perpetrator and therefore in no position to report the perpetrator (even supposing someone were prepared to listen). The violation is frequently submerged in silence. Similarly when a soldier rapes a civilian in a highly militarized zone, the victim is left with no channels through which to pursue accountability, justice, or redress – particularly where the army carries as much political weight as in northern Uganda, and where those who should be prepared to listen are not.

To make matters worse, President Museveni, the person best placed to call the perpetrators to account, was himself, as Commander-in-Chief, part of the institution from which the perpetrators emerged. When the personalisation of politics in Uganda is considered, in which individuals such as the President assume a disproportionately important role akin to that of a father-figure in the popular imagination, then the fact of being violated by one or more representatives of the institutions which are an extension of this figure's power does indeed seem analogous to a form of incest. If on top of this, those representatives are co-opted from the victim's own clan or ethnic group, as was generally the case with Home-guards and some members of the UPDF, then the incestuous nature of the act, and its psychological consequences for the victim and society/community, are further aggravated.

Protection as violation is not without political repercussions. IOM argued that;

> while the government's efforts in deploying soldiers in Northern Uganda may have been done in good faith, the people's 'protector', the UPDF, is instead perceived to be causing more harm than good. The popular opinion is that with soldiers being rela-

tively rich they have used this position to lure young girls into sex, break up families by seducing poor desperate women and then harassing the husbands. This is an important stumbling block in the peace process as these actions malign the well-intentioned government intervention.[223]

As UNOCHA noted, 'The sense of alienation from the central government is already very high'. Echoing Behrend's portrayal of Gulu as 'a city 'occupied' by the NRA' UNOCHA continued that 'The UPDF has in many ways comported itself as an occupying force in hostile territory' (Weeks, 2002: 12). While UNOCHA was not categorical that the protected villages had violated principle 6 ('The prohibition of arbitrary displacement includes displacement (a) when based on policies of apartheid, 'ethnic cleansing' or similar practice ... (e) when it is used as collective punishment'), neither did it wholly exclude the possibility. Instead it noted that 'it will be important for the government of Uganda to require a high level of accountability from its civilian and military officials, to ensure that matters of ethnicity do not *per se* impinge on decision-making regarding the Acholi displaced' (Weeks, 2002: 29).

Coming in 2002, this latter recommendation could not undo years of damage to individual and collective psyches in northern Uganda. The Government's failure to deal with the high levels of impunity enjoyed by the UPDF seemed to many people in northern Uganda to be an implicit authorisation of that abuse, further proof that the Government shared in the devaluation of the Acholi. In terms of the political stability of the area the impact of the double and triple violations which took place under the guise of protection was in this regard graver than the atrocities of the LRA. It was an entirely logical (though not necessarily correct) step for people to conclude that the Government's intentions were dark, if not genocidal. This was simply and starkly captured by a youth who, at a youth conference held in Gulu district, argued, 'we live by chance, die by design'.[224]

Notes

1. I alternate between referring to them as 'protected villages' and as 'camps'. Although 'protected villages' is such a clear misnomer that to use it risks making a mockery of people's experiences, this ambiguity is part of their reality. This diverges from Amnesty International's decision to use the term 'camps' in an attempt to minimise the political connotations associated with the alternatives (see Amnesty International 1999: 13).
2. UNOCHA used these figures in its 1999 *Consolidated Appeal.*
3. UNHCU 14 July 2000.
4. FEWS 8 August 2002.
5. All these figures have to be treated as indicative rather than absolute. The last census in the north was conducted in 1991. Even the figures of WFP, which keeps some record from its food distributions, fluctuate month by month.
6. WFP, 12 March 2002, *WFP Operations in Gulu District, Northern Uganda,* p.4.
7. ARLPI, *An Overview of the Situation in Acholiland,* January 2003.
8. IRIN, 14 March 2003.
9. NRC figures were 47,170 for 2000 (Cited in ARLPI, July 2001, p28).

10. August 1998 pilot, Cwero.
11. Gulu market, January 1999.
12. One contribution to this was Els de Temmerman's book, *Aboke Girls,* published in 2001 and translated into dozens of foreign languages.
13. Our findings were consistent with those of Amnesty International (1999), Human Rights Focus (February 2002, p18–23), and ARLPI (July 2001, p7) all of which documented methods of forcible displacement including beatings, burning down homes, shelling villages, shooting and raping.
14. Awere pilot, August 1998.
15. Armoured personnel carrier manufactured in South Africa, infamous for its use by the SADF during the apartheid era.
16. Odek Pilot, 1998.
17. Cwero Pilot, August 1998.
18. Atiak Pilot, August 1998.
19. Interview with elder, Gulu 4 August 1998.
20. Anaka Pilot, August 1998.
21. Awer, August 1998.
22. Visit to Awer, 17 December 1998.
23. Idem..
24. Odek, 14 December 1998.
25. Palaro, 20 January 2000.
26. I confirmed this during a field visit to Palaro, 27 December 1999.
27. Pagak, January 2000.
28. Atiak, August 1998.
29. Mendes, April 1998.
30. Girling still records these as a major feature of Acholi compounds in the 1950s (Girling 1960; 45).
31. 26 March 2000.
32. IRIN, 30 June 2004, *6,000 IDPs Homeless After Fire Guts Pabbo Camp.*
33. PANA, 23 March 2000, *Uganda Gets Multi-Million Dollar Food Aid Programme.* ARLPI, July 2001, p27.
34. Pabbo, August 1998.
35. Girling describes the Rwodi Kweri themselves as a spontaneous innovation in response to the scattering of kin groups under British Administration in the 1920s and 1930s (Girling 1960: 193).
36. Cwero Pilot, August 1998.
37. Atiak, August 1998.
38. Pabbo, 7 April 1999.
39. Pabbo, 11 December 1999.
40. Pabbo, 10 March 2000. For further discussion of perceptions of Local Councils in the camps, see Finnström, 2003: 129.
41. *UNOCHA Humanitarian Update – Uganda, January 2002,* Vol. IV issue I.
42. Awere, 17 January 1999.
43. Awer, 20 November 1999.
44. Atiak, October – November 1998.
45. http://hrw.org/reports/1999/uganda/Uganweb-02.htm
46. Interview with secondary school teachers, Gulu High School, 13 August 1998.
47. Pabbo report, 1 March 1999.
48. Cwero, March 2000.
49. Pabbo, 3 August 1999.
50. Gulu Municipality, December 1998.
51. Monthly camp reports, 1999–2000. Prices were checked in camp markets every third month. Fluctuations in price were by area and season. Inflation was very low over the period the data was collected.

52. The lower value is the lower number of sacks per acre by the lower price obtainable per bag. The higher value is the higher number of sacks per acre by the highest cost per bag.
53. Atiak, 11 May 1999.
54. By May 1999 it cost Ush 2000 for a litre in Palaro.
55. Odek, 28 February 1999.
56. See also Gulu District Development Plan, 1996/97.
57. Idem, section 6.1.1. p 50.
58. Awer Pilot, August 1998.
59. *Conflict and Means of Livelihoods* research, 1999, also ACORD, February 2001, p 11.
60. www.idpproject.org: 'Profile of Internal Displacement: Uganda', 11 October 2002, p 78.
61. Pabbo, 2 September 1999.
62. Medical Superintendent, Lacor Hospital, 19 January 1998.
63. AVSI figures for the period July 1998 to December 2001, 8 March 2002.
64. Estimates vary widely; WFP quotes a UNICEF figure of 40,000 for 1988-1999, and an ICRC figure of 4,000 amputees for the same period (WFP, 1999: 10).
65. Atiak pilot, August 1998. For discussion of landmines as symbols of the global character of the war see Finnström, 2003: 274.
66. Awere, 20 February 2000.
67. Atiak and Biabia pilots, August 1998.
68. Girling describes how a man 'attains his maximum status...when he takes part in the hunting ... This was also an affirmation of his adulthood' (Girling, 1960: 161).
69. Awer Camp, 3 August 1998.
70. Anaka, 9 August 1999.
71. Anaka, 18 April 1999.
72. Awac, 24 December 1999.
73. Pabbo, 2 April 1999.
74. Anaka, 10 July 1999 – Source LCIII office. (An example of the clash of authority systems)
75. UNDMT Technical Group Status Report – undated, early 2002.
76. Palaro Pilot, 30 July 1998.
77. Visit to Gulu, January 1998.
78. Pabbo Pilot, 30 July 1998.
79. Awac Pilot, August 1998.
80. Awere, 27 April 1999.
81. Visit to Coo-pe Kwene, in January 1998.
82. Atiak, 14 November 1998.
83. Atiak, August 1998.
84. Odek, 14 December 1998.
85. Pabbo, 30 October 1998.
86. Anaka, June 1999.
87. Palaro Pilot, 30 July 1998.
88. Palaro, 28 February 1999.
89. Awer, July 1998.
90. Awere Pilot, 28 July 1998.
91. Pabbo, 1 June 1999.
92. Atiak, 22 December 1998.
93. Palaro, May 1999.
94. Pabbo, 4 November 1999.
95. Palaro, 1 May 1999.
96. Palaro, 1 April 1998.
97. Pabbo, 1 June 1999.
98. Palaro, 1 September 1999.
99. Odek, 14 December 1998

100. CRS also made distributions (Awer, 31 August 1999).
101. Cwero, December 1998, Awer, December 1998.
102. Awer, June 1998.
103. Atiak, 30 March 1999.
104. Atiak, 11 May 1999.
105. Odek, 3 July 1999.
106. Awer, 25 August 1999.
107. Palaro, 8 November 1999.
108. IOM, 2001, section 2.1.8.1.
109. ARLPI, July 2001, p22.
110. UNDMT *Technical Group Status Report: Preparatory Planning for Displaced Persons,* undated (but late 2001/early 2002).
111. It was widely believed that the Ebola virus had been brought back from Congo by UPDF soldiers taken there to fight Kabila's forces.
112. Justice and Peace chronology, December 2001.
113. *Standard Operating Procedures for IDP Camp Decongestion* – undated
114. Personal observation during visit to Kitgum district, August 2006
115. UNHCR, *Assessment of IDP Movement/Return and Protection Concerns,* December 2006
116. In a discussion with youth in Gulu, 6 June 1998, I was told that the reserve forces, under Salim Saleh, were troops who had been 'demobilised' in the period 1992 to 1995 but had since been recalled to duty and were now said to be 'the ones manning the posts in the protected villages, while the 'real' UPDF are seated in the barracks doing business and collecting war bonuses'.
117. Atiak, 30 March 1999.
118. See also ARLPI, July 2001, p8.
119. Pabbo, 12 April 1999.
120. Pabbo, 17 May 1999.
121. Various camp reports (COPE).
122. For discussion of other initiatives involving Salim Saleh see Finnström, 2003: 238.
123. Atoo Hills, 22 January 1994.
124. Awach pilot, August 1998.
125. Workshop on Primary Education organised by the Ministry of Education. Report from a participant (Cwero).
126. Awach pilot, August 1998.
127. Cwero pilot, August 1998.
128. Parabongo (728 pupils, 7 teachers), Jimo (568 pupils, 8 teachers).
129. Pagak school (987 pupils, 19 teachers), Kaladima (434 pupils, 8 teachers).
130. Awer, 10 October 1998.
131. Pabbo, September 1999.
132. Awere, 26 October 1999.
133. Palaro, 13 November 1999.
134. Gulu, 6 March 02.
135. Palaro Pilot, 30 July 1998.
136. Odek field notes, July 1998.
137. Awach Pilot, August 1998.
138. Cwero, August 1998.
139. Diocesan Aids Prevention Officer, Gulu, 20 January 1998.
140. Atiak, August 1998.
141. Pupil headcount organised by the Ministry of Education and Sports from 22 to 27 March 1999.
142. The national figure for P1-7 enrolment in 2001 was 3,334,402 males (51.14 per cent) and 3,185,141 females (48.8 per cent) www.education.go.ug/Factfile_2001.htm
143. IOM, 2001, table 6.

144. 1998 Workshop on Primary Education organised by the Ministry of Education. Report from a participant (Cwero).
145. Odek Field notes, July 1998.
146. Cwero, 19 April 1999.
147. Odek, 24 June 1999.
148. Awere, 1 October 1999.
149. Cwero pilot, August 1998.
150. Awach pilot, August 1998.
151. District Education Officer, 6 March 2002.
152. Education Officer in charge of Sport, Gulu District, 4 March 2002.
153. Awac, Awere, Atiak Technical College etc.
154. Headmaster, Gulu Central High School, Gulu town, 6 March 2002.
155. Gulu 5 March 02.
156. Headmaster, Layibi, March 02.
157. Awere, 9 January 2000.
158. Education Officer in charge of Sport, Gulu, 4 March 2002.
159. Headmaster, Pabo Secondary School, 5 March 02.
160. Termly fees were Ush 57,050 to which you had to add an optional Ush 10,000 for lunch in schools and Ush 18,000 for school uniforms.
161. Keyo SS, 13 March 2002.
162. Gulu, March 2002.
163. Pabo SS, March 2002. National enrolment figures in Government Secondary schools for 2004 show males 211,244 (56.9 per cent) and females 159,563 (43.1 per cent) www .education.go.ug?final%20Factfile%202s004.htm
164. Visit to Coo-pe, 19 January 1998.
165. Awere pilot, 29 July 1998.
166. Medical Superintendent, 19 January 1998.
167. Ibid, 19 January 1998).
168. Atiak-Biabia pilot, August 1998.
169. Odek, 14 December 1998.
170. Acet, 25 October 1999.
171. Anaka camp, October 1999.
172. Biabia, June 1999.
173. Awer, 25 August 1999.
174. Acet, 30 April 1999.
175. Secretary for Women's Affairs, Anaka, September 1998.
176. Awer, 13 December 1998.
177. Pabbo, August 1998.
178. This was described as 'very deep and near the bone. When you press the skin it doesn't jump back. It is not treatable in hospital – if you take it there either you get sent home or the hospital calls a traditional healer to operate. They cut you open to get the pus out' (Atiak, August 1998).
179. Anaka, August 1998.
180. Awer, August 1998. Girling (1960: 161) talks of 'female *ajwaka,* medicine women or herbalists', with no mention of male equivalents.
181. Pabbo, August 1998.
182. Atiak, August 1998.
183. For many illnesses the traditional healer keeps the patients in his compound until they are cured – and/or have paid.
184. Awer, August 1998.
185. Atiak, 11 May 1999.
186. Awer, August 1998.
187. Mendes, 1998.
188. Awere pilot, 29 July 1998. Note the use of the term 'local', as discussed in Chapter 4.

189. Visit to Awer, 13 October 1998.
190. Awer, September 1998.
191. Atiak, August 1998. This compared to Ush 54,000 salary + food allowance for a UPDF private.
192. Palaro pilot, 30 July 1998.
193. Atiak, August 1998.
194. Odek, 12 November 1998.
195. Awer, January 2000.
196. Pabbo, 6 March 2000.
197. *Sunday Monitor,* 24 May 1998, 'UPDF Men Eating Our Chicken – Lira People'.
198. Palaro, 19 December 1998.
199. KM E-newsletter 15, 23 May 2002.
200. Palaro, 20 January 2000.
201. Visit to Cwero, 15 December 1998.
202. Awach pilot, August 1999.
203. Acet, 7 June 1999.
204. Palaro, 1 April 1999.
205. Atiak, August 1998.
206. Acanling, 24 September 1999.
207. Awer report, 12 July 1998.
208. Gulu, September 1999.
209. *The New Vision,* 11 April 1998, 'Wamala Offers To Be Caned for Zeu'.
210. Atiak, August 1998.
211. Awer, 3 December 1998.
212. *The Monitor,* 1 March 1998, 'Time for UPDF to Come Clean'.
213. *The Monitor,* 2 March 1998, 'UPDF, Kony: Who is Burning Out?'
214. Awer, 14 December 1999.
215. Awere, 25 October 1999.
216. Awac, 20 July 1999.
217. *New Vision,* 14 June 2004,' Commanders to Face Court Martial over Massacres'.
218. Pagak, February 2000.
219. Atiak, August 1998.
220. Odek pilot, 21 July 1998.
221. Awere pilot, 29 July 1998.
222. Notes on visit to Awer, 13 October 1998.
223. IOM study, section 2.2.6.
224. 'Youth at the Cross-Roads: Which way forward?' Youth Conference, District Council Hall, 22 January 1999.

6

PROTECTION AS DEBILITATION

'Staying in the camps is a miserable life. Actually you are in prison within your own country. Have you been to a camp? They are so congested. Sanitary provisions are not adequate. People are from different places resulting in immorality, drunkenness'.[1]

Introduction

The violation of a wide range of human rights resulted in such a 'miserable life' for those in the 'protected villages' that the question inevitably arises as to why people put up with it rather than returning to their homes at the earliest opportunity. For the number in camps always increased when security deteriorated, but when the security situation improved dramatically (January to late December 1999, for example), the camps remained congested. A baseline survey of Awach conducted in November 1999, after nearly a year of relatively good security, found that in one parish only ten households – all elderly people – had returned home.[2] There was thus a time lag between improvements in security and peoples' decision to return to home areas.

One factor holding people back was the lack of a clear signal from Government. As UNOCHA reported 'There is no clear sense on the part of the displaced population of its official status, and in particular of whether it is authorized to return home' (Weeks 2002: 19). In meetings between military commanders and camp residents 'the local community asked the commander of the Home guard, Pagak detach, to tell them about the security situation in the area and when people would be allowed to go back home'.[3] To return home without such authorisation was to risk coming under suspicion as rebel collaborators and suffer the consequences. Having experienced military force in the process of coming into the protected villages, few were willing to incur similar force by trying to leave spontaneously. People were also held back by uncertainties about the broader security situation, and by the practical need to have a base in the camps while rebuilding in their home area. This was partly to minimise risk, partly to maintain access to the resources and basic services available in camps. To the extent they existed at all, food relief, education and health were all directed towards the protected villages. UNDMT reported in late 2001 that: 'With few exceptions, no significant assistance is presently being provided to re-habilitate roads, schools and other infrastructure in sub-counties or parishes or between these and the main trading centres. Several months would be required for agencies to re-orientate their assistance strategies and to shift personnel and resources away from care-and-maintenance to return and resettlement'.[4] Fur-thermore, as described in Chapter 5, Part III, parents had been obliged to invest their own labour in building up a key element of the infrastructure of the camps, the schools.

However, these factors do not adequately explain why people did not return home when circumstances improved. This chapter considers the nature of the immediate and cumulative impact of war, displacement and their associated vi-olations, and argues that people became too debilitated, physically, psychologi-cally and, ultimately, culturally, to break out of the situation and go home. In short, they really were 'in prison' in their own country. A key to the complexity of these different dimensions of debilitation is that they did not simply happen to people. Through their choices of short-term survival strategies people dam-aged their own longer-term prospects, and thus became implicated in their own debilitation. Impacts did not just happen to them, but also through them.

Physical Debilitation

> While needs have significantly increased, overall resources have remained at their pre-2000 level, resulting in sizeable shortfalls, a lack of basic services and undue human agony.[5]

At its most basic, displacement into protected villages caused hunger and mal-nutrition. An ICRC study in 2000 found that the longer people stayed in camps the less food they had. The hunger gap increased from 2.7 months for new resi-dents to 3.49 for those who had stayed over two years; while new camp residents averaged 1.93 meals per day, this fell to only 1.6 for those residents who had been there for more than two years.[6] WFP rations were supposed to provide 25 per cent of cereal needs, and 30 per cent of pulses and oil, but in practice deliveries were erratic, as in the example of Cwero (Table 6.1).

The average period between deliveries of food aid over this nineteen-month period was 54 days. The longest wait was 105 days, the shortest 21. Predictabil-ity and consistency (amongst the minimum standards for delivery of humanitar-ian relief set by Sphere Project) were hardly the order of the day. Furthermore, content and amounts fluctuated dramatically. Over the period 4 September 1998 to 14 May 1999 the maize delivered equated to approximately 0.3kg/hh/day or 0.08kg/pp/day, or 20 per cent of the minimum requirement (a caloric intake of 2100Kcal/day requires approximately 70g of beans (+/- 250kcal), 50g of oil (+/-

Table 6.1 Food Relief to Cwero Camp, September 1998 to March 2000

Date	Days since previous ration	Oil (ltr)	pp/day[7]	Maize (kg)	pp/day	Beans (kg)	Cowpeas (kg)
04-Sep-98		0		5.1[8]		0	3
13-Nov-98	70	0	0	5.1	0.078	4	0
10-Feb-99	91	1.5	0	5.1	0.060	3	0
23-Apr-99	72	1.5	0.0045	5.1	0.075	0	0
14-May-99	21	0.3	0.0155	4	1.190	1 pp	0
15-Jun-99	32	0.3	0.0020	3	0.027	0	3–8kg
16-Jul-99	33	0.3	0.0091	3	0.091	0	1.2
26-Aug-99	41	0.3	0.0016	4	0.073	3	0
07-Oct-99	42	0	0.0016	2.5	0.095	0	0
08-Nov-99	32	0.3	0.0000	3	0.078	0	2.5
Mar-00	105	0	0.0006	10.5	0.029	0	0
Average	53.9	0.45	0.0035	4.58	0.180	1.111	0.411

420kcal), and 400g of maize (+/- 1500kcal). With hugely irregular supplies there were long periods in which food aid did nothing to solve peoples' problems. Even when supplies did arrive, crude registration mechanisms (see Chapter 5, Part III) resulted in large households receiving less per person than small ones.

Three-monthly nutritional surveys conducted in the camps by ACF and Oxfam from November 1996, revealed that, despite the efforts of WFP and its implementing partners 'to ensure displaced persons are provided with access to a basic diet', 50 per cent of children under the age of five were stunted, and 30 per cent were wasted or underweight for their age. Malnutrition was clearly exacerbated by displacement. An ACF-U.S.A. nutritional survey in Kitgum in December 1999 found that global malnutrition rates among children aged six to fifty-nine months differed between the non-displaced, who appeared to benefit dramatically from the relative peace of 1999 (levels dropped from 6.7 per cent in March 1999 to 3.5 per cent in December), and those living in the camps (whose levels dropped only from 7 per cent to 6.6 per cent over the same period). Consequences for the displaced were also clear. In 1999 WFP reported that 'In the camps corneal ulceration and childhood blindness caused by Vitamin A deficiency is widespread, as are deficiencies of Vitamin B and iron. Both have contributed to growth retardation, mental as well as physical, with women and girls being especially prone to malnutrition as a result of household food allocation patterns favouring males' (WFP, 1999: 17).[9]

Following renewed insecurity from February to March 2002, malnutrition rates soared. A nutritional survey conducted by WFP and its implementing partners[10] found global malnutrition rates of 32 and 18 per cent among children under the age of five in Anaka and Pabo respectively,[11] further confirmation of the extent to which the camps created both malnutrition and dependency. This exacerbated the already serious problem of mental and physical growth retardation noted back in 1999 – effectively a whole new generation was being physiologically 'dumbed down'.

One response of the relief agencies was to set up supplementary feeding schemes. ACF did so for 13,000 children in nineteen camps in 1999. In Atiak, they had 560 children on their register, and a small number of adults:

> The dry ration they give to these children are ground soya beans mixed in the ratio 1 jug: 1 mini Plastic cup (LAPWOTI in local language) of sugar and in addition to that they give one piece of soap. They give these once a week ... Action Faim have their staff with white T-shirt with writing 'Action against malnutrition' and the abbreviation "SFC" meaning Supplementary Feeding Centre. Among the adults found are mostly females some with the cases of T.B. which made them to lose appetite.[12]

World Vision also had schemes in several camps, including Pabo and Atiak. In Pabo Oxfam operated a centre for malnourished children – 'but only on Fridays and Saturdays. World Vision Gulu branch also carried out similar tests on malnourished children three times in July 1998 and the worst affected children were transported to Lacor hospital in Gulu'.

It was not just the young who were malnourished and in poor health. As the late medical superintendent of Lacor Hospital noted, 'there has been a serious rise in malaria, partly due to breakdown in public health services, partly as people are sleeping in the bush' (see Chapter 5 for discussion of such temporary shelters),[13] 'in addition to malaria, malnutrition, TB and trauma have all increased over the last 5 years'.[14] There were also outbreaks of cholera (see Chapter 5). IOM found in 2001 that 30 per cent of a sample of 3,769 Gulu IDP camp residents, irrespective of sex and age, reported being sick during the month before their survey, suggestive of the general state of (ill) health of the population.

A more qualitative insight into peoples' major health concerns can be gained from a workshop I conducted with fourteen male and twenty-three female traditional healers in Gulu in June 1999. In a ranking exercise conducted as a group they indicated that they dealt most frequently with (in order of perceived priority): pelvic inflammation, upper respiratory tract infection (URTI), sexually transmitted infections (STIs) and HIV/AIDS, TB, miscarriages, convulsions and malaria, impotence/infertility and mental problems. When each healer was subsequently interviewed individually and the cases they had dealt with in the preceding week were listed, a somewhat different ranking emerged (Table 6.2).

Herpes zoster and induced abortion had not been mentioned when discussing as a group, and impotence and infertility, which collectively the healers had ranked almost bottom, emerged as the third most important issue they dealt with when questioned individually. It is also striking how many of the issues appeared to be related to sexual health and/or to be symptoms of HIV infection. Pelvic inflammation, the number one complaint, is frequently a symptom or after-effect of the STIs which are ranked number two. Whereas impotence has

Table 6.2 Ranking of Illnesses Treated in 961 Patients by 37 Traditional Healers in Gulu District in the Week 14–20 June 1999

Illness	Ranking	Number of cases (m = 416, f = 545)	As % of total
Pelvic Inflammation	1	186	19.4
STIs and AIDS	2	146	15.2
Impotence and Infertility	3	137	14.3
Convulsions and Malaria	4	131	13.6
Upper Respiratory Tract Infection	5	115	12.0
TB	6	79	8.2
Herpes Zoster	7	67	7.0
Miscarriages	8	53	5.5
Mental Problems	9	34	3.5
Induced Abortions	10	13	1.4
TOTAL		961	100.00

many possible causes, female infertility is also often linked to a wide range of infections, including STIs. TB and Herpes Zoster are both closely associated with HIV. Miscarriages are also at times linked with STIs. From this point of view, nearly half of the cases seen were potentially related to sexual or reproductive health problems – and while not all these sexual health problems are necessarily evidence of HIV, having an STI can increase vulnerability to HIV infection.

Physical injuries were also very evident. IOM found in 2001 that of 3,769 Gulu IDP camp residents surveyed, 282 or an extraordinary 7.5 per cent, had suffered an injury in the month prior to the survey. Of these, 161 were caused by gunshots (IOM 2001, table 11). Landmine incidents were ongoing during the period of the research, as were cases where children died after picking up unexploded ordinance which then blew up (see Chapter 5). While there is no systematic data on deaths in the camps where we conducted fieldwork, anecdotal evidence suggested that deaths amongst children and young adults were high (Table 6.3).

Such a list suggests that people were dying very young, with malaria a major killer among small children, and TB, AIDS and poisoning as major causes of premature deaths among adults.

While deaths and injuries did not compare to situations such as the Rwanda genocide, they were nonetheless significant relative to the size of the population. Gersony records about 1,000 war injuries leading to hospitalisation over the period January 1996 to March 1997 alone. And contrary to his estimate that deaths throughout the war 'would be measured in the tens of thousands, rather than in the hundreds of thousands',[15] the EU in its resolution of July 2000 estimated the total number of deaths at over 100,000 (point E).

Table 6.3 List of Deaths Recorded by Fieldworkers in Awer and Pagak Camps, July1999 to March 2000, Sorted by Age of Deceased

Date	Sex	Age	Cause of Death
17-Jul-99	F	0.66	Sickle Cell Anaemia
28-Dec-99	M	0.66	Malaria
15-Jan-00	?	0.66	Malaria
14-Aug-99	?	1.5	Malaria
27-Mar-00	?	2	Malaria
06-Jul-99	?	2.5	Malaria
14-Aug-99	?	3	Malaria
12-Dec-99	M	3	Malaria
07-Jan-00	?	3	Took poison left in house by parents
14-Aug-99	?	5	Malaria
09-Mar-00	?	5	Malaria
25-Sep-99	?	7	Malaria
10-Oct-99	M	15	Poison (Suicide)
24-Jan-00	F	25	Died in child birth (as did the child)
13-Jul-99	?	30	Continuous vomiting of blood
02-Sep-99	M	31	Pneumonia
17-Dec-99	M	31	TB which lasted long
18-Sep-99	M	33	Died after long illness
27-Jul-99	F	35	Died in Lacor Hospital, cause unknown
11-Mar-00	F	37	AIDS (Died in Gulu hospital)
06-Jul-99	F	40	AIDS
30-Aug-99	M	41	Unknown
03-Sep-99	M	41	Given poison in the local drink (*lujutu*)
25-Dec-99	M	42	UPDF Soldier killed in Bundibugyo, brought to Pagak for burial
13-Sep-99	F	45	Hit on head by falling branch
10-Oct-99	M	45	Poison
17-Mar-00	M	52	Poison (old *mzee*, died in Lacor Hospital)
07-Oct-99	M	56	Poison
15-Dec-99	F	63	AIDS

Psychological Debilitation

The debilitation caused by the impact of the war and camp life was not just physical but also psychological. Indications of psychological ill-health ranged from complaints seen by doctors and healers, to a number of behaviour patterns, many of them self-destructive. The medical superintendent of Lacor Hospital, for example, reported seeing a marked rise in the number of women with symptoms of anxiety, such as lack of sleep, loss of appetite, and palpitations, some of which he attributed to their having to shoulder greater responsibilities. Traditional healers identified mental health problems as 3.5 per cent of their case-load – a level which rises substantially if some of the physical symptoms they deal with, such as impotence (Table 6.2), are regarded as somatic symptoms of psychological stress. The most dramatic indications of psychological stress found through fieldwork were, however, high levels of suicide and poisoning, as well as alcoholism and interpersonal violence.

Suicide

Information on suicides emerged in three stages. Over the main data collection phase (mid-1998 to March 2000) thirty-six accounts of attempted suicide were collected, of which twenty-one were successful and fifteen failed. The predominant method used (seventeen cases) was to swallow pesticides or insecticides, either straight from the bottle or pack, or by washing seeds which had been sprayed with pesticide and then drinking the water.[16] Hanging was also common (5), while overdoses of medications (2) and swallowing watch batteries (2) were less common. Although fifteen attempts failed, this was generally because other people realised what was happening and were able to administer a combination of raw eggs and cooking oil which forced the person to vomit up the poison.

We supplemented this data with figures from Gulu Police Station. For the period 1998 to 2001 they had records of 27 successful suicides, of which we were able to analyse 25 (m=15, f=10). There were noticeable gendered differences, with 12 men hanging themselves compared to only 2 women. On the other hand 4 women took poison compared to only 1 man, and 3 women swallowed batteries compared to only 1 man

Such findings prompted further discussions in Pabo and Acet camps in March 2002. Additional examples were put forward and respondents identified an upwards trend. Officials in Pabo informed me that 'Suicide cases are very rampant. People use sibacol pesticide and watch batteries. Yesterday a woman swallowed two cells [watch batteries] and was admitted to Lacor ... it is something which can happen anytime'.[17] When I spontaneously raised the issue with five members of a self-help group in Acet they were able to give accounts of four attempts which had taken place in the weeks immediately preceding our discussions. This was despite the fact that suicide is frowned upon in Acholi culture. When asked 'what happens if someone kills themselves?' the answer was that

> if you hang yourself the tree will be cut down. There is also a law remaining from colonial times that the police are supposed to beat the body of the deceased person. Traditionally, it was also believed that suicide was a bad omen and could result in many spirits haunting people. The first person to see the body after the person has died has to go through a cleansing ritual. They will also put a piece of grass or a leaf on the body to symbolise burial.

It was also the case that, traditionally, the family of the deceased had to be compensated by whoever was believed to have triggered the suicide, and that, notwithstanding the punitive approach introduced by the colonialists, funeral rites would be performed normally. The fact that few of these traditions appeared to be operating suggests that these mechanisms had either been overwhelmed by the rising levels of suicide, or had become irrelevant given the changing causes of suicide, or a combination of the two.

With few exceptions, suicide attempts appeared to relate to intergenerational tensions and an inability or unwillingness to meet gendered expectations,[18] which in turn were linked with the dynamics of war and mental health problems. Amongst adolescents in particular, suicide seems to have been perceived as the only escape from domination by adults. One young woman killed herself because her family were forcing her to get married to someone against her will. They were intending to use the bridewealth, which would be paid for her, to enable their son to pay bridewealth for his wife-to-be – a process sometimes referred to as 'recycling'. In another case the girl was two months pregnant by one of her teachers (as shown in Chapter 5, adolescent girls would often take poison in an attempt to abort children they had conceived with their teachers).

Many women appeared to reach a point of desperation at their economic situation, often aggravated by their husband's behaviour (using money for alcohol was frequently mentioned), as in the following account;

> Patricia Atim committed suicide ... at around 1:00 A.M. in the morning ... According to the witness she was six months pregnant. Patricia picked a quarrel with her husband with bitter words inclusive (The husband's occupation is transporting people on bicycles to their different destinations for money and such a man is described as a *boda-boda* man. His bicycle is also termed as *boda-boda*). After the exchange of words, her husband removed some of her money and yet she (Patricia) had actually decided she would use that money when she gave birth to her new-born baby in the near future. When she found out that she wouldn't be able to handle the situation any more she decided to go and borrow money from one of her woman friends in the pretence that she wanted to buy some medicine from the clinic.

> Well, she was offered a little money all right, but instead of using this money on what she had requested it for, she bought chlorophinical capsules and swallowed all that much at a go. The medicine in return started affecting this young lady and she was then taken to the hospital – but the medical personnel could do nothing to rescue her life and in the end she passed away.

> Afterwards the medical personnel demanded twenty thousand shilling (about £9.00) for removing the dead child inside her womb. The parents of the deceased refused to pay the money demanded by the medical personnel saying that after all 'Patricia is already dead and so is her child so paying that money wouldn't be worth it'. The relatives of Patricia took her body for burial in a village outside Anaka. My wife was there in the funeral rite on the 27/10/98. She told me that the child was removed from the mother's womb by a 72-year-old woman.[19]

Another 'successful' suicide had been caught stealing from her step-sister's granary and was expected to replace the stolen sesame and to slaughter a goat in compensation. When in late November 1998 a group of seven women in Pabo camp all tried to commit suicide by swallowing Furadan (a pesticide), they were found in time, 'rescued', and asked to explain themselves. They stated that their husbands were drinking away all the money realised from selling rice, leaving them in abject poverty, and that their husbands were bringing co-wives despite the first wife already living in appalling conditions. This spate of attempted suicides led to a ban on the sale of Furadan in Pabo camp in early December 1998, but this did not prevent another woman in Pabo from attempting suicide about a month later. She also failed, and when asked to explain herself stated that she had tried to kill herself 'because of the husband drinking 10 bottles of beer daily and leaving her to starve together with her children'.

Often the visible prompt to the women's suicides is something men do to women. The invisible underlying theme is a frustration at their resultant inability to meet their gendered expectations of themselves. Women taught to nurture their children, cannot. Women taught that when their husbands take a second wife, they as the first wife will be able to sit back a bit, cannot when the household economy is in tatters. And so on. Similarly, for men, the majority of suicides are explained in terms of an inability to live up to gendered social expectations. Just how important this is as an explanation for individual and social dysfunction, and how closely this is related to the dynamics of war, humiliation and militarization, is explored further in Chapter 7.

Heavy Drinking

Suicides are just the sharp tip of an iceberg of psychological symptoms arising in part from the war. Heavy drinking was much more widespread. Although the connections with war-related stress are less immediately discernible, one professor attending a peace meeting in Gulu in 1998, placed alcohol at the very heart of his analysis, arguing that 'To bring peace we need respect for one another, to drop the use of alcohol, and to stop aiming to go into the army or into exile'.[20] While few people gave alcohol such a central place in their analysis of war, it was widely recognised by soldiers and civilians alike as a factor in the spread of HIV. When discussing the rise in HIV rates in Gulu district non-commissioned officers rated alcohol as the sixth major risk factor. Soldiers' wives rated alcohol as the seventh major cause (Table 6.3), and traditional healers also saw alcohol abuse as a major factor. It was an obvious nexus for soldier-civilian relationships. In Awac, with Gwengdia detach nearby, boys who wanted money for drink would seek to get girls for soldiers. The Awac Parent-Teacher-Association (PTA) wanted to stop young girls from going to the market to sell home-brewed alcohol as it exposed them to the attentions of soldiers. As already mentioned, men's drinking was seen as the cause for many women's attempted and successful suicides.

Drinking was also believed to be threatening education. When a police liaison officer addressed a mass meeting in Attiak-Biabia, he listed 'drunkenness among men and women' as one of the main problems confronting the education sector.[21] When Awac Displaced School PTA met their Local Councillor they identified 'over-drinking' by teachers (along with the problem of soldiers taking pupils as their wives) as a cause for poor performance by the pupils, and proposed that 'Any teachers found drinking during lesson hours must be handled before the court'.[22] Similarly, when the Minister for Education and Sports addressed people in Awere he made a point of stressing that 'some Headmasters are really misusing the UPE funds ... [they] are drinking, anyhow, without thinking that this money is given by the Government for uplifting the standard of education'.[23] One secondary school teacher described how 'Some of the teachers take alcohol too early in the day, resulting in disciplinary cases regarding neglect of duties. The rate of drinking has gone up'.[24] The District Education Officer implicitly acknowledged the problem when he argued that 'We need inspectors' houses, stores and offices in every county ... [this] would lead to drunken teachers and teachers who have not prepared [their lessons] being caught in the act'.[25] The problem was seen to lie not just with teachers. At a Parents' Day at Acet P7, 13 December 1999, the headmaster pleaded with them because he felt that 'some parents have left [neglected] teaching their children from [at] home because of drunkardness, and lack of seriousness in teaching children'.

The impact of alcohol featured heavily in many of the fieldworkers' reports. There is the case of the government official who attended 'a grand end of year party'. When he 'was going back home after taking a lot of booze at the party, he rode his motorcycle and when he reached the junction near Co-operative Bank he failed to make a bend at the corner. Instead he crashed at a commercial building in front of him – and died instantly'.[26] Another story involves a man aged sixty-five who was drunk: 'When he was walking towards his house [in broad daylight], he came across a woman aged about 54 lying down resting. Without any exchange of words, K___ kept standing, unzipped his trouser and began urinating over the woman! Finished. No fight erupted. Elders ruled that K___ should pay three bars of soap for the woman to clean herself of urine'.[27]

Cultural Debilitation

Although psychological debilitation is a more complex expression of the impact of the situation than a simple concern with physical impact, it still focuses on the individual rather than on the society more broadly. Yet many saw links between the two. Teachers, for example, would argue that:

> the war has led to moral disintegration and lack of moral discipline. The students are more and more difficult to handle. Partly because class sizes have increased. [Partly because] Those who have been abducted may have spent two or three years in the bush, [and] some have lost interest in studying – it depends on the individual. One child may be willing to learn but have no sponsor, some see only black clouds. Also there are many non-educated role-models, such as business men. Also the government is planning to cut grants and look at loan schemes instead.[28]

An ACORD report described how 'there is cultural demoralization of the displaced living in the camps: prostitution, divorce and early sexual relationships among young children have become another way of earning an income to survive in the camp' (ACORD 2001; 17). The Acholi Religious Leaders talked

of a 'collapse of cultural and moral values' and of how 'as one moves through
any of the displaced camps, one of the most depressing sights is to see scores of
unattended children everywhere, idle youth loitering about and men drinking alcohol'. They went on to argue that 'Cramming together people in a small space
is seen in all camps as another main reason for the lack of respect that children
show towards their parents' (ARLPI 2001: 17). IOM reported that people in three
focus group discussions believed it was 'loss of parental control over children
[which] resulted into prostitution, child pregnancy, drunkenness and theft'. Furthermore, they consistently reported a loss of parental control over children 'who
end up learning bad behaviour like theft, disrespecting elders and general indiscipline' (IOM, 2001: 1). Such assumptions pervaded public discourse:

> On the 22/12/98 WORLD VISION INTERNATIONAL organised an end of year
> party for traumatised children, street-children, and other school children supported
> by the organisation. The party was at Boma ground near Acholi Inn with the RDC
> being guest of honour.
>
> Food, drinks, biscuits, sweets was served to more than 4,000 children who were in
> attendance. During the party the LCIII chairperson appealed for respect from the
> children especially in the form of greeting the people whenever they meet them. He
> further stressed that these days children ignore advice from the elderly people and
> thus do the wrong things instead of the right ones.[29]

Ironically, even the supposedly idle youth brought the question of prostitution into the lyrics of *lukeme* songs composed while 'loitering about':

> Min Akello Muhora (The mother of Akello is a slut)
> Min Aumony Malaya (The mother of Aumony is a prostitute)
> Oh Latuiri Muhora (Oh that child is a slut)

Discourses of breakdown thus resonated with a wide range of people living
inside the war zone who saw overcrowded living conditions as vectors not just
for bacteria and viruses, but, insofar as they resulted in various practices which
would not have been tolerated under other circumstances, as a vector for social
breakdown and moral disintegration. It was duly echoed by external observers.
UNOCHA argued that 'Displacement has put social relations and basic cultural
values under severe stress', and that 'the socialization into violence of young
people has grave implications for the future of the society as a whole'. Like
the Religious Leaders, they found that 'The conditions of destitution and the
idleness to which young people in the camps are subjected are also having a profoundly disruptive influence on the society' (Weeks 2002: 28). In effect, an unacknowledged consensus emerged that there was a breakdown going on, although
perspectives differed on what exactly was getting broken. Teachers saw moral
breakdown in the youth, youth saw it in women, parents saw it in teachers (and
their own children), and religious leaders noted it in 'men drinking alcohol'.
    Some of the fears such discourses reflected were belied to an extent by observ-
able behaviours. There was, for example, a widely prevalent belief that returned
abductees were wild and disruptive as a result of their traumatic experiences, as
in the following statement by a head-teacher:

We have quite many abducted students. They are very difficult to handle because we have to make sure other students don't call them 'rebels'. If they become annoyed they can be very dangerous. Last year we had to dismiss one. When he came here he was annoyed by a friend. Peace was brought but an hour later he took a knife and cut his friend on the throat (both were from Kitgum). He ran away into the bush. We called the parents and had to dismiss him.

However, when pushed on the number of returnee students currently attending his school, the same head-teacher had no idea, suggesting that few returnees warrant particular attention, and that they were not as 'difficult to handle' as first suggested. When pressed on this he admitted that 'We don't have figures for the overall number, they fear to be identified. In the first place they sneak back and go to private schools, then they get admitted here. I think the entire population is traumatised, psychologically some see violence as the solution to the problem'.[30]

This belief that returnees were a problem coupled with an inability to identify who the returnees actually were was common amongst the head-teachers I interviewed. It was just one of numerous examples of a disjuncture between discourse and reality. If there were total social breakdown, why would people attempting suicide be rescued – and reprimanded for trying to kill themselves? If students were truly de-motivated, why would they bother to come back from suspension in order to take their exams? Why would some steal in order to pay their school fees?[31] Why would seventeen of the twenty-three students in the newly re-opened Keyo Secondary School (see Chapter 5) have been digging in the fields on the morning of the day we interviewed them in order to raise their own school fees? Four of them were not eating lunch – in order to save money. They also had dramatic aspirations, which included being teachers, doctors, a minister for education (f), an army major, and Secretary of the OAU.[32] How could teachers complaining of youth idleness and lack of motivation explain such behaviours, let alone the burgeoning of private secondary schools to meet the demand the public sector could not deal with?[33] Furthermore, if there really were 'idleness' among the youth, what accounted for the range of associations formed by those unable to attend school? Or for the numerous *Lukeme* groups with their spiky commentaries on current social and political problems? Why was this practice such a threat that attempts were made (unsuccessfully) to bring it under the control of the Movement?[34] Why was there such a range of goods for sale in the market, however pitiful the amounts may seem? (Chapter 5) These are all indicators of initiative which somewhat belie the preferred account of the camps as sites of idleness and breakdown. As Finnström also observed, they demonstrate 'the younger generation's unconditional struggle for a comprehensible life in the midst of war and displacement' (2003: 15).

Nonetheless, if asked to be specific, people could point to a long list of concrete indicators of breakdown: living in camps, many norms no longer held sway and people were doing things which would not have been accepted under other circumstances. Physical segregation of the sexes, as practiced in traditional homesteads, had largely broken down and there was a serious lack of privacy. Whereas in normal times boys would build their own huts from the age of eleven or twelve, in the camps whole families lived in one hut, resulting in exposure of children to their parents' sexual activities.[35] Parents taking refuge in the bush at night no longer had oversight of their children, who as a result were 'faced with various ways of behaviour from different peers. The children find a place to hide [at night] and spend time in each other's company, rather than sitting around the household fire being educated by the parents (they separate in this way because of different levels of risk of abduction)'.[36]

Those able to send children to school had far less say in their children's socialisation than would traditionally have been the case. Informal socialisation mechanisms, such as story-telling at the household hearth (wang oo – see Chapter 7) were blocked, and traditional authority systems were overlaid with those of the Local Council system, camp administrators, and military structures. Parents were unwilling or unable to help young people to marry in the way they would have done in the past (see Chapter 7), yet young girls were at times being turned into camp followers by their own parents. Children were being abducted and forced to kill, girls were committing suicide because their teachers had made them pregnant, under-age boys because they had made under-age girls pregnant. Teachers were drinking too early in the day, women were swallowing pesticide in protest at the untenable positions they were left in by their husbands' over-drinking, and fear of HIV created a climate of inter-personal distrust.

In effect, the various discourses of moral, social and cultural breakdown (which were very similar to the concerns expressed by the LRA to justify the creation of a 'new Acholi'), although at times exaggerated, sought to do justice to a level of complexity and breadth of impact not captured in individual physical and psychological debilitation. For the sake of clarity I shall group what these discourses sought to capture under the concept of cultural debilitation. I shall use this to refer not only to the weakening or disappearance of what people considered their traditional practices, but also to the adoption of new practices, which were at odds with and made a return to pre-conflict social relations more difficult. Examples of practices under threat included burial and funeral rites, restorative justice, and various song and dance forms. Examples of new practices ranged from changing economic roles arising from external interventions, to changed relationships between the military and civilian populations.

Burial and Funeral Rites

Conflict and displacement had created many obstacles to burying the deceased in what had been the customary manner. From Awer it was reported that

> The system of funerals before we came to the camp was that if a person dies she or he is left to remain for three to four days depending on sex. A man would remain for three days and a woman for four, with people gathering to mourn and give their condolences to the family of the deceased. They would converse and eat and drink. Then later on the last funeral is organised where many relatives are invited to come and attend. That will be the time when many animals lost their lives. People eat and drink for at least two days, and this would mark the end.

Since we moved to the camp this has changed. When a person dies, religious leaders are invited to come and conduct prayers. Everybody within the surrounding area gathers to pray and food is organised for those who attended the prayer and that normally marks the end of the funeral rites.[37] Not too much food and drink are taken.[38]

Displacement and insecurity meant people could not travel to attend burials and funeral rites. Previously such rituals 'involved all relatives, but now not all relatives are involved because they are scattered'.[39] For similar reasons it was at times difficult or impossible to bury the bodies in the original homestead: 'When someone dies the body is quickly taken to the deserted home and buried and the people have to come back to the camp for mourning. That is when news of the rebels is consistent. However, when the situation allows, then the people can stay for a while'.[40]

A further obstacle was economic – people simply did not have the means to host the large gatherings which had previously been the norm; 'we don't have the material to prepare a funeral, so it is not organised these days'.[41] Most complex was where a person had been killed by a known person, for then the funeral rites would not be organised until compensation (*culo kwor*) had been paid by the offender's clan.

Breakdown of Restorative Justice

According to 'tradition', as reported by an elder, 'If a crime is committed, the guilty party sincerely acknowledges responsibility for the crime in public and repents without fear or shame. Paying compensation is the responsibility of the family and the clan of wrongdoer, therefore discipline is a collective responsibility and the whole family and the clan expect, and demand it'.[42] This claim was borne out in at least one instance where a powerful clan member attempted to pay a contribution on behalf of his entire sub-clan, only to have his offer rejected: 'Omwony-Ogaba tried to pay the whole 28,000 for Parwach sub-clan for the *culo kwor* of Puranga clan. However, it was rejected by the sub-clan leader who said it is not the rightful procedure. As it is a clan issue even a rich person has to allow the clan to pay a contribution'.[43]

Thus if a person was killed intentionally, then the perpetrator's clan traditionally had to pay compensation (*culo kwor*) to re-establish communication between the clans of victim and perpetrator (see also Girling, 1960: 66, Finnström, 2003: 290–296). By involving not just the offender but also his or her family and clan members, compensation thus also served as a mechanism for the restoration of social cohesion. Even if the killing were accidental, such as in a traffic accident, *lim kwo* would be paid. *Lim Kwo* could also be paid if important animals had been killed. This could be in the form of goats, cows or cash equivalent.[44] The exact amounts would be specified by local elders.

In principle the Local Council system introduced in 1986, which extended from village level (LC 1) upwards and in which local councils and local courts were linked, superseded such traditional justice. Appeals were supposed to move upwards, from the LCI to the LCII to the LCIII courts, through the Grade II and

Grade I courts to the Chief Magistrate and on to the High Court, the Court of Appeal/Constitutional Court, and finally the Supreme Court. In practice, the new system had partially displaced but not satisfactorily replaced the old, leaving something of a vacuum, the extent of which differed from place to place. In Palaro, a camp in a very rural setting, the response to the theft of a goat was to take the culprit to the council of elders and make him pay compensation. In Gulu town, by contrast, the theft of a bicycle from a market place prompted an outburst of mob justice:

> Then people took off after the man and he was caught in about one mile from the market. When he was arrested people beat him from there up to the market. After that the LC of Vanguard ran and invited the highway police to prevent people due to their shoutingness. When the highway police came, they grabbed the thief and took him to the jail and he died from police there because people had over-beaten him.[45]

Such mob-justice was a far cry from the idealised vision of Acholi restorative justice put forward by various actors in northern Uganda (see below). Another example from Gulu town suggests that mob violence could be provoked by a number of issues. One day there was considerable commotion opposite my flat in Gulu, and I saw that one of the small eating places opposite my flat had been torn down. Thinking that it might have been knocked down on grounds of hygiene control or some such, we went and asked what had happened. As I noted afterwards

> It turned out that a man and woman had been caught having sex inside the restaurant, at around midday. Not only that, but they were doing it on the very table which customers eat their meals off. Even worse, the back of the hut faces over the Muslim cemetery, and so it was the Muslims who were most irate, this being the second time it had happened apparently. So the place was ripped down completely. As we were standing there the local councillor, a short man, came up and said 'you see, these people, just fucking at midday!' I had to laugh; it is so funny to hear people here saying 'fuck', cos the language is generally so very correct. As we were standing contemplating the scene three women came towards the place, one of them I was told was the woman who had been caught in the act – 'you see, these Baganda, they like a lot of sex, anytime, anyplace … Really!'[46]

When local justice was discussed at the ACORD conference in September 1999, some felt that the LC system did not work well and that the traditional system was more appropriate and should be revived. Some saw LC courts as an abusive imposition on the people of Uganda, which merged political and judicial establishments. Some argued that the Acholi system of social reconciliation was superior, since a murderer could not simply pay his way out of a charge but had to reconcile with the victim's family. It was noted that the modern and traditional structures operated on different value systems (for example the respect given to age) and had different functions which are difficult to align with each other.

However, reviving traditional processes of compensation in a context of displacement was also somewhat unrealistic. Many forms of compensation (notably cattle) were no longer feasible, at least not in the form set out by the elders.

For cash-strapped camp dwellers seeking to earn money through *leja-leja* the likelihood of raising the cash equivalent of cattle was very small. In 2002 a cow cost 20,000/= in Kitgum, and 50,000/= in Gulu. Furthermore, as described in Chapter 5, Part I, in the process of displacement most clans were significantly dispersed and thrown together with other clan groupings, making it very difficult for the collective processes described to take place.

Dance and Song

Dancing and singing, which many saw as cornerstones of Acholi culture, were not uniformly affected by the conflict. *Larakaraka,* a courtship dance for youth, traditionally performed in large gatherings, with men grouped by clan, and women able to circulate from group to group, was still very popular, although cardboard was being used instead of skins for the costume (see also Girling, 1960: 68). *Dingidingi,* performed by young people to entertain visitors, had not been very affected either. *Apiti,* a dance of married women performed to praise someone, for example at election time, was still in use by women's groups (Chapter 5, Part II). Other dance forms were more affected. *Bwola,* the royal dance, supposedly performed for the chief by older and more skilful dancers, was increasingly used to celebrate non-Acholi (e.g. a visit by the Archbishop of Uganda, 2002) and danced by younger people: 'there is a fear because of the problems of the last fifteen years that older people might die and younger people be left without the skills'. In the villages its use was very limited. 'Major costume parts such as the ostrich feathers are very difficult to get, even the skins, because the wildlife authorities are now very hard on hunting'. *Otole,* a war dance involving both men and women, had become uncommon and costumes had changed: 'culturally women used to put on *ceno,* a piece of thread to cover the private parts, but their chests would be bare. But now, with modernisation, they can even wear T-shirts'.

One type of performance affected by political changes was *aguma.* This involves groups of youth playing home-made finger-pianos (*lukeme*) and stringed instruments (*adungu*) to accompany their own lyrics. Different groups come together for sessions which go throughout the night ('transnight'). *Aguma* thus has the dual function of creating opportunities to meet members of the opposite sex, but also to pass comments on topical social and political issues. As one respondent noted, 'it is also used to make people aware of issues, so if [for example] someone is caught having sex with animals it will be sung [about]. It should shape youth in appropriate morals and life skills as an adult'. Often songs are irreverent and poke fun at the authorities, and could include topics such as the UPDF's failure to respond when the rebels came.[47] While this local musical form remained popular in the camps, the authorities, perhaps inevitably, sought to bring its potential for articulating subaltern viewpoints under their control (El Bushra and Dolan, 2002). In 1998, it was reported from Palaro that *lukeme* dance was prohibited, 'as it was detrimental to school regulations'. In July 1999 a competition was organised with sponsorship from the chairman of Laroo Division and the NRM Secretariat. While all *lukeme* groups were free to enter, they could only sing on four topics selected by the organisers – including either a praise song for Museveni, or a song in praise of Universal Primary Education.

Overall, people noted: 'there is no serious cultural dance taking place … In general, cultural dances have been halted because of insecurity'. Typically, dances such as *apiti* for women and *lukeme* for the youth would only be performed 'when government officials come to the area'.[48] Respondents in Awer felt that 'The Acholi culture is dying and diluted'. They argued that

> The true Acholi culture has changed in so many ways from the original one which was known by our fathers and grandparents. Say for instance, when we consider cultural activities normally the present generation are not completely interested in the culture. For many cases you find very few people participating in cultural dances, they are considered to be useless, instead people go for discos and those who go for the cultural dances are said to be backward. In this way you find the culture is dying and diluted … Most of the elders today do not know what these cultural activities are. So instead of directing the children correctly, normally the children do what they think can satisfy themselves.[49]

In practice:

> The only source of learning to dance now is through schools and participation in music festivals. Some primary schools cannot even perform, even though the curriculum states that it should be done. There is in fact a fine for schools which do not send a team for the district competitions. As far as secondary schools are concerned, only two schools have participated in the last few years. It is though part of the extra curricular activities.

It was felt that there had been a decline in interest. Asked how teams for such competitions got chosen, it appeared that

> … when a circular comes then those interested are asked to register with the concerned person, they are then trained and a selection for the team is made. Much less than 25% will register. For example, in Gulu High School there are 600 pupils, but only about 60 will register, of whom 45 will finally participate. If it continues like this for a number of years then our culture will continue dying. There is also the fact that the styles have become more varied over recent years, partly because of some element of modernisation.

In summary, dance as a repository of cultural identity came under a number of pressures. Some of these were part of wider processes of 'modernisation'; others were very northern Uganda specific. Turning them to use in ceremonies to welcome outsiders meant that they partially shifted from being a marker of Acholi identity to becoming a vehicle of incorporation of the outsider. In doing so they simultaneously symbolised the assimilation of Acholi with the 'outside'. When built into music competitions they were part of a much wider cultural syllabus, which included 'Original composition, Sight singing, Drama, Traditional dance (*Bwola, Lyel, Larakaraka*), Traditional folk song, Instrumental composition *Adungu/Lukeme (Aguma)*, Creative dance, Solo involving *Nanya* and flute'.[50] By taking dance out of informal spaces and bringing it instead into the school curriculum, it was becoming less and less available to non-school-goers, who, as shown in Chapter 5, Part III, formed the majority of young people despite the introduction of Universal Primary Education. It was perhaps not surprising that some people felt that their culture was being 'diluted'.

External Interventions which 'Diluted' Culture

This was further aggravated by the introduction, through NGO and Government interventions, of new practices and forms of organisation into people's lives. These seemed to work actively to challenge existing modes of organisation and thereby to constitute a form of 're-socialisation'. For impoverished displaced people, they were difficult to resist. At times this was an inevitable outcome of the 'humanitarian imperative'; people were in camps so that is where assistance went. However, even service provision was structured in ways that would have a longer-term influence on social structure and practice. Thus HIV/AIDS education was targeted at youth, not their parents. WFP gave food assistance for primary schools, but none for secondary schools, a decision which could not be justified on numerical grounds – there were after all only about 5,000 secondary school students in the whole district, and even if the availability of free food had made it feasible for more students to study at this level, that would have meant fewer mouths to feed in the villages. On the other hand, the construction of schools in the camps helped to consolidate them and make return to home areas more difficult. As shown in Chapter 5, Part II, people in the camps were 'learning the importance of working in a group rather than in isolation as an individual',[51] and they were notably more organised where NGOs were present to catalyse the process. Some interventions, such as the distribution of assistance, obliged people to organise themselves in certain ways, ostensibly for ease of administration:

> Before seed distribution takes place, the agency group the people in groups of 12 people from the different parishes. They therefore give plots to the groups. The groups identify the seeds they are interested to plant. Fund for the purchase of the seed is therefore awaited; then seed procurement takes place. This has even been the working logistics of World Vision and Catholic Relief Services. People are taught how to plant seeds in line, use of how to apply pesticides in case of pest outbreak. The procurement of the pesticides is all carried out by the NGOs.[52]

Where people were able to farm, they risked losing control of their own produce:

> Despite threats of insecurity, the camp population were able to carry on with other activities such as digging in the long distance places. The beans harvest has been very high in the camp. World Vision International has embarked on purchasing beans from the farmers at 250 shillings per kg and maize at 45 shillings per kg. They are convincing the camp population that if the insecurity persists then those food stuffs will be looted from the camp population by the rebels, and yet the World Vision's main intention is to ferry those items and store them in town and then later distribute them to the camp population in the form of relief.[53]

NGOs' emphasis on teaching people how to survive on very little land, rather than helping them to get back onto the land they already knew how to manage (Chapter 5, Part II), suggested an underlying 'modernisation' agenda, and a preparedness to sanction de facto land alienation. In at least one place WFP intervened to form a so-called 'primary grouping' of farmers to pool their produce before selling it. WFP subsequently purchased a total of 600 tonnes of food for distribution. The relationship between this ostensibly pragmatic arrangement, and the wider re-shaping of the rural economy, was identified by WFP, who believed that 'The creation and encouragement of primary societies [farmer associations] to pool agricultural produce may be made easier by the gradual urbanization (or, more accurately, peri-urbanization) around trading centres, including IDP camps' (WFP, 1999: 22).

Even the re-stocking of cattle, which initially appeared to be in support of a revival of traditional ways of life, in fact further subverted them. There were various small cattle-stocking schemes, sometimes combined with micro-finance. Under many such schemes cattle were given to women, as in March 1999 when forty-five head of cattle were given to three women's groups in Acet. As the fieldworker explained it, 'These cattle were given by the government under the policy of restocking the cattle raided by Karamojong. The Women's councillor for Odek sub-county, was the one who brought the cattle to these women's groups'.[54] In Pabo, NSARWU, an organisation headed by Janet Museveni, the President's wife, organised to donate forty-five head of cattle to Pabo Combined Women's Group, as part of a NURP exercise to re-stock northern Uganda. At the beginning of August 1999 the District Veterinary Officer organised the group 'to build a kraal for keeping the 45 cattles to be given to them soon'. The women contributed 10,000/= per member, to serve 'for buying of spray pumps and veterinary drugs for handling the animals in question. Part of the money will be used for catering for the services of the Veterinary doctor who inspects these animals. Mr. Okupot who represented the office of the First Lady was there physically and confirmed the above requirements. The beneficiaries therefore responded well in raising the money'. Some three weeks later the coordinator of NSARWU returned to oversee the distribution of the cattle, which this time were not 'long-horned Ankole cattles but local breeds being purchased from Adjumani district. 3 bulls are meant for running the 45 heifers. If the heifers give birth to female calves, they should be given to the next household in order to reach everybody in the sub county'.

The direct connection between the donations of cattle and key individuals (in one case, from the relevant women's councillor, in the other, from the President's wife herself) is striking, as is the fact that the cattle are given primarily to women, who traditionally would not have been in charge of cattle. This ignored the increasing economic desperation of men, as evidenced by, amongst other things, the trend of men moving into what had previously been women's areas of work (such as traditional healing) (Chapter 5, Part IV), and contributed to a larger dynamic of externally encouraged shifts in gender roles and relations.

Although this may have been an attempt to win support for Museveni through patronage to women, it is doubtful whether people's loyalty could be bought through such methods. When the MP for Aswa County toured his constituency from 3rd to 6th March 2000, and aired a Government plan to restock the Acholi with cattle 'robbed off by the Karamojong and NRA in the past', most people saw this as an attempt to buy peoples' votes:

> There is nothing much the people want other than peace for they have been in problems for so long and if the war has not yet ended having cattle is still useless. They [people listening to the speeches] said the cattle they had [had in the past] was not given to them by any previous government instead their own works as a result of peace prevailing by then [i.e. at that time].[55]

As the cattle restocking exercises exemplify, NGO and Government interventions were not just of an economic nature, but extended into the cultural domain. At times this included consolidating a particular view of history. A good example of this was the commemoration of the Atiak massacre, an incident in which several hundred technical school students had been killed in 1995. In 1999 a memorial stone was built and the Anglican Bishop was invited to celebrate mass. A major event was developed, which also served as a highly successful fund-raising exercise for a new technical college (Lwani Memorial College), with contributions in cash and kind received from local government officials, NGOs, embassies, and local groups.

Changing Military–Civilian Relationships

Many people saw relationships between soldiers and civilian women as a major indicator of cultural debilitation, and as an explanation for the spread of HIV and resultant physical debilitation which appeared to be threatening Uganda's much hailed success in controlling the spread of HIV/AIDS.[56] Although some figures suggest that overall HIV+ rates declined in Gulu in the mid 1990s, the sharpness of the drop (from 25 per cent recorded amongst pregnant women in Gulu district in 1993 to 13.6 per cent in 1997) raises questions about the reliability of the data. Furthermore, perhaps the more important indicator was that the figures for Gulu district had risen from among the lowest to the fourth highest in the country.[57] Whether in discussion with soldiers' wives in Gulu Barracks, HIV positive women in a self-help group, or traditional healers, 'war' emerged as their overall explanation for this. This issue was further examined with the soldiers' wives, as set out in Table 6.9 below.[58]

The linkage with the war is unambiguous in the top four reasons. Taking the others in turn it is possible to link them in also. People passed through Gulu on business which was not necessarily to do with the war, but many of the business activities were in fact part of the war economy – building roads for military patrols, boreholes for displaced camps, marketing produce from block farms etc. Many people would argue that an increase in availability of sexual services was a symptom of the economic pressures which themselves arose from the violence of war. Even 'alcoholism and discos' may not be unrelated, with both offering a form of escapism from the otherwise unrelenting pressures of the war situation. Ignorance about HIV/AIDS was at least partially due to the lack of sensitisation by government and NGO workers, which in turn was at least partly attribut-

Table 6.4 Explanations Given by Soldiers' Wives in Gulu Barracks in Answer to the Question 'Why Do You Think the HIV Infection Rate in Gulu Has Risen To Be One of the Highest in the Country?'

Ranking	Explanations
1	Crowding of people in urban areas due to search for security
2	Confining people in camps
3	Many soldiers from different parts of Uganda
4	Abduction
5	Many people passing through Gulu on business
6	Economic pressure due to violence (e.g. if your father gets killed and you become an orphan you have to get a man to look after you)
7	Alcoholism and discos
8	Ignorance about the dangers of HIV/AIDS
9	Many war widows
10	Older people having sex with young people by promising to pay school fees

able to insecurity preventing travel. War widows were obviously a result of war, and while the practice of older people using economic power to obtain sexual favours was not peculiar to war, the poverty which made this an option to be considered by young people had undoubtedly been aggravated by the war.

The HIV positive women explained their own infection in a number of ways (Table 6.5).

Table 6.5 Women's Stated Reasons for Their Own Infection with HIV, as Given by 116 Members of an ACORD Assisted Support Group for People Living With AIDS

Women's stated reasons for HIV infection	Number	%
Polygamy	31	26.7
Displacement	23	19.8
Inheritance	14	12.1
Cross-Infection	8	6.9
Prostitution	7	6.0
Separation	6	5.2
Rape	6	5.2
Peer Group	6	5.2
Multiple Partners	4	3.4
Husband	4	3.4
Unknown	3	2.6
LRA	2	1.7
Casual Sex	2	1.7
TOTAL	116	100

The belief of 20 per cent of respondents that 'displacement' was the cause of their infection is broadly shared with the soldiers' wives, who see urban overcrowding and people being confined in the camps as two of the major explanations for the rising rate of HIV infection.[59] Although large numbers blame polygamy and wife-inheritance for their own infection, suggesting 'cultural' factors as the major explanation alongside displacement, when the data used to compile the table is further examined it also points to a strong relationship between militarization and the spread of HIV. Of the 116 women, 48.3 per cent had had soldiers as their former partners or were in relationships with soldiers. Of the seven who stated rape as the reason for their infection, four had been raped by soldiers. Two of the four husbands who were blamed for their wives' infection had been soldiers. Three of the six who believed they had become infected as a result of 'separation' from their partners [i.e. because their partners had become infected while away from home and then brought the infection home] had been married to soldiers. Although such figures cannot replace epidemiological surveys, they do suggest further avenues of enquiry.

Traditional healers in Gulu, who claimed to have seen an increase in STIs and AIDS cases over the years, attributed this to:

- rape by soldiers
- too many mobile soldiers [i.e. soldiers who were not based in one barracks for a longer period of time]
- confinement in camps
- poverty/hunger leading to prostitution
- redundancy leading to alcohol abuse and careless sex
- rape by other civilians
- having to sleep in many different places in search for security increases chance of sexual encounters (e.g. *alup*, night commuters)
- low morals during discos
- only soldiers having a sure income, which is something women look for
- infected people deliberately setting out to infect others
- resistance to condom use/ignorance about need for condoms

Although the military are by no means the only cause identified, the explicit connection the healers made between between rising levels of STIs/HIV and the military echoed the words of the late medical superintendent at Lacor hospital; 'There are also a lot of sexual health problems from rapes and from young girls going with soldiers to get food and money'.[60]

Although at times based on rumour (such as the one that soldiers known to be HIV positive were instructed to rape), the connection was not without grounds. Even if there were no rape or intention to spread HIV involved, the military would be an obvious vector as their mode of organisation and operation created both incentives and opportunities for multiple sexual partners. Despite UPDF official policy being that no soldier was allowed to have a wife while on mobile duty (i.e. when stationed outside the main barracks), in practice they could take wives with them when deployed to rural detaches, or take local women there. Indeed, many rural detaches had small settlements adjacent to them where sex and alcohol were sold. These consisted of a mixture of local women and women who had been left behind when soldiers were re-deployed elsewhere – these latter being known as 'camp followers'. In discussion at one such detach, the soldiers described how when they were first deployed, those who had no wife with them would stroll through these settlements, and choose themselves a woman whom they would then take to stay with them as their 'wives' inside the detach until they were transferred elsewhere. This included getting an identity card issued to show that the woman was the 'wife' of the man concerned.[61] Thus military strategy intersected with the policy of moving people to 'protected villages' to increase contacts between military and civilians as most had a detach stationed within them or nearby. In the larger camps, when insurgency levels were high, such military units formed an important addition to the population.

There was generally a financial transaction involving not just the soldier and the woman, but also the woman's parents. According to the soldiers in Gweng-dia detach, 'Parents normally follow their daughters to the barracks just a few days after you take her inside. Some of them keep coming back for more money'. Their wives gave the example of one woman from Gwengdia who was herself in Gwengdia 'detach' and had six daughters spread around other detaches. The soldiers' wives reported that 'Sometimes old soldiers bring young girls of 16 years as their wives: their boss (the commander) just said that if they have brought in their wife then it is not his business to interfere with it'. Although the average age of our focus group respondents was 28.5, and the average age of marriage was 21, six of the fifteen women had themselves been married below the age of 18 (12, 13, 14, 14, 15 and 17 respectively).[62]

Evidently, for women in the desperate circumstances created by the war and life in the camps, becoming a 'camp follower' may have been the only realistic option – and a decision in which not only were they at times encouraged by their parents, but in which the wider community was believed to have a vested interest, despite the loud discourse of moral disapproval. Indeed, in a day-to-day sense the small settlements on the edge of military barracks served as a buffer between the soldiers and civilians in the village as a whole, although in the longer term they were clearly a potential vector for HIV transmission between the two, as women moved in and out of them. Asked whether the commander of the detach was making any effort to stop the women staying on the fringes of the detach, the soldiers' wives said the civilians living nearby had told the commanding officer not to chase them – because if the prostitutes were not around the soldiers would disturb their women. As one argued, the prostitutes were there 'to assist those soldiers inside who don't have wives'.

Many civilians feared the presence of soldiers. One field-worker wrote, 'I believe and have seen beyond doubt that being wives of soldiers doesn't create a sense of security instead it worsens the affinity [likelihood] of catching Aids. This is because soldiers are care-free people in society'. Many were deeply concerned to try and limit the exposure of young women to soldiers. When the

Local Councillor for Awac paid a visit to Awac Displaced School in July 1999, the Parent-Teacher-Association identified (amongst other things) two major problems relating to the soldiers in the area, namely 'Soldiers taking pupils for being house wives and not being followed up by Law', and 'Parents sending school girls to sell local [alcoholic] brew in the Market thus exposing them to the soldiers'.[63] Similarly, when the Minister of Education and Sports addressed the people of Awere camp in October 1999 he was reported as saying that 'Home-guards … are now spoiling the women of civilians. If any commits himself to taking the wife of the civilian, he must be taken to court. Not only Home-guards but soldiers must respect civilians'. He also made much of the fact that even soldiers (along with teachers and businessmen) would be taken to court if they 'played with school girls'.[64]

Civilian concerns about the military had some basis, if our discussions with soldiers and their wives in Gwengdia are anything to go by. They presented the need for men to have an outlet for sexual frustrations as natural – and therefore undeniable and to be accommodated. This discourse was also evident in Gulu barracks, where many soldiers kept their official wives. Both men and women argued that separation in the course of duty resulted in sexual frustration for both. Soldiers dealt with this by opting for prostitutes or taking other partners, as described above, and their women also described taking other partners – sometimes to satisfy sexual needs, but also to find an alternative source of economic support if their partners were away for a long period. Further reasons given by the women for changing partners included 'misunderstandings and indiscipline', the death of a husband, tribalism by in-laws (i.e. they tell their son to get a wife from his own village), status of husband, barrenness (the husband takes another wife to give him a child), and change of place of work (mobility). Men were believed to change partners for similar reasons: indiscipline, admiring ladies of a lighter colour, tribalism (get someone from your own tribe), the need for children, and 'being seduced by civilian women'.

Despite the considerable frankness with which respondents described behaviours and motivations, at another level their interpersonal relations were far from straightforward. As well as HIV-promoting patterns of multiple partnerships and short-term sexual relations based on physical and economic needs, it appeared that normative discourses of marriage and fidelity were a further obstacle to HIV prevention. Condom use would be taken as evidence of mistrust – in both directions. If the wife asked the husband to wear a condom it could be because she did not trust him to have been faithful to her, or because she herself had been unfaithful to her husband in his absence. Compounding these factors was a lack of medical information or treatment (Chapter 5), and the fact that HIV was only one risk amongst many facing the soldiers. Both commissioned and non-commissioned officers ranked HIV/AIDs as less of a risk to their health than the risks associated with being a soldier (Table 6.6).

The threat of death through HIV infection appeared to play a much smaller part in the imaginings of many soldiers than did the more immediate threats of war related injuries and death.

Table 6.6 Ranking of Risks to Health as Given in Two Focus Groups with Members of the UPDF, 3–4 June 1999

Ranking	Commissioned Officers	Ranking	Non-Commissioned Officers
1	Illnesses such as malaria	1	Landmines
2	Landmines	2	Gunshots
3	Gunshots	3	Ambush
4	Fighting/Combat	4	Accidents
5	Ambushes	5	Thieves
6	HIV/AIDS	6	Alcohol
7	Accidents (e.g. road accidents)	7	AIDS and 'Bad Friends'
8	Snakebites while in the bush	8	Indiscipline
9		9	Poor Command
10		10	Poor Hygiene

The central role of money in military-civilian relationships was clear. As recipients of a monthly salary, the military stationed in such rural areas – where the majority of men had no source of income at all due to their displacement – occupied a particular position in the sex-money nexus created by the acute impoverishment of the war zone, especially within the camps. Civilian men would complain that there was no market for them (i.e. women were not interested in them), and the soldiers reported that unlike many civilian men, who were described as 'mukono gamo' (literally 'hands glued', i.e. tight with money), they could provide for their women, even if only on a temporary basis while stationed in the area. Furthermore, the soldiers argued that 'Soldiers are not very economical; they use money on women anyhow ... Civilians don't have money because of this type of war; people have been chased from villages to these types of camp'. They noted that when waiting for their crops to mature civilians did not have any money, whereas as soldiers they had a regular monthly income, whatever the season. Thus, 'whereas a civilian wife at this point can be seen buying only greens in the market, a soldier's wife will be out buying meat on a daily basis. It therefore becomes very easy to woo a woman'.[65] When the time came for the soldiers to be transferred, they would leave many of the local women behind in the settlement adjacent to the detach, to await the next set of soldiers to be posted. Asked how they felt when they had to leave these 'wives', one soldier said 'it is very painful because you have dropped money there'.

For some civilian men it was less a question of soldiers' money than of women's (im)morality. As one argued:

> To get a wife by civilians despite the presence of [an] army detach depends on the morals of women in an area. Normally, a well sound economical man just disputes [competes with] soldiers easily and defeats them. Culturally, rural women don't have the affinity of loving a person of unknown destination. It is only immoral ones that switch to consumption of soldiers.

Another observed that 'Normally wives eloped by soldiers are abandoned in case of [the soldier's] transfer to another station. Very few cases lead to permanent marriage. One must note that women who go to soldiers are prostitutes'.

The question of what was actually happening in Gulu in terms of HIV prevalence and incidence rates, and the place of militarization in these, is an open one. On the one hand the literature about HIV indicates that militaries tend to have higher levels of HIV infection than the general population (Foreman, 2002: 1–3), and as has been explored, there are numerous points at which the Ugandan army intersects with civilians, whether through voluntary encounters or in instances of rape of the civilian population. On the other hand, figures from the sentinel sites in Gulu show a drop in prevalence throughout the 1990s. However, it should be stressed that the actual epidemiology of HIV in the war zone, although important in terms of physical debilitation, is not the central issue here. What is key to the discussion is the evidently widespread perception of linkages between HIV and changing social practices, the central place of militarization within this, and the way military-civilian relationships were seen as indicative of cultural debilitation. This latter is particularly important given that militarization is offered by the government as *the* solution to the problem of war.

Discussion

The picture which emerges thus far is one of various degrees of physical and psychological debilitation, linked to discourses – and to a certain degree realities – of cultural debilitation. Acts of war obviously had an instant impact in terms of physical injuries such as gun-shot wounds, mines, bombs and miscarriages as a result of bomb blasts, and the state of displacement resulted in malnutrition and related illnesses. There was also a direct relationship between physical and psychological debilitation. Physical ill-health (or the threat of it) caused psychological stress, which in turn was somatised into more physical symptoms and behaviours. For example, people committed suicide not because they necessarily were HIV+, but because of fear that they might be (see Chapter 7). The stress of the idea alone was enough to prompt drastic steps. Physical hardship, loss of livelihoods, loss of relatives, shelter, livestock, repeated displacements, sleeping in the bush, constant fear of abduction and landmines, trying to buy security by selling children to soldiers, were other self-evident psychological stressors.

Many impacts, which looked like the result of a discrete incident (Patricia Atim kills herself because her money is taken), were in fact not. Rather they were the outcome of an accumulation of traumatic experiences which, for most people, continued over the entire period of the war (see Chapter 3). This was further complicated by the fact that the actions people took in response to such cumulative debilitation, while at times successful, at times contributed to further debilitation. Thus one person brewing alcohol in order to feed her own children, could meet the needs of an alcoholic man who as a result would not have money to feed his own children. The account of Patricia Atim's suicide, given above, offers a subtle example of such complexity. The loss of the money she had saved up was almost certainly not the only cause, but rather the proverbial straw that broke the camel's back. Having had her money taken by her husband, she has to borrow the very tiny amounts needed to bring about her own death, an indicator of her desperate economic situation. Her actions undoubtedly threaten her family with further debilitation. Once she is dead, the medical staff refuse to remove the foetus from her womb; not only has poverty reduced the scope for compassion (the medical staff are unwilling to do the operation without additional payment), but it has removed the space for her parents to grieve. At the very moment of their loss, they have to make an economic calculation. There is no space in the poverty of camp life for grief to override the day-to-day concerns of the living.

The relationship between militarization and the risk of HIV further exemplifies the ways in which debilitation was not just about the physical environment created by war and displacement, nor was it simply about the cumulative impact of multiple instances of war-related violence, important though both these were. It also related to economic strategies which served short-term survival needs, but made the medium to long term terminally insecure. Marrying a soldier could potentially give the woman a more reliable economic base, and also reduce the number of mouths her own family had to feed, but also carried increased risks of becoming HIV positive. Where HIV/AIDS did occur, it was the result of a complex interplay of conflict, displacement, impoverishment and militarization, a whole range of economic, physical, psychological and emotional needs and imperatives which arose from this over time, and the way in which these eventually altered patterns of behaviour, thinking and self-perception in a manner which actually accelerated debilitation, and which continued to inform the shape of life inside the war zone even once the primary victims of violence were long gone. In other words, the common assumption that impacts only happened *to* people, rather than also happening *through* them, simply did not hold.

Another coping strategy, the necessary internalisation and hiding away of grief (rather than its overt expression), which occurs in the face of a relentless stream of traumatic incidents and circumstances (experienced first-hand or witnessed second-hand), also seems likely to have negative consequences. In my own fieldwork I developed a very 'thick skin' within about three months, but my subsequent experience of how difficult it proved to be to even just to go over data I had collected (with the protection of a seemingly thick skin), suggests that this emotional numbing was illusory. All the experiences heard about or witnessed, even if barely acknowledged at the time, seemed to have been deposited somewhere in my memory, able to foreground themselves when the absolute need to suppress them was no longer there. And this was just when witnessing at second-hand. For people who are unable to escape the relentless accumulation of such experiences, and who have little occasion on which these things can be vented in some relatively harmless way, it seems probable that another means of expression will eventually be found. When traditional healers in Gulu and camp officials in Pabo were asked 'why do men overdrink?' they used almost identical language: 'Firstly, redundancy, feelings of powerlessness, they cannot live as they used to do when they had full control ... Powerlessness is based on the fact that men cannot cope with what happened whereas they used to be fully occupied. They find that people who were beneath them socially are now above them'. Asked whether this sense of redundancy was more of a problem for older or younger men, the camp officials answered 'it is common to all age brackets – because the children feel the powerlessness'.[66] This transfer of impact across generations epitomises the complexity of impacts and the extent to which they become self-perpetuating.

Signs of Resilience?

At one level, as I have argued, beliefs about social and cultural breakdown or dilution were not always fully supported by the evidence, or at least there was evidence to qualify the picture painted. At another these discourses were shorthand for the complex interaction between people's debilitation and their adaptive responses to it, the broader impact of this on society, and a sense of its irreversibility. They reflected a loss of social predictability; people were breaking a range of social taboos, whether in the interests of survival (e.g. the mother who placed her six daughters in six different detaches), or in the interests of taking their own lives in suicide attempts. The discourses thus served as an indicator of fear of loss of control – for example, by adults over youth and by (male) youth over women – and of fear that the changes were irreversible. They can thus be read as the closest most people could come to admitting their own personal sense of failure or psychological distress.

At yet another level, these statements and discourses could be read as signs of resistance to social breakdown which qualify the very picture of absolute collapse which they purport to portray. The key feature in this regard is that they allocate responsibility for what has gone wrong to the people most affected by what has gone wrong. The assertion is made, for example, that it is parents who have lost control over children – rather than an alternative explanation, namely that soldiers have taken control of those children. Women's decision to become prostitutes is seen as moral weakness rather than as a personal sacrifice made to prevent their children starving. It is children who are said to be disrespectful rather than adults who are abusive.

While such assertions were disempowering for those being blamed, they were empowering for those doing the blaming. Whereas focusing blame on the LRA would at least partially externalise blame,[67] and thereby lessen the possibility of addressing the situation, the language of moral, cultural and social breakdown, by internalising responsibility, allowed some sense of control, or at least the possibility of regaining control over a chaotic situation. Reversing moral collapse, re-instilling traditional values, re-integrating traumatised youth, picking fallen women off the floor, all are within the realms of the feasible – unlike other aspects of the war situation, such as the rebels, or the army, or the food distributions, which were externally controlled, and therefore, in a literal sense, out of control.

Conclusions

This chapter began with the question of why people did not take advantage of long lulls in the armed violence to return to their homes, and I proposed that, having been forced into the camps in the first place, there would have been risks in leaving them on an unauthorised basis. There would also have been no access to the assistance needed to tide people over until they could begin harvesting again. Furthermore, to move back home would have been to lose the benefits of the considerable amounts of energy they had been obliged to invest in consolidating the protected villages. As such, it was scarcely a choice between two more or less equal options, and it could be said that conditions in the protected villages created a metaphorical prison.

But in addition to these considerations, something far deeper had happened. In the name of 'protection', people actually underwent a gradual process of ever more complex forms of debilitation. Physical debilitation presented some very practical obstacles to returning home. The physical capacity and strength to re-open fields that had lain fallow for several years was diminished in many households. Thousands of children had suffered permanent physical and mental damage due to malnutrition, and premature deaths had left some households without a provider. The intellectual and physical bases for reconstruction were thus compromised. In many instances this was worsened by the effects of psychological debilitation arising from multiple violations over time. Although often hidden, these were at times externalised, as in the case of alcoholism or even suicides, whether of heads of households or of youth. At an even more profound level, various institutions had been undermined and people had adapted their behaviours to their circumstances in ways which contributed both further physical and psychological debilitation, and to a sense of cultural debilitation.[68]

Although these processes of debilitation were not necessarily as sequential as this articulation makes them appear, each of them made the other less easily reversible. When physical debilitation was compounded by psychological problems both became more difficult to deal with. When the cultural context within which such issues would otherwise be dealt with was debilitated, they became still less amenable to solutions. The longer these processes continued, therefore, the less reversible they appeared to be and the more they militated against the possibility of an easy return. Living under a situation of protection which was a form of violation in its own right thus created further metaphorical chains which people could not shake off.

From this perspective, many of the interventions in northern Uganda were wholly inadequate, for they tended to break down violations into discrete acts (e.g. having been raped) or issues (e.g. lack of sanitation) which could be quantified, thus allowing the illusion that their impacts could also be managed, addressed and reversed. Physical debilitation, in particular, was targeted through various forms of assistance, such as food relief, supplementary feeding, seeds and tools, demonstration plots and prosthetics, and thus made to seem at least partly reversible (even if physical stunting and mental retardation were not).

Th humanitarians' simple and fundamentally static model of the people affected – they were OK before something bad happened to them, they would be OK again after the damage has been fixed – could not bring people's health back to the status quo ante, to life as it was before, because it could not accommodate the reality of truly relentless processes of physical and psychological violation, in which there was no time for recovery from discrete incidents. Most interventions – notwithstanding some very limited attempts at trauma counselling – failed to conceptualise, let alone address, the self-reinforcing interplay of physical, psychological and cultural debilitation, which relentless violation provokes.

Many people in the camps were therefore not only themselves debilitated to a point where it became very difficult to return to their homes even when the opportunity to do so presented itself, but they were unlikely to receive assistance of a kind which adequately addressed the complexities of this debilitation. Notwithstanding the fact that the very discourses of breakdown could be interpreted as signs of resistance to the changes wrought by debilitation, for some the situation seemed irreversible.

Notes

1. District Education Officer, Gulu, March 2002.
2. Ongiertho Emmanuel, November 1999: 2.
3. Awer, 20 November 1999.
4. UNDMT report, undated, point 5.1. Whereas when people moved to the camps they could sometimes return home to recover crops which were still developing when they left, by the second year of camp life the fields had not been ploughed or planted and had reverted to bush, requiring considerable labour to clear it again.
5. UNOCHA, February 2001, *Secondment of NRC standby staff member to UNOCHA in Uganda.*
6. ICRC, June 2000.
7. Calculated as 4.6 persons per household on the basis of camp population figures and household numbers provided by one of the camp leaders involved in food distributions in Cwero. This gives a slightly higher ration per person than under the WFP's own calculation which, until May 1999 was of 5 people per household, regardless of the actual number.
8. = 25/4.9.
9. Prolonged vitamin and iron deficiencies (as opposed to inadequate calories) are believed to have serious effects on mental capacity.
10. Ministry of Health, Action Against Hunger U.S. (ACF), and Norwegian Refugee Council.
11. FEWS NET: *Uganda – Monthly Food Security Update,* 27 February 2003.
12. Atiak, 25 March 1999.

13. A report from Patongo Health Centre in Pader district showed that between December 2001 and January 2002 80 people had died of malaria in that health centre alone. KM E-newsletter No 5, 15 February 2002.

14. Interviewed in Lacor Hospital, January 1998.

15. Gersony, 1997: 48.

16. In Chapter 5 it was noted that seeds handed out in the camps were accompanied by a warning that 'the seeds are dusted with poison therefore it should not be eaten'.

17. Sibacol is used against worms on crops such as onions, tomatoes and cabbages, also around banana trees. Some people use it to try and catch birds and edible rats, but of course this is dangerous as the poison is then inside the meat.

18. Girling noted that 'Several of the rare cases of suicide of which I heard occurred among childless wives' (1960; 27) which both suggests that there has been an increase in rate, and further supports a close relationship between suicide and inability to meet gendered expectations.

19. 26 October 1998, Anaka.

20. *Bedo Piny Pi Kuc,* 26 June 1998, Gulu.

21. Attiak-Biabia, 21 September 1999.

22. Awac, 9 July 1999.

23. Awere, 1 October 1999.

24. Awac Senior Secondary School, March 02.

25. It is important not to assume that it is because they are teachers that some are drinking heavily – one headmaster interviewed noted that one of his teachers had started drinking heavily only after his wife had been killed in cross-fire.

26. Gulu Municipality report, December 1998.

27. Anaka, 27 February 2000.

28. Interview with secondary school teachers, Gulu High School, 13 August 1998.

29. Report from Gulu Municipality, December 1998.

30. St Joseph's College Layibi, March 2002.

31. Gulu Municipality, September 1999.

32. Keyo SS, interview with students, 13 March 2002. Whether these aspirations should be interpreted at face value, or as indicating a dark sense of humour, or poking fun at the researchers, is an open question. Whichever of these it is, when combined with the other indicators of initiative, it does not correspond to the vision of apathy and demotivation portrayed by many teachers.

33. This is not to deny that many potential students, particularly those living far outside the district capitals where the secondary schools are all located, are faced with insuperable practical difficulties which make it impossible to pursue secondary schooling.

34. For full discussion of this, see El Bushra, Judy and Dolan C (2002).

35. Notes from visit to Coo-Pe, 19 January 1998.

36. Atiak, August 1998.

37. Last rites could be conducted long after the death and burial of persons. Thus the funeral rites of one fieldworker's wife and daughter, both of whom had been killed by fire from a UPDF mamba, took place at least two years after their actual deaths (Awere, 6 April 2000). Given the importance attributed to performing this symbolic laying to rest, it seems likely that last rites will be a significant feature of any post-conflict context.

38. Awer, July 1998.

39. Atiak, August 1998.

40. Palaro Pilot, 30 July 1998.

41. Awach, August 1998.

42. 28 September 1999.

43. Odek, 9 December 1999.

44. Notes on traditional dances, Gulu, 12 March 2002.

45. 3 July 1999.

46. 5 February 1999.
47. In this context Okot p'Bitek's 'Song of Lawino' is pertinent. Lawino contrasts her experience of formal education, which made her feel like 'stale bread on a rubbish heap', to how she felt when dancing with her peer group;
    'We joined the line of friends
    And danced among our age-mates
    And sang songs we understood,
    Relevant and meaningful songs,
    Songs about ourselves (p'Bitek, 1985; 79)
48. Palaro pilot, 30 July 1998.
49. Awer, June 1998.
50. Awer, 6 June 1999.
51. Odek, 14 December 1998.
52. Pabo, 30 October 1998.
53. Awer, 3 November 1998.
54. However, the necessary support was not given and by August of the same year the forty-five cattle given in March had all died.
55. Awach, 3 March 2000.
56. An article in *The Lancet* in July 2002 questioned the empirical basis for such a success claim and warned against extrapolating policy lessons from the Ugandan case to other countries facing high HIV levels (Parkhurst, 2002).
57. UNAIDS/WHO *Epidemiological Fact Sheet,* 2000 Update, p12.
58. Research conducted by the COPE team in collaboration with the ACORD HIV/AIDS prevention programme in Gulu. Reported on at the September 1999 conference.
59. Kitgum district, which, at least until 2002, had far less displaced camps, did not experience a similarly severe rise in infection levels.
60. Lacor Hospital, Gulu, January 1998.
61. Gwengdia detach, 7 June 1999. One widow of a deceased soldier explained, 'they give them the identification letter called 'Kihali'... It is just a small card with the numbers of your husband. So when for real you are married they give you that card with the army number of your husband. If you are somebody who was not married you can also stay there [i.e. live with the soldier] but there is no help that they give to you [i.e. you will get no financial compensation if the soldier dies for any reason]'.
62. Gwengdia 'detach', 7 June 1999.
63. Awac, 9 July 1999
64. Awere, 1 October 1999
65. The image of soldiers' women leading a life of relative luxury was countered by civilians who, when asked 'what happens to women who marry soldiers?', answered 'they want women to build for them (Mama Nwoya huts), carry luggage, provide sex. Some get taken up to the DRC, some get abandoned along the way. Other women will follow their husbands from place to place'. One respondent knew a woman who had tried to follow her husband, but had eventually given up and found him, a distant relative, to help her re-settle. She was now in the terminal stages of illness (Discussion in Pabo, 5 March 2002).
66. Pabo, 5 March 02
67. This can only be partially successful insofar as many of the LRA are drawn from the same population, described as 'our children', and as such, in a moral sense, 'within' that population.
68. I would thus suggest that the diminution of cultural and social agency which Finnström argues will eventually happen (Finnström, 2003: 191), had already begun to do so.

7

PROTECTION AS HUMILIATION[1]

✦ ❧❧❧❧ ✦

Introduction

Up to this point I have talked about how, under the guise of 'protection', civilians in the war zone in reality experienced massive violation of rights, and resultant physical, psychological and cultural debilitation. I have also talked about how this debilitation, and people's adaptive responses to it, militated against their return from displacement to their homes. This chapter focusses on how these dynamics of violation and debilitation affected men in particular. It argues that violation and debilitation were closely linked to a sense of humiliation, and a collapse of masculinities, and that men's responses to this collapse further contributed to the perpetuation of the situation.

Masculinities collapsed in two senses. Firstly, a hegemonic masculinity emerged in the face of which the space for alternative masculinities largely disappeared. Secondly, although the war consolidated expectations of hegemonic masculinity, it simultaneously undermined men's lived experiences of their own masculinity, thereby aggravating a process set in motion by colonialism. Unable to live up to the model, which involved particular relationships of power over women and youth, but neither offered nor allowed to develop any recognised alternative, men's aspirations and expectations were thwarted, and they experienced social and often physical impotence and resultant humiliation. In the face of this collapse of their own masculinity, some resorted to acts of violence. This could be against themselves, in forms such as alcohol abuse and suicide, but also against others, as seen in domestic violence, mob justice, and joining armed forces, whether government or rebel.

The model of masculinity that men ascribed to also made them more vulnerable to violence meted out by other men, in that it created incentives for armed forces to exercise violence on the civilian population in ways which actively undermined civilian men's sense of self. The state shared an interest in allowing these processes, as they generated a sense of control over both civilians and army, both of which were necessary for national and geo-strategic purposes. This unfortunate synergy of the psychological needs of individuals and the political needs of the state, reinforced the dynamics of conflict and violence and also propped up what was in some key respects a weak state, notably through facilitating ongoing militarization and creating obstacles to the pursuit of non-violent solutions.

The Hegemonic Model of Masculinity

To make the case that there is a relationship between a hegemonic model of masculinity and the self-destructive behaviours outlined in the previous chapter, I draw initially on the findings of a workshop which considered various forms of discrimination and social exclusion in northern Uganda, and their relationship to conflict.[2] This brought together the staff of the ACORD Gulu office, the COPE fieldworkers and research assistants. From the nineteen male and five female participants, it was apparent that a powerful admixture of pre-colonial, colonial and post-colonial messages had led to a normative model of masculinity which combined a range of characteristics and behaviours, primarily defined by the extent to which they differed from stereotypes of women and youth. These polarised stereotypes of what women, youth and men were like then informed what they should do, how they should relate to one another, and what their respective positions and roles in society should be.[3]

What Women Are (Supposed To Be) Like

Workshop participants argued that it is generally assumed that women differ from men, that they are weaker, incapable and a burden, a position legitimised by the Biblical story in Genesis that man was created first, woman from his rib, and the saying that women are the 'weaker vessels'. The assumption that women are therefore more controllable is reflected in the account of abduction given in Chapter 4, in which boys were chained together whereas girls were not. Participants had been brought up to believe that women cannot perform to the level of men, and must conform to the culture of their husbands. Women are regarded as unfit for formal education, and it is argued that education of women is a waste of family resources because they get married and move elsewhere. Technical institutions are regarded as being for men only.

Women are often portrayed as being like children, without knowledge or skills, or as jealous gossipers and busybodies who are not to be trusted and who are unable to be in solidarity with one another. There are sayings in Acholi that 'Women are always cats who seek sympathy', and that 'when there is constant drizzling it is like women quarrelling'. They are also likely to be blamed for domestic wrangles and misfortune in the family and organisations – as noted in Chapter 5, one cause of male impotence is believed to be a mother touching her son's private parts within the first three days of his life.

Once bridewealth has been paid and a woman marries, the woman is supposed to leave the parental home and move to the husband's home, where she is considered the subordinate and the property/asset of the husband. She loses her own clan identity on marriage but does not fully assume the clan identity of her husband, and is viewed as an outsider and therefore not to be trusted (On a historical note, Girling noted in research conducted in 1951 that 'until her children have grown she has few rights and apart from her husband has no close relationships with members of the village' (1960: 25)).

Women do the domestic work for the family and can be beaten if they do not show respect to men (Girling wrote that 'The beating of young wives to train them is regarded as the duty of the husband' (1960; 32)). Historically, women were not allowed to eat certain foods such as chicken, and, according to WFP, women and girls remain 'prone to malnutrition as a result of household food allocation patterns favouring males' (WFP, 1999: 17). They are not supposed to initiate divorce, which is seen as the prerogative of men. Women tend to be regarded by men as there to produce children, which then belong to men; if a woman divorces she has to leave any children behind (Girling describes how, if after some time a woman failed to produce children, she 'may be returned to her father and another must be provided in her place'. He also argues that 'As a mother of a child and as the mistress of a household she [a woman] achieves the highest status possible for a woman in Acholi society. The more children she bears, the greater the respect she will enjoy ...' (1960: 21–24)).

Women's voices are often ignored and they are denied ownership of family assets. To this day women do not participate in clan meetings or the traditional leadership, which is all male, and if they do the elders will ask 'what are women doing here in our meeting?' (see Chapter 4 for Kony's view of Betty Bigombe's participation in the 1994 peace talks). That women are to be put back in their place if they overstep their limits is clear from an Acholi saying which translates as 'when the hen crows it must be slaughtered'.

What Youth Are (Supposed To Be) Like

Workshop participants noted that 'Unmarried young people are perceived as UNABLE to participate in political life' and that whereas 'all adults are responsible (because they have children and houses and run homes)', youth are stereotyped as 'irresponsible, disrespectful, impatient, extravagant, arrogant, fun-lovers who are ineffective at work' and who 'like leisure at the expense of work'. Such stereotypes were evident at a seminar on Human Rights and Democracy organised by Uganda Young Democrats (see Chapter 3), where the vice-president of the Democratic Party was reported as saying that 'since independence the youth have not been prepared to use their resources for the nation's benefit ... The youth have power but need tuning. If they are not utilised, they can run amok".[4] Stereotypes were further demonstrated in a speech given in Awere by the Minister for Education and Sport: 'He told the youth to be active. They must not be sitting free without work. They must start projects which the government will help them with. They must not be wasting time dancing disco. They must see that they are studying very well at schools. They must be careful with AIDS'.[5]

Unmarried participants in the ACORD workshop, who according to this model were still youth, felt that these stereotypes were used to ensure that 'development is the domain of adults alone', in other words that youth had no access to power. Adults claim their experience counts more and tell youth 'Don't start climbing trees from the top.' Youth ideas 'are not listened to' and they are 'kept in limbo about vital information'. 'Youths' complaints and requests are ignored' and 'adults are slow to react on decisions important to the youth'.[6] Given this tendency for adults to look down on youth, it was therefore probably no accident that when the LRA representative welcomed the delegation led by Mrs Betty Bigombe in 1994 he stressed that it was as young people that the LRA were ready to talk with Government representatives and elders to reach a compromise which would enable them to come out of the bush (Chapter 4).

A strong youth voice was generally absent in the major civil society groupings which emerged over the course of the war, but when given a voice, as in the Uganda Young Democrats seminar, young people appeared to have more radical critiques of the situation than their elders. When we asked young people to identify the main actors in the war, they were able, despite having no access to media other than the radio and the occasional newspaper, to identify both actors and their interests in the conflict, as shown in the findings from one such group discussion with eleven youths (average age 22) as set out in Table 7.1.

While this table shows considerable insight into the complexities of the situation, very few of the youth's insights would be carried to a national level. While the members of the group involved in the above discussion were unusually highly-educated (nine of the eleven had attained Senior 4 (GCE/GCSE 'O' level)), none of them was likely to go any further due to various constraints(see below).

What Men Are (Supposed To Be) Like

As men are defined in part by how they differ from women, it is clear that they are supposed to be richer, stronger, more capable, knowledgeable and skilled, trustworthy, and able to work in solidarity with one another etc. As they are also defined by how they differ from youth, they should also be responsible, respectful, patient, moderate, humble, serious, and effective. Males are supposed to take priority in education and all other benefits. Boys are regarded as better and brighter – indeed, traditionally a man may take another wife if the first only delivers girl children. Having paid bridewealth, men – who are richer, more educated and own other assets as well – are able to exercise power over their wives.

Masculine Roles

The three main strands of the masculine role are marriage, followed by provision for and protection of the household thereby created. While socialisation into masculinity begins at a very early age and relies on creating difference be-

Table 7.1 Actors Identified by 11 Members of a Youth Group in Gulu District, 8 February 1999

ACTOR/ PLAYER	*Actions keeping war going*	*Actions to bring peace*
Sudan Government	– supporting rebels through giving weapons and things like transport, food, training	
UPDF	– need war allowances – delaying tactics (no immediate response to rebel attacks) – contracting individuals to finish the war (e.g. Salim Saleh)	– fight with the rebels if they come across them – protect civilians and their properties – escort vehicles – rescue abducted children from LRA and hand them over to World Vision and GUSCO
Rebels	– forced recruitment of children – looting food to allow survival – prefer to die fighting than surrender due to the many atrocities they have committed – target civilians, dodge government troops	
President and other government officials	– underestimate the rebels' strength – President refuses peace talks with rebels	
Collaborators	– benefit from materials and goods from rebels – feed rebels with information on strategies and deployment of Government soldiers – provide material support to rebels	
Weapons manufacturers/ sellers (e.g. Britain, South Africa, Americans)	– encourage war in order to create a market for their manufactured weapons – have double standards; they sell weapons to one side and the antidote to the other	
Uganda Government	– Unequal treatment of different categories of soldiers by the government, for example better treatment (e.g. prompt payment of salaries and allowances to mobile troops and not to the militia) – Weak security arrangements in camps for displaced people exposes them to abduction by rebels – support to SPLA	

tween men and women, its full achievement is impossible without making the transition to adulthood by way of marriage and thereby marking the difference between youth and adults. It is not sufficient to be an economic provider; a man has to be a married provider. Although any young man who has a source of income will come under heavy pressure to support members of his immediate and extended family, he will continue to be seen as a youth or 'boy' – and as such not to be taken seriously – until he has married and fathered children (see also Finnström, 2003: 309). Marriage is therefore the key to the other two, and it cannot take place without payment of bridewealth.[7]

Having achieved this position of husbands and fathers (preferably educated, to confirm the idea that men are more knowledgeable and skilled than women), men are expected to exercise considerable control over wife and children, their right to do so based on successfully making material provision for them, as well as protecting them. They are also entitled to control the youth. Thus attaining adult masculinity gives men power over other (unmarried) men as well as women.

This normative model of masculinity is therefore inherently relational. Connell has argued that 'masculinity' does not exist except in contrast with 'femininity' (1995: 68), I would add that it is only brought fully into focus through the contrast with 'youth'. Although the experience of being subordinate to adult men is shared by women and youth alike, the nature of the relationship is quite different. Whereas men are supposedly powerful by contrast with women, they cannot have the power without the women as the primary markers of masculinity centre around their relationship with women. The power over other men, by contrast, rests in excluding them from the equation on the basis of their not being married.

In summary, the hegemonic model rests on a clear distinction being drawn between male and female characteristics, as well as between 'youth' and 'adults'. It is also entirely dependent on marriage, the only possible way to transition from youth to adult status. At its simplest it can therefore be described as based on sexism, heterosexism, ethnocentrism and adultism, entailing considerable economic responsibilities and a particular relationship with the state.[8] The model of marriage-provision-protection is hegemonic in that it largely precludes alternatives and is buttressed by major forms of social and political power. It is normative in that men are taught they should aspire to and judge themselves by it, and state and society in turn judge and assess them against it – before either validating, or belittling and punishing them.

The Gap between Model and Reality: Inability To Fulfil External and Internalised Expectations

That the model of masculinity still held sway was evident from various indicators, including access to secondary education. In 2001, Awac Secondary School had 36 girls and 151 boys. In 2002, Awere Secondary School had 123 girls and 273 boys, while Lukome had 32 girls and 70 boys. One teacher explained these differentials as the product of parents' attitudes, which he claimed resulted in girls being 'given less material support and more domestic work (e.g. collecting water, grinding, cooking)'. Another felt that

> On average the boys perform better than the girls, especially in science subjects ... There is also the problem of drop-outs; for girls this is firstly due to pregnancies ..., secondly school fees, thirdly elopement. For boys it is firstly due to school fees, secondly domestic problems such as being orphans who are also trying to take responsibility for siblings, thirdly fear of defilement cases.[9]

Despite such biases in favour of men, they were by and large unable to live up to the hegemonic model. There was a large and growing disjuncture between men's lived expectations of masculinity, which were contained in the hegemonic model, and lived experiences, which, in the context of ongoing war, heavy militarization and internal displacement, were largely of a failure to come close to that model. The key disjuncture was between the lived expectation of marriage, and the lived experience that it was very difficult to do so, but it extended to all the other expectations outlined. Along with marriage, the acquisition of knowledge and skills, and the provision for and protection of wife/wives and children, all became increasingly difficult.

Acquisition of Knowledge

The prospects of becoming 'knowledgeable' were limited. Both formal and informal education were severely affected by the war, with no secondary schooling available outside district capitals, and extremely limited access to tertiary education (Chapter 5, Part III). Indeed, the statistics for people from northern Uganda attaining tertiary education are an extra-ordinary indicator of the extent to which they, and therefore their region, had been marginalised from the national mainstream: university students from local secondary schools from all fourteen northern districts amounted to only 120 out of a national total of 20,000.[10] With such low involvement in tertiary education and the resultant exclusion from employment opportunities, their critical voices were unlikely to be heard at a national level. For the very few who succeeded in completing secondary education, the job opportunities were limited, the more so as policies of decentralisation had led to many government positions being awarded on the basis of ethnicity. For those who failed to get tertiary education, this could be a source of tension with those older people who perceived themselves as better educated because they 'grew up when education was at its peak under the British'.

On the other hand, it was also possible for those who did acquire some formal education to experience tensions with their elders, for formal education was by no means universally regarded as a 'good thing'. Indeed, in the eyes of one respondent – himself a teacher in a local primary school – it undermined processes of informal socialisation and therefore contributed to the cultural dilution discussed in Chapter 6:

> The formal education has brought a lot of changes on the culture in all aspects. The informal education was concerned with true cultural activities. All the boys' educa-

tion was left with their fathers. In order to become a man a boy must go through that. All girls' education was left with their mothers. Any girl to become a woman must pass through that. But now the formal education has taken over the education of children from their parents. It talks of the curriculum, syllabus and in an organised institution of learning like schools. This has made our culture dying and diluted.[11]

From this perspective, wherein education, culture and masculinity are seen as interdependent, the rise of the formal education model made it difficult if not impossible for a boy to become a man. This resonates with the writings of Okot p'Bitek, an Acholi writer whose *Song of Lawino*, first published in 1966, is in many respects a commentary on social change. In describing her husband Ocol's extensive formal education, Lawino, a rural woman whom he has left behind as he goes to travel, concludes that all the reading has 'killed' her man 'In the ways of his people'. Worse still

'... his actions and behaviour
Are to please somebody else.
Like a woman trying to please her husband!
My husband has become a woman!'

Lawino regards education as a wilderness, a 'Dark Forest of Books', and she makes an explicit connection between education and the loss of masculinity, not just of her husband, but of youth in general:

For all our young men
Were finished in the forest,
Their manhood was finished
In the class-rooms,
Their testicles
Were smashed
With large books! (p'Bitek 1985: 116–117)

In short, p'Bitek, through Lawino, articulated the concerns of those who felt that young men seeking masculinity through formal education was a misguided enterprise, as it effectively destroyed their independence and therefore their 'manhood'. Logically, given that one component of the adult man's roles is to educate and socialise his sons, when 'organised institutions of learning' take over these roles for a large part of every day, they also undermine the masculinity of adult fathers. This is perhaps most pointedly the case where schools become the only place in which cultural dances are taught (see Chapter 6).

Most respondents did not make such explicit connections, but nonetheless lamented the loss of one of the focal points of informal education, the household hearth (*wang oo*) around which old and young would sit in the evening, exchanging information and knowledge. Under curfew or when hiding in the bush in an attempt to avoid abduction, there was no prospect of this taking place (Chapter 6). Even if there were no curfew, it was very difficult in the more congested camps to sit around an open fire when there was barely space to walk between closely spaced and thatch-roofed huts (Chapter 5). Similarly, for the thousands of children who 'commuted' into the major towns every night this route to socialisation had been cut off. In summary, both formal and informal education were drastically curtailed, particularly from 1996 onwards. The 'informal' route to masculinity was gone, and the formal one had not replaced it, leaving youth unable to pursue either route towards adult masculinity.[12]

Marriage

Although there had long been men too poor to pay the bridewealth (Girling, 1960: 167), this was now the case for the vast majority. As Finnström also reports (2003: 24), I neither heard of nor witnessed a single wedding inside the protected villages throughout my fieldwork. The economic basis for the hegemonic combination of marriage (the essential passage to adulthood), and the subsequent provision and protection of the household, was substantially worsened by the war. Marriage based upon payment of bridewealth, hitherto a key mechanism for creating social cohesion, was felt to have changed considerably.[13] With very little access to subsistence farming, education, employment and cash income opportunities (Chapters 2, 5), the possibilities of making bridewealth payments necessary for marriage were seriously curtailed, not least by competition from the military who had more money (Chapter 6). Whereas prior to the war many families held wealth in the form of livestock, this economic guarantee of marriage had been largely removed by cattle rustling and raiding (Chapter 2), prompting one youth to write:

'Shall we marry?
Really when our animals
Scuffled their ways
To the so-called strongmen
With dry woods on their shoulders
That burnt the whole village fallow land
Even introduced us to beg
For the mouths from neighbours?'

The removal of cattle would have been less of an issue had it been possible to produce and sell surpluses for a cash dowry. However, the military situation and the protected village policy both drastically curtailed subsistence and cash-crop farming. Although curfews and restrictions on movement were not applied consistently in these villages, people were generally unable to return to their own lands to farm and able to use only lands immediately around the protected village itself. Hunting and gathering of wild foods, a further source of food and a fall-back position for generating cash income, was frequently outlawed and always dangerous (Chapter 5).

The picture was therefore bleak, as captured in the following fairly typical responses to the question of whether marriage practices had changed; 'There is a totally great change. Mostly there is no marriage these days just because of money in addition no respect for parents and no proper land for cultivation.'[14]

The Atiak fieldworker described how before the camps the suitor would pay bridewealth before the woman moved in with him:

> Now people first collect the girl from her parents illegally, then pay for the dowry later on. [in the past] Most of the girl's relatives would be invited to come, while nowadays it is done secretly as if buying something from the shop. If people [LRA] hear about dowry they will organise to come and loot it. So they [the parents] just take money, depending on the girl's education, family status, e.g. 850,000 for an S4 lady. Payment for interrupting education by getting a woman pregnant is called 'Obal Kwan' [Spoiled Studies i.e. the woman's education is terminated or interrupted as she is not allowed to attend school while pregnant].

It was not just a matter of bridewealth, but also of parental involvement. Girling found that as early as 1951 this was an area in which parents in theory had considerable control over their children's marriage (1960: 70) but in which in reality 'about 50 per cent of all Acholi unions, excluding widow inheritance' were 'marriage by elopement' (1960: 74). Nonetheless, even in the late 1990s the perception that parents should control marriage remained prevalent:

> Marriage ceremonies is completely changed from the ones of the past. It was the duty of the two parents from both sides to accept first before a boy and girl were allowed to get married.[15] Both families must be well known to one another for the good things that they do, like a home with a lot of food, animals (goats, cows etc.), hard-working and are not wizards. With all that good things mentioned above one is allowed to get married. But now a girl may decide to be eloped to a boy without the prior knowledge of their parents and the same with a boy.[16]

In camps where dozens of villages had been brought together (Chapter 5, Part I) parents often simply did not know the prospective in-laws. Without the involvement of the wider family in the marriage arrangements, the obligations which went with such involvement could be sidestepped. Thus; 'the soldiers could go with your daughter without fulfilling the needs of the parents of the girl. Many girls got pregnant and go to the would-be husband. The parents of both the boy and girl would just allow their son/daughter to marry and stay together without dowry, for fear of AIDS epidemic'.[17] In short, both young men who could not get married, and older men who could not control their children's marriage choices, felt their masculinity was undermined. Even where the match was between two civilians, some regarded it bleakly;

> In the end you find that this kind of family does not last longer, it has resulted into a very high level of prostitution. A boy and a girl may decide to come together when they are below the expected age of maturity and this kind of family ends up by not being in a position to maintain themselves properly and eventually they separate.[18]

Provision

As the last quotation suggests, for those who managed to marry, the prospects of providing adequately for wife and children were eroded. Economic context and lack of schooling available made it very difficult to pay school fees and associated costs, thus undermining one of the key responsibilities of the 'masculine' role. Even more basic, ensuring their dependents' health and nutrition became impossible. Fathers could only watch helplessly as a whole generation of physically, mentally and psychologically stunted children was created in the camps (Chapter 6). The psychological impact on men was captured graphically in a *New Vision* report, which, under the headline of 'A Camp of Living Dead', described how

> ... repeated humiliations of camp residents have contributed to loss of pride and self-esteem. How can such residents be expected to assert their dignity when they must bend knees in order to collect 16 kilograms of posho? How can a husband speak with confidence before his wife when other men provide his daily sustenance? How can parents discipline children when the little ones' distended stomach and sunken eyes speak of meals eaten five days ago?[19]

Physical Protection

The third key aspect of the masculine role, physical protection, was largely taken out of the hands of individual men and placed in the hands of the state. Men were now supposed to earn protection for themselves, their wives and children, by relating to the state as loyal citizens who put their trust in the state to protect their interests and were themselves prepared to take up arms whether as soldiers in the army, or as members of local defence units. Participation in *mchaka-mchaka,* or political education courses, was one means of demonstrating loyalty to the state (Chapter 5). Yet this contract between state and citizen, never firmly established in the first place, was seriously undermined by the context of war and violation. Despite a military presence in many of the 'protected villages', rebels raided with impunity, seizing men, women, children and properties at will (Chapters 2, 3, 5). While the state still denied the individual the right to protect his own family (for example by refusing to allow people to leave the protected villages and move back to their home areas), it failed to provide a satisfactory substitute. There was often no response to civilian demands for protection, and even where rebel raids could be predicted, such as after relief deliveries, adequate protection was rare (Chapter 5). Although men could become directly involved in providing physical protection through joining the Home-guard or local defence units, and there were periodic recruitment drives to bolster the Home-guards, there were also widespread fears that young men recruited as Home-guards would be forced into the army and sent far afield, for example to the DRC or Sudan (Chapters 3, 5).

Further Threats to Sense of Masculinity

To this very simple picture of how the basic parameters of masculinity became impossible to fulfil, it is important to add some more insidious ways in which men's self-esteem was undermined. Some of these were products of immediate circumstances, others were rooted in a much longer history. An immediate problem for many men, was that while the protected villages with their high population densities may have increased sexual opportunities for some, they also created a number of obstacles aside from the economic ones outlined. At a most basic level, accommodation in protected villages was overcrowded and did not allow the privacy which characterised pre-war settlement and accommodation patterns. For male youths who engaged in sexual activity with female counterparts there was, over and above the risk of HIV/AIDS, a high risk of being accused of defilement (sex with an under-age female) with the risk of a six or seven years prison sentence if convicted, and very costly out-of-court settlements to avoid such a sentence.

More historically rooted threats to men's self-esteem came from external and internalised ethnocentrism and racism. A long history of north-south opposition, British divide-and-rule tactics of singling out Acholi men for service in the military, and widespread perceptions of Acholi involvement in extreme violence and brutality under Obote II, contributed to a reputation for militarism and violence played upon by southerners to justify the imposition of harsh military control on northerners.[20] As described in Chapter 3, it was also part of the portrayal of the LRA. While this national reputation for militarism sat uneasily with elements of Acholi self-perception such as being well able to reconcile with others and resolve differences through discussion, it blended almost seamlessly with wider ethnocentrist and racist discourses equating northerners with primitivism and backwardness. It was not uncommon to meet people in Kampala who would explain how they had overcome their belief that northerners are 'less than human' – or who still retained such views (see also Finnström, 2003; 112–116). Given that many continued to see Acholi and the LRA as synonymous, and that the LRA was regarded as crazy and dehumanised, the prompts for such beliefs were far from disappearing. As some Acholi youth recounted, 'if you are in Kampala you get a lot of names. For example, if you lose your temper someone might say "Kony is cross"'.

Among the negative messages workshop participants had heard as young children, were that people from northern Uganda were 'primitive', 'backwards', 'poor', 'illiterate' 'swine'. This fitted into a wider colonial racist discourse under which people recalled being told as children that black people were viewed as 'evil', 'animals', 'cannibals', 'monkeys, 'devils' and 'spirits' who 'don't have souls or feelings'. Furthermore, that 'they are dark and ugly', 'smell bad and dirty', and are 'jealous', 'uncooperative', 'backwards', 'unintelligent' and 'associated with disease'. Some were told they were 'supposed to be servants' who were 'not entitled to anything', and 'should be puppets (to be used and thrown at will)' (ACORD 2000).

As in all such cases of widely prevalent discriminatory stereotypes, it is difficult to identify individual sources of such statements. Some are clearly linked with the colonial period. Written in 1966, Okot p'Bitek's *Song of Ocol* is at one level a treatment of exactly these issues. Having been accused by his wife Lawino of having lost his manhood as a result of the white man's influence (see above), Ocol responds in a way which demonstrates the extent to which he has internalised those influences. He disparages 'Africa', as the 'Idle giant', which is

'Diseased with a chronic illness, Choking with black ignorance ... Stuck in the stagnant mud Of superstitions ... Timid, Unadventurous' (1985: 125–126). It is noteworthy that Ocol talks of Africa as a he (1985: 125), whereas European commentators, in a further emasculation of 'Africa' (and by association 'Africans'), generally talk of the continent as feminine. The editor of the 1985 edition of *Song of Lawino,* for example, writes that 'Traditional remedies should have some place in Africa, but they cannot solve all her medical problems' (1985: 30).

The parallels between p'Bitek's words of 1966, and what the workshop participants recalled in 2000, suggest that, once internalised, such negative imagery has a life of its own. And as the feminisation of Africa by p'Bitek's editor demonstrates, the sources are often barely visible. In a sense they become less of an issue than the question of how the underlying and tenacious legacies of ethnocentric and racist discourses compound the more immediate causes of suspicion and hostility at group level, destroy self-esteem and self respect at individual level, and how these in turn feed violence and conflict.

'Gender' Discourse and Practice

That the parameters of models of masculinity and femininity had long been in a state of flux is suggested by Girling's observation from fieldwork conducted in 1951 that 'the status of women has increased in relation to that of men. Women own property of their own, including livestock ... They manufacture distilled liquor and pots for sale ... Women beaten by their husbands have the right of appeal to the Government Chiefs' (1960: 194). That rights-based discourses, such as the notion that women should be educated, were still only trickling down nearly fifty years later, was clear. Although a major male-female imbalance remained at secondary level, there were efforts to address it at primary level, with reports of visits to villages specifically to promote Universal Primary Education and within that, girls' education.[21] In a speech given by a district school inspector in Cwero, the fieldworker noted that:

> On gender balance he mentioned that a female child's education must be considered important as those of a male child ... He went on to say that in the past girls' education was ignored and he used an Acholi proverb [to prove that this should no longer be the case] 'Gwok ma dako bene mako lee' [Even the female dog can catch an animal].[22]

However, although more subtly than the racist and ethnocentric discourses, this more modern rights-based one of 'gender', when over-simplified into a zero-sum game of women's rights versus men's rights, paradoxically also served to undermine men's sense of masculinity. Sometimes a 'gender perspective' could lead to a near-blanket dismissal of all men, as in the following description of the impact of war in Gulu, given by a Kampala-based women's organisation:

> One indicator of women's economic initiative is the number of activities being undertaken by individual women or groups of women in the form of self-help projects ... The majority of men on the other hand have failed to cope with the rapidly changing situation. In situations where farming cannot be practised like in Gulu town, many

men have failed to find alternative economic survival mechanisms and have taken to heavy drinking out of frustration. Some have resorted to performing previously despised jobs like general sale of labour to perform menial tasks.[23]

Men are implicitly labelled as having no economic initiative, in contrast to the women, and are explicitly described as 'failing'. There is no praise for those who have eaten humble pie and taken on menial tasks. Rather it is presented almost in the same breath as heavy drinking. And there is no discussion of men who have moved into what were previously regarded as women's areas of activity (such as traditional healing), nor about the numerous male youth groupings seeking to create some economic enterprise against all odds – *boda-boda* cyclists, agricultural groups etc., as documented in Chapter 5, groups which belie the dual stereotype of idle men – and idle youth.

When the Government's political education course (*mchaka-mchaka*) talked about human rights (Chapter 5), the emphasis was on the rights of women. In the interests of the project of 'equality', some interventions showed a lack of understanding for the relational aspects of gender and effectively emasculated men. As documented in Chapter 6, many of the cattle-restocking initiatives similarly furnished women with heads of cattle, heedless of the fact that this was traditionally a masculine area of activity. WFP at one point had a policy of distributing food exclusively through women, but then found that men controlled the food's distribution at home (WFP 1999: 21). Such interventions almost certainly worsened day-to-day relations between men and women – thus detracting from any positive impact they may have had on the supposed beneficiaries, the women.

Militarization

A further thorn in the side of men unable to achieve the model of provider and protector was the large military presence, a constant reminder of civilian men's failures. As discussed in Chapter 6, Government soldiers were present in all protected villages and were economically powerful by comparison with the majority of civilians, whose 'hands are tied'. They also exercised visible control over their women, as in Gulu barracks, where soldiers' wives were not free to move in and out of the barracks except at very limited times of the day, while their husbands could move in and out relatively freely.[24] Some parents encouraged their children to become soldiers' wives (Dolan 2000) and some believed that youth were attracted to joining the army in order to get 'free women' (ACORD 2000).

In these circumstances, joining the Government forces represented a dramatic shift in power relations in favour of militarised men, and probably a significant incentive for the continuation of the conflict. For male recruits to the LRA, on the other hand, access to women was closely controlled (Chapter 4). Indeed, the establishment of a controlled sexuality and thus 'purity' in response to the breakdown of 'traditional' morality, was a stated concern of Joseph Kony and part of his wider project of establishing a 'New Acholi'. As such, joining the LRA was less of an assured route to satisfying this particular dimension of a thwarted masculinity.

The Impact of the Emergence of a Hegemonic Model

In northern Uganda civilian men's ability to achieve key elements in the normative model of masculinity into which they had been socialised went into protracted crisis. With their capacity to create a family and then provide for and protect it much reduced, they experienced a loss of domestic and political power, and also could not exercise military power. Given that many of the features of this model were sexist, patriarchal, and adultist, this may at first glance seem a good thing, but it had numerous negative ramifications, not only for the immediate individuals and their families, but also for the wider society.

However difficult to attain, the model was strongly self-reinforcing, and precluded the development of alternatives. The more people struggled to attain it, the less open they were to non-patriarchal, non-oppressive alternatives. In this sense there was a 'collapse' of multiple masculinities, mirrored by the emergence of a single hegemonic one.

The second area of impact was on individuals who sought and yet failed to live up to the model. While men who were able to conform to the model benefited to an extent in terms of the power they could wield over women, children and youth, it is as important to see that the expectations (particularly economic ones) were onerous and indeed many men expressed a sense of being oppressed by them. Not only were they almost impossible to meet in the northern Ugandan context, but the struggle to do so left men with little possibility of pursuing individual aspirations.

To break out of these expectations was not really an option: men were unable to achieve the model, but they could not afford not to try to live up to it. The social and political acceptance which came from being seen to conform to the norm, and the access to a variety of resources which this facilitated, was critical. As Kabeer has argued, access to intangible resources (solidarity, contacts, information, political clout) 'is likely to be particularly critical in situations where market or state provision of social security is missing or where access to these institutions is imperfectly distributed' (1994: 280).

Trapped by the model, and by their inability to achieve it, there was inevitably considerable frustration. There is much evidence that this 'thwarting' of aspirations and expectations can result in various forms of violence against the self and others. Moore defines thwarting 'as the inability to sustain or properly take up a gendered subject position, resulting in a crisis, real or imagined, of self-representation and/or social evaluation' ... 'thwarting can also be the result of contradictions arising from the taking up of multiple subject positions, and the pressure of multiple expectations about self-identity or social presentation' (1994: 66).[25] Foreman makes the same argument when he argues that 'fear of ridicule, of being seen as 'less than a man', lies behind much of the violence men inflict on strangers or their wives' (Foreman 1999: 20). Equally, he argues that resentment is often manifested in anger and violence towards women and other men' (ibid, 1999: 14). Zur argues that in the Guatemalan context 'The humiliation of not being able to protect and provide for their families ... led to anger and resentment, which some men took out on their wives'. She further argues that these processes 'contributed to a loss of identity as a male' (1998: 103).

The belittlement felt by men is evident in the statement from a group of teachers, that 'As teachers we are just like kids, you just cry while your parents are fighting. You can make a noise but you won't be heard by anybody'.[26] If teachers, despite their education and position, felt unheard and reduced to the status of children, how much more so the average and poorly educated civilian living in a protected village?

Many symptoms of ill-health documented in Chapter 6, notably impotence, heavy drinking, and cases of suicide, can be interpreted as related to a loss of masculinity. In the overall ranking, impotence and fertility together were the third most important illnesses treated. When the data was disaggregated by gender, however, male impotence emerged as the number one complaint.

The healers suggested that impotence had increased as a result of fear of STIs/HIV, increasing alcohol abuse, and increasing redundancy, and that returned abductees were often impotent due to their experiences (see Chapter 4 for LRA treatment of impotence). Impotence was also explained as due to 'women's curses'. Because the population was scattered in the camps they were unable to perform clan rituals, but their use of *Tedo Bwoc,* which was specifically for impotence, had increased in recent years. When asked again why they thought this was the case, confinement, lack of food/money, pressure by army, loss of social norms, and increased levels of violence were added to the above list (*Tumu Kir,* a cleansing ritual conducted after a domestic dispute, was said to have increased for the same reasons).

The identification of 'increasing alcohol abuse' as one factor in impotence adds a further twist to the discussion of psychological debilitation. It was noted in Chapter 6 that 'redundancy', 'powerlessness' and an inability to 'live as they used to do when they had full control' (in other words, social impotence) were factors leading to over-drinking. Here it is seen that alcohol is regarded as causing physical impotence, suggesting a direct link, indeed a vicious circle, between men's social and physical impotence.

It is striking, given the apparent prevalence of male impotence and attempts to cure it, that in *group* discussion of the major health issues (before each healer

Table 7.2 Ranking of Illnesses Treated in 416 Male Patients by 37 Traditional Healers in Gulu District in the Week 14–20 June 1999

Illness	Ranking	Number of cases	As % of total
Impotence	1	81	19.5
Backache	2	66	15.9
Convulsion/Malaria	3	60	14.4
STDs/AIDS	4	57	13.7
Upper Respiratory Tract Infection	5	50	12.0
TB	6	49	11.8
Herpes Zoster	7	28	6.7
Mental Problems	8	25	6.0
TOTAL		416	100.00

was interviewed individually to establish his or her caseload in the preceding week) impotence was ranked as one of the least important health problems. This suggests a collective shame regarding this symptom – and symbol – of the emasculation of men in the war zone (Girling, after all, described how sterility for men and barrenness for women were regarded as 'the greatest afflictions any person can suffer among the Acholi' (Girling, 1960: 160)).

Whereas explanations for over-drinking embrace the loss of masculinity in the widest sense of a loss of social power and control, explanations given for men's suicides are much more directly focused on their unsatisfactory relations with women (Table 7.3)

Table 7.3 Methods and Reasons for Suicides/Suicide Attempts among Men

Age	Method	Succeed/ Fail	Reason
Unknown	Furadan	S	Feared that his wife had slept with his uncle who was suspected to be HIV positive
Unknown	Batteries	F	Not known
Unknown	Furadan	S	The wife of the deceased indicated that the late had had a love affair with a woman who was an AIDS victim
Adolescent	Cibacol	S	Unrequited love
18	hanging from mango tree	S	Feared paying 100,000/= fine and 7 year prison sentence for defiling 15-year-old girl
27	poison in food	S	Had been infected with syphilis by wife when she returned after having left him for two years – he killed her with the same poison he used to kill himself
Adult	Insecticide	S	He was ill with AIDS, not able to stay with woman he was in love with as her relatives prevented it
Adult	Batteries	S	Felt he was not taken seriously by his wife
20	Cibacol	S	Parents would not pay his school fees but paid those of his siblings
42	Hanging	S	His wife committed adultery, he beat her nearly to death and then hung himself
36	Rat poison	F	He is lame, frustrated because he felt his disability prevented him from getting a wife
15	Poison	S	Feared 7 years prison sentence for defiling 13-year-old girl
Adult	Poison	F	His wife was barren – he wanted his sperm back. He threatened to cut her open with a *panga* in an attempt to recover his sperm.
Boy	Hanging	F	He had been arrested by UPDF because of lack of ID card
Adult	Hanging	S	Mental health problems – he thought his brothers and wife wanted to kill him

In only three of the above cases is there no obvious connection with the person's relations with a woman/women. Twelve of the fifteen cases were directly attributed to a failure to achieve the hegemonic model of marriage and of control over women. In three cases relations were complicated by HIV infection. In two the youths killed themselves rather than face seven years in prison for sleeping with an under-age girl. In the remaining five cases the person seems not to have felt validated; the woman either rejected his advances, did not appear to take him seriously, cuckolded him, infected him with an STI, or did not bear children. In one case the man felt unable to attract a wife due to his disability.

For young men in particular, the question of defilement was a central factor in suicide. One fieldworker described the case of an 18-year-old male who committed suicide by hanging himself after being caught having intercourse with his niece, a girl aged fifteen. He told his friend that he feared that 'he was going to be put to prison for seven years and paying 1,000,000 shillings for the spoiling of the study of Alice. Hence he thought locally to hang himself from a mango tree at 6.30pm on the 8/5/99 very close to his house'.

That failure to achieve the gender norms was a central cause of suicide was also confirmed in various group discussions in Pabo and Acet camp (March 2002). In Acet the group recalled four recent cases of suicide, all connected to inter-gender tensions – and respondents agreed that if you cannot marry you also cannot get taken seriously, and that this resulted in psychological problems.[27] The first case concerned a father of five who 'had fought with his wife and gone to stay with his uncle. Previously he had been abusing the wife and the uncle had tried to stop him. Eventually the uncle beat him with a panga, causing him a dislocated shoulder and knee'. The second had taken place the previous night: 'Last night a man was to inherit his brother's wife.[28] His own wife didn't want this to happen and quarrelled a lot, so he took Ambush (a pesticide for termites). He threatened to beat the wife if she raised the alarm and he disappeared into the bush. She did though raise the alarm and he was captured'. The third example was of an old man of some eighty years, whose wife had died some time back: 'He brought another woman. There were some quarrels in the house. The woman left him. The same day he took poison (also Ambush). He was rescued by being fed raw eggs and oil which made him vomit … His reasons are that the second woman took all his money, he feels he cannot survive without that money'. The fourth concerned a mature woman who:

> … drank poison in October last year. People were rumour mongering that she was being run by a young man.[29] Her own husband was in Kampala and he had sent her back to cultivate and was supporting her … The LCs and elders decided to counsel the woman and the young man. People were seeing the way they behaved. It reached a time when the boy started to talk with a young girl and the woman was enraged … Now she knew people knew, so she drank poison, but she was rescued and did not die.

The last case is interesting in that it again simultaneously confirms and yet qualifies the picture created by discourses of breakdown. While the ostensible reason for the woman's suicide was jealousy, it was also linked to the intervention of the wider community. To try and control this couple's behaviour, which 'people were seeing', the LCs and elders 'decided to counsel the woman and the young man', an intervention which prompted the young man to make sure he was seen talking with a young woman more in his own age group. The fact that 'now she knew people knew' is part of the reason the woman drank the poison. Clearly the elders had not lost all their authority for they took it upon themselves to speak to a young man who was 'running' a woman old enough to be his mother – and he listened to them. Paradoxically, therefore, the relationship could be a symptom of the breakdown of social controls, but the suicide was a symptom of an at least partially successful attempt to reassert them.

Following this exposition of recent cases, the discussion in Acet Camp moved on to possible explanations for what was perceived to be an increasing suicide rate. The primary argument was that 'frequency has increased due to the frustration of living in the camps.' At a practical level the fact that cotton and tobacco growing had been reactivated meant that more pesticide was available, making it 'easier to commit suicide' (see Chapter 6), but upon further discussion it became clear that living in the camps created very specific problems. It was felt that suicide attempts were predominantly amongst youth and young women, in part because camp life had shifted the parameters of relationships:

> Very few people are able to marry, there is no means. Also staying in the camps has led to promiscuity, therefore people don't think of permanent partners. High levels of promiscuity leads to distrust, you don't know the other person's HIV status.
>
> In the past every home had elders and parents. Now they don't have that. There is no sitting together to provide corrective measures. So you get a combination of frustration, pleasure in sex, and lack of correction. This minimises the potential to create families.
>
> In the past it was the responsibility of the father to help organise marriage. Now the father will refuse to waste resources (for example, if he does not approve of the proposed wife), this also creates frustration leading to suicide.[30]

A good example of the complex HIV-loss of trust-suicide nexus comes from a case in Pagak camp in July 1998:

> A man called Simon committed suicide from Pagak camp on 07/07/98 in the evening after quarrelling with the uncle that his uncle was in love with his [Simon's] woman. Later they fought seriously and he went and bought Furadine which is a poison and took it that evening. He did that because the uncle was a suspect of AIDS virus.

Officials in Pabbo confirmed the broad picture of adolescents reacting to excessive attempts at control: in their opinion suicide among young people was mainly caused when a parent corrected or reprimanded a child – especially in the case of girls – and they gave the example of a girl who killed herself when her father stopped her from marrying a close relative she was in love with. They also argued that it was not just youth; 'Even men [can commit suicide] when they quarrel with their wives'. Asked why elderly men would kill themselves, they answered 'in one case he was quarrelling with one of his wives and she was quarrelling and insulting him – he killed himself'. In another case 'One man suspected his wife was running [having sexual relations with] another man. Once he came home and heard her talking to a man inside the house. Instead of checking who it was, he picked a rope and hung himself'.[31]

In short, many suicides are either a reaction to attempts by others to exercise control over him or her, or to a failure to achieve control by the person committing suicide. For men, the question of masculinity is at the core of the matter in both cases. The destruction of men's sense of their masculinity, and the behaviours which result are also implicated in women's suicides, as both undermine women's sense of their femininity. If the explanations for women's suicide attempts are recalled (Chapter 6), it is clear that a self-perpetuating dynamic is set up: men's aspirations are thwarted such that, for example, they turn to drink to drown their sorrows, as a result their wives' aspirations are also thwarted, causing them to swallow pesticides and watch-batteries as their final solution.

Domestic Violence

Further evidence of a sense of loss of control, and therefore of masculinity, can be seen in high levels of domestic violence, and in the treatment of youth. In one incident a non-Acholi businessman 'went to his mother-in-law to demand for refund of his money since the wife had become pregnant with another man ... but the mother-in-law said there was no money for refund'. He later returned with a panga and attacked her and her younger daughter, inflicting injuries of which they both later died: 'When the woman's son arrived on the same day that his mother died he rushed to the house of his mother's attacker and immediately began to attack young children in revenge for the death of his mother and sister ...'

It would be hard to find a clearer example of the causal relationship between humiliation and domestic violence than this explosion of inter-personal violence by a man who was humiliated both by his wife becoming pregnant by another man and by his mother-in-law's refusal to repay the bridewealth. In one somewhat unusual case, a man was believed to have acted out his humiliation and anger by raping the nephew of the woman he thought had infected him with HIV, an extreme example of a wider tendency for adult men to take out their frustrations on youth and children.

That the psychological dynamics go beyond the arena of domestic violence and into the social and political arena is suggested not just by instances of mob justice (see Chapter 6, for the case of a man being beaten to death after he stole a bicycle), but by workshop participants who argue a link between the experience of humiliation and the perpetuation of war: 'the local population lose their human dignity; they feel unprotected by the national army and or rebel forces and that their lives are not valued. They become aggressive in self-preservation'. Furthermore, 'people who get victimised take sides in the war with the spirit of revenging the atrocities against them or their families'.[32] From the discussion about discrimination about youth, it was clear the participants also made a connection between individuals' frustrated aspirations and decisions to join armed groups: 'they defy culture by joining war in order to achieve what they have been denied', and 'since they are denied economic opportunity by elders the youth take short cuts through taking up arms'.[33] As the comments of one female respondent in Acet camp suggest, it is the denial of marriage, that core element of adult masculinity, which is at the heart of many frustrations:

> It is very difficult for attitudes to change regarding the importance of the status of being married. As a result some youth migrate to urban centres. Others join the military forces, they fight and die there. My fear is that because of this attitude and the fact that many remain unmarried, what kind of future are we looking at? Attitudinal change is very important. Unmarried persons must be accepted. They should be appreciated as having potential.[34]

Increased Male Vulnerability to Violence

The discussion up to this point has emphasised how the thwarting of the aspirations and expectations created by the model of masculinity is itself a form of psychological violence which in turn produces a reaction in the form of physical violence against the self and others. Insofar as some men seek to overcome thwarting by joining military forces it can also be considered a factor in perpetuating the dynamics of conflict.

It is also important to look at the situation the other way round and demonstrate how the hegemonic model of masculinity also makes men more vulnerable to physical violence by others. Paradoxical though it may seem, the closer a man comes to achieving the model, the greater his vulnerability to violence at the hands of other men – particularly at the hands of men whose own masculinity is in need of a quick fix. Because civilian men's sense of achieved masculinity is so fragile in the war zone, it is an easy target for military violence, notably in the form of violence against the women and children whom a 'real man' is supposed to be able to protect. Rape of women (wives, daughters and sisters), rape of men (themselves, brothers, fathers, sons), and abduction of their children, all constitute direct attacks, not just on the immediate victims, but also on the 'achieved masculinity' and sense of self of their husbands, fathers, brothers and sons.[35]

While rape occurs at the hands of all parties, it is particularly bitter when the rapists are the very men to whom civilians have been told to entrust the protection role. One fieldworker reported how on 7th February 2000 members of the UPDF entered a village in his area and raped a 70-year-old woman. On the 8th a 29-year-old was raped, on the 9th a 43-year-old and a 30-year-old. In the latter case 'The husband tried to boycott the wife [i.e. not have intercourse with her] but his parents advised him not to beat the wife because it wasn't her need (wish) to meet the soldier. In conclusion, people in the camp and the few who go to collect food are really very worried and not happy because these (soldiers) are more harmful than rebels'.

In some instances the army did discipline soldiers (see Chapter 5), at times provoking the guilty party to extreme steps, such as a Home guard who, having raped a civilian woman, shot himself rather than face military discipline. More often, when soldiers guarding civilians broke discipline, there was no redress. As one fieldworker reported,

> The UPDF soldiers based at A__ detach are giving a lot of embarrassment to the people in the camp by beating and raping. On the 10-2-00 a UPDF soldier came to the place of Agnes at night and hid himself behind the house. When Agnes was asleep he opened the door and flashed a torch. He then landed on the neck of the women and wanted to have sex with her forcefully but Agnes began to shout loudly for help. Then Ay__ who is the cousin sister rushed to find out what was wrong with Agnes. On hearing foot steps coming from the neighbouring houses the soldier ran away.

> The following morning the LCs followed the case up to the barracks and the woman identified one of the soldiers named O. But the Commanding Officer ... argued that the statement given by the woman was wrong because O did not go out that day. The case ended there just like that.

When in February 1999 a young woman was raped and shot dead by an army soldier, her relatives (impoverished subsistence farmers) were told by the army's public relations office to obtain a signed statement from the soldier's commanding officer before they would take action. Faced with this intimidation they were unable to take action, and by August there was still no progress on the case (personal interview with the relatives). As workshop participants noted, 'when a woman is raped, the husband feels inactive to stand up and bring change (disempowered). He was supposed to protect her, but soldiers continue raping'.[36] While rape of men was less common, it had occurred, with particular prevalence in the early 1990s, when respondents reported an increase in STDs, allegedly due to 'indiscriminate rape of men (*tek gungu*) and women by NRA' (see Chapter 3, see also Finnström, 2003: 252). The stigma attached was even higher than for female rape, and workshop participants described how 'when a man is raped it takes away his manhood and he fails to act to bring change'.[37] The late medical superintendent at Lacor hospital pointed out that 'It [male rape] was used by the Government soldiers as a weapon. The anger goes very deep, the men cannot talk about it, it is the women who bring it up. Male rape is a major cause of people's anger against the army.[38]

Overall, then, the army, while ostensibly responsible for the protection which civilians were no longer permitted to provide, in fact attacked women, children and men and allowed them to be attacked – and civilian men could do little or nothing about it. The model of masculinity made non-combatant men vulnerable to the use of violence by combatants, and the process of undermining men's sense of masculinity became a key channel for some men to exercise power over other men. Interactions between combatants and non-combatants around masculinity became something of a zero sum game; the civilian's loss in masculinity was the combatant's gain. In short, it was possible for particular tactics to simultaneously reinforce the sense of masculinity of the perpetrator and undermine that of the victim.

State Benefits from the Hegemonic Model

The above discussion of hegemonic masculinity illuminates the complex interaction between individual behaviour, social norms and group intentions. It is highly unlikely that individuals involved in acts which undermine other men's sense of masculinity do not understand this impact of their actions. But what is the role of the state? Is it plausible that the state, through military and other channels, deliberately manipulates the hegemonic model, and the vulnerabilities it creates in many men (civilian and soldier alike), as a means to military and political ends?

Several major elements of the state's behaviour in northern Uganda suggest this may be the case. Certainly militarization of the north (Chapter 3) can be seen as consolidating the model. The state's own behaviour consistently modelled 'masculinity' in its crudest sense, promoting a militarist approach to dealing with the LRA, certainly in terms of its rhetoric and visible militarization, and in its belittling of attempts to model alternative forms of masculinity based on practices of negotiation, reconciliation and non-violence (Chapter 4).

At the same time, the creation of the camps – for which the state was also responsible – made the model of masculinity less and less possible to achieve. The state therefore had a central role in creating the conditions for thwarting and humiliation. To the extent that it did not deal with numerous acts of violence and abuse against civilians, including rape, abduction and looting, and was itself a frequent perpetrator of such acts, the state actively contributed to this thwarting (Chapter 5).

There were several perceptible benefits to the state from simultaneously promoting a model of masculinity and undermining its achievement. Given a belief system which portrayed the north as a threat to the south, the state might see benefit in the creation of a disempowered male population which turned violence on itself rather than against the state, and in the maintenance of a context of violence which justified military intervention and the strengthening of army control over the civilian population in the area (this is explored further in Chapters 8 and 9). From a more strategic perspective, the Ugandan state may have seen benefits in sustaining a context of conflict which helped to justify the maintenance of a large military force for deployment in other regional theatres of war (most recently the DRC and South Sudan). From such a perspective, addressing the situation of northern Uganda would not be a relevant consideration. Indeed, the creation of a context which empowered military and disempowered civilians could be seen as strategically justified. Having once created large military forces, it is also necessary to control them. The selective way in which discipline was applied to soldiers who engaged in acts of violence against civilians suggests that playing on soldiers' sense of masculinity was used both to reward and control them. This parallels in many respects Zur's findings from Guatemala that 'Having set in motion the conditions to create patrollers' feelings of alienation, the army and its local cohorts proceeded to manipulate them, promoting the patrols, with their emphasis on violence, as a new space for the reassertion of male dominance' (Zur, 1998: 103).

Discussion

This chapter has used a psychological model of thwarting to elaborate on some of the behaviours documented in preceding chapters. Individual psychological debilitation and behaviours are shown to be not just a symptom of individual weakness, but a set of reactions to the thwarting of aspirations for which there are many parallel examples. Thwarting is linked to the wider social and political dynamics within the war zone, and itself contributes to the perpetuation of the dynamics of violence.

Men's lived experiences and their lived expectations are two very different things. To conflate the two is to miss a psychological dynamic that is profoundly important to the understanding of violence and conflict, as it is in the disjuncture between the two that the seeds of violence are to be found.[39] Whereas in a peacetime context it was possible for a majority of men to attain a reasonably close match between expectations and experiences, war sees an increasing heterogeneity of experiences with growing polarisation between those who are able to attain the markers of masculinity and exercise the power which these bring and those who are unable to fulfil expectations and are thus deeply disempowered. Some (most clearly the youth) have little power whether in the domestic or the political/public sphere; others exercise considerable power in their domestic sphere over their wives and children, but little power over other men; others (notably military) exercise power in all spheres and over both men and women.

Paradoxically the increasing heterogeneity of experience goes hand-in-hand with a further homogenising of expectations; while marriage and fatherhood, provision and protection become harder to achieve, they become more rather than less desirable as they appear to provide anchors and points of leverage in the midst of economic, social and political disorientation created by war. Attainment of different components of the model creates a hierarchy among men – and a man's position in this hierarchy is not wholly static. Although it becomes ever more difficult to do this in a civilian context, and levels of domestic violence bear witness to this, it remains possible in principle to attain a full masculine identity, and social expectations remain fully in support of this. Individuals subscribe to the model for economic and psychological survival reasons, and their families have a vested interest in ensuring that they do so for economic security reasons. Militarism provides a route for some, with full support from a state policy of increasing militarization and associated recruitment drives into Home-guards, militias and the army itself. It should be noted, however, that in many respects the military route to achieving masculinity is an illusory one. After all, the stability of the military hierarchy, depends on the capacity of upper ranks to maintain control over the lower ranks (frequently through techniques of humiliation or 'discipline'). While the latter may be able to demonstrate their power over even quite successful civilian counterparts, they are doing this from within an institution within which they themselves are quite weak – and often humiliated. In short, what is given with one hand (the promise of achieving masculinity vis-à-vis civilian counterparts), is taken with the other as, vis-à-vis their superiors, the militarized foot-soldiers remain weak and subaltern.

Within this militarized space the possibility of multiple masculinities largely collapses. The destruction of education opportunities removes one avenue for alternative forms of achievement, as does the destruction of an economic environment in which it is possible to become somebody through wealth. Attempts to promote alternative visions of how to resolve the situation are ridiculed both implicitly by policies of non-protective militarization and explicitly by the utterances of various key leadership figures. With this ever narrower horizon and ever smaller windows of opportunity, people are left with each other as sources of identity and power.

For this model of masculinity is inherently relational, not just between men and women, but between men and men, particularly between 'youths' and 'adults', as differentiated by marriage. While masculinity is articulated in terms of how it differs from femininity, between men it is lived as a zero sum game, which allows power differentials to be established between them, notably between military and civilian men. Whereas women cannot be removed from the achievement of a masculine identity, the removal of other men is a key part of that process. The very sources of power for men contained in the prevalent model of masculinity are also the roots of their vulnerability, generating the possibility of any man being both a perpetrator and a victim of violence. It is therefore not surprising that the bundle of ideas that goes to make up masculinity exercises such a hold over men – sufficient to prompt many into acts of suicide when they find that they cannot succeed within the only sphere of influence which remains open to them, and to prompt others into acts such as rape and pillaging which they imagine demonstrate their power relative to other men but in fact merely prove that they themselves continue to occupy a position of humiliation and subordination.

Within the civilian population, it is the thwarting of men's wish to achieve masculinity which appears to reduce them to acts of domestic violence; violence becomes a last resort of those who are unable to achieve 'masculinity'. Within the military, the institutional framework, and the removal of soldiers from more general social networks, to an extent promotes the use of violence as an easy route to masculinity. Those in the military gain in domestic power over women as they are in a stronger position to provide economically and to protect militarily; at the same time they enjoy military power and social status over other men. The resort to violence by the military can be seen as a conscious or subconscious strategy to exercise control over civilians, which is effective in that it strengthens the perpetrator's masculinity through weakening that of the victim. That this vulnerability is deliberately targeted is clear from many descriptions of rape in war situations in which the husband or father is forced to watch their wife or daughter being raped. In other words, it is not merely the sexual act which is gratifying, but the capacity to humiliate another man at the same time. Furthermore, the perpetrators' individual aspirations to power over others (for they, too, are by and large from opportunity-deprived backgrounds) coincide neatly with the state's need for control over the population in general.

The normative model is thus shown to have considerable destructive power which can be manipulated by the state for purposes of social control and creating more space for political and military manoeuvre – and the nexus of 'masculinity', power, violence and conflict begins to come into focus. Within this nexus it is impossible to dissociate power relations between individual men from the power relationships existing between individual men and the state. The gap between individual psychology and state level power-plays is bridged.

Conclusions

In conclusion, a scrutiny of masculinities in the war zone illuminates the connections between protection as violation, protection as debilitation, and protection as humiliation. It also goes some way to explaining behaviours in the war zone as well as contributing part of the answer to the question of how and why the situation is perpetuated. It identifies a psychological dynamic which very few men escape. Rather than being instances of individual moral weakness, the various behaviours identified in the preceding chapters and elaborated here, are individual expressions of the psychological dynamics provoked by broad processes of social and political subordination within the national context. The concern with individual behaviour, which permeates discourses of 'breakdown', is validated in the sense that something is broken (men's masculine identity), and this is visible in individual behaviour, but it is relativised in that explanatory causes are found in bigger dynamics for which the individual has little responsibility and over which he/she exercises little or no control. As such there is little value in judging or 'blaming the victim'.

The construct of masculinity is a key nexus linking the individual with the social and, beyond that, with the political at the national level: while individual men lose control over themselves and their households, other actors, notably the state and NGOs, increase it. Paradoxically, therefore, the firming-up of the hegemonic model and the narrowing range of permissible masculinities, suggests that what people are experiencing is not so much a social breakdown as a tightening of social control, and that the use of masculinities by men to exercise power over other men is a key part of this process.

This interpretation also raises a number of further questions. If, as has been suggested, the state benefits in some discernible ways from the hegemonic model and has played a key role in creating the conditions of violation, debilitation and change whereby people's attempts to live up to it are thwarted, then what name can be given to these processes, and how do they relate not just to the continuation of this war, but to the nature of today's wars more broadly? These questions are explored further in the next chapter.

Notes

1. Many arguments in this chapter were first developed in Dolan (2003).
2. ACORD 2000.
3. These generally confirmed my own observations, and were subsequently affirmed in further research on Gender and Conflict in 2001 (ACORD 2002: Annex 1).
4. *New Vision,* 8 June 1998, 'Kony: DP attacks Albright'.
5. Awere, 1 October 1999.
6. ACORD 2000.
7. The importance of marriage in defining these power relations is brought into sharp focus by the fact that when the head of one major Acholi clan, Rwot Achana, died in 1999 and was to be succeeded by his unmarried son, this could not take place without the chief-to-be's sister playing the role of surrogate wife. Symbolically, at least, he had to be married to be regarded as an adult worthy of assuming the responsibilities and powers of a chief.
8. I do not attempt to explore the historical development of this dominant model, though the Christian influence is clear. For a discussion of how western ideals of masculinity 'have been exported through colonialism to mingle with local notions of masculinity' (Oxfam 1997: 4), see Cornwall and Lindisfarne (1994).
9. Gulu Central High School, 6 March 2002.
10. COWI, Volume 1, July 1999, pp94, 207–209. This figure does not include students from those districts who have completed secondary education elsewhere in the country.
11. Report from Awer camp, June 1998.
12. In one instance where a Functional Adult Literacy Campaign was launched in Bungatira sub-county, only one of the 122 participants was a man (KM E-newsletter 15, 23 May 2002).
13. Only one of ten fieldworkers claimed there had been no change (Odek pilot report, 21 July 1998).
14. Awach, August 1998.
15. Girling writes 'Fathers have the right to control the marriages of their children ... A son may not marry without the consent of his father' (1960: 33).
16. Awer, June 1998.
17. Palaro pilot report, 30 July 1998. When two people stay together without the man paying bridewealth it is known as *Poro* (see also Girling, 1960: 70).
18. Awer, June 1998.
19. *New Vision,* 25 February 1998.
20. Finnström explicitly writes 'against the claim that the Acholi are more prone to war than other people' (2003: 35).
21. Odek, 31 July 1999.
22. Cwero, 23 July 1999.
23. ISIS-WICCE, 2000, p1.
24. The soldiers' wives reported being largely confined to the barracks in Gulu. There is what is known as 'small gate' through which they can pass, but the times were very restricted:
    Monday   1–5 P.M.
    Tuesday 1–2 P.M.
    Thursday 1–2 P.M..
    Saturday 1–2 P.M.
    Sunday   7 A.M.–1.30 P.M.
    Women trying to enter outside those times would have difficulty being allowed in. Soldiers were free to rent houses outside but were supposed to sleep in the barracks where they could be on-call for active duty.
25. For a similar use of the term some thirty years earlier, see John Griffin (1964: 109–110).
26. Interview with secondary school teachers, Gulu High School, 13 August 1998.

27. Acet Camp, 1 March 2002.
28. This refers to the practice of wife inheritance, whereby in the event of a man's death, his wife is expected to become the wife to her deceased husband's brother. With the rise of HIV/AIDS this was coming under increasing question.
29. That is to say, was having a sexual relationship with.
30. Acet, 1 March 2002.
31. Pabo, 5 March 2002.
32. ACORD 2000.
33. An argument also made by Large (1997).
34. Acet Camp, 1 March 2002.
35. The term 'victim' here is used in the sense adopted by the South African Truth and Reconciliation Commission, namely to include relatives and dependants of victims of direct abuse and violence (Goldblatt and Meintjes, 1998: 34).
36. ACORD 2000.
37. ACORD 2000.
38. Lacor Hospital, Gulu, January 1998.
39. The implications of this for theorising masculinities are explored further in Dolan 2003.

8

SOCIAL TORTURE AND THE CONTINUATION OF WAR

❦

Introduction

In Chapter 1 I argued that the situation in northern Uganda should be considered primarily as one of social torture rather than war. I proposed that the identification of torture, rather than hanging on the question of perpetrator intentions, requires an assessment also of impacts, actors, benefits and functions, and justificatory processes and mechanisms. I also proposed that although social torture shares key features with individual torture, it can be analytically distinguished from individual torture along a number of parameters. These include that it is low rather than high intensity, it impacts on society as a whole rather than being focused on individuals and their immediate associates and families, and it is geographically extensive and time indifferent rather than place and time-bound. Furthermore, rather than a readily identifiable and limited group of perpetrators linked to the state, it involves multiple state and non-state actors and becomes to a degree self-perpetuating. It also differs to an extent from individual torture in that its justifications are in the public domain in the form of public discourses, whereas much of the justification done in individual torture is at the level of individual psychology, even if it to an extent draws on public discourses.

In this chapter I consider how each of the proposed constituent elements of a social torture model, and those aspects which distinguish it from individual torture, are demonstrated in the preceding chapters. I argue that states typically induced through torture of individuals, are to be found in the population in general, as are various behaviours akin to those found in victims of individual torture. These include perpetrators blaming the victim, victims blaming themselves, victims associating with perpetrators, and also other forms of victim behaviour which fit a diagnosis of Post-Traumatic Stress Disorder arising from torture. I then scrutinise the multiple actors in social torture together with the nature and motives for their involvement. Taking the distinction between perpetrators, bystanders and victims as my starting point, I consider the actors to be not just the LRA and UPDF, but also the Government more broadly insofar as it made the policy decisions which created and maintained the context for social torture. I also look at where institutions and organisations such as churches, aid and development donors, media, humanitarian and human rights organisations, fit in the perpetrator-bystander spectrum. Particular attention is paid to international NGOs and Inter-Governmental Organisations, who in failing to fulfil the humanitarian imperative to protect and assist, played bystander roles which at times merged with those of perpetrators.

The functions of social torture can be seen to include meeting the immediate and day-to-day psychological, economic and political needs and interests of visible perpetrators and complicit bystanders. But within a wider process of historical change and the struggle of the Government to build and hold onto state power in the face of shifting pressures from both above and below, social torture in northern Uganda also served a more strategic function. Rather than excluding the Acholi from the national polity, it would ultimately bring about their subordinate inclusion. By this I mean the inclusion of the north as an integral part of the Ugandan polity, but on subordinate terms set by the Government in the south. The relatively high visibility of this process, by intimidating other sections of the national population, in turn helped in exercising control over the country as a whole. It was also part and parcel of a third area of struggle for the Government, namely negotiating the terms of its own engagement with the international community.

Turning to the question of how, notwithstanding their role in a larger dynamic, it was possible for these actors to justify what they did to themselves and their constituencies, I argue that this was achieved through the use of public discourses and conscious silences, both of which render the underlying dynamics invisible. The discourses of intra-ethnic war, terrorism and humanitarian crisis, together with their accompanying silences, are taken as the principal examples.

The discussion focuses on how low intensity and wide impact, geographical extension and time indifference, multiple actors and functions, and justification through public discourses all distinguish social from individual torture. It is these features individually and in combination that offer an explanation for the question with which this book begins, 'why, when many people say they wish it would end, does a situation such as that in northern Uganda continue?

Impacts and Methods

That states of debilitation, dependency, dread and disorientation have been induced not just in a number of individuals, but in the population as a whole within the war zone, has been amply demonstrated in the preceding chapters. All the elements of debilitation outlined in the introduction were prominent features of life in the 'protected villages', which one respondent described as like being 'in prison within your own country'.[1] In Chapter 6 it was shown that hunger increased the longer people stayed in the camps. The number of meals people ate per day decreased due to inadequate and erratic relief supplies, and the resort to subsistence production became ever more difficult over time. Lack of sleep and fatigue were inevitable when people spent nights in fear of raids and abduction, and were further aggravated when, in an attempt to evade capture, people hid in the bush in makeshift hideouts (*alup*) or, alternatively, walked several hours each night to take shelter on the terraces of buildings in town before returning to their homes in the morning. In the 'protected villages' themselves, the quality of shelter was poor, particularly in terms of over-crowding and the very real risk of fire. There was a serious lack of medical provision (Chapter 5) and beatings were numerous, whether in the form of domestic violence, school disciplinary measures, or at the hands of various military forces. The impact on physical and mental health in the camp populations, as described in Chapters 6 and 7, was unmistakable and constituted a case of mass debilitation.

Enforced dependency was most visible at an economic level; as described in Chapters 3 and 5, over the course of the period 1987 to 2006 the backbone of the traditional household was broken, several times over. Already weakened by years of under-investment from the national level relative to other areas of the country (WFP, 1999: 30), Gulu and Kitgum districts experienced a major direct blow in the looting and slaughter of livestock in the late 1980s, which removed people's main form of capital and with it their ability to weather difficult economic times, finance large one-off expenditures and maintain social cohesion through marriage, burial and compensation practices (Chapters 6 and 7).

The formation of the protected villages from the mid-1990s onwards was a further blow. From their very inception they further undermined the agricultural subsistence capacity of the majority of rural households, resulting in the need for 'substantial humanitarian assistance … provided on an ongoing basis by the international community' (Weeks, 2002: 4). The 'socio-economic collapse of the north' was such that, 'Despite the humanitarian assistance they have received… the overall picture is one of severe destitution: of a population accustomed over generations to a situation of relative self-reliance and even prosperity that has been reduced to **dependency, idleness** and **debilitating uncertainty** with respect to what the future may hold for them and their children [emphases added]' (idem: 4). Dependency was enforced in the sense that people were restricted in their movement and thus in their opportunities to seek alternative forms of livelihood (Chapter 5). It became entrenched to the extent that children born in the camps grew up without learning the agricultural skills they would otherwise have acquired, and so were at a disadvantage should they eventually be allowed to return to their land. Dependency was also psychological, as social structures and (already weakened) traditional authority systems were further undermined by the relocation into camps in which dozens of clans were thrown together unceremoniously (Chapter 5). Militarization and displacement, and the living conditions in the camps further stripped people of status and dignity, culminat-

ing in thwarted aspirations to adult masculinity and femininity, and the emasculation of heads of households and traditional leadership (Chapters 6 and 7).
Paradoxically people came to see the very mechanisms that had thwarted them
and created their dependency (e.g. militarization) as the means to escape it, and
thus they joined military forces, a move that was only likely to further consolidate their psychological dependency (Chapter 7).

Dread or 'a constant state of fear and anxiety' aptly describes the state of
mind induced in most inhabitants of the war zone. As Finnström argues, 'Continued stress and existential uncertainty about the near future were central aspects of everyday life' (2003: 19). Camp dwellers not only lived under constant
threat of raids by the LRA, but the fear that this generated was compounded by
anxiety about whether the soldiers supposedly protecting them would in fact
do so, as well as about whether the soldiers might become abusers themselves.
Rumours such as the one that HIV-positive soldiers had been instructed to rape
civilians fuelled such dread (Chapter 6). Those travelling from one place to another moved in fear of coming under attack or being blown up by a landmine.
Those in school slept in fear of abduction or forcible conscription. Those in
camps feared being burnt alive if the tightly packed grass-roofed huts should
catch fire by accident or be set alight intentionally by the rebels.[2] Endless reit-
erations of the position that the LRA existed through abduction of children,
combined with ever-changing accounts of what the LRA was doing (Chapter 4),
fuelled a sense of dread which drove tens of thousands to seek shelter in town
every night, and tens of thousands more to hide in mosquito-infested hideaways
in the bush (Chapter 5), rather than sleeping in their houses in the 'protected
villages'.

From when the protected villages were established in 1996, people were kept
in doubt about when – indeed whether or not – they would be released to return
home. Often there were mixed signals. In early 2002, for example, there was talk
of 'decongesting' the camps, policies which would have allowed some people to
return to cultivate in their home areas while still retaining some aspects of the
'protected villages' (Chapter 5). Before this ever was concretised, the military
geared up for Operation Iron Fist, the result of which was ultimately an escalation in LRA activity and a burgeoning of the camp populations, resulting in further congestion rather than de-congestion (Chapters 3 and 5). More generally,
there was a long-term pattern of repeatedly raised and dashed hopes, as each of
the numerous phases to the conflict began with acute violence, which gradually
reduced – though it never disappeared – until a failed peace initiative released
a renewed wave of ever more intensive violence from those who were part of
the preceding war, but not of the 'peace process' (Chapters 3 and 4). Given this
roller-coaster history of broken deadlines for military solutions (Chapter 3),
and broken promises for negotiated ones (Chapter 4), in which peace seemed
round the corner one day but rebels were launching Rocket-Propelled Grenades
from inside Gulu town the next,[3] people doubted whether any of the efforts to
bring the war to an end and thereby release them from its stranglehold were
either serious or would bear fruit.

Uncertainty about the macro-picture compounded daily uncertainties about physical injury (would there be an attack by the LRA, harassment by the UPDF?), hunger (when would WFP deliver the next relief supplies, and how much would be given? (Chapter 6)), ill-health (was the Ebola outbreak really an accident? – Chapter 3; would there be access to care? (Chapter 5)), abduction and forcible recruitment, and death. Equally it was difficult to know which of the conflicting orders and prohibitions from LRA and Government (Chapter 4) to take heed of. Just as the true composition of the LRA and the nature of its links with the LRM remained something of a mystery throughout, it was similarly unclear just how many troops the Government had in place. The identities and agendas of soldiers involved in specific acts of violence within Gulu and Kitgum districts were often never fully established as either LRA or UPDF. In an alleged rebel attack on a bus, the ostensible rebels all wore UPDF uniform,[4] and some soldiers even admitted to disguising themselves as rebels (Chapter 5). People thus had to live with profound ambiguities and constantly ask themselves 'is X a rebel collaborator? Or perhaps a government internal security operative?'[5]

Ongoing and pervasive uncertainty undermined people's capacity to determine their own allegiances, provoking additional disorientation. Further complexity was added by the fact that many people had relatives on both sides and/or had experienced ill-treatment at the hands of both sides. It was not unusual to have an abducted brother in the LRA and a cousin in the UPDF, to have lost cattle to the NRA and food relief to the LRA. As one fieldworker put it:

> At least in one way or the other, the majority of Acholi people have suffered either in the hands of the Government army or in the hands of the LRA.... there were mass killings of the people of Acholiland, worst was done by government soldiers. This was before 1994. Later on it was followed by LRA killings ... So every family in Acholiland at least has suffered from either [one or other] of the two armies.[6]

In practice therefore, many found it hard to give support to either side. The same fieldworker later reported; 'pressure is being mounted on the civilian [population] by both the UPDF and the LRA, making it threatened, sickly. People are so confused that some of them do not know which direction to take; the LRA or the UPDF, of which to them it is the same animal wearing different clothes'.[7]

At a village level it was uncertain who would be in control from one day to the next. To make matters still less clear, returned abductees were recruited into the Home-guard and army. Thus the LRA, the UPDF and the LDUs all contained people from the area, former victims now in the position of visible perpetrators. And while the various armed forces were the visible perpetrators, they were not necessarily the only ones – they were after all generally acting under orders (excuses of individual indiscipline notwithstanding) and with various forms of external support. This inability to identify an unambiguous enemy sustained the sense of being out of control already generated by the lack of any trusted authorities to turn to for protection. Traditional authority structures and justice mechanisms had been displaced but only very partially replaced with 'modern' alternatives (see Chapters 5 and 6). Underpinning these day-to-day tensions was a fundamental tension between nationalist and ethnic identities. The Government could lay some claim to people's support by virtue of models of citizen-ship, the LRA by its image as an 'Acholi' organisation. All these factors meant there were not just multiple players but also multiple experiences, identities and loyalties (see Chapters 5 and 7). This combination stretched personal loyalties of civilians to breaking point, reinforced a collective loss of identity and self-esteem, furthered the internalisation of blame, lessened capacity to organise a coherent response or resistance to what was being done, and offers some expla-nation to the otherwise vexed question of how an entire social group allowed itself to be tortured (Chapter 6).

Further Symptoms of Torture

The symptoms of torture also included behaviours that could be placed under the rubric of Post-Traumatic Stress Disorder. As discussed in the introduction, the language of 'trauma' was widely used within the area. The fact that psychic numbing and emotional anaesthesia are frequently symptoms of torture throws further light on the findings from the traditional healers outlined in Chapters 6 and 7. It is possible that the male impotence which they dealt with on a day-to-day basis was a sign of such emotional anaesthesia. The high rates of alcohol abuse which the women attempting suicide accused their husbands of, may also have served as a form of self-administered anaesthetic against the trauma of ongoing social torture.

A number of other striking features of people's behaviour in the war zone also become more comprehensible once the possibility that they may be symptoms of torture is allowed. One is the way in which, when there was a lull in the fighting, as in 1999, people were eager to believe that peace had come. This was despite the fact that there was no evidence that this was anything other than a lull, which could end at any time (as indeed it did after the signing of the Carter Center brokered peace accord between the Governments of Sudan and Uganda). As one Member of Parliament said in September 1999, 'People say there is peace now, but it is just that Kony has not appeared for several months. However the lull may become permanent'.[8] While such optimism in response to lulls in the violence could be taken as an indicator of people's resilience, it may plausibly be read as a symptom of trauma, specifically a case of disorientation insofar as people had lost their sense of the larger pattern despite years of similar dynamics.

It is also striking that civil society in northern Uganda was relatively slow to organise in order to draw attention to its plight. This can plausibly be seen as a symptom of disorientation and psychological debilitation, which prevented the development of pro-active and constructive responses. In this regard it is noteworthy that two of the most prominent organisations in terms of work-ing for peace, namely the diaspora grouping Kacokke Madit, and the religious grouping ARLPI (Acholi Religious Leaders Peace Initiative), both enjoyed struc-tural features which lessened their susceptibility to disorientation and debili-tation. As a diaspora grouping with headquarters in London, Kacokke Madit benefited from a certain distance from the day-to-day ups and downs of living and working inside the war zone. As religious leaders, the members of ARLPI, while working at the heart of the war zone, had national and international institutional frameworks, as well as religious duties and rituals, which provided a certain level of continuity and constancy in the midst of uncertainty (even if, as argued below, the level of explicit support provided was disappointing). They also enjoyed a degree of economic security, which was not available to the civilian population at large. This is by no means to underestimate the tremendous pressures and stresses under which both organisations and individuals within them were put, simply to suggest that they were better placed than others to develop pro-active responses.[9]

Examples of the victims being blamed for their misfortune were numerous. One UPDF 4th Division Commander 'blamed Acholi leaders for the continued war being waged by Lord's Resistance Army rebels. He said some leaders are using the situation to expand their political careers, while others simply keep quiet ...'[10] WFP argued that there was 'a lack of local capacity amid a population whose civil society linkages are weak and whose expectations of 'top down' (Government and/or aid agency) assistance have inhibited self-reliance'(WFP, 1999: 32). Such attributions of blame were compounded by numerous instances of Acholi blaming each other and themselves. Chapter 5 described the case of women being admonished by the Ministry of Health Nutrition Unit on how to feed their children a more balanced diet – as if their children's malnutrition arose from a poor grasp of domestic science rather than from enforced displacement. In Chapter 6, I described how people appeared to have internalised blame, or at least to lay it at the feet of their fellow citizens, for 'moral' breakdown, rather than seeking explanations in the broader political situation.

Many of the churches and related institutions located responsibility squarely with their congregations. At a 1998 graduation ceremony for seminarians the Catholic Bishop noted that '"Peace is not in our area due to lack of love for God." He called on the people of Gulu to love their neighbours'.[11] When the new Anglican bishop of Northern Uganda diocese was installed, he said 'the 12 year rebellion in the region can only be solved through love. "Love begets respect, opens avenues for dialogue and solves all disputes without spilling blood,"... He said the Acholi are divided and only love can reconcile them'.[12] When he made a pastoral visit to Pabbo camp later that year 'he told the congregation to love one another as oneself and learn to forgive each other. In short, a message of reconciliation was preached'.[13] Similar messages were preached by religious leaders of all denominations (e.g. The Life Ministry from Kampala), as well as those associated with them (e.g. the Anglican Mothers Union).[14] Even Acholi MPs at times hectored their own constituency; 'The first requirement now is for the Acholi to come together to understand the conflict, recognise past attempts to bring it to an end, scrutinise their own responsibilities in the situation, before acting. The Acholi are in very deep; they must put up the ladders and climb out'.[15] One contributor to the Kacokke Madit e-newsletter stated that he was writing 'after a lot of thoughts and reflections on how other people in and outside Uganda view the Acholi community. Everyone living in Uganda knows how the Acholis are taken. The black image seems to be brought by ourselves' (KM E-newsletter No 8, 13 March 2002).

Joseph Kony, however, challenged this pattern of blaming the general population for a lack of love and self-reliance, choosing to turn the spotlight instead on the leadership. In a message given to some girl abductees to carry home he

> ... condemned the religious leaders in the north for their indifference towards the pathetic plight of the *wananchi* [ordinary people]. 'We the LRA/M are unhappy with you because of all the evil things done to God's people in Uganda,' Kony said in a letter addressed to bishops, priests and the faithful ... Kony accuses religious leaders of looking on as the *wananchi* are bundled up and forcefully herded into concentration camps. Kony's letter said the young and adults die daily of disease and hunger.[16]

Actors

When considering the model of perpetrators, bystanders and victims, as set out in the introduction, and recognising that the term perpetrator encompasses not only 'the torturers themselves, but also those who are in charge of a system which perpetrates torture.' (Staub 1990:106), then the perpetrators in northern Uganda would include both LRA and UPDF and their leaderships, but also extend to include the Ugandan Government insofar as it planned and authorised the execution of various measures in the war zone, ranging from public displays of purposive violence (see Illustration 8.1), to, most notably for the purposes of this study, the policy of 'protected villages'.

The Anglican and Catholic churches could be considered bystanders (those who either observe directly or at least are aware that torture is being committed, but take no action to prevent or stop it) insofar as, despite some members (ARLPI) being key actors for peace at the local level, the institutions as a whole made limited use of their considerable potential to raise awareness at national level through their congregations and at international levels through their respective institutional structures. From a human rights perspective the donors also come in for considerable criticism for their lack of action. In its *1999 World Report* Human Rights Watch reported that 'Robust and consistent human rights-related messages from the EU were the exception rather than the rule', and that 'U.S. criticism of Uganda's human rights practices became increasingly muted'.[17] *The Monitor* quoted directly from the report that the donors' "increased rhetoric about the need to respect political freedoms and the rights of civil society in Uganda was rarely matched by any specific action".[18] Smaller donors were often uncritical on rights issues, and of interventions derived from the mainstream account. For example, when the Norwegian minister for development and human rights visited northern Uganda 'She praised the traditional means of solving conflict currently advocated by the leaders there ... [and] pledged more assistance to the centre through Red Barnet, an NGO assisting former Kony rebel captives'.[19]

But it is the nature of the involvement by International NGO (INGOs) and Inter-Governmental Organisations (IGOs) in these dynamics of social torture which deserves particular attention at this point. It may be argued that it is unfair to critique humanitarians by suggesting they have a role in social torture, and that they have done the best possible given their mandates and capacities. Certainly it is not easy to question the validity of humanitarian interventions – my own attempts to do so have frequently provoked the furious riposte 'what would you do then, let them die?' However, humanitarian interventions in northern Uganda can be critiqued in terms of their own stated missions and shared commitments to the humanitarian imperative. This critique relates directly to the concept of social torture and the related categories of perpetrator and bystander.

Humanitarian Missions and Mandate

Some major organisations operating in northern Uganda shape their work by focusing on particular target groups. World Vision, for example, describes itself as 'a Christian relief and development organisation working for the well being of all people, especially children'.[20] Save the Children (who work through Red Barnet in Northern Uganda) 'fights for children in the U.K. and around the world who suffer from poverty, disease, injustice and violence ... as an organisation for children, we try to view the world through children's eyes'.[21] UNICEF takes the *Convention on the Rights of the Child* as its framework.[22] Other organisations are more explicitly focused on particular types of assistance: Action Against Hunger's mission 'is to save lives by combating hunger, malnutrition and the associated distress that endanger the lives of children, women and men living in situations of war, conflict, and natural disaster'.[23] The crux of the WFP's somewhat tautological mission statement is 'the elimination of the need for food aid' – through the provision of food aid 'for social and humanitarian protection'.[24]

What unites these somewhat different missions and approaches, however, is a commitment to a set of overarching humanitarian principles, as set out in the *Humanitarian Charter* of The Sphere Project. This project, which many of the agencies active in northern Uganda were themselves involved in and sponsored (see The Sphere Project, 2004: 315 for full list of sponsors), attempts to establish principles and minimum standards for agencies involved in humanitarian work. In the *Charter* the humanitarian imperative is understood as; 'the belief that all possible steps should be taken to prevent or alleviate human suffering arising out of conflict or calamity, and that civilians so affected have a right to protection and assistance' (The Sphere Project, 2004: 16). In addition to establishing that humanitarianism involves a dual-focus on protection and assistance, the *Charter* also 'affirms the fundamental importance' of a number of principles, the first of which is 'The right to a life *of dignity*' (emphasis added). It acknowledges that this right 'is reflected in the legal measures concerning the right to life, to an adequate standard of living and to freedom from cruel, inhuman or degrading treatment or punishment' (idem: 17). *The Humanitarian Charter* thus borrows directly from, and therefore implies a commitment to, the *1987 Convention Against Torture and Other Cruel, Inhuman or Degrading Treatment or Punishment,* which is discussed in Chapter 1.

Failures in Assistance and Protection

And yet, in northern Uganda there was a collective failure to assure a right to life with dignity – if anything international NGOs (and some national ones) contributed to the consolidation of living conditions which were inimical to such a life and which created the context within which social torture occurs. Partly this was because of their tardy arrival – Catholic Relief Services (CRS), for example, while describing northern Uganda as a complex emergency which began in 1989, only opened their office in Gulu seven years later.[25] More importantly, when they finally did become operational, INGOs and IGOs consolidated conditions of indignity because of the nature of their assistance interventions. Some examples have been given in earlier chapters. WFP food relief was unpredictable and wholly inadequate, and World Vision established demonstration plots for people without access to land rather than promoting conditions under which they could return to their own land (Chapter 5). Hunger Alert (a national NGO) gave cattle to women rather than men and therefore further weakened men socially and psychologically. UNICEF focused its attention on returned abductees and for many years successfully ignored both adult abductions and child soldiers in the UPDF (Chapter 4). Others focused on the provision of schools within the protected villages rather than promoting return to places of origin, and so on. Infrastructure such as schools, clinics and water points, literally concretised the policy of internal displacement rather than resolving it. To the extent that protected villages were sites of loss of human dignity, such forms of assistance verged on a perpetrator role.

Furthermore, the focus on assistance activities was at the expense of meeting the first leg of the humanitarian imperative, namely the right to protection. If by protection we understand the effort – generally through the application of pressure on the relevant parties – to ensure that citizens enjoy their access to rights such as basic services, physical security and the rule of law, rights for which the state and its associated institutions are responsible, then the performance of the humanitarian community was mixed at best. When alleged thieves were killed extra-judicially and their bodies displayed to the public none of the INGOs made any protest to the authorities.

Broadly speaking there was an inverse relationship between such organisations' level of operations, scale and capacities in terms of funding and staffing, and their willingness to speak up about those aspects of the situation which involved criticism of the Government of Uganda. Thus local NGOs, notably Peoples' Voices for Peace, Human Rights Focus, Acholi Religious Leaders Peace

Initiative, and Concerned Parents Association, were by far the most outspoken. National organisations such as ISIS-WICCE, Jamii Ya Kupatanisha, Refugee Law Project, were more cautious, though by 2003 and early 2004 some important reports had been published.[26] International NGOs, who arguably by virtue of the funding they brought to northern Uganda, as well as the scale of their domestic constituencies, were in a stronger position to speak up and to have an impact, were yet more cautious, as can be seen from their websites which, almost without exception, continue to give considerable prominence to accounts of the LRA's atrocities, and make almost no reference to Government policies or abuses as a factor in human suffering.[27] When the INGOs did speak out, it was in very diffuse fashion with no single organisation prepared to take a strong stance. This changed somewhat in May 2002, partly in response to Operation Iron Fist, when some forty local and international organisations joined a loose advocacy coalition known as CSOPNU (Civil Society Organisations for Peace in Northern Uganda). This allowed them to conduct advocacy without any organisation taking sole responsibility for the messages put out, but the initial momentum demonstrated in a number of position papers[28] was not sustained, and by mid-2006 the coalition was in disarray. Nonetheless it was an attempt which contrasted favourably with Inter-Governmental Organisations such as WFP, UNOCHA and UNICEF, which appeared wholly unwilling to make critical public statements, and generally laid the blame for all suffering at the feet of the LRA.

The classic defence of bystanders is to argue that they did not know what was happening. Certainly international visitors to Uganda were unlikely to reach the war zone unless they had work there, and the cappuccino bars, internet cafes and mobile phones of Kampala often persuaded them that all was well, particularly if they had seen Kampala in the mid-1980s. UN visitors and donors who reached the war zone were generally prevented by their organisations' insurance policies from travelling to the most affected areas,[29] and NGO staff were often immobilised as their policies disallowed the use of military escorts (WFP 1999: 28).

Notwithstanding all these provisos, humanitarians in northern Uganda could not claim ignorance. There was, as Allen points out (2005b), an extensive literature about the failings of humanitarianism just across the border in southern Sudan. More concretely there was also detailed documentation provided by the local NGOs mentioned above (Human Rights Focus's 2002 report *Between Two Fires*, for example, focused specifically on human rights abuses in the displaced camps). By the late 1990s, a number of reports had been commissioned which looked at some of the complexities of the situation rather than focusing solely on the abuses of one actor (e.g. Gersony 1997, Amnesty International 1999, WFP 1999, COWI 1999, Weeks 2002).

The Amnesty International report of 1999 explicitly balanced the organisation's earlier critique of LRA abuses (see Amnesty International, 1997) by concentrating on Government violations. It argued that, whilst the authorities had not intrinsically violated international human rights or humanitarian law when they created the camps, they had nevertheless failed in their obligations under international humanitarian law 'to provide protection, in terms of physical conditions and safety from human rights abuse', had failed to take steps to minimise displacement, and had 'not taken effective steps to bring to an end the situation that has caused displacement in the first place'. It concluded that 'This all raises serious questions about whether continuing action to compel people to leave the countryside remains consistent with international law' (Amnesty International, 1999: summary).[30]

Weeks' 2002 consultancy report for OCHA, the UN organisation intended to provide coordination to all humanitarian actors in emergency situations, was researched at the time Operation Iron Fist was getting underway. It did not flinch from documenting problems with the Government's approaches, not least that 'In all too many cases, the military are themselves the source of insecurity, committing acts of brutality and lawlessness against civilians that rival those of the LRA' (Weeks, 2002: 4). Such reports were important in nuancing the one-sided picture of the LRA as bearing sole responsibility for human suffering. The NURP II report is striking in this regard, for it emphasises the reasons for generalised trauma in the civilian population and makes the point that these are not specific to northern Uganda:

> ... the districts of Gulu and Kitgum were found to be the most affected ... It should be noted that conflict and conflict situations directly create trauma conditions that people experience. Inability to access basic social services; uncertainty about what the future might bring; physical effects (mutilation and rape) and social damage (orphanhood); and psychological impact (children seeing violence) are some of the countless conditions which populations in conflict and (sometimes) post conflict situations experience. These are the conditions in which the Government often fails to meet basic needs of the people of Northern Uganda ... It was established that there was only a variation of intensity, otherwise in one way or the other, everybody was found to be traumatised (COWI, 1999; 68).

There was also one striking (internal) report which scrutinised the role of the major humanitarian actor at the time, the WFP. Writing in 1999 the consultant explored the fact that 'tension still remains between the government's broader political concern to control the population (for example, through the protected villages/camps) and the potential co-opting of the aid programme to this end' (WFP 1999: 18). In reviewing WFP's handling of this tension, he came to the conclusion that:

> In almost all issues relating to individual or group protection there is a difficult balance between the provision of humanitarian assistance and the implicit sanctioning of illegal action. This was nowhere more apparent than in the formation of the 'protected villages', effectively sanctioned by WFP through its close collaboration with the authorities in providing assistance and advice on registration, locations and common services.

He points out that WFP failed to act on the fact that government rights abuses were a key factor in forcing people out of their homes, or on 'the lack of reasonable steps taken by the authorities first, to minimize displacement and second, to create conditions in which it can be brought to an end as quickly as possible' (WFP 1999: 25). He goes on to highlight how 'The modalities of the relief operation have been almost entirely dependent on priorities set by a military strategy pursued by the UPDF' (WFP 1999: 31), and how 'the role of convoy soldiers after a while became that of ensuring orderliness at distributions, rather than safe delivery along the road ... This was not only inappropriate ... but also underlined the WFP-government-army axis in the eyes of recipients' (WFP 1999: 33). In short, 'The programme as a whole was not designed around protection concerns, other than the general assumption (not necessarily proven) that camps were safer than outlying villages ... WFP may have too readily fallen in line with government policy, in effect becoming both provider and legitimizer of a villagization policy' (WFP 1999: 33).

There is, however, no evidence that this highly critical view had any influence on the subsequent work of WFP. While WFP's proposal for the period 1 April 2005 to 31 March 2008 is quite explicit and detailed in setting out the impact of displacement on the population, it reverts to analysing the causes solely in terms of LRA activities,[31] with no mention of the Government's actions as a causal factor, nor any attempt to address the problems of complicity identified by the consultant.

The discrepancy which this example highlights between the analytical capacities of individuals working within the humanitarian sector and the actions of the organisations with which they were associated, was not unusual. In the 1999 conference in Gulu, at which many humanitarian aid workers participated, an alternative 'reconciliation agenda' identifying more than eighteen issues of concern was drawn up, but had little observable influence on subsequent humanitarian practice.

From various conversations with aid workers it appeared that as well as allowing the 'saving lives' argument to override the 'with dignity' element of the basic principle, the fact that organisational missions focused on target groups or technical expertise provided a structural excuse for not taking a broad view of the overall dynamic. For many aid workers it was just a case of doing what they were good at. In the many cases where organisations such as Action Against Hunger were actually the implementing partners for IGOs such as WFP, responsibility for policy decisions was largely delegated upwards. Thus NGO workers often saw themselves as simply implementing the policies of others – a classic recipe for avoidance of responsibility.[32] The fact that there were human rights organisations highlighting rights abuses provided a further structural excuse for humanitarian aid workers who expressed the view that 'politics' was not their business – and when people saw that Amnesty International's 1999 report critiquing the Government drew absolutely no response, this perhaps contributed to a sense that even if you did speak out, it would make no difference.

In summary, the findings presented suggest that neither INGOs nor IGOs could claim to have taken all the 'possible steps' on assistance or protection, which their own humanitarian charter committed them to. In addition to failings in the kinds of assistance provided, they failed to raise awareness of major factors leading to the complex emergency they were responding to, despite the information being available in both public and internal documentation. From a social torture perspective, the types of assistance provided may have saved some lives, but did not assure the right to a life of dignity. In the process of saving lives they often consolidated conditions of indignity and as such can be considered as placing the humanitarians in a perpetrator role. And if bystanders are defined by their decision to keep silent about the wrongs which they witness, then the failures of the humanitarian NGOs to speak up on behalf of the poor and to make a noise about the violence and injustices arising from the State's failures (as well as the LRA's), amounted to the adoption of a bystander position and role.

One possible conclusion to draw would be that the humanitarian imperative is fundamentally flawed in that it can be twisted to suit purposes which are far from humanitarian. It seems that just as the Hippocratic Oath provides a convenient excuse for the doctor to work with the torturer by keeping his victims alive, so the humanitarian imperative can be used to keep people alive while doing little to resolve their situation and indeed legitimising the government policies which are partially responsible for it. Additionally the 'obligation to provide humanitarian assistance wherever it is needed' (The Sphere Project, 2004: 317) is evidently applied in highly selective fashion and on the basis of non-humanitarian criteria – for if humanitarian need had been the principal criteria, then northern Uganda would have attracted humanitarian interventions far earlier than it did.

A more optimistic conclusion is that there is considerable mileage for those who subscribe to the *Humanitarian Charter* to address situations of social torture, but only if they begin to address the protection and assistance dimensions simultaneously, for as we have seen, assistance without protection can only contribute to the problem rather than resolve it, just as protection without assistance also has severe limitations.[33]

Benefits and Functions

While the costs to the population were manifest, it is evident that the situation of social torture had benefits and served multiple functions for the actors involved. Alongside the overt ones of coercing direct victims into particular behaviours (e.g. yielding a confession, handing over information about 'rebel co-ordinators'), there were a number of less obvious, but ultimately more important economic, psychological, military and political functions.

Economic

As Betty Bigombe noted in the 1994 peace talks, 'There are others who think that if this thing [i.e. the war] ends, they will have nothing to lean on'. That people found economic opportunities in the midst of extreme poverty is demonstrated in Chapter 5, where multiple instances of petty corruption were noted, including the pocketing of extra ration cards, the sale of relief goods to business men by relief workers, the theft and sale of medicines by medical staff, the diversion of funds from block farming to building property in Kampala, and the pocketing of wages from 'ghost teachers'. It would also appear that displacement-induced poverty, and the resultant lack of money with which to transport products to market, made some farmers a captive target group for intrepid produce buyers.

For individuals in the military the economic benefits ranged from relatively petty business interests such as the sale of illegally logged timber to opportunities for petty corruption such as the pocketing of 'ghost soldier' wages (Chapter 5). For the military as an institution the benefits in terms of justifying increasing the defence budget were not unimportant.

For INGOs, over and above the substantial basics of relief assistance (Chapter 5), the situation created a number of opportunities. One striking example was the focus on the psycho-social needs of returned abducted children. The 10,000 or so abducted prior to 2002, the majority of whom had returned, provided a defined, high profile and relatively limited target group, as well as a self-evident vehicle for the promotion of the rights of the child by organisations such as UNICEF and the campaign against the use of child soldiers. A number of local NGOs – with international NGOs with a mandate on children close behind – emerged to fill the niche thus created.[34]

Another niche the NGOs largely created and then expanded to fill was the re-invention of traditional leadership. Empirically speaking, given that the formation of an 'Acholi' identity was in many respects a relatively recent phenomenon resulting from the Arab slave trade from the mid-1800s (Atkinson 1989) and the ministrations of the Catholic Church in the 1920s (Allen, 394), the polarisation into 'modern' and 'traditional' was deeply problematic (see also Behrend, 1999: 5, and Finnström (2003: Chapter 2) for a counter-position). Yet international organisations played an important part in projecting an idealised and de-historicised vision of the traditional leadership as the solution to the situation in the north. Writing for AVSI, one consultant wrote that, 'In response to years of war, Acholi elders and tribal leaders have worked to reinstate the prayers and ceremonies once used by their ancestors in the face of adversity. Their purpose is to seek reconciliation, to pacify the land and to recall the values that have been at the core of the Acholi culture since time immemorial' (Bramucci, 2001: 11). A UNICEF document argued that:

> Despite the weakening of traditional culture in Acholiland, especially in the IDP camps, elders still have considerable influence at community level. They play a central, unifying role in rituals such as cleansing ceremonies (e.g. after abduction) and reconciliations after disputes between individuals, families and clans. They also have a crucial role to play in helping communities fractured by many years of conflict to heal their wounds, and in helping the older and the younger generations of Acholis to listen to and learn from one another. (Williams et al. 2001: 38)

Such dichotomisation of 'modern' and 'traditional', and the idea of an Acholi culture with pre-modern roots, were very real and potent sources of political mobilisation and authority and created numerous possibilities for a range of

Government, religious and civilian actors, all of whom sought to use the legitimacy associated with an involvement in the notion of tradition to achieve their
own distinctly contemporary ends.

For Government, the co-optation of traditional leadership, which would otherwise retain a worrying potential for dissent, was quite important. Reviving the
traditional structures also created a useful counterpoint to the churches which
were becoming increasingly vocal at that point. At a meeting between the Belgian Government, local government officials and ACORD on 2 June 1999, the
then Minister for northern Uganda said: 'As Government we have lost several
opportunities in this war. I'm in a precarious position. This should not be seen
as a government initiative, but the truth of the matter is that it [the initiative to
revive traditional leadership] came from us'.

For NGOs such as ACORD and Red Barnet, working on strengthening traditional leadership was a far less demanding task than confronting and challenging
the inadequacies of modern leadership, which were legion. On a more positive
note, it created a new voice for civil society, alongside NGOs and religious leaders. In doing so they found some support from civilians who did not wish to
acknowledge the reality of social and political change, and were unwilling to ad-
mit that it was impossible to go back to an idealised pre-colonial time in which
there was no such thing as a national state impinging on local realities.

As it turned out, once the traditional leaders had been restored their role in
reconciliation was by no means as dramatic as had been forecast. When ARLPI
reviewed their contribution to the Amnesty process they found that it was minimal.[35] Perhaps because of these failings the traditional leaders became a target
for further NGO interventions, and a channel for non-traditional conflict-trans-
formation technologies. Despite the fact that traditional leaders had been restored because of their supposed wisdom in dealing with reconciliation issues,
the British NGO Responding To Conflict held a workshop for them from 4 to
8 February 2002 'aimed at strengthening and building skills of the chiefs and
community leaders in conflict analysis/handling, negotiating, and arbitration'.[36]
Another economic niche had been found – and the blurring between 'modern'
and 'traditional' was fully achieved.

Psychological

Although it is doubtful whether violence was made acceptable to the public at
large, Uganda had a long history of aggression, and an ideology of antagonism
between different ethnic groups which was nurtured throughout the colonial and
post-colonial period. The persistent and devastating violence experienced under
Idi Amin in the 1970s, Obote II and the Luwero triangle in the early 1980s,[37] as
well as severe economic difficulties and substantial social change which accompanied it, was likely to give rise to the psychological need for some groups to
shore up their own sense of identity and position in the world by means of a devalued 'other' (as suggested by Staub), and to create the necessary preconditions
for scapegoating and devaluation of the Acholi. The blame for the Luwero trian-

gle massacres, for example, was generally allocated to the national army domi-nated at the time by northerners, and, as shown in Chapter 7, many southerners would agree that they were brought up to believe that the northerners were less than human. As recorded in Chapter 5, some northerners felt that 'Many Ugan-dans, especially in the south, dismiss this tragedy, just saying that '... they are having what they deserve. It's their turn now. When they have enough ... they'll stop' (Murru, 1998: 11). In the 1990s ethnic tensions were further invigorated to an extent by (World Bank sponsored) decentralisation, under which it became more difficult for civil servants to work outside their home areas.

President Museveni's Movement system was monolithic rather than pluralist; there was a strong respect for authority and a remarkable emphasis on the power of the individual, particularly in the case of President Museveni himself, whom one might regard as seeking to develop a 'Big Man' cult (Chapter 4).[38] His insis-tence on a military solution to the northern war, as well as developments in the war itself (in particular the formation of ethnic militias in 2003), furnish further evidence of an ethnicised psychology of aggression, humiliation and devalu-ation (see Chapter 4). In the case of northern Uganda, the devaluation which enabled the creation of 'protected villages' in the first place, was deepened over time as basic supports to dignity such as hygiene or a good set of clothes were stripped away, and as economic and psychological dependency were induced by life in the camps. The perpetrator thus gained further grounds to feel superior and reinforce his or her devaluation of the 'other'.

While the Government and southern Ugandans benefited psychologically from devaluing the Acholi, it is plausible that the international 'bystanders' in turn benefited from watching this process of devaluation. Though this could not be fully investigated, observing the perpetrators' misdemeanours (which con-firm their prejudices about their former colonial subjects' 'primitive tribalism'), may have re-assured the bystanders themselves of their own moral superiority and consolidated the existence of an inferior 'other'. In other words, devalua-tion by southerners inside Uganda may have allowed devaluation of Uganda as a whole by those from outside, a devaluation which may in turn have been used to legitimate the bystanders' subordination of the perpetrators at a higher level.

Political

As this last point suggests, the psychological functions of social torture are inti-mately linked to its political ones. In Uganda, a political unit which is little over one hundred years old, processes of state and nation-building are still ongoing, along lines drawn both literally and figuratively by former colonial powers and neo-colonial interests. Literally in the sense of international borders and the leg-acy of internal divisions played upon by the colonisers and internalised by the colonised, and figuratively in the sense of 'modernisation' and more recent notions of 'democracy', 'good governance', 'structural adjustment' etc. as propagated under the rubric of 'globalisation'.[39] These created three identifiable struggles for an incumbent Government seeking to establish and exercise control.

The first was to achieve the subordinate inclusion of the northern parts of the country. By this I mean the inclusion of the north as an integral part of the Ugandan polity, but on subordinate terms set by the Government in the south. The second was to maintain control over the rest of the country, and the third was between the Government and the wider international 'community' over the terms of the Ugandan State's inclusion in *that* community. This latter struggle is one in which the cards were *a priori* heavily stacked in the donors' favour, and in which the Government was, generally speaking, a subordinate party seeking to become less subordinate.

Given this need to fight on internal and external fronts simultaneously, social torture under the guise of 'war' could be seen as a rational strategy, and 'protected villages' a weapon of choice. On the internal front it has several functions analogous to those of individual torture. Within the war zone, Finnström has suggested the protected villages entail 'an imposed redefinition' from citizen to subject and eventually to object 'as human agency is increasingly restricted' (2003: 183). I would add that, just as individual torture breaks down the suspected political dissident, so social torture breaks down the sub-national social cohesion which is regarded as an obstacle to the project of national unity. It creates the opportunity substantially to alter and weaken local organisational structures while also sustaining and even building up military forces – with support from international agencies whose concern with good governance melts away when confronted with humanitarian need. The clan units which collectively constitute the 'tribe' are effectively dispersed into the protected villages, traditional socialisation mechanisms are disrupted, old sources of identity are stripped away and new ones (controlled by the Government) are put in their place. Demonisation of individuals (Joseph Kony, 'the Dreadful Dreadlocked One' – see Chapter 4) and sub-groups, and militarization in the name of pacification, provide important opportunities for social engineering and control. The exclusion of subgroups from the benefits of power, for the purposes of ensuring their subordinate inclusion in the system, is key to the process.[40] War within the 'excluded' populations is furthered, which justifies further militarization in the interests of pacification by the State.

Social torture was not just about breaking down society in the north, but also about the larger national picture. Cohen notes of individual torture that 'Fear inside [the country where torture is perpetrated] depends on knowledge [of torture] and uncertainty: who will be picked up next?' (Cohen, 2001: 19). Similarly, the function of social torture was not only the subordination of people in the north, but also, through the intimidation of others with the knowledge that they too could be at risk of such treatment if they step out of line, the shoring up of national-level political control. During my visit in January 2004, I found it not uncommon for people in Soroti to comment on how their ethnic group, the Teso, had accepted things as they were and were getting on with economic activity rather than concerning themselves with the political arena the way the Acholi did.[41] In this context the constant coverage of the LRA and the UPDF in the Government's newspaper, the *New Vision*, makes more sense – they were neither out of sight nor out of mind at a national level, even though the majority of the Ugandan population had never been near this particular war zone. The war in the north thus met a specific need to subordinate one part of the country over which control was somewhat shaky, and at the same time contributed to the wider process of maintaining a grip on the country as a whole. It is noteworthy that, no sooner had peace talks begun in mid-2006 than Government military activity was greatly increased in neighbouring Karamoja, ostensibly in the interests of a disarmament process.

On the external front, social torture – with all its obfuscatory ambiguities and shifting dynamics – could be regarded as a useful instrument in the struggle of the subordinate party (the Government of Uganda) to achieve greater parity with its donors. As the analysis highlights, in social torture international 'bystanders' play a central role in defining the parameters of what it is possible for the Government to do in its own 'backyard'. The perpetrators can only operate with the permission of the 'bystanders'; by granting that permission, the bystanders become complicit in the perpetration. Nowhere is this more evident than in Museveni's referral of LRA members to the International Criminal Court (demanding permission), and their subsequent (mis)handling of this (becoming complicit in perpetuating his version of events).

This complicity creates a paradox which is at the heart of the success of social torture: The Government needs northern Uganda – indeed, its continued inclusion in the polity is a *sine qua non* for the Government of Uganda, just as the international community needs the Government of Uganda. Were threats of secession such as that made by the Catholic priest (Chapter 3) to be realised, it would be a disaster for the state in terms of the loss of domestic and international room for manoeuvre which would result. At the same time the bystanders, even as they display their power vis-à-vis the perpetrators, make themselves vulnerable to awkward questions from their domestic constituencies. If, for example, the true situations in the IDP camps were to become widely known, this would represent a serious threat to the image disseminated by the World Bank of Uganda as 'the main example of successful African post-conflict recovery'.[42] To question the Ugandan Government's record would be to question the integrity of the donors who had long held up this record as exemplary. The threat of such questioning gave the perpetrators a certain leverage over the bystanders, who now had a shared vested interest in the success myth. In effect complicity in social torture under the alibi of 'war' deprived them of any moral high ground from which to attack the Government and thus lessened the power differential between the Government and its sponsors. When after nearly twenty years the UN's special representative on humanitarian affairs succeeded in drawing attention to the situation, all the emphasis was put on the 'humanitarian crisis', and by the nature of the humanitarian interventions which ensued, the long political history which had led inexorably to this 'crisis' continued to be largely ignored. It remains to be seen whether, by creating pressure to resolve the humanitarian issues, the international community's belated intervention will also create pressure to resolve the underlying governance problems.

Justifications for Action and Inaction

From individual torture we know that perpetrators have to justify their actions
both to themselves and to others. We also know that self-justification is inti-
mately linked to the need to validate the self, and is generally achieved through the
devaluation and dehumanisation of the 'other' (both the victim and the larger
social or political group he or she represents). Equally bystanders have to justify
their inaction, and often draw on value systems shared with perpetrators to do
so. As well as this psychological function for perpetrators and bystanders, such
justifications based on devaluation contribute directly to the humiliation and
belittlement of the victim. As such perpetrator justifications play a dual role.

In social torture, the need to justify action and inaction goes beyond the individual's need to feel psychologically comfortable; institutions and organisations
need to persuade their constituencies and the general public that what they are
doing is acceptable. The principal means by which this is achieved is through
shaping discourses, which purvey only those aspects of a situation which confirm
their own story and activities, and ignore or silence those which are in contradic-
tion. And just as in individual torture, such discourses exacerbate the humiliation and belittlement of the victims.

In northern Uganda these discourses focused primarily on the abuses of non-
state actors, as is exemplified in the preface to a report on *Women's Experiences
of Armed Conflict in Uganda, Gulu District 1986–1999*: 'Rebel groups in parts of
Gulu, Kitgum and other parts of Northern Uganda and the activities of the Karamojong cattle rustlers on their neighbouring districts have collectively made the
people in these areas despair as they see their human rights become meaningless
privileges in the face of perpetrators' (ISIS-WICCE, 2000: vi). Within this larger
discourse on non-state actors, the principal emphasis was on the LRA. The various images of the LRA, which all implied that the LRA had no political agenda,
were visible in the various derogatory labels applied to the LRA by Government,
academics, NGOs and media (Chapter 4). These had the immediate purpose
of dehumanising and humiliating the LRA, humiliation which further fuelled
the violence (see Chapters 4, 7). But reports that the LRA was irrational, led by
a madman of Acholi origin who abducted, killed and enslaved for sexual purposes those of his own ethnic group (particularly children), and who was seeking to breed a new Acholi and kill off the 'old' ones, did not just nourish the view
that this was an intra-ethnic conflict and, within that, a war about children, but
also fuelled a vision of anarchy and primitivism, characteristics that were extended
by association to the Acholi ethnic group that the LRA is largely drawn from, a
group with an anterior history of being devalued and dehumanised (Chapter 7).
As one elder noted during the ACORD conference in 1999, 'the war has greatly
degraded the Acholi in the eyes of other Ugandans, who view them as murderers,
stupid, and senseless. Acholi elders have had to swallow this condemnation'.

With this focus on the LRA, the discourses drew on and reflected the predominant explanations of conflict in the immediate post-cold war period as found
in academic discourses on internal and intra-ethnic war – and their links with

notions of anarchy and primitivism. These were then overlaid with the language
of terrorism and humanitarian emergency.

Justifying Action

As well as the immediate function of devaluation, the intra-ethnic/terrorist/hu-
manitarian discourses justified the pursuit of a military solution by the Government, and, particularly insofar as the LRA were seen as 'terrorists', allowed the
Government of Uganda to position itself in the larger 'war on terror', and the
U.S. Government to justify an extension of military support to the Government
of Uganda. Within this, they reinforced impunity for a whole range of human
rights abuses at the hands of various elements of Government, and justified the
creation of 'protected villages', which were presented as purely a response to
the behaviour of the LRA. Asserting that the LRA was made up primarily of
children and abductees silenced the actual scale and military effectiveness of the
LRA, and was used to legitimise military activity, which had nothing to do with
the interests of the child and everything to do with wider geo-political processes.
It ignored the fact that at the beginning of 2002, a possible maximum of 1,000
of those 9,818 children still remained in the hands of the LRA, and that it might
be somewhat disproportionate to send ten thousand soldiers into South Sudan
in the hope of finding those one thousand unaccounted children.

For international NGOs, who argued that 'the conflict with the LRA is essentially between Acholis, and [that] the peace-building process must involve
the Acholi people at all levels' (Williams et al. 2001: 44), the portrayal of the
war as intra-ethnic and therefore as a localised problem requiring localised solutions, was central to their interventions for peace, which remained limited to addressing the relationship between the LRA and Acholi civilians through reviving
traditional leadership and conflict resolution mechanisms (despite the evidence
that Joseph Kony despised the traditional leaders – see Chapter 4). It also allowed the NGOs to focus on the victims of 'intra-ethnic' abuse, the abducted
children, and to argue that they would need a particular kind of reintegration
(a view internalised by many students and teachers despite the fact that most
students and teachers in secondary schools were not even aware when there were
returned abductees in their midst (see Chapter 6). The naming of the EU's assistance programme as the 'Acholiland Programme' exemplified this broader pattern of donors and humanitarians contributing to ethnicising the situation and
to creating 'the Acholi' as a homogeneous grouping in which all were assumed
to share the same viewpoint and needs.

When, in 2002, the upsurge in violence resulting from Operation Iron Fist
was put together with extremely high levels of internal displacement (also presented as caused entirely by the LRA), an ahistorical 'humanitarian crisis' was
generated which was primarily to the benefit of UN agencies and INGOs. The
number of organisations providing relief in the camps had by this point rocketed
from five in 1996 to over sixty. NGOs issued a statement in which they argued
that 'the current armed conflict in the region is destroying the gains made from

years of rehabilitation in the sub-region, with communities previously self-sufficient now unable to cope'.[43] This was correct in the sense that the needs were great, but inaccurate in its implication that the situation had arisen after 'years of rehabilitation'. The reality of sixteen years of gradually escalating violence and humanitarian need, along with the accompanying attempts by civil society to find non-military solutions, was negated at the stroke of a pen.

Justifying Inaction

The use of intra-ethnic/terrorist/humanitarian crisis discourses to justify certain forms of action obscured the way they also had the effect of justifying bystander inaction in the face of social torture both to themselves and to their respective constituencies. For, regarded in isolation, many of the interventions were unobjectionable; who, after all, would quibble with providing psychological assistance to a child who has been brutalised? They were justified on the basis that 'we are doing X because the situation (as presented by us) demands it'.

Yet this meant that there was no argument that 'we are doing X rather than Y for this and this reason' because the discourses had cast silence over certain issues and thereby established a number of areas of inaction. For example, the involvement of members of other ethnic groups, which should have signalled that the LRA was a symptom of Uganda-wide problems for which the Government bore a share of responsibility, was never mentioned. The Government tendency to talk of the LRA as a 'cult-like' and irrational group threw a veil of silence over the ways in which the Government had itself undermined various peace initiatives (Chapter 4) and how such an 'irrational' group had maintained an effective relationship with the Government of Sudan over an extended period of time.[44] It also foreclosed the possibility that there might be some members of the LRA with legitimate grievances and grounds for negotiation. In February 1998, for example, the UPDF 4th Division Commander 'rejected the idea of peace talks with Joseph Kony's Lord Resistant Army rebels – because their struggle is aimless',[45] a position echoed six years later by the British Minister for International Development, who reportedly doubted 'that calls to bring the LRA to the negotiating table could realistically be expected to evoke any meaningful response. 'Given the history of LRA activities, it seems to be more of a cult than a political organisation,' he told IRIN. 'It's hard to see what there is to reason with.'[46] By extension, there was no place for the Acholi to have legitimate grievances, for the LRA had became a metaphor for the Acholi, and the demonisation of the LRA by Government and international institutions alike, assisted in the demonisation of the Acholi as an ethnic group.

Discourses focused on children abducted by the LRA allowed inaction on adult returnees (the 20,000 adults taken by the LRA accounted for two-thirds of all abductions), as well as inaction on the rights of the several hundred thousand children who had been lucky enough not to be abducted but were nevertheless traumatised by the situation in general.[47] It perpetuated inaction on the UPDF's multiple failures/reluctance to bring the LRA under control, as well as on the abuses perpetrated by the Government and its armed forces in the name of protection. These included the recruitment of children into the UPDF[48] and the existence of child wives of UPDF soldiers (with several divisions based in northern Uganda, these latter were surely more than the average of 116 girls per year abducted by the LRA over the period 1986 to 2001 (total 1,741)).

The discourses thus enabled inaction on the fact that 'protection' had long been a violation of all categories of human rights (Chapter 5), and served to hide a long-term process of physical and psychological debilitation. They allowed inaction on the economic dependency and political restructuring (e.g. the re-ethnicisation of governance through decentralisation), the introduction of discourses of control under the guise of 'rights', and the undermining of all aspects of socialisation into local culture. They also allowed inaction on the use of 'protected villages' as sites of de- and re-socialisation (Chapters 5 and 6), most dramatically evidenced in child suicides and the fundamental undermining of adult masculinities and the resultant humiliation of men (Chapter 7). While the number of organisations providing relief in the camps rocketed, there was no corresponding increase in calls for the camps to be dismantled.

In short, the discourses did not question the Government's agenda for northern Uganda, and they absolved the Government, donors and INGOs alike of responsibility for the continuation of the situation. It seems plausible that donors also found the fiction of intra-ethnic war convenient, for it obscured the extent of their interest in the status quo in Uganda and their corresponding failure to exercise their potential to influence the situation. It left undisturbed the image they had constructed of post-1986 Uganda as a success story, an exemplar of the wisdom of structural adjustment, good governance and the African 'renaissance'. It meant that the conceptual strictures and political strait-jacket of the 'intra-ethnic' model could be left undisturbed, and helped to ensure the continued ignorance of their constituents overseas, many of whom (even those who considered themselves 'well-informed'), did not know what they did not know (i.e. they did not know what they were not being told), and would not have welcomed their view of beneficent humanitarianism being shaken. For INGOs the focus on humanitarian assistance needs not only justified the humanitarian scramble for northern Uganda, it effectively de-historicised the entire conflict and thereby legitimised the INGOs' inaction during the sixteen years build-up to the (predictable) 'crisis'. The discourses thus structured both thinking and intervention, typically resulting in many interventions to address the needs of a minority of victims, against a staggering lack of action on the torture of the majority.

Discussion

Low Intensity but Wide Impact

Social Torture is low intensity in the sense that the processes are not always readily discernible, and its impacts are not always immediately visible, yet they are felt by the majority of the population. Because the experience and impact of social torture is so generalised, it is difficult to pick out the individual victim and much suffering effectively is rendered invisible. Thus the impact on the young and old of being forcibly uprooted from their homes became less and less discernible as these processes increasingly affected the majority of the population and thus became the norm. Equally the impact on significant numbers of children of having their parents abducted, was not highlighted, nor was the impact on parents of having their children abducted. Neither children nor adults knew if those taken were still alive, even fifteen years after abduction took place (see Chapter 6). Like the families of the disappeared in Latin America discussed by Melamed et al. (1990: 25) they could therefore justifiably be considered the indirect victims of torture, or victims by association. Equally, the population in general was exposed to repeated cycles of hope and despair, as peace initiatives held out false promise of a resolution. This cross-generational transmission of impact was pinpointed by camp officials in Pabbo when they argued that a sense of being redundant and powerless was as much of a problem for younger as for older men 'because the children feel the powerlessness [of the adults]'[49] (see Chapters 6 and 7). Finnström also brings the Acholi concept of *cen,* roughly translated as ghostly vengeance, to bear on this discussion, noting how it will 'expand socially, in space and time, and to other people', such that traumatic experiences become part of 'the structuring of social life, group identity and collective memory' (2003: 219).

This low intensity contributes to the perpetuation of the situation insofar as the majority of its impacts are never addressed, for in what is effectively an externally determined psycho-social triage system, agencies deal only with the most visible victims. Their interventions do not acknowledge the depth to which many other individuals have also been affected. Were they to look at these other individuals in more manageable isolation, they might not hesitate to describe them as torture victims. In yet another paradoxical reversal of perceptions, the 'helpers' become unable to see the trees for the wood. As such the interventions needed to break the process of social torture are never initiated.

Geographically Extensive and Time-Indifferent

Unlike individual torture which is concentrated in very specific locations, which even if known are kept screened from public view, social torture is geographically extensive, for the entire 'war zone', and all the protected villages within it, can be considered a site of social torture. Furthermore, some of the processes integral to social torture, such as devaluation of the victims, continue for Acholi who travel outside the war zone whether to other parts of Uganda or further afield. Those coming to the U.K., for example, continue to see the mainstream account of the situation being disseminated to the public through the media and the publicity of international NGOs. Whereas for the individual who has been tortured in a cell, exiting from that cell offers a degree of physical and time distance from the events which took place inside the cell, this option is less clear-cut for those subjected to social torture. Indeed, the difficulty in pinning down the process to a clearly defined place and time also suggests that multi-local interventions will be required to break it. It is not enough to intervene just in Gulu or Kitgum; efforts also have to be made in other sites, whether these be Kampala, London or Washington.

Multiple Actors

The situation also continues because it involves a larger number of actors than is conventionally understood in war situations. Whereas most interventions take the two actor (LRA-GoU) model as their starting point, the social torture model suggests that churches, NGOs, INGOs, media and IGOs, as well as the civilian population, all need to be considered as important contributors to the dynamics. The discussion of interventions in the name of the humanitarian imperative throws into question the notion of passive bystanders: the relationship between perpetrators' actions and those of bystanders suggests that ultimately the distinction between the two breaks down. Just as the doctors described by Staub shift between bystander and perpetrator positions with disturbing ease (1990: 68), so the humanitarian agencies in Northern Uganda demonstrated the fundamentally fluid interrelationship between the two roles.

Whereas Staub sees the perpetrators as 'those who are in charge of a system which perpetrates torture,' and he regards bystanders as in some way outside this system, the WFP example suggests that some apparent 'bystanders' in fact play an integral part in enabling and contributing to the system. Insofar as WFP provided for and legitimised 'illegal action', it had a systemic importance from the very early days of the protected villages strategy. It could therefore be considered a demonstrably complicit bystander, a position shared by many of the NGOs who worked in the camps, effectively enabling and legitimising a villagisation policy whose benefits in terms of protecting the population were never demonstrated, and whose costs to the population were manifest.

Although at any given point in time it is possible to pinpoint perpetrators, victims and bystanders, over time many people traverse all three positions, creating a fluidity that is at the heart of what keeps conflict going, in part because so many people are both impacted on and themselves implicated, in part because existing mechanisms of accountability, such as the *Convention Against Torture* or the International Criminal Court, cannot accommodate this fluidity, complexity and range of culpabilities.

Multiple Functions

Interventions to break these dynamics would have to address the various psychological, economic and political and functions which continuation of 'war' serves for many of these actors. Not only is the range of those concerned quite wide (from those most visibly involved such as the LRA and the Government, to those more generally associated with attempts to address the problem such as churches, IGOs and INGOs), but the different functions are in fact interrelated. In the process of meeting their psychological needs, perpetrators generate a further need to justify their actions and inactions to themselves and others. When these justifications are externalised in the form of public discourses such as that of 'intra-ethnic war' and 'Acholi backwardness', they in turn generate a particular pattern of interventions such as the re-invention of traditional leadership and the 'rescue' of abducted children (Chapters 6 and 8), and the associated establishment and consolidation of economic and political interests (over and above the petty economic opportunities which the context creates for soldiers and rebels alike: see Chapter 5). The political economies established as a result of meeting micro-interests fit the overall political function of sustaining a process of subordination for as long as possible rather than rushing to achieve it as an end, for while some of these interventions appear to deal with the negative impacts of social torture, their own survival, paradoxically, lies in the continuation of social torture.

For as long as the Government continues to struggle to hold together the country, and to the extent that the process of subordinating the north helped to do this, it made sense for the Government of Uganda to draw out the social torture for as long as possible – hence the time indifference described above. If the subordination of the north were to be fully achieved, alternative mechanisms would have to be found for keeping the other fragments of the country under control. It was therefore more important to sustain the process of subordination of the Acholi as a means to the end of keeping control elsewhere, than it was to achieve complete subordination of the Acholi as an end in itself. Just as in individual torture the perpetrator seeks to keep the victim alive, so in social torture. This would explain President Museveni's alleged refusal to accept offers from the U.S. Government to deal with Joseph Kony once and for all.[50] By extension, the tensions between Government and civilians over the terms of their inclusion in the Ugandan polity would not go away even if the LRA in its existing form were to come to an end. Further expressions of dissent would emerge, just as the LRA itself emerged from the remnants of the UPDA and the HSM. Indeed, the referral to the International Criminal Court, in which the focus is on LRA perpetrators to the almost total exclusion of UPDF ones, can be seen as yet another catalyst of such dissent. Equally the struggle of the Government to assert itself on the international stage would not come to an end even if the north of the country were eventually brought to subordinated inclusion.

In an important sense, therefore, although the language of perpetrators, victims and bystanders, which was generated in large part in response to the Nazi genocide of the Jews,[51] has application to the situation in Northern Uganda, there must be reservations about describing the camps as 'concentration camps' or the war in the north as 'genocide', as does the LRM. Subordinate inclusion by way of social torture differs from genocide in two important respects; it targets groups for subordination rather than elimination, and it is an ongoing (modifiable) process rather than in any sense a 'final solution'. Indeed, for the Government in particular, it is of more use as a means than as an end.

Social Torture Acquires Its Own Momentum

Perhaps the most disturbing feature of the social torture dynamic is that it acquires its own momentum which does not require the continued involvement of the original perpetrators. This can be seen in physical and mental stunting as a result of prolonged malnutrition; while the 20,000 or so abducted children are seen as a threat to stability, in reality it is the half million or more children growing up in the camps under such conditions who are a much bigger 'time bomb' threatening future processes of economic production and political participation. As noted in Chapters 5 and 7, very few young people will benefit from tertiary education and the resultant employment opportunities it opens up. Equally, the spread of HIV may further undermine these basic processes, by cutting through the ranks of the trained and skilled, as well as productive manual labour.

In the medium term, the violation which people experience in the camps does not just deepen their impoverishment and accompanying physical and psychological debilitation; these in turn become a source of violence. While some resort to abuse of self, many others, as suggested by the literature on torture and violence, cope with their own oppression by oppressing others (Staub 1995, Gilligan 2000). If 'difficult life conditions' create a psychological need to re-establish self-esteem through the degradation of others, how much more so the experience of social torture itself? People's sense of security, of 'positive identity' (both individual and group), and of 'connection to others' are all at risk in the war zone, as is 'a meaningful comprehension of reality, a sense of how the world is ordered and of one's place in it'. Many victims of social torture thus are likely to come to feel psychological needs similar to those which led the perpetrators of social torture to oppress them. Meeting these needs is often achieved through abusive actions, which, as Chapters 6 and 7 show, generally exacerbate the poverty and debilitation of those abused. In short, the former objects of torture can become its agents.

When those who were oppressed become perpetrators themselves, they do not always turn on their own oppressors – they are more likely to displace their anger to others less powerful than themselves. This can be seen in the proliferation of 'small men': subordinated adult men seeking to regain their self-respect by turning against women and subordinating youth. Indeed, the locally internalised discourse around returned abductees (see Chapter 6), exemplifies a wider discourse within the war zone of 'youth' as a category of 'others' who have energy, are no longer fully under the control of their parents/society at large, and are under severe economic pressures to become involved in lives of crime (see Chapters 6 and 7). This discourse turns them into people who need to be helped – and thereby brought back under the control of adults. Some of the youth in particular came to see being recruited into the military as the only way out of the impasse of poverty and of oppression by their own elders. Paradoxically therefore, one of the mechanisms which thwarts the achievement of civilian men's adult identity, becomes seen as the means to regain it, despite the fact that in reality it is more likely to consolidate psychological dependency than to break it, and is almost certain to feed into the further escalation of violence.

This apparently voluntary militarization of some oppressed youth, who as soldiers become involved in various abuses, is also a good example of the formation of perpetrators out of former victims, and further underlines the argument that the categories of perpetrators, bystanders and victims are fluid rather than fixed. It is also an indicator of the extent to which an atmosphere of fear and distrust, coupled with the physical disruption caused by displacement, creates barriers to alternative, non-violent/non-abusive routes out of the position of victim.

Such an analysis raises complex questions of agency. It might be argued that to talk of an abstract concept, social torture, acquiring an independent momentum, is to belittle the agency of those most affected, and that only some changes in peoples' behaviours are directly attributable to the interventions of various external actors, while others (such as voluntarily joining the armed forces) are their own (chosen) adaptive responses to the debilitation arising from multiple violations over an extended period of time. This distinction, however, is in many respects an artificial one, which rests on an illusion of choice. The widespread debilitation and vulnerability which were such a prominent feature of the protected villages effectively reduced the options available to people, such that even if they appeared to be 'choosing' to behave in a particular way, it would be generous in the extreme (and more accurately a form of moral escapism) to describe this as a 'free choice'.

In the context of such a severely circumscribed set of choices, the introduction of alternative practices by external actors, whether in the field of demonstration plots, cattle for women, or political re-education, became easier as people had little realistic option but to go along with them. As such the camps acted as crucibles for and accelerators of social change – on terms set by outsiders. Long-standing props for socialisation, and thus for 'moral' behaviour, had been removed. Economic survival strategies were established in a context in which the economic dependency of the population as a whole was being systemically consolidated. Attempts by elders to regain a degree of political control at a local level were going against the flow of long-term national processes of political change.

Social Torture is Justified in Public Discourses, which then Become Instruments of Social Torture

When partial representations of reality were allowed to pass muster as total explanations, they did not just set the terms of debate and intervention in northern Uganda as a whole, they also became part of the distortions which helped to keep the dynamic going. Rather than simply a reaction to social torture, the public discourses were an integral part of it. These externalisations of psychological process into the public arena, together with their related institutional practices and silences (and 'forgetting'), were not just crucial to enabling inaction and legitimating the visible perpetrators. In generating interventions which left real needs unattended, they aggravated both physical and psychological processes of debilitation. In disregarding (and thereby suppressing) alternative voices and interpretations (often the voices of the tortured), they themselves became a form of further psychological violence and therefore an instrument of social torture and subordination in that they further weakened people's sense of control over their own lives and environment. As Zur says of what happened to the widows of *la violencia* in Guatemala: 'The "official truth" undermines alternatives, deliberately violating people's memories. The violence to people's memories, though less tangible than the physical violence from which it is not entirely separate, affects victims for years because the violence is internalized' (Zur,1998: 170).

Not only did the discourses of intra-ethnic war and humanitarian crisis present a skewed and partial version of reality while laying claim to objective and moral 'truth', but they were often generated by the very people who were supposed to be helping, people who should have known better. That their silences induced despair was evident when religious leaders complained that

> ... many of these facts we are mentioning are systematically silenced or distorted. We are told that the insecurity is soon coming to an end, that so many rebels have been killed. The truth is that things are just getting worse by the day, people are often left unprotected and that many abductees (mostly children) are the ones being killed in armed confrontations. Given the seriousness of this situation, we the religious leaders wonder why this great tragedy unfolding in Northern Uganda hardly features in the international news.[52]

Comparing media coverage of their situation with that given to other contexts they noted that; 'Two children killed in Israel will appear in the front page of all world newspapers, while hundreds of children killed in Northern Uganda seem to be nobody's concern' (ARLPI Press release, 31 January 2003).

The sense that such coverage devalued the Acholi was sharpened by the duplicity of those perpetuating the discourses, for many of those living inside the war zone were aware that lack of international attention was not due to lack of knowledge. The title of ARLPI's report on the camps (*Let My People Go: The Forgotten Plight of the People in the Displaced Camps in Acholi'* (ARLPI, 2001)), for example, implied that the problem was not that nobody knew what was going on, but rather that they had 'forgotten'. One human rights activist I interviewed put it bluntly:

> The international community also has a portion of the blame, especially the international press who subscribe to government policy when reporting on Uganda [he specifically mentioned the BBC at this point] ... Diplomats who have been here have a lot of information, but they don't go public with it, except when they are about to leave [a former U.S. ambassador was mentioned here] ... For the love of our people we have to fight our intellectual dishonesty.[53]

The fact that 'helpers' knew the reality but persisted in presenting a very partial version of it to their international audiences, positioned them simultaneously as 'helpers' and co-perpetrators, a duplicity which added to people's sense of disorientation and dread. As well as playing a supporting function, the discourses and those who generated them were thus further instruments of social torture in their own right.

Conclusions

This chapter has sought to elaborate the multiple dimensions of a social and political process which, taken together, constitute a form of torture. The range of actors responsible for inducing debilitation, dependency, dread and disorientation is not limited to the LRA and GoU, but is considerably wider. A correspondingly wide set of benefits and functions are addressed by social torture, and this is justified through a number of key discourses and entrenched through the interventions these discourses legitimise. Key areas of discourse established to serve these purposes are those of intra-ethnic war and, related to that, of the war being about 10,000 children rather than 800,000 people, and of humanitarian rather than political crisis.

When looking at wider processes of social and political change, the fighting between GoU and LRA forces becomes only one of several key elements of the situation. Ethnic groups such as the Acholi are uncomfortable with nationhood, and the state is uneasy with yet contributes to the persistence of ethnic identities. There are also tensions between the Government and national population, and between the Government and international community. Long-established donor states are reluctant to cede power to emerging states, while the Government of Uganda, as a relative newcomer, still seeks to consolidate its power. 'Bystanders' in these struggles, most obviously the international NGOs, are pulled selectively into supporting various elements of these processes, and, in allowing this to happen, they compromise their value claims and therefore potentially their funding base.

Taking all these different elements into account, it is possible to see that the fundamental process in Northern Uganda is one of social torture, a process which contributes to the subordination and inclusion of the Acholi by the Government and of the Government by the international community. The key to the perpetuation of social torture lay in maintaining the cover provided by the LRA-GoU war. For in a reversal of what we generally expect, rather than torture being used to prosecute war, war in Northern Uganda was being used as the disguise under which to prosecute social torture. It was a successful disguise, to the extent that when people wished the situation would end they think solely in terms of the LRA-GoU war ending. When the disguise is stripped away, two of the more paradoxical features of the situation become more comprehensible. The Government's refusal to dismantle the protected villages despite their long-standing failure to achieve their stated objectives of protection and containment, for example, can be attributed to the success of the protected villages in contributing to the subordination of the civilian population. Similarly the Government's reluctance to engage in negotiations with the LRA (or to allow civil society actors such as ARLPI to pursue a non-military solution) and its 'failure' to achieve a decisive military victory make sense if it is recognised that success in either option would have stripped away the cover provided by the war.

Notes

1. District Education Officer, Gulu, March 2002.
2. In the Barlonyo massacre of February 2004, for example, people were reportedly forced into their huts, which were then set alight.
3. This was the case in December 1999 when, within days of the signing of the peace accord in Nairobi between GoS and GoU, the LRA attacked the Resident District Commissioner's house in Gulu using an RPG.
4. *The Sunday Monitor,* 17 May 1998, 'Fire and Death on Black Wednesday'.
5. In this regard, my own experience with research assistants was illuminating. One of the most forthcoming about the LRA also turned out to be a Government Internal Security Operative (see Introduction).
6. Awer, 27 July 1998.
7. Awer, 17 December 1998.
8. Hon Owiny Dollo, MP, Gulu Conference, September 29 1999.
9. There is some evidence from the literature on individual torture that people with a well-developed political position are better positioned to resist torture than those who lack such a framework within which to make sense of what has happened to them (Summerfield 1990, Zur 1998).
10. *New Vision,* 13 June 1998, 'Wamala Criticises Acholi On Kony War'.
11. *New Vision,* 1 June 1998, 'Army Repulses Kony Attack'.
12. *The Monitor,* 21 May 1998, 'Kony War Needs Love – Bishop'.
13. Visit on 8 November 1998, Pabbo report, 23 November 1998.
14. Awach report, March 2000, Pabbo Report; 5 January 1999
15. Hon Owiny Dollo, MP, Gulu Conference, 29 September 1999.
16. *The Monitor,* 18 July 1998, 'Kony Condemns Gulu Clergymen'.
17. www.hrw.org/worldreport99/africa/africa3.html .
18. *The Monitor,* 22 December 1999, 'U.S. Rights Group Hits at NRM Again'.
19. *New Vision,* 3 February 1998, 'More Food for North'.
20. www.wvi.org/wvi/about_us/who_we_are.htm
21. www.savethechildren.org.uk/scuk/jsp/aboutus
22. www.unicef.org/whatwedo/index.html
23. www.actionagainsthunger.org/who/history.html
24. It was the first UN organisation to develop a mission statement, which runs to some two pages (www.wfp.org/policies/Introduction/mission).
25. www.crs.org/about us/who we are/index.cfm
26. HURIPEC 2003, RLP 2004.
27. For example, see http://www.christianaid.org.uk and then search 'Uganda'.
28. http://www.csopnu.org
29. With the exception of WFP, UN agencies lacked risk insurance for Phase IV security areas.
30. There was no government response to the 'more than 40 extra-judicial killings, dozens of rape cases and torture by the UPDF soldiers and Police' – *The Monitor,* 21 June 1999, *Silence on Rights Report Won't Help.*
31. WFP/EB-1/2005/7-B/2 (22 December 2004), available on www.wfp.org pp 5–10.
32. Action Against Hunger's website specifically directs the reader to see 'The Opinion of the United Nations World Food Program on Our Work In Uganda'. (www.actionagainst

hunger.org/who/history.html). This shows a somewhat worrying desire to be seen to please authority, particularly if we consider Milgram's experiment in which he found that authority figures could override people's moral concern not to inflict pain on others (Stanley Milgram, 1974: *Obedience to Authority; An Experimental View*).

33. For an exploration of how the concept of 'humanitarian protection' was being put into operation in Northern Uganda, see Dolan and Hovil (2006).

34. Local NGOs included CPA (Concerned Parents Association), set up by parents of children abducted from Aboke to work for their return, and GUSCO (Gulu Support the Children Organisation) and KICWA (Kitgum Concerned Women's Association), both of which established reception centres for returned abductees in Gulu and Kitgum districts respectively. These worked closely with World Vision, which also had a reception centre for returned abductees, and Red Barnet (Save the Children Denmark).

35. ARLPI, *Seventy Times Seven*, Section 5, 2002.

36. KM E-newsletter No 5, 15 February 2002.

37. A revisionist interpretation of what happened in the Luwero triangle is to be found in HURIPEC, 30 October 2003.

38. One example of the way this image of the President as all powerful was internalised by civilians includes the story of an ACORD fieldworker whose wife had been killed in crossfire between the UPDF and LRA. After trying for some time to get some compensation from the UPDF, he assured me that he would go to Museveni himself to get the matter sorted out. Similarly, the *New Vision* reported that the five children of a bus driver killed in an LRA ambush, would approach the President personally for help with their studies (*New Vision*, 26 April 2004: 'Driver's Kids Seek Presidential Help')

39. As the case of hunting (Chapter 5) illustrates, people's practices came under pressure from war-related factors (UPDF, rebels), but also from a broader change in socio-economic organisation: the former 'wilderness' was now a managed national park with armed game rangers.

40. I describe the process as one of subordinate inclusion rather than social exclusion because in some respects the latter term has been brought into the language of the political mainstream and is now used for any group that is not enjoying the fruits of an otherwise problem-free socio-economic and political dispensation. Subordinate inclusion shows that what is at stake is a dynamic in which power is predicated on the mutual dependence of the powerful and the subordinate and in which the essence is inclusion rather than exclusion.

41. Personal observations in discussion with range of local NGO respondents, Soroti, January 2004.

42. See http://www.worldbank.org/research/conflict/papers/uganda.htm (cited in Allen, 2005b: 18).

43. IRIN, 4 October 2002.

44. This compares closely with the relationship between the supposedly irrational RUF in Sierra Leone and Charles Taylor in Liberia (Keen, 2005).

45. *The Monitor*, 23 February 1998, 'UPDF Boss Says No Peace-Talks'.

46. IRIN, 7 April 2004, 'Extend Amnesty for Northern Rebels U.K. Minister Tells Government'.

47. If one considers that children under the age of 18 accounted for at least 50 per cent or 400,000 of the total population of Gulu and Kitgum districts, and that 220,000 of these were aged between 8 and 18 (i.e., were at risk of abduction), then the 800 or so children abducted every year accounted or at most 0.4 per cent of children at risk of abduction (i.e. aged 8–18), and 0.2 per cent of the child population as a whole (aged 1–18). As noted in Chapter 5, there was little attention given to the orphans of victims of the war or AIDS.

48. When UNICEF finally surveyed the UPDF's Lugore training camp in 2003, they found 10 per cent of recruits were 'probably' under the age of 18 – IRIN, 13 November 2003: *Uganda Should Do More to Stop Child Soldier Recruitment – UNICEF.*

49. Pabo, 5 March 02.
50. I and others have on a number of occasions asked people with links to the U.S. military why they did not simply use a missile strike to 'take out' Kony, and the answer was consistently that the offer had been made and turned down.
51. See for example, Raul Hilberg's *Perpetrators, Victims, Bystanders: The Jewish Catastrophe 1933–1945*.
52. ARLPI Press release, 31 January 2003.
53. Human Rights Focus, Gulu, January 1998.

9

CONCLUSIONS

The mainstream discourse around today's wars, which broadly speaking has shaped both interpretations of and interventions into the situation in northern Uganda, tends to see them as internal, irrational and driven primarily by greed. This case study of the LRA-GoU situation offers a counter-narrative; it suggests that war can in fact be a disguise for a more complex and far reaching process of social torture. In relationship to the *Convention Against Torture,* the model of Social Torture, by drawing on and integrating what I termed the 'building blocks of a counter-narrative', broadens the lens through which to identify and address the phenomenon of torture. In regard to addressing situations of protracted conflict such as that found in northern Uganda, the model also suggests a far broader range of interventions than is generally considered.

Social Torture Offers a Counter-Narrative to the Mainstream Discourse

Social Torture is a counter-narrative which embraces complexity and rejects over-simplification. The range of local, national and international actors involved, the intersection of multiple economic and political motivations with psychological needs arising from cycles of oppression and subordination, and the transnational nature of justificatory public discourses and value systems, cannot be easily accommodated in the depoliticising binary oppositions (such as 'internal-external', 'greed-grievance' and 'rational-irrational') which underpin the mainstream discourse of internal war. By explicitly seeking to integrate this complexity, Social Torture offers a multi-dimensional explanation for situations of protracted 'war', an explanation which includes and links together numerous elements of existing literature such as the constructed nature of war, the political economy of humanitarian assistance, globalisation and global governance, discourse theory and psychoanalytic theory as applied to the phenomenon of violence. As such it places emphasis on the systemic nature of the process. This is represented in Diagram 9.1 below. It is also a counter-narrative in the sense that much of this complexity is identified through taking a 'bottom up' rather than 'top-down' approach.

When dichotomised conceptions of who the actors are (e.g. Government versus Rebels, insiders versus outsiders, perpetrators versus victims, military versus civilian) give way to a more comprehensive and fluid range of actors, then the causal and locational internal-external oppositions embedded in internal models of war fall away. The catalysts and dynamos of today's wars are neither exclusively within the war zone, nor simply external to it. Importantly, they are located in both – and, as the analysis of discourses exemplifies – in the interactions, influences and mutual dependency between the (geographically) internal and external. The cast of actors involved in creating and perpetuating the dynamics of war extends well beyond the evident military groupings, to also include international governments and donors, multi-lateral organisations, religious groupings, international and national NGOs and media, 'victims' and diasporas, and academics and policy makers.

It is not just the range of actors which breaks down a clear internal-external differentiation, but the nature of the relations between them. Despite suffixes

Diagram 9.1 An Elaborated Model of Social Torture

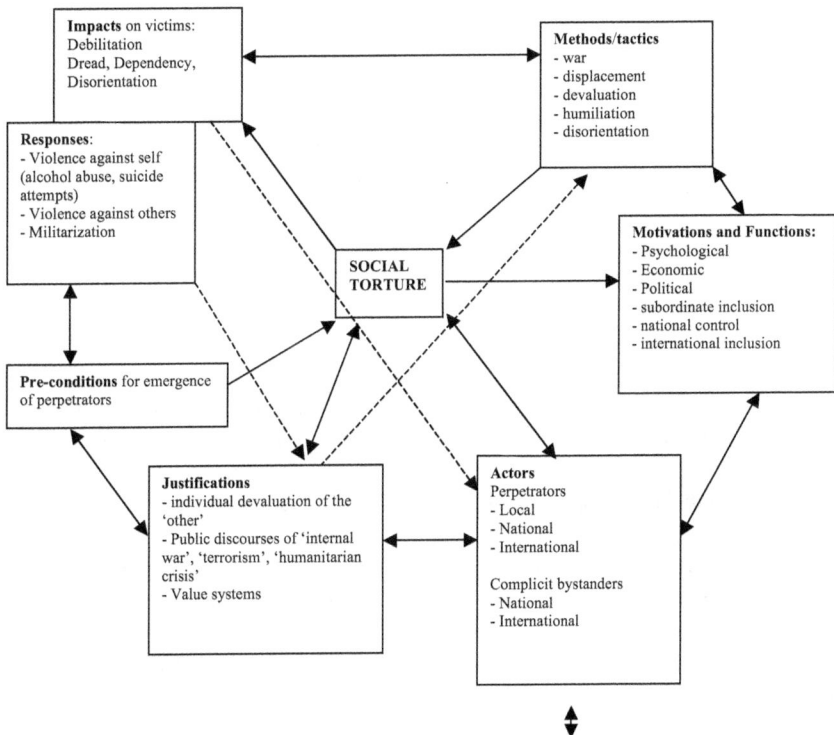

such as 'national' and 'international', they do not neatly divide up into oppositional categories defined by geographic origin, as they are inter-dependent and
multi-local in terms of their operations and decision-making. Furthermore, the
hierarchy of power is not stable; whereas in the basic model of perpetrator-
bystander-victim the perpetrator is the most powerful (and indeed, it is this
power which turns others into bystanders), in social torture the most visible
'perpetrators' (Government of Uganda) are in many respects subordinate to key
'bystanders' ('external' states). At the same time though, perpetrators are able
to exercise leverage over the bystanders because, by virtue of their own inaction, the bystanders become complicit. This complicity puts perpetrators and
bystanders in a shared position vis-à-vis external constituencies such that they
jointly generate and perpetuate the discourses which serve to mask the true nature of what is going on.

Interdependence extends to value systems, indeed some actors draw on conceptual frameworks that explicitly transcend or disregard geographic boundaries,
such as traditionalism versus modernism, Africanism versus Arabism, Christianity versus Islam, deism versus animism, neo-colonialism versus independence.
Even where they appear to correspond to prejudices about geographic origin
(e.g. traditionalists from 'Africa', modernisers from 'the West'), such conceptual
forces are in reality always inter-linked, as demonstrated by the revival of traditional Acholi leadership (Chapter 8), an ostensibly local initiative which was
catalysed by an expatriate and funded by foreign donors.

Such interdependence puts a question mark over the 'new wars' analyses
which explain war as due in part to the internal weaknesses of states. Kaldor, for
example, argues that the 'haves' derive their strength from access to the new
technologies and the espousal of multiculturalism and associated liberal values, while the 'have nots' are weakened by lack of access to the benefits of the
new interconnectedness, and by their espousal of what Kaldor variously terms
'particularism', 'exclusivism' and 'identity politics' (2001: 75). In other words,
blame is placed at the door of the weak states, whose weakness is reflected in
their having made two unwise, but unrelated, choices.

While the Ugandan state is in important senses weak – particularly in its
dependence on external funding – this is not due to a lack of perspicacity on
its part, but to the paucity of means at its disposal with which to establish and
maintain control over its population. The reality of social torture and subordinate inclusion, notably the mass violation and debilitation in camps, and the use
of hegemonic masculinities and identity politics to humiliate and devalue, are
reflections of that relative poverty and powerlessness. While elements of these
dynamics demonstrate that the state has some capacity to resist international
pressures insofar as it uses the ambiguities of social torture, and the complicity
of bystanders, to compromise its donors and thereby lessen the power imbalance
with them, they also ensure the state's continued weakness, as the bystander
states will use their knowledge of what is going on as a source of leverage (aid
conditionalities) on the perpetrator state, and thereby help to keep the state
itself in a weak and subordinate position with limited options for exercising

control over its population. Both perpetrator and bystander states are therefore caught in a situation of mutual dependence of their joint making.

This mutual dependence in turn suggests that, far from the idea of a post-Cold War vacuum where previously there was a 'world order', there is in fact an equally systemic quality to today's wars. The failure of the 'weak states' argument is therefore not so much a descriptive as an analytical one – the weakness is well described but its systemic nature is not well identified. The weak states do not espouse particularism, exclusivism and identity politics in opposition to multiculturalism and associated liberal values, but rather with the covert support (arguably the permission) of the supposed purveyors of 'cosmopolitan' values. The situation thus appears closer to Duffield's notion of 'subordinating forms of North-South integration' (Duffield, 2001: 5).

Greed–Grievance

The model of social torture furthermore suggests that the pursuit of a single overarching motivation in explanation of today's wars (or any war for that matter) is a flawed enterprise. Even if, for the sake of argument, 'greed' and 'grievance' did represent the whole gamut of possible motivations, which of the two would be regarded as the real motivation in cases where grievances arise out of a failure to satisfy greed? And even supposing that one of the two could be identified as the primary motivation, it still remains to correctly determine the quality of the greed or the grievance. For example, one explanation offered for some of today's wars is that people are angry at being kept out or excluded from the global system and its benefits. The LRA by contrast appear angry at the Acholi being drawn into or included in that system with no discussion of the terms of their (subordinate) inclusion. And perhaps most importantly, even if greed or grievance could be identified as the cause for a war beginning, they do not offer a satisfactory explanation for why wars continue. For the motivations of actors are not uni-dimensional; the perpetrators combine psychological wants and needs with economic and political interests. Nor are motivations static; if the experience of oppression or victimisation within a given context gives rise to the need to oppress/perpetrate in turn, then what drives people, and their resultant positions in the dynamics of war, changes over time. As I argue in Chapter 8, even the elaboration of a simple perpetrator-victim binary model into a marginally more complex triangle of perpetrator-victim-bystander fails to accommodate the reality that over time people can shift between these respective positions. While terms such as 'perpetrator', 'bystander' and 'victim' have descriptive validity at a particular point in time, they cannot capture this changing positionality over time or the changing motivations associated with each.

The role of motivation is further qualified by the simple reality that the majority of the people who are most impacted on find themselves in a war rather than deciding to go to war. Where the resultant economic imperatives and psychological dynamics drive people to self-destructive actions or violence-escalating behaviours, these must to an important extent be regarded as independent of questions of 'rationally' articulated motivations or intentions based on self-interest. And as the psychology of denial suggests, people can simultaneously know and not-know what they are seeing or doing, a key function of which is to protect their sense of their own moral identity. It is thus possible for humanitarians who come into such contexts to continue to believe that they are still 'doing good', when objectively their activities are already doing some harm. In short, humanitarians' expressed motivations for going to the war zone are not directly correlated to the actual impact of their actions.

Furthermore, the self-destructive and violence-escalating behaviours of some people living in the war zone may appear irrational in that they do not serve those individuals' best interests, but they create opportunities for others to pursue their 'rational' economic and political interests in the form, for example, of certain INGO interventions. As such there is no de facto division between individual and group psychology and political economy, or indeed between 'rational' and 'irrational'. The incorporation of the psychologies of oppression and denial into an analysis of war, and in particular the recognition that over time these will have some influence on peoples' positions and behaviours within such wars, qualifies Keegan's argument that today's wars are the result of long-suppressed hostilities and tensions being able to come to the surface following the end of the Cold War (Keegan, 1998: 66). Without denying that there are hostilities whose origins people trace back to pre-colonial times, the Uganda case suggests that they have since evolved through multiple phases of colonial and post-colonial divide and rule and resultant cycles of oppression and victimisation. Today's hostilities thus build on historical tensions, but cannot be reduced to them.

These psychological cycles and their associated political economies also suggest that searching for the 'root causes' of today's wars, as was attempted by many analysing 'complex emergencies' in the 1990s, is problematic. They seem to indicate that, as an evaluation of humanitarian responses to the Rwanda Genocide concluded, 'recent events result from a cumulation of events of the past, with one factor forming a building block for the next, and all actors and factors interrelating and interacting' (Millwood, 1996: 13). If some of today's perpetrators were yesterday's victims, and some of today's victims will be tomorrow's perpetrators, then it is more important to examine the interweaving of complex events and processes, and the multiple truths for those who live these causes and effects, than to search for specific 'root causes'. The iterative nature of cause and effect is well captured in the idea of a 'vicious cycle' of deprivation and violence (see Moore: 1996: 1).

While the various components of the mainstream discourse on 'internal war' both implicitly and at times explicitly depoliticise the present, they themselves constitute a conceptual and political force in the here and now. As I have shown in Chapters 4 and 8, important elements of the mainstream discourse were reflected in the way northern Uganda was portrayed, with the LRA-GoU war presented as internal and intra-ethnic, and the LRA as irrational terrorists or greed-driven bandits, and as *the* problem rather than *a* problem. The 'humanitarian crisis' that people are portrayed as having brought upon themselves in intra-ethnic wars provides a mantle under which international actors can intervene. In this respect the discourses of internal war ignore the agency and role of various actors, and by ignoring key psychological dynamics, negate the complex subjectivities of the many people who live through such situations. In silencing them, such discourses directly contribute to their further subordination and thereby contribute to what Nader calls an 'ideology of harmony', in which the portrayal of violence as irrational is used as a form of social control (Nader, 1992). The mainstream discourse of internal war, as operationalised in northern Uganda, thus played a role in shaping the dynamics of the very phenomenon it purports to be describing and analysing.

In the process, such discourses obscure meaningful analysis of the national and international political economy of conflicts in the post-Cold War era. Although works such as those of Keen (1994), Duffield (1994, 2000), Richards (1996) and Kaldor (2001), indicated that there were vested 'external' interests in areas affected by war, and indeed in the prosecution of warfare itself, the mainstream discourse gave this little attention. The humanitarian nature and intention of any international intervention was assumed and reasserted in nearly every branch of the discourse. On this basis alone, the mainstream discourse on war can be seen to form an integral part of the broader development discourse and the 'international relations of dominance and subordination' (Abrahamsen, 2000; viii), which it supports.

Similarly the discourse on 'internal war', which, like that on good governance and democracy, coincided with the end of the Cold War and filled the need for alternative legitimations for and modes of foreign intervention. In one sense the already oversimplified view of Cold War proxy wars were simply reversed. Just as these were portrayed as externally driven ones which had no internal energy of their own, so post-Cold War wars could not be explained as proxy and therefore logically had to be internally driven with no impulse from outside. In this way, the notion of 'internal wars' did not threaten the historic oversimplifications of the 'proxy war' model, indeed it confirmed them and prevented too close a scrutiny of other (non-Cold War related) dynamics of the Cold War era. As such, the visions of post-Cold war conflicts as internal are like the wider discourse on development in that they obscure 'the interconnectedness of states and political forces in the global era' (Abrahamsen, 2000: xi).

In summary, the discourse of internal wars, generated by some actors and used by others to intervene in – and thereby exercise a degree of control over – areas to which they claim to be 'outsiders', effectively masks the complexities of today's wars. By maintaining simplistic oppositions such as 'internal-external', 'rational-irrational' it stifles the possibility of multi-dimensional explanations and the more effective interventions which such explanations could generate. Rather than explaining the problem of wars and their continuation, they are used by 'bystanders' to elaborate policy and practice. In generating inappropriate interventions and silencing the subjectivities of those most concerned they contribute to the devaluation of the latter and as such are component of the dynamics of social torture in today's wars zones, a form of discursive violence which underpins the more visible physical forms of violence. The very existence of this discourse belies the picture it seeks to portray of war as internal, for its usage constitutes a traceable linkage between the local and international, the 'inside' and 'outside'. Any meaningful understanding of war thus has to include an analysis of the analyses of war and the degree to which, through discursive violence, they underpin physical violence.

Social Torture Goes beyond the *Convention Against Torture*

One question raised by broadening what is placed under the rubric of torture, and who is considered to be involved, is whether the integrity and condemnatory power of the term 'torture' will be weakened, either conceptually or in terms of action taken against perpetrators. For social torture, or torture on a mass scale, does not describe the behaviour of a few individuals, rather it involves a systemic process and dynamic which is enabled by a range of actors, including governments, multi-laterals, NGOs and academics.

At a conceptual level it can be argued that the content ascribed to terms such as torture is not fixed; it can and should change over time to reflect shifts in understanding. For example, what is considered child abuse in the present, has changed dramatically in the last few decades as a result of changed understandings of the impacts of various forms of behaviour, such as physical beating, on a child's development. In countries such as the U.K., sexual orientations which only a few decades ago put people at risk of imprisonment, have in the last ten years or so come to be recognised as legitimate grounds for claiming membership of a particular social group – and therefore can be used as grounds for claiming asylum.

It is also important to reiterate that the definition of torture given in Article 1 of the *Convention Against Torture* is broad enough to include much of what I have placed under the rubric of social torture, and that in Article 3 'flagrant or mass violations of human rights' in an asylum seeker's country of origin are stipulated as possible grounds for considering the person at risk of torture. There is nothing to suggest that this excludes the mass violations of human rights entailed in the forcible displacement of populations, or in the Government's failures to protect physical security and provide access to basic education and health care. Although it might be argued that later articles in the convention (Articles 10–13) put considerable emphasis on torture in situations of 'arrest, detention or imprisonment', many would regard the situation in the protected villages, with their tight curfews and risk of shooting if caught outside the camps, as akin to imprisonment.

However, the concept of social torture goes beyond what is addressed by the *Convention Against Torture* in several respects. Firstly, the range of actors is larger and more complex, and the nature of their involvement more nuanced than a rigid perpetrator-victim distinction suggests. I have argued that there are many actors who are neither hands-on torturers, nor passive bystanders, whose moment of involvement may be transient relative to its impact and who may not even go near the war zone itself, but who are complicit insofar as their actions enable the conditions in which social torture can take place. In addition, many are non-state actors who have not signed up to any formal obligations. The restricted Convention model of the perpetrator group as those public officials who personally inflict physical torture and those who authorise this, cannot be used to hold the majority of actors accountable, though it might be argued that, as Article 1 includes not just those acts inflicted by or at the instigation of public officials or other persons acting in an official capacity, but also those acts inflicted with the 'consent or acquiescence' of such persons, it partially accommodates bystanders as well as visible perpetrators. Whereas consent requires a verbal or written 'yes', acquiescence requires the absence of a 'no!' As such the concept of acquiescence, to an extent, coincides with that of the bystander who does nothing despite having the capacity to do otherwise.

Secondly, the categories of perpetrator, bystander and victim are shown to be fluid, such that, over time, as victims seek to deal with their situation by becoming perpetrators, membership of the perpetrator group is likely to grow, creating a simple problem of scale for those seeking to deal with torture through legal prosecution.

Thirdly, the legal definition of torture takes the fact that pain is 'intentionally inflicted on a person' as its starting point and therefore focuses primarily on the identification and demonstration of conscious intention to harm, whereas in the identification of Social Torture the intention to inflict pain on a person cannot be used as a criterion. For it is argued that social torture succeeds precisely because of its ability to combine and create synergy between unconscious wants and needs and various economic and political interests. While the intentions of individuals and institutions are not eliminated from the picture, they are not the critical issue, indeed they cannot be the critical issue as social torture is at least in part defined by the involvement of bystanders who do not – arguably cannot – acknowledge their own complicity. Social Torture relies on the fact that people have psychological mechanisms, and generate discourses to externalise these, specifically to convince themselves and others that they had no bad intention (critics of humanitarianism, for example, are likely to temper their criticism by acknowledging that even if the humanitarians do harm, they do so with the best of intentions). As the saying goes, 'the road to hell is paved with good intentions'.

To ascertain which intention is the issue is thus extremely difficult, especially once a situation has been ongoing for nearly two decades. For example, should we focus on the intention to do harm or the intention to benefit from somebody else's doing harm? Even if people pursue their interests 'rationally' once they find themselves in a given situation, this does not automatically equate to having intentionally created that situation, though it may contribute to wanting to perpetuate it. Such ambiguities around intention highlight the practical limitations of seeking to address the complex realities of mass torture through exclusively legal frameworks: peoples' actions are not reducible to intention, and the burden of proof of intention is very hard to meet, the more so when working in a war zone. It is for this reason that social torture is identified through the composite of acts committed, responses to them, benefits derived from it, legitimations used by those involved, and situations arising from it, rather than through a scrutiny of intentions.

There is some risk that the practical, conceptual and logistical constraints on the identification of intention in social torture will be interpreted to mean that the analysis of the multiple forms of involvement and causal responsibility is wrong. This though would be a *non-sequitur*. The mismatch between available legal mechanisms, which can only handle very limited numbers of actors, and the realities of social torture, which involve a whole spectrum of them, does not necessarily demonstrate limitations in the analysis of social torture, rather it reflects the known constraints of the available legal mechanisms.

Sticking with a narrow definition of torture and responses to it would also condemn us to inadequate responses to situations such as northern Uganda. A narrow vision of visible perpetrators, which by its silence absolves the many other partially responsible parties, simply adds to the tensions which are a part of what keeps conflict going for it can quickly appear closer to scapegoating than justice, and to demonstrate complicity rather than a search for truth and justice. It may fail to address the grievances of the many who suffer at the hands of 'minor' perpetrators, never see and are therefore not so concerned with the 'major' instigators behind the minor ones. It may thus be more of a hindrance than a help in the cause of peace making and post-conflict reconciliation.

To deal with the limitations of a legal approach requires a shift in emphasis, away from preoccupations with intention to harm and towards a concern with responsibilities for harm. If the multiple ways in which a wide range of actors contribute to the perpetuation of war in situations such as northern Uganda are acknowledged, then an actionable hierarchy of responsibilities can be established. This is necessary both to deal with the range of actors involved, and their locations – for there is a need to focus not just on physical visibility *in* the war zone but also on responsibility *for* the war zone.

In this hierarchy, causal responsibility is shared by many, while moral responsibility can only be attributed to a sub-section of these, and legal or criminal responsibility applies to a smaller sub-section still. Causal responsibility does no more than establish the link between an action and its consequences (e.g. a person gives money in good faith to an aid agency which misspends it), whereas moral responsibility is relative to an actor's capacity to have done otherwise, a capacity which itself is a function of that actor's access to resources such as information, economic, political, and social power, psychological resilience, and so on. Those who enjoy access to such resources and choose not to use them have greater moral responsibility. It is thus important to distinguish between a witness who sees but is powerless to intervene, and a bystander who sees yet chooses not to use their power to intervene. The relationship between causal and moral responsibility is not fixed as the resources available can change. Legal responsibility is always likely to remain restricted in practice, for to vest excessive hopes in top-heavy legal institutions such as the ICC is to guarantee that only a tiny fraction of those involved in perpetuating suffering are held to account, and to ensure that wider questions of causal and moral responsibility are never addressed.

Each type of responsibility requires a very different set of responses or interventions: *punishment is reserved* for legal responsibility through existing criminal justice processes, whereas *expressions of disapproval* are pertinent for moral responsibility (voting for another party, or withholding funding would be obvious mechanisms), and *supportive* interventions (e.g. providing more and better information) for those who are causally responsible but cannot easily be held morally responsible, let alone legally.

Establishing an actor's moral responsibility, on the basis of their capacity to have done differently than they did, might ultimately prove more useful than a legal process. For if some actors rely heavily on a domestic economic support base or political constituency, and many of their supporters/constituents would not want their own moral self-image destroyed by association with the immoral actions/inactions of those they sponsor, then holding such actors morally responsible for predictable harm arising from their actions or inactions could create very real pressures for changes in approach. Highlighting an actor's capacity to have done otherwise would also be particularly useful in the pursuit of those who have done harm through inaction.

This creates an onus to improve the quality and quantity of certain types of information available to actors, in particular about the predictability of the harm which has been done, for if the dynamics whereby harm is done are better understood, and harm – whether through action or 'inaction' – therefore becomes more predictable, the capacity to hold actors to account will be increased.

Social Torture Suggests the Need for More Comprehensive Interventions

By highlighting the systemic aspects of today's 'wars', social torture demonstrates, as does Galtung's term 'structural violence', that something which people considered acceptable in fact is not, and that actors have responsibilities which are frequently left unacknowledged and for which they cannot be held accountable through existing legal mechanisms. This analysis should serve not just to hold actors to account, but also to create a shift in understanding and the resultant interventions. It obliges people to re-assess a situation that they observe. Whereas understanding such a situation as primarily one of war prompts interventions which are inevitably partial and frequently inappropriate, if the 'war' can be placed in its larger context of social torture then the reasons why neither a military solution nor a negotiated settlement between the LRA and the GoU has been achieved (and why even if they were they would be insufficient), can be better understood.

The social torture analysis also brings into focus some parallels with situations which are generally not associated with today's 'wars'. Thus, for example, it is possible to see how as the dynamic of social torture deepens, and people resort to self-destructive behaviours, the protected villages in northern Uganda may increasingly resemble the ghettos of North America, which Castells describes as 'part of an earthly hell' in which America 'is systemically reproducing its deepest pattern of social exclusion, inter-racial hostility, and interpersonal violence' (Castells, 1998: 148). Similarly it confirms Gilligan's model of violence, not just in terms of the psychoanalytic insight he offers between patterns of humiliation, shame and violence, but also the political economy of ensuring that such cycles are perpetuated rather than broken.

Rather than regarding war as an aberration, it is necessary to situate it in broader processes of social and political change. The recognition of multiple dimensions and parallels with 'non-war' situations also offers a far greater range of entry points into the complex task of bringing such situations to an end, entry points which may include but should certainly go beyond those which are generally pursued to deal with war. Rather than peace hinging on how you deal with one reclusive figure, such as Joseph Kony, or one sub-group of traumatised people, such as returned abductees, it becomes clear that meaningful peace also involves addressing the multiple and systemic causal forces implicated in the perpetuation of social torture and the war which disguises it.

Rather than focusing solely on the absence of 'rationality' of some actors, it is important to scrutinise the form and potency of discourses of others, whether at local, national or international level. Rather than simply trying to identify the political agenda of one group, it is also important to establish the complex of psychological needs and economic interests of all those involved, whether as military, donors, civil society or humanitarians, as Keen has demonstrated with regard to Sierra Leone (Keen, 2005). Perhaps most important is to explore how best to address the impacts of nearly twenty years of violation, debilitation and humiliation, impacts which contribute to the self-perpetuating momentum of social torture whereby victims become perpetrators along the lines suggested by Gilligan (Gilligan, 2000). In particular the patterns of devaluation and humiliation, which are such a feature of the dynamic and which offer a potent explanation for behaviours in both the civilian population and the LRA, need to be broken. This requires psycho-social approaches to address questions of self-esteem, interventions into discourses of masculinity and femininity, and both political and developmental interventions to address inequalities at a national level. These should create an economic climate within which non-violent masculinities can be developed and within which the Government's sense of control is secured. If these can be put in place, then a number of the actors in social torture will find alternative and less harmful ways to meet the needs of economics and institutional survival.

In conclusion, a Social Torture analysis offers considerably more opportunities for action than the simple mainstream model of binary war. If the range of actors is widened, then there is more scope to influence them and less hangs on one individual or one grouping. Equally, if the theatres of any given war are multiple and global, this creates more points of intervention, many of them more accessible than the war zone itself. While northern Uganda works particularly well as a case study of social torture insofar as it combines extremes of violation and inaction in the 'protected villages', the use of justificatory discourses and silences, the involvement of a multi- and trans-national cast of actors, and a particular structural relationship between the State, LRA, civil society and international community, the model of social torture could potentially be applied to the analysis of many other situations of protracted conflict and socio-political change, not least if they are generally thought of as 'internal' conflicts. Sierra Leone, for example, shares certain key features, such as a prolonged state of uncertainty in which people did not know whom to turn to, supposed protectors turned into oppressors, and war served as a cover for a range of other economic and political projects (Keen, 2005). But as war is only one of any number of potential disguises for processes of systemic subordination, social torture could also be used more broadly to look at situations where people's right to life with dignity is denied in systemic fashion, and where their confinement produces behaviours which are then used to dehumanise and devalue them and justify their further confinement; contemporary examples might include the North American ghettos described by Castells, and the protracted situation of the Palestinians. Further situations in which the fine line between camp, 'protected village' and prison suggests parallels with northern Uganda are to be found in numerous refugee settings around the world; if to leave the camp means to risk landing in prison,[1] then the camp effectively has become an extension of prison.

Notes

1. As is the case for Congolese refugees in refugee camps in Tanzania.

ANNEX A

TESTIMONY OF AN LRA SOLDIER WHO RETURNED UNDER AMNESTY, OCTOBER 2001. RECORDED APRIL 2002, KAMPALA

A Comment on the Integrity of This Testimony

In elaborating my understanding of the LRA in Chapter 4, I drew heavily on the testimony which follows. Some may feel that I am relying unduly on this source. After all, as Behrend argues, field research in a war zone is complicated by the way mass media affects

> what we have up to now called ethnographic reality. They create *feedback*. Ethnographic reality can no loner be assumed to be 'authentic'; rather, we anthropologists must consider how it is produced – and what models it imitates' … It is already becoming apparent that in future, anthropologists will increasingly be confronted with an (ethnographic) reality that they themselves (together with the subjects of their research) have created (1999: 5).

I myself was quite sceptical and wary of using Jacob's testimony. He was clearly very aware of portrayals and perceptions of the LRA. Nevertheless, there are several reasons to be confident that Jacob's account, although necessarily subjective and quite possibly informed by 'feedback', offers valid insights into the LRA. Its sheer length, complexity, and level of detail would be difficult to simulate – to do so would have required access to extraordinary amounts of documentation. Less visible from the printed page is the extent to which he was positioning himself vis-à-vis mainstream perceptions of the LRA, shifting between 'we' and 'they' depending on what was being discussed, also protecting friends who remained in the LRA by censoring some parts of the story, and insisting on the inclusion of certain details which would signal to those who had also been there that this was a first-hand account. Had the story been fake it is unlikely that he would have been able to simulate those behaviour patterns in the telling of it.

He also had a considerable sense of urgency about telling his story. Several previous attempts to work with journalists had failed as they did not have time for the level of detail he wanted to give. After leaving Uganda I tried for many months to keep in contact with Jacob, with no response. I hesitated about making his account public, fearing it might damage him in Uganda. It came as a severe shock to learn in October 2003 that he was already dead. It took a further four months to establish that his death had occurred only a few months after recording his testimony. I learned that the UPDF had taken him to a barracks in Koro (just outside Gulu town), apparently to persuade him to join them. When after three days he still refused, they killed him.

For ease of reference I have divided the account into a number of sections:

Section 1: Abduction
Section 2: Integration into the LRA in Sudan
Section 3: Life in the LRA
Section 4: Escape and return

These are followed by a number of further sections which reflect where we digressed from the primary account in order to fill in the picture of specific aspects of the LRA.

Section 5: Treatment of 'stragglers'
Section 6: Control exercised over people's sex lives
Section 7: LRA sick bays
Section 8: Herbal remedies used by the LRA
Section 9: Organisational chart of the LRA for the year 1999–2000
Section 10: The four holy spirits guiding Joseph Kony
Section 11: The Yards
Section 12: The Controllers
Section 13: Items kept in the Yards

An Aye: I am the one[1]

Section 1

1.1: Abduction

I will not forget my days when I remember November 15 1995 when I was abducted from my home village and taken to live in captivity far away from home for many years in Southern Sudan. I am called Yakobo Engena born in 1969. In my village where I came from I was staying with my parents, but now I am living alone in Gulu town without parents (they are all gone/deceased – my father died in 1990, my mother died in 1994; when abducted I was staying with my paternal aunt in Acaba trading centre).

I still remember the way I was taken to the bush by the rebel Lord's Resistance Army. It was on Friday evening at around 10.00 o'clock when the rebels entered my village well armed with a group of brave men who were selected for the mission. I was already asleep in my hut as I had cycled more than 40km that day. When these people came to one of the trading centres near my home it was already night and they first went to attack Acaba Technical Institute where they captured 200 students. Some managed to escape capture by running down into the village. Many of the students jumped from the windows and others from the doors, and some got wounded at this time as they tried to escape. The rebels split up throughout the village with some looking for more children to be captured and others continuing to burn houses and loot the properties of the civilian community. They looted clinics, shops and other important places.

The abducted children were ordered to carry with them food and looted properties in the convoy. The convoy moved from place to place where they needed to go and they continued disturbing the peace of the civilian's. In the process many children were taken from their homes and parents. As we moved from Acaba where I was abducted towards Minakulu, this process continued. Every person captured was tied in chains for fear that they might escape. We were told to hurry to move very quickly to catch up with time before crossing the main road heading from Kampala to Gulu at a place called Bad Cati (sleeve of shirt). When we approached the main road everybody was made to stop and wait until the rebel commanders had gone ahead to check that nothing would happen when people crossed the road. We then started moving until everybody had crossed and then continued walking some distances, about 200 yards.

There was a young boy in front of me carrying 45 kilos of sugar and I was carrying 25kg bag of sugar and three pairs of shoes. The young boy was almost collapsing from the combination of load he was carrying on his head and the speed at which he had to walk out of the UPDF soldiers who were following up to rescue the abducted children. One of the rebels came nearer to me and told me to exchange the heavy load the younger boy was carrying with mine. By bad luck during the exchange of these heavy loads one of the bags got torn and about 2.5kg of sugar poured down onto the ground. I tried my level best to control the torn sack but it happened that it had already poured. Three rebel commanders who were guarding us came to me and asked me what had happened. I told them I'm sorry but the bag was not properly tied so the mistake (accident) occurred.

These commanders were not at all sympathetic to me, instead they started beating me terribly. After this I was terribly beaten. Laker Lucky, the commander leading the convoy, came and ordered me to be shot later. However, when I was at my last hour, they discovered I was a technician, so he told the soldiers not to kill me but to watch me closely because I seemed to be one of the people who wants to escape (I later stayed with him until we reached Sudan and we became friendly). If I should try to escape at anytime I was to be finished without any further discussion.

By now we were in the bush heading down to a place called Okule in Minakulu, some 20km from home and we were already getting tired of walking long distances. We were also hungry but nobody cared, they simply ordered us to move until we reached the final destination where we were supposed to be taken that day. There was no stopping whether for short or long call, people had to defecate as they were walking. The whole 150 boys were chained together. The 50 ladies were not chained together but were made to carry crates of beer, sodas, radio cassettes, and other looted properties. Before we reached Okule the rebels set many houses ablaze. Goats and chickens were looted.

We were hoping that many people captured were going to be released because we included elders, people with white hair whose duties were mainly to carry looted properties. However, two old men who were frustrated at walking all the way collapsed on the ground and, although we were almost reaching the first final destination of the day's journey where we were going to spend the night, they were then beaten to death with axes. And that was the end of these two men.

We reached our destination at around 5.00pm on 16th November. The place was called Opuk in Okule parish in Minakulu county. The home we stayed in belongs to a man who worked as a coordinator for the LRA. He would gather military information about UPDF soldiers, and could also be sent to town to purchase other important things the LRA wanted to be taken to Sudan or for military use, such as gum boots, clothes and other essential commodities.

While I was in Okule parish it turned out that one of this man's sons was married to a girl from my home village of Acaba. She was a lady called Doreen. When Doreen saw me she was shocked to find me in such a desperate situation. She had no chance to talk to me but gradually she managed to push information to the commander that 'before you here I have a brother to me and you have captured him'. She asked 'why couldn't you leave this boy?' but the commander ignored the young lady completely.

When it was already coming to around 7.00pm we were divided to different positions for protection under military guard. During the night all the boys were put together in a single roomed house (*ot lum*). The girls were put in another house. The next morning when everybody was complaining about the way we were squeezed together that night. The rope was untied for the night and fixed again in the morning.

17th November: Some few people were then released (3 old men and one lady who had a disease of the legs). The most important looted goods were then carried along the rest was left behind and collected by the civilians in that area. We then proceeded until we reached another village where we got the information that UPDF were making a follow-up to rescue the abducted children. So we then had to hurry for more distances in case of attack by the UPDF soldiers and other militias who were controlling the area between Minakulu and the Saint Thomas Senior Secondary School. Immediately Some soldiers were immediately selected to go and investigate whether the information was correct. When nothing happened we eventually stopped to rest and cook food before being told to proceed. We were now heading to a place called Koch, and the UPDF had already noticed the LRA movements.

We continued moving for some distance until we reached the place where we were supposed to spend the night (Koch). On arrival we found the overall commander of the operation, Mr John Matata Okello with some other comanders (eg. Murefo and others) based here, and they were lying under a big tree reading newspapers which had been brought to them by local coordinators. We were then registered by Matata and from there were allocated to different units of Sinia brigade. Some were taken into 'Headquarters', others to Teranga battalion, others to Hoka battalion, and others to Siba. I was taken to Teranga battalion headed by a man called Odong Latek.

We proceeded again and when we stopped for the night we made a camp with Headquarters at the centre and the other battalion units spread around at a distance of about 30 metres. Officers ordered us to make small thatched shelters for the night for them. We then cooked some of the food we had been carrying, ate and slept the night outside on the ground.

The following morning (18th) we had an attack by the UPDF soldiers who had been sent from Gulu and Koro military defence. They found us where we had been sleeping. We (the abductees) were still newcomers who could not participate in the battle and we were moved away from the battlefield heading towards Bobi. Others were selected to carry the wounded people down to the sick bay in Koch. The LRA battled with the UPDF leaving a number of casualties on both sides. The fighting took almost two hours, and eventually the UPDF were defeated. Many UPDF soldiers were wounded and some died. The remains which they took from the UPDF soldiers, such as clothings, uniforms, gumboots, guns, were then put to fire [burnt], not carried with them. LRA soldiers who died were just left; they only covered them with leaves and prayed for their souls. The ones who were wounded were carried along on stretchers to be taken to the sick bay (in Koch) where they were supposed to be given treatment until when they were cured.

The convoy then continued moving until I found that we were already crossing the main road coming from Gulu to Bobi, from west to east. We continued from there until we reached Tegot Ato hill (where there is a radio transmitter) where UPDF soldiers caught up with us and launched another heavy offensive against LRA. From there many UPDF soldiers died and some LRA soldiers also died and the wounded LRA soldiers were taken to a sick bay in Tegot Ato.

On leaving Tegot Ato we proceeded towards the north where by the time we were about to cross the main road we met together with the anti-personnel carrier named Mamba, which fired a lot of bullets onto the LRA convoy. So people had to retreat and in the process some18 school boys who had been captured from Acaba Technical Institute managed to escape. That night (18th) the commanders gathered together the remaining abductees and other soldiers who ran for fear of bullets the Mamba was shooting and we slept there in that village called Abere, Lalogi division (Omoro county).

The following morning (19th) we were then taken to somebody's home where we the abductees were gathered together. The commander in charge of the convoy, Mr John Okello Matata, checked on the number of abductees before a radio message was sent to Joseph Kony about what had happened the previous day. Kony asked him why he had decided to ignore his orders and the military option which he was supposed to carry out, and added that that was why Matata had caused the convoy to enter into a UPDF ambush. This conversation made Matata very angry. Young officers were deployed around that home in Abere because the home was fenced, and they were ordered to go and bring heaps of sticks which were used to beat us terribly. Nobody was allowed to cry and if you did that would be the end of you. We were beaten until nobody could walk. Two boys who did cry were shot to death on the spot. Their bodies were just picked up and dropped near the home. That is where I got wounded on my back, a wound which took three months to get cured, and the scar of which can still be seen today.

After this action we were ordered together with the convoy to leave the place that very morning (19th). We continued until we were about to cross the road leading to Odek, a point where again there was suspicion of military ambush ahead. The LRA soldiers decided to penetrate the ambush by force and they managed. So we ran in a hail of bullets until we managed to cross to the other side of the Odek road (from west to east) for about two miles. From there we proceeded up to Aswa Ranch which we reached at around midday. Everybody was very tired and they decided to spend the night there.

From Aswa Ranch we went to Anaka. At this point we were no longer tied together. We spent two days in Anaka where again there was another battle in which we lost five soldiers. It was now approaching the time for fasting and we proceeded deep into Murchison Falls Park where we spent fourteen days fasting. We were just staying in a bushy covered area where we were being taught the policy of LRA. After the prayers then we had to leave. People were sent to loot in Anaka trading centre. Some went to the mission, others went to Anaka hospital and health centre in the centre where they looted drugs, micro-scopes and other medical apparatus. That was on the 22nd of December. We went down to the no-man's land heading towards Adjumani and we stopped on the way in Kabarega National Park where we spent two days and we again moved east towards Pabbo with UPDF in close pursuit. They launched a further offensive where a helicopter gunship was sent to come and patrol from above while the infantry were pushing forwards to rescue the abducted children.

On 25th December 1995 UPDF launched another attack on the LRA. By this time we were back in Aswa and two of our officers got wounded; one called Ojara Signaler was wounded in his thighs and another fellow called Smart was wounded on his legs. They were both taken to the sick bay in Tegot Ogili (Kitgum) where they were supposed to get treatment. The following day we headed back west and crossed a rocky area full of running water bordering Kitgum and Gulu. We then crossed the Kitgum-Gulu road and headed back towards Anaka.

Just before we could reach our destination in Anaka a lady in the LRA who was rumoured to be trying to engage herself to two army officers was shot dead under a big mango tree with a silenced gun. We left her lying in her own blood. Everybody was called to see the dead body to let everyone know that if you commit any of these offences then you will be killed directly.

1.2. Journey to Sudan (December 1995/January 1996)

When we reached the area near Pabbo we looted bags and bags of rice. We took goats and salt from the village. Then we turned back towards Kitgum district, crossing to Lagile. We proceeded up to Pajule. We crossed to Patongo. Then we went and spent the night on the mountain called Got Ogili where we went and checked on people who were taken to the bay for treatment. From there another fellow called Odong Richard was killed because he was found making plans with his friends as to how they could escape from the convoy. He was killed using Lukile [see below] and left lying on the rocks.

That evening we were taken on top of the mountain where we made a big fire and people were addressed by Matata Okello. He told us about the current war they were undertaking inside Uganda, and that we would be heading back to Sudan before long. We then spent the night there.

The following day we came down [from the mountain] and crossed to a place called Omiyanyima before crossing the river Pager and heading towards Padibe. When we were there a message was received from Joseph Kony in Sudan for the LRAs who were in Uganda to return back to Sudan. From this point LRA commanders had to make arrangements for us to move safely back to Sudan. Soldiers were selected to go and loot properties, food and other important things both to help us on the way and to be taken to the people inside Sudan.

For the journey to Sudan we were lined up in eight rows. We were again attacked by UPDF on the way, but LRA managed to open the way by fire. We continued moving heading towards the Atebe River which marks the Uganda-Sudan border, and a helicopter gunship was sent again to come and check on the direction LRA was heading – by this time civilians were complaining a lot that the government is leaving the children to be taken down to Sudan without steps being taken to rescue them. So the helicopter had to fire some bullets at the moving convoy and the LRA also fired their guns to threaten the helicopter from controlling them and to allow them to continue moving ahead. Thereafter the commanders decided that people should start running ahead because there were soldiers following after the LRA.

This time they were on the way to cross the border to Sudan. Before reaching the river Atebe, people suffered a lot because there was a scarcity of water. Some became so tired they could not continue moving and were killed by the blocking forces [see below], their bodies simply left behind. The majority though continued until we reached the river Atebe. The river had very deep water that was not easy for us to cross. So they used a long rope where people would climb to cross the river to the other side. Two people were drowned in the process of crossing.

After we had crossed the Atebe river it was already 6.00pm. The commander John Matata Okello ordered the properties and military arms they were carrying along with them to be checked, as well as the number of abductees, because when they reached the camp they would have to present a working report to the Chairman (Joseph Kony) as to how the operation had proceeded down inside Uganda. Having found that some commanders had mishandled the abductees such that many were no longer present, and that some of the properties were also missing, he ordered a terrible beating for some of the officers until some of the properties which had been hidden among them were rescued. Some also lost their rank because of their misbehaviour during this operation.

1.3 Arrival in Sudan

We then moved to an area called Limwu, there was nobody there, we only found remnants of pangas and hoes, ruined houses left there by the SPLA. It was dry season and extremely hot. There was absolutely no water and many children died during the one day we took moving from the border up to Aru. The commander survived by drinking sodas which had been looted sometime back. We crossed to a place called Aweno Olwiyo until eventually we reached the Government of Sudan military post at a place called Issac where we were welcomed and given different types of food to eat. After the message that we had arrived had reached the LRA headquarters some six lorries were brought to collect us up to the LRA camp in a place called Aru, a distance of some 9 kilometres. The lorries belonged to the Government of Sudan. They made several journeys to collect the abductees and soldiers to the camp.

Section 2: Integration into the LRA in Sudan

2.1: Arrival in Aru Camp (18 January 1996)

We reached Aru on 18th January 1996 at around 5pm in the evening. Aru camp was built on both sides of the Nimule-Juba road about 58km from Juba. Gilver and Stokri were on the west side of the road, Sinia was on the east. Control Altar extended across the road, but with Kony's headquarters on the west side.

We were gathered together to wait for our friends whom we had left behind to come and join us. When we were now all together we were addressed by commanders from different units telling us why we had been brought to their camp. They told us we were brought to be trained and to become soldiers because we have to work hard and make sure we go back and overrun Museveni's government.

The convoy which I had been abducted by was that of Sinia brigade. We met different people from different tribes. I even met my tribal men who had been abducted earlier and taken to Palutaka (in Pajok, Sudan). By this time they were used to the camp. They were able to tell us how they were maintaining their life and about the conditions in the Sudan. They even advised us not to be worried about home because if you continued worrying a lot about home then you could either die or you may fall sick, and they warned us that if the commanders notice you have that intention of going back then they will decide to kill you instead. We were then released to go to our brigade Sinia where we were allocated to various positions. For example some went to Brigade Headquarters, others to Teranga Battalion, Hoka Battalion, Siba Battalion [see organisational chart]. Then people were divided and taken to stay with their commanders who were heading the brigade.

The following morning on the 19th January 1996 we were then gathered so that the adjutants, Regimental Sergeant Majors (RSM) and brigade admin could collect information about our particulars. They asked us our names, district, home village, parish, parents, qualifications, age/dob. All this was noted down in their particular book, which was then used for the Parade State (Roll Call) which took place each morning, early enough for the information to reach the Brigade Headquarters by 8.30am. They in turn had to take the information to the overall Headquarters, where it was processed before being taken to Joseph Kony by 10.00am each morning. During the Parade State details of any sickness, deaths, births, absence without leave, duties, loss of weapons, food distribution would all be noted and steps taken later in the day to address these. As such those abductees who arrived in Aru in poor condition physically eventually received some treatment, but it was not immediate upon arrival.[2]

200 had been abducted initially from Acaba. Of these 18 escaped but many others were added as we moved: by the time we reached Aru in January we totalled about 1500. 2 elderly men had been killed near Acaba for being too weak to continue, 1 twentyfive year old man was killed in Got Ogili for trying to escape, 2 children drowned crossing the river Atebe, and a further 50 or so children had died of thirst in the march to river Atebe and across the border in the Limwo area.

2.2: 1st Meeting with Joseph Kony, 20 January 1996

The following day on the 20th January Joseph Kony was invited by the Brigade Commander John Okello Mutata to come and address the newly arrived abductees. Other high ranking officers like Ottii Lagony, Beba-beba, Celestine Akury, Buk, Nyeko Tolbert (Chief Personnel Administrator at the time), Mr Odego (Military administrator from West Nile), the Secretary to the Chairman, Mr Paul Okodi, Field Commander Omona (who was the former UNLA signaler at the rank of Corporal), and junior officers like Lucky Laker, and Major Otullu, were amongst the officers who attended the ceremony in Sinia Brigade.

When Joseph Kony came to address us he was a major general by rank. He told us 'we have not brought you here to kill you, but because we want you to be trained and become soldiers so that we can go back and launch offensives against Museveni's regime which is oppressing the population of northern Uganda'. He talked of the Uganda Government killing off innocent civilians in Uganda, capturing civilians who were then taken to Luzira, and persecuting and poisoning ex-soldiers who were taken to Luzira after the military takeover from the late

Major General Tito Okello Lutwa. He added that 'now that you are brought to Sudan here get to know we are in suffering and you must change yourselves and your faith to be a true rebel who will work hard, train, and have his guns ready to go back and fight against UPDF' (By then it was still called NRA [changed in 1996]).

2.3: *Joseph Kony's Regulations*

We were also instructed by JK that there were some regulations we were supposed to follow:

- Whoever is brought from Uganda must undergo smearing with shea nut oil and ashes, after which you have to stay for three days without washing. You will then be allowed to greet and eat together with fellow LRA because they will assume you are now part of them.
- You are not supposed to hold a gun or any bullets before training
- Nobody is allowed to go out of the defense [the camp] without informing the authorities. Also nobody is allowed to shoot the gun because many times soldiers have been hurting themselves by either shooting their legs, their hands or one another in what we call 'mistakes'.
- You are not allowed to eat certain types of food and fruits, e.g. mango, oranges, lemon, edible rats, pork, honey, sheep, duck, eggs (only children up to age 5 can eat eggs) etc. Why? Because the Holy Spirit believed that the opposing enemies of LRA such as the NRA for example, would use these items for witchcraft to overrun the strength of LRA (for example, if you ate honey you would be wounded immediately you are in battle). So LRA had to counter the enemy plans by using their own witchcrafts by stopping their militants from either eating or using the above items as foodstuffs.
- No stealing; if you are caught stealing you may either be killed or terribly punished .
- You are not allowed to fall in love with any girl or woman unless it is authorised by the military council. This is to control the rate of unwanted pregnancies and prostititution within the camps.
- You have to respect your mother and father. Now that you have been taken to any of the officers or commanders then you must bear in your mind that is now your father or mother. Because if you don't respect then you will find yourself in difficulty and you may continue suffering because of your misbehaviour within your 'family'. No ladies or other women are allowed to share houses with their commanders or have sexual relations with any commander before they have gone together to swear before the yard.
- Any LRA is not allowed to get married or in touch with any foreign lady be it a Sudanese, or otherwise. If you happen to commit such then you would either be killed or deserve a terrible punishment for the same.[3]
- All the tribes who joined the LRA were termed to be the new Acholi community, '*Acholi Manyen*' who were fighting against the government because

they have their own agenda. They were informed that the people who are now taken to Sudan might in fact be safer than people who were left behind in Uganda because of the happenings which were taking place inside Uganda. For example, cases of homosexuality, ladies being taken by UPDF soldiers, problems of money causing many girls to become prostitutes, in the end you find lots of people dying of AIDS disease. So the few people who are in Sudan could be safer than those left behind.

- LRA is carrying a holy spirit war so LRA are well versed with their prayers, their way of belief, to God, such that LRA is the only chosen people of God who are fighting using the assistance from the Holy Spirit.
- LRA as a rebel movement has no room to spare for our enemies because whenever we go for battle we kill, we murder, we rob, and loot without being sympathetic to our enemies. That is why most people fear LRA atrocities.

JK said LRA is a Movement which stands for itself. We will make sure we fight until we overrun the Government of Museveni. He also said 'LRA and their objectives will not accept any Ugandan government decision unless the conditions which made LRA go down to the bush are fulfilled (i.e. the ten commandments). We shall only have dialogue with the Government of Uganda under certain conditions, including that the Government will apologise to the LRA for the long war and for the insults they have made about LRA. And that is because M7 last time said he cannot negotiate dialogue with the criminals'. Kony commented that if the elites of the Acholi tribe continue supporting M7's government then they will be the sufferers because when two elephants fight it is the grass which suffers. So the Acholi community should open their eyes to know that some people are betraying them by trying to promote war against the LRA.

This was the speech he made while addressing us in Sinia brigade when we were first arrived in Aru camp in Sudan. The Brigade Commander of Sinia was then ordered to 'recruit' us again since we are new faces and we need to be welcomed and to know the policy of LRA such that no-one amongst us would try to escape from the camp back to Uganda.

2.4: Initiation Into LRA and Military Training

The following morning on the 21st of January we were again called for assembly. Some of us had already been beaten down in Uganda and we managed not to be beaten again because John Matata Okello said these people were already beaten as a sign of recruitment, but 17 others were selected and were terribly beaten with canes and sticks by a group of young children aged 15 and below who had been abducted sometime back and were now well versed with the situation. Two people died on the spot. They were just taken and thrown to the bush without burial. They got rotten there. That was the end of them.

We then immediately started training how to dismantle and reassemble guns. After which we continued training, we were taken for target practice and then for field-craft training e.g. how to take cover, how to assault the enemies. Parades were also conducted and we were assured that to be a good army you must first of all know how to parade very well. There was also training on how to use other machines like SPG9 recoiler guns, grenades, V10 recoiler guns, LMG (local machine gun), SMG (sub-machine gun), as well as on how to use mines of different types. Most of us got used to how to shoot guns.

Section 3: Life in the LRA

3.1: *Shortages of food and water (January/February 1996)*

The major problems we were facing were that there was not enough food or water. We were all taken under guard whenever we were going to the water well, which was some 3km away from the camp. After some days a group of four boys managed to escape from the water well. They were followed and were nowhere to be seen. So order was put forward that nobody is allowed to go to the water well until time is scheduled for everybody. So we experienced difficulties of thirst and we improvised another strategy of carrying water in small jerrycans to help us whenever there was no time to go and fetch water.

Talking about the problem of food, Sinia Brigade had never cultivated enough food for their brigade, both because they had been operating for quite a long time inside Uganda and because by that time Aru was still a new camp made after the LRA was attacked in Palutake. As a result many of us had nothing to eat with the exception of cooked sorghum which was divided into little quantities for us to chew before sleeping for the night. During the day you could find the abductees in the old potato gardens removing the left-over tubers that they would then chew or roast during the evening when people are gathered together.

I stayed together with 13 other boys in the home of an old man called Mr Omwa.[4] Because of the food shortage these thirteen boys decided to go and pick a certain tuber called *oye*. When they brought this plant they chopped it into pieces and cooked it to eat. After eating this all thirteen boys died one after the other and had to be taken and buried down in the bush. This happened because although *oye* is eaten by some tribes in southern Sudan it requires a lot of processing to make it safe to eat: It is first chopped into pieces which are left in running water. After some time these are then dried in sunshine and cut into smaller pieces and then pounded in a pestle and mortar to make flour. This is then mingled like maize flour to make bread. Without this process it remains poisonous. Myself and four other boys who were staying another officer called Ojuk who was in charge of us did not eat this tuber so we escaped dying from this poisonous food.

After the death of these thirteen boys a report was sent to Joseph Kony and as a result he had to order that nobody should be found trying to dig any tuber or cooking it to be eaten. In addition to this kind of eating of raw food and various leaves of sweet potatoes, cassava and other possible leaves, there was also an outbreak of the epidemic named cholera in Sinia brigade, causing the death of more than 200 people. There was no possibility of medical assistance that we could get because the camp was still a new place LRA had just come to and they were still trying to make proper connection with the Sudan government.

After these events a message was sent to the Sudanese Government and they decided to start sending lorries to bring food and other assistance to LRA camp in Aru. By the time food was brought many people had died due to malnutrition. When the food arrived people started to practice their appetites once again, but ate too much too quickly. This also gave us many problems because some people were roasting sorghum flour which gave many people stomach problems. There was another break-out of cholera and a further twenty five people died although there was enough food for everybody. These problems further reduced the number of children who had been abducted and brought to Sinia Brigade. Many of the abductees continued to be weakened because there was a lot of work to be done putting up new buildings, which involved going to collect bamboos from a long distance, for example moving a distance of 6km to and fro when you were already weak. Some eight children died on the way.

3.2: Food raids in Dinka villages, March 1996

In March 1996 another plan was brought forward by the military committee, that since children were dying in large numbers and they don't enjoy the food-stuff brought from the Sudanese Government we must start going down deep in the village to look for a variety of foods and other plantation crops like cassava stems, millet, sorghum, beans, maize and cowpeas to be planted in gardens they had cultivated. So people worked very hard to make sure they had dug large plantations to plant all these crops.

Thereafter many people were sent to go down in the village and raid food from the Dinkas' area. They sent about 200 soldiers and 150 abductees down to the village. When they reached the village I was among them: we went into the village, we roamed the village, we attacked the Dinka by shooting them with guns, we killed five Dinkas, we burned houses.[5] After which we gathered a lot of sorghum which had been hidden inside anti-hills on the mountain. We even got white ants, and honey sealed in pots. We collected them all and brought them back to the commander. We even got stools which were made by the Dinka, as well as lion-skins, donkey skins, bows and arrows; all these things we carried along with us. The operation took two days because we were searching for more food from neighbouring villages in a place called Captain Cook. After finishing the operation a message was sent to Joseph Kony that we have got a lot of things here: 'We have got all possible foodstuffs you had sent us to look for'. So he replied 'if what you have collected is enough then you can come back now'.

On our way back to the camp we had a shortage of water because we had gone deeply into a barren land occupied by the Dinka, and when we left the Dinka's place we were carrying heavy loads. That was at eight o'clock in the morning. By ten o'clock in the morning things changed. Some of the children started collapsing because they were now thirsty and nobody could help because they had little water. So you find that some just decided to go and sleep under a bushy tree in search of a cool position.

Others continued moving hoping that they will get water because they were told that some people were bringing water to rescue the situation. A message was sent to JK and people from different positions in the camp who had sent children to go and collect food for them immediately decided to collect water and rush to the rescue of those children.

Unfortunately some of the children were already very weak and people in the convoy decided to take them and lay them under the shade of trees while other people continued moving. Now, the rescue team which was sent from Aru camp came slowly by slowly because the land was full of depressions which made it difficult for them to move quickly to catch up in time to assist their brothers. When they managed to reach the position at around midday the people who were already unconscious were left behind and the people who could still continue moving were rescued and continued moving although they were very tired. I too was very tired but I prayed to God that he should help me and not let me die in the wilderness. And he did good and helped me. Until when I was brought water and I had to drink, that is when I felt I was alive.

It was so hot that even those who brought water for us were at risk of dying because the water they brought got finished and they also began to suffer. Three ladies and one man called Mr Acel Calo Apar missed dying narrowly although he was a commander and had commanded those who had brought water to rescue the children and various men who had gone for the operation.

The nine people who were left behind lay there until in the evening when all of them revived and when the Dinkas came in pursuit of the LRA they collected all the nine children and took them along with them. They kept these children properly until they found a way of sending a message to the GOU and a helicopter was sent and nine children were brought back to Uganda here (1996). Before I left LRA when I was still in the bush I heard one of the boys talking in Radio Uganda explaining the problem they got when they were sent to go and collect food in that area of Captain Cook. I was thus able to confirm that the nine children never died although they had been left behind and nobody had gone back to check on them.

When we arrived back at the camp the food we had collected was divided among the different places in the camp where Joseph Kony thought there was too much problem of food. From this time people began staying more comfortably. Although Government of Sudan was supplying more food LRA would supplement this by going to attack the neighbouring villages within Sudan in SPLA areas for more food support (the seeds which had been collected in the raids described above were not yet ready for harvesting).

3.3: Arrival of members of WNBF, 17 March 1996

On 17th March 1996 a group of 270 soldiers headed by a commander called lt Col Juma Oris from WNBF came from Yei and joined LRA in Aru camp.[6] When they came they were warmly welcomed. After two days a parade was organised to welcome the WNBF, at which introductions were made between commanders of the two forces. LRA also expressed their opinion about the joined forces and they commented that they had joined hands to work together to make sure they overthrow Museveni's government.

3.4: Juma Oris Day, 7 April 1996

Time came when it was approaching the celebration for the day for one of the spirits called Juma Oris (not the same as the person who brought WNBF soldiers on 17 March). That was on the 7th April 1996 when everybody was gathered for the assembly to receive information from the Holy Spirit and to celebrate the day the Holy Spirit appeared to LRA commanders inside Uganda at a place in the bush near Lacekocot which the LRA called Bethlehem.

Joseph Kony said 'we are soon going to expect an attack from the NRA', and he said 'we shall lose some of our officers here because they do not fully support our Movement, although they are the full commanders within LRA'. He also stressed that 'when this war will come then we have to select only 250 men to go for the battle. If we exceed that number even by one person then the war will turn against us'. He also told the congregation that there were some abductees brought here who were anti-LRA Movement, and he called these 'anti-LRA supporters' although they were within the LRA camp. These abductees suffered the most because they were all the time suspected of wanting to escape at any time from the LRA Movement.

By then the field commander was Mr Omona and the Chief of Operations and Training was Mr Ottii Lagony. On that day, Lagony as a very senior officer, was responsible for hosting the other high ranking officers from the whole camp and the celebration took place at his home.[7] People gathered there, ate food and drank tea. There was strictly no alcohol and no smoking because 'a guerilla man has to be alert at all times'.[8] There was no marijuana either. After the ceremony people prayed and some continued enjoying themselves but already everyone was discussing about the report which was revealed by Malaika in the Yard earlier that day.

3.5: Attack by NRA/SPLA, 9 April 1996

The following day people were gathered up in a field where all the military weapons were exhibited to be checked and cleaned and tested because LRA was suspecting a heavy offensive from NRA/SPLA. The WNBF soldiers who had joined LRA were also present to assist LRA fight against the NRA/SPLA. Soon after this a standby of 150 was selected to go and attack NRA/SPLA before they could reach the defense in Aru

These people they took two days going to where they were supposed to put their defense and wait for NRA/SPLA in order to disorganise their plan of coming. But when they entered the defense of the incoming NRA/SPLA they fought. As the NRA offensive was very heavy the LRAs decided to retreat back to come and defend their camp. That is where we lost one of our commanders called Lieutenant Ojuk whom I was staying together with.

After that encounter between LRA and NRA/SPLA, the enemy continued to come with their heavy offensive towards the LRA camp. They had heavy artilleries, tanks, mambas (anti-personnel carriers), and all sorts of guns. In the evening they attacked the LRA camp in Aru with a combination of heavy shelling and infantry coming from both sides of the defense. Eventually the NRA/SPLA succeeded in overrunning the LRA camp.

They burnt the palace of Joseph Kony, the ammunition stores full of weapons brought from Juba and other food stores which were brought for the people, as well as burning other houses. The NRA/SPLA entered the camp from different sides until LRA and WNBF had to abandon the camp. The NRA/SPLA ambushed the lorry which was carrying LRA properties to be taken to Juba and they burned it off, leaving the lorry on the road. They also set heavy ambushes on the way from Aru to Jebeleen where they killed even many of the Sudanese Government soldiers who were now retreating towards Juba.

Many people died in this war and many properties were also left because a day before the attack the Government of Sudan had sent tonnes of food and ammunition to LRA and war broke when these things were being divided to various positions within the camps and most of the things were left after the attack. Many people fled the camp and made their way independently to Jebeleen.

Some of the LRA soldiers led by a commander called Tabuleh decided to come back to fight against NRA/SPLA in an attempt to recover the camp again. But they never managed because the NRA had overrun the camp due to some of the LRA commanders who became too frightened. But on the other side NRA was already on their feet to withdraw the artilleries and other ammunitions back. This was revealed by one of the participants who was on the NRA side and was again recaptured by LRA when they came for operations in Uganda and he was taken to Sudan. He revealed this information that if LRA had tightened their belt for a little time then NRA/SPLA were not going to overrun the camp.

For myself, I was with my commander Mr John Okello Matata working on shelling 120 mm artillery. We tried our best to shell the battle but when we found that the camp was now overrun we came together with Tabuleh and he told us to leave the camp because almost every part of the camp was now overtaken by NRA/SPLA. We then had to leave everything in complete destruction, though we managed to dismantle some of the artillery guns.

We left and started moving slowly by slowly. Anti-personnel artillery were shelling the camp and throwing other bombs towards where we were. I carried my RPG bomb on my back leaving all my properties and I started following the people who had gone earlier, especially women and children who were already on the way to Jebeleen. Since many people had not expected this attack to have happened that evening on 9th April some of them got confused because they had left a lot of their properties behind and they decided to try and come and collect them. But unfortunately some of the people who came back lost their lives in the process.

The following morning everybody had to shift from Aru up to Jebeleen (a distance of 22km). Some of the abductees who were very weak were also left in the defense in Aru and when the NRA/SPLA overran the defense they rescued all of them and they were all repatriated back to Uganda. When we reached Jebeleen NRA/SPLA had not completed their offensive against LRA so they continued pursuing LRA until they reached up to Jebeleen where they wanted to overrun the Government of Sudan camps as well as the new LRA camp.

As soon as the Sudan Government knew that Aru was overrun and that LRA had now come to Jebeleen, full lorries of ammunitions, food supply, jackets, uniforms were shifted to Jebeleen where LRA was camping. The Government monitoring office in the Government force situated on mount Jebeleen also sent a report that the NRA was now approaching the LRA led by an NRA commander known as Firepower. So a standby of different classes was then selected and I was selected among the first group who went to attack the NRA/SPLA who were by then already camped on the mountain at a distance called 39 (ranging from Juba) (those markers go up to Soroti following the old Arab trading routes). (Jebeleen is 33km south east of Juba, distance 39 is south of Jebeleen). When we reached a position where we knew our enemies were now nearby we dug our trenches (andarchies). Immediately the enemies started attacking us with mortars, tanks, APCs, and other weapons. Eventually they stopped and we then managed to sleep that night.

The following morning NRA/SPLA soldiers and other militias brought from Uganda had already covered the lowland part of Jebeleen. LRA sent more troops to come and attack other sides which were already occupied by the enemies. The Sudan Government, knowning that NRA/SPLA were going to try to overrun their defense on Mount Jebeleen, managed to send two helicopters which were countershelling the NRA/SPLA army which were by now located up on the mountain around 39. When the helicopters came to shell the mountain 39 a second time the NRA/SPLA managed to shoot one of them down.

The remaining helicopter returned to Juba and informed the Sudan army of the loss of the other one, at which point the Sudan Government ordered their commanders to send heavy artilleries and many of their soldiers to come and support LRA against the NRA/SPLA offensive. 3 lorries full of soldiers came from Juba. They were deployed in Jebeleen. Another 4 lorries were taken to 39 where the war was waged very heavily for about five days until UPDF soldiers were finally expelled from Jebeleen. Many of them died in Jebeleen. For example nine tanks were captured and burned out. Four tanks whose operators had run away were then taken to Juba by the Sudanese army. From that day LRA and Sudan army became one and began to share all their military plans due to the hard work they had done to help overcome the NRA/SPLA attack.

3.6: *Jebeleen, April 10th 1996*

It was after this battle that LRA again shifted its base and made their full camp in Jebeleen where they stayed there for the next three years. We moved there on 10th April 1996 straight after the battles were over. We continued staying in

Jebeleen until January 1999, which gave LRA a lot of experience about various offensives and Sudan took a lot of interest in LRA, giving LRA the opportunity of making a lot of ambushes and burning most of the SPLA vehicles which were supplying food and arms brought from Uganda.

3.7: Offensives in Uganda

LRA often moved from Jebeleen down to Uganda to come and do operations inside the country. Immediately after the heavy atrocity LRA committed inside Uganda by killing two hundred people in Atiak, as well as cutting off ears and mouths, the GoU published a letter which was sent to the United Nations accusing LRA of the atrocities they had done inside Uganda. This brought a lot of dislike of the LRA from the communities inside Uganda as well as from the UPDF.

At this time LRA was organising to come and launch another offensive in Uganda. The operation was made clear to all the soldiers. We had three weeks of rehearsal in Jebeleen, after which the whole convoy had to come down to Uganda heavily entering Gulu via Atiak in January 1997. When they entered Uganda they fought heavily and this was the time when UPDF soldiers were heavily ferried to go and camp in different parts of Gulu commanded by the present Army Commander Kazini.

LRA fought several battles using different strategies inside Uganda over a period of almost three months, during which we lost some of the LRA officers including the army commander called Mr Opiro Agula. These battles which were heavily fought in Gulu caused fear to the GoU and the President himself had to come to Gulu and shift his headquarters to Gulu until the war was over (By that time Col Wasswa was 4th Division Commander). Then, when other officers were still continuing the operation with soldiers inside Uganda, Kony and some of his nearest officers decided to go back to Sudan to look for more assistance in arms and food to be brought to the soldiers who were still operating inside Uganda. Another group was selected to ferry all these things down to Uganda and Kony remained in Sudan to settle other matters of military administration.

After a short time a new programme was drawn and as such the defense was transferred one kilometre ahead towards Juba. They moved the defense, which was now known as Jebeleen II, because Jebeleen I was very near to that of the Sudanese military defense. The UPDF were already aware of this position so as a military man you have to change. Also children were moving between the two camps and causing confusion. Putting a greater distance between the two camps made it more difficult for people to move between them without being noticed. So, the camp was transferred and people started building in the various positions identified by the military committee for the brigades.

3.8: Visit of Ugandan Delegation, June 1997

Another accusation was put onto LRA that they were abducting a lot of children, including the Aboke girls, of which a good number have been taken to the rebel held base in Jebeleen. Then immediately a delegation from Uganda concerned to go right up deep in the bush to check whether the accusation put on LRA was correct. And indeed a group of people like Owiny Dollo, Sister Raquele and others colleagues came up to Jebeleen with some of the Sudan security and they went up to the front-line in search of the Aboke girls and young children under 15 years of age.

But soon after the information was sent to LRA by the Sudan Government LRA decided to hide the Aboke girls and children under 15. So when Raquele went to the front line (by then the commander whom they found there was called Lagira and he was the real man who abducted these girls from Aboke girls school) they had hidden these girls and young children in the bush for quite a period of time. It was only after the visitors had returned back to Juba that these children were then told to come back to the camp.

Unfortunately Raquele and the colleagues managed to get one girl who was from Aboke, but this lady refused to talk to Raquele in fear of being killed. When Raquele returned from the front line with her colleagues they came to Joseph Kony's palace where she pleaded with Kony to accept the release of the Aboke girls who were now in the camp. But Kony and his commanders did not allow the decision which Raquele and her colleagues had asked for. They confirmed that the few numbers of girls she wanted were there but they were not going to be freed.

At this point one of the girls appeared to Raquele and the colleagues. Raquele asked the girl, who was crying, 'now that they have got you here what is your decision?' The girl said 'I want to go back home and if possible I must go together with you'. Kony ordered that if Raquele decided to take along this lady with her they should both be shot, and the delegation had to leave.

As soon as Raquele had left for Juba this girl was called up to Kony's palace. She was questioned and then she was taken to the COT Mr Ottii Lagony, to decide on why the lady appeared to these people who had come from Juba. She was then ordered to be killed and within short time she was beaten then taken to the bush and killed. This was because LRA was keeping these girls for political reasons.

In another incident two other ladies, one called Catherine who was the head girl of Aboke girls, tried to organise with two of her friends to escape back to Uganda. But when their plan was discovered the two ladies were stoned to death by the younger children (the third lady was a young one who revealed the information and so was not killed).[9]

3.9: Revision of standing orders, 1 December 1998

This took place on Whistle Day, 1ˢᵗ December 1998: this is the day when one time LRA was inside Uganda and there was a heavy operation on LRA. So there was no time for anybody to talk to one another because the soldiers after them were in large numbers. So time for fasting came when LRA were still operating inside Uganda and wars were also after them, so they couldn't talk to each other because they had to sit and fast for a period of time then everyone had to whistle to one another in case they wanted to communicate. And that day is still remembered by LRA and known as Whistle Day.

Before this revision Joseph Kony was unhappy with the behaviour of some of his commanders and he used the revision of standing orders to demote some people and promote others as a way of tightening discipline and stopping people from discussing issues, a process which threatened many people. Ottii Lagony was demoted from army commander to a mere 2nd Lieutenant. Okello Matata was appointed the second chairman to JK and to replace Ottii Lagony. Banya was to follow Matata. Ottii Vincent was made Chief Intelligence Officer. Kolo Okello continued to work as the political commissar of the LRA/M. Owor Lakati was appointed Brigadier General, and Nyeko Tolbert was appointed Chief of Staff. Buk Oringa was appointed brigade commander of Stokri. Major Odongo was appointed brigade commander of Control Altar. Caesar Acellam was appointed Brigade Commander of Sinia, and Lieutenant Colonel Bunia was appointed brigade commander of Gilver.

3.10: Explosion of ammunition store (November 1999)

We continued staying in Jebeleen for some months and a mysterious happening took place there. One afternoon at about two o'clock some boys who were seated in front of the ammunition stores as guards set fire to a charge and the whole stores containing a wide range of newly delivered stock of ammunitions got burnt down completely. Nothing was rescued. There were big explosions because some explosives like mines, grenades and shells were contained there. People had to run away until the explosions were over because they feared the deadly explosive anti-aircraft missile called SAM7.

The initial interrogation and investigation made did not give everybody a good understanding about what had happened, whether there was an enemy infiltration or some sort of sabotage. Eventually it was confirmed that it was some of the boys guarding the store who had set fire to it. This made the suppliers very angry since it was a great loss and what they had given to LRA had not yet been utilised. Therefore it became one of several issues causing the Sudanese Government to lose interest in the LRA as they realised that despite the many times they had been supporting LRA a lot of their military equipment had been wasted.

3.11: Attack on civilians near LRA camp (December 1999)

Another thing which made the Sudanese lose interest in the LRA while the LRA was in Jebeleen was that in late December 1999 there was a large attack on the Sudanese civilians who were staying near to the LRA camp and this was claimed to have been the SPLA who had attacked the civilians but after investigation it was proved the civilian attack was by the LRA because Trinkle Brigade, commanded by Brigadier Owor Lakati of LRA thought the civilian community who were living on the suspected side would be a possible chance for the enemies to come and attack them, so they decided to chase them out of that place; several houses were burnt down, children, men and women were shot dead. Other people escaped.

The following day we went to the village where the incident had occurred, we found that there were some dead bodies lying, some of the children burnt and others were still burning in the burning houses. Another woman I saw was shot from the door while she was trying to escape. She was shot from behind together with the child and she fell down and they both died. She had just come for a Christmas celebration and she was preparing the following morning to go back to her home in Juba (I knew the husband who was a Sudanese soldier).

This brought a lot of misunderstanding between the LRA and the civilian population in southern Sudan, and LRA at this time was hated by the civil society in Juba and elsewhere in Sudan. This also gives a clear picture of the kind of thing LRA had been doing down in Uganda. Although they may say the atrocities attributed to them are not their doing, an example like this makes a clear meaning of what LRA normally do whenever they go down to Uganda for operation. On this issue, it should be noted that people would even return from operations in Uganda and recount everything they had done, including killing people and attacking military positions.

The Sudanese Government eventually came and gave the LRA five days to withdraw their camp from Jebeleen to Nisitu. They even sent five lorries from Juba to come and assist LRA in transportation of their properties from Jebeleen to Nisitu. Five days later there was nobody to be seen in Jebeleen, although immediately after the LRA left the Sudanese Government sent six lorries of troops to occupy the position which LRA had left behind. Since the transfer was so quick many properties and crops in the garden were left behind, and the civilians living in the area came and picked those things.

3.12: Move to Nisitu (January 2000)

When we reached Nisitu people stayed there for a a few weeks and the military committee, with information from the Sudanese Government, decided to go deep 15km in the bush but not before Joseph Kony and some of his officers took a walk down to the bush. He had informed the people during the time when he was conducting prayers in the Yard that he would be going out in the wilderness to pray about what had happened abruptly and he would receive some of the information from the Holy Spirit to guide LRA as to what to be done for the near future and what will come in the near future. So he went and he took two days in the wilderness.

After he had come back he told everybody his journey had been to go and see where the new camp would be put. Each and everybody should get ready with their hoes, pangas, sickles, to go down and start building the new camp because the camp in Nisitu was not large enough to accommodate all the people who had come from Jebeleen. And people went down into the bush again to start making new houses for the camp, which was known as Lubanga Tek.

3.13: Lubanga Tek (February 2000):

The plan for the camp was already drawn according to the usual arrangement. The headquarters were at the very centre, guarded by a new brigade called Trinkle made up of men selected by the chairman, Joseph Kony. There was then a circle of high ranking officers, then commanding officers including majors, captains, other officers from lieutenant to second lieutenant, warrant officers to corporals. Control Altar became a brigade on a slightly higher level than Gilver, Sinia and Stokri.

I came late to Lubanga Tek because when I reached Nisitu my woman was already pregnant and about to deliver. After she delivered I had to make a follow up to the new camp where I built two huts and I was staying in the communication centre under the control of the director of signals called Lumumba Martin.

The place we were settling in was quite overgrown although the area had been settled by the SPLA maybe twenty years earlier. We found the remnants of ruined huts which were settled by the SPLA, ammunitions which were left behind, cages for small hens, granaries, grinding stones and the like. We also found the land was fertile for cultivation. There was a nearby river called river Kit which was helping people with water. We found the area was full of wild animals which people would hunt. These factors made the place to be more suitable for the stay of the people. The weather of the place was too cold because it was yet new and it was fully covered with big trees which created a lot of dew. People found it difficult at the beginning, but as time went on people started cutting trees, making charcoal, digging to plant crops and so we adapted to the conditions of the area.

Now, the Sudan government was still wondering why we decided to transfer from Nisitu to Lubanga tek without their notice, but they continued sending food aid, uniforms, and other assistance like medical care down to the bush to help people. We had two lorries, one was a Hino ZY, the other a Fuso truck. We also had three Toyota Landcruisers – one for the chairman, one for the second chairman, and one was given to the LRA representatives (ambassadors).

Since LRA/M was maintained by the Holy Spirit, each and every time they go to another camp they always make sure a yard is built within a few days. Until it is built people go pray under a big tree chosen to provide enough shelter to cover the whole congregation.

Lubanga Tek was four days walk from Uganda.

3.14: The move to Bin Rwot, April 2000

At this time LRA was frequently changing their plans and they had caused a lot of problems to themselves and they were now a long distance from Jebeleen, such that it was not easy for them to walk to Uganda. Despite this the LRA still continued although they were far away from the border. At a certain point a decision was made to open another camp called Bin Rwot, which was another 9 miles between Sindru road and Lubanga Tek.

As in the move to Lubanga Tek people went there together with Joseph Kony in the wilderness where they prayed for four days in search of a better position which the Holy Spirit would recommend as suitable for another defence to be built there. In this place the Holy Spirit released a message to the LRA commanders telling them to have two defences. In case of any attack one would come up quickly to rescue the other and all the military arms and weapons were to be kept in both of these defences. This new camp, known as Bin Rwot, was then opened.

Grass thatched houses were built and women, children and men were taken to live there. Some of them also participated in planting large fields for crops like simsim, cowpeas, beans and cassava plantations and keeping domestic animals within the camp. This place was well enjoyed by the people because there were a lot of wild animals which they could hunt, and set traps for. Meat was not a problem to people living there. So people enjoyed this area because it was like living in the village.

At this time there were no constant wars or going out to operation as had been the case in the past, although a good number of soldiers could be sent out to go and patrol at a distance of ten kilometres from all directions to ensure that no enemy would infiltrate the camp. At the same time some of the LRA were operating widely inside Uganda and a few were also operating elsewhere in Sudan. There was a lot of hard work LRA was doing within both camps to sustain themselves since the Government of Sudan had already stopped giving supplies.

Although the relationship between the Government of Sudan and LRA worsened, for a number of political reasons the LRA got organised and Joseph Kony went to Nisitu camp with his commanders and met with the Sudanese army. For the first time, they discussed a lot of issues concerning the current situation of the LRA. This was done together with delegates who had come from the Carter Center, but they did not come to any agreement. After which the delegation went back to Khartoum with promises the LRA had made. After a little time they came again and met with Joseph Kony on the same issues. These were as follows:

- LRA should renounce rebellion and talk peace with the Uganda government (dialogue)
- They were told to release any abducted children who were 15 years old and below which had been taken to battle at any time, as this is against the children's rights.
- LRA should release the commonly wanted Aboke girls if they were to continue with their war properly.
- The atrocities committed by the LRA inside Uganda, for example burning houses, looting, killing people and many others should stop
- LRA should be transferred 1000km far away from the border of Uganda and Sudan and that would mean LRA would be taken beyond Khartoum for resettlement.

- Sudan should stop supplies of food, uniforms and ammunitions to LRA because this would be another way of stopping LRA from attacking the military and civilian communities inside Uganda.

At this time LRA was in some dilemmas about whether or not to accept the conditions which the Carter Center and the Khartoum Government had put forward. After some months JK decided to call some of the political wing who had their main offices in Khartoum, to come back to the bush and join hands together with others. But only two of the members responded to his calls back to come back to the bush at a place called Lubanga Tek. After which they had to continue up to Bin Rwot where they were had to build their homes. The other political members refused to come back because they had confirmed rumours about what had recently been done by the LRA Movement leaders in Jebeleen, namely the recent killing of the late Army Commander Ottii Lagony. In fact the Sudanese security told them that they need not come back to the bush. As a result two of the politicians remained in Khartoum until they had processed their tickets and were flown to Nairobi.

3.15: Breakdown of Relations with Government of Sudan

The Movement secretariat which was the head office in Khartoum was then closed and another office was opened in Juba. At this time things were not normal but LRA was watching what may come again because there was no way to keep all parties satisfied. The Sudan government tried to support LRA with some food aid, especially to help the innocent people like children, women and men who no longer knew what was going on. Although the Sudanese Government continued to support LRA, the JK understood this to be a deception/trick behind which efforts were being made to capture him and some of his commanders.

Joseph Kony decided to stop receiving supplies of food, arms and uniforms from Juba, saying things like 'any food being brought by Arabs must not be accepted because they may be poisoned'. He even decided to refuse messages and information from the Sudanese Government although there was still contact with the Carter Center. So he continued to stay settled in his camps in Lubanga Tek and Bin Rwot, without any more assistance from the Government. Kony and his commanders turned against the Government programme because they were told that if they refused all the conditions set for them, then United Nations troops were to be brought up to Juba to disarm Kony and his rebel group. They might include troops from Libya, Sudan, Egypt, Uganda, Tanzania, Rwanda.

At this time Kony stopped most soldiers in the camp from moving between Lubanga Tek and the Sudanese Military Camp. As a result there was little communication between some of the LRA commanders and the Sudanese army commanders, although it continued at a low level because this was the only way the LRA could get a market for selling their produce they had, such as charcoal, and also allowed them to purchase other essential commodities like sugar, salt, drugs, clothing and fuel for their vehicles.

3.16: *Building links with Equatoria Defence Forces (2000)*

After all these occasions JK wrote a letter of recommendation of the LRA Movement and three of his commanders (Ottii Vincent, Owor Lakati and one other) took it to their former companions who were soldiers of the Equatorial Defence Forces led by Commander Kenyi in southern Sudan. The EDF's base is situated at a place called Upper Talanka. At the first meeting the EDF and LRA soldiers decided to dialogue with each other although they had had some conflicts in the early 1990s.

For the second meeting some LRA officers were sent to meet with their EDF counterparts in another EDF camp in a place called Agoro on the Sudan side of the border. At this meeting they sat together and agreed with each other on some of the reasons why LRA wanted to join with them. LRA, in reaction to the insult from the Sudan Government, wrote a letter stating that they were ready at any time to fight against the Sudanese Government if any attempt was made to send external troops to come and disarm them from within their camp.

But since the EDF had a strong connection with the Sudanese Government and were getting their supplies from them they decided to send a copy of this LRA letter the Government of Sudan. When this letter reached the Government the Sudan, their security decided to call Kony. He initially refused to meet with them, but later was persuaded by his commanders and they went and met with the Sudanese officers.

During their meeting, at which they were supposed to discuss among other things the current political issues taking place, the Sudanese Security also produced a copy of the statement which had been sent to them by the EDF about what LRA was proposing to do, namely to launch an attack against Sudanese Government soldiers.

There was no way the LRA could deny this evidence and they had to apologise for they never thought this would have reached that level, but they were not happy with the tricks played on them by the Sudan Government because when they meet they can talk important issues and agree on them, but on the other side Sudan Government will only be giving them a carrot and [simultaneously coming with] a stick behind.

3.17: *LRA drawback*

Actually there was now a total drawback in the LRA programmes. So they decided to start other activities to unite everybody who are in the camp. They started traditional teachings about village life in Uganda and differences in how people are undertaking culture these days. Some of the LRA who were operating inside Uganda were already blocked inside by the UPDF. So Kony sent a message to them to try hard if they could penetrate their own way then they had to come back. Some few numbers came back to Sudan while others continued operating inside Uganda.

The remaining people who were led by the commanders, for example Lieutenant Colonel Onen Kamdulu, started making dialogue with some of the civil population in the year 2000. They succeeded and they were welcomed by the UPDF soldiers and Government of Uganda to continue with the dialogue and some of the soldiers who were operating on the other side led by Lieutenant Colonel Tabuleh came together and the dialogue continued.

At a certain point in 2001 Kamdulu's group were given their camp in Pabbo with a Landrover vehicle [in] which they were allowed to freely move from their defense then go into Gulu town. The UPDF at all times were responding to the LRA's demands. For example, they gave Kamdulu mobile telephones which would help them at all times to talk and coordinate the affairs of the dialogue.

In October 2001 these people decided to go back to Sudan because Kony sent the information from Sudan that the dialogue being undertaken by Kamdulu and his group was not proper. For this matter Kamdulu must first of all go back to Sudan and then they will make another arrangement. Before these people could leave to go back to Sudan they decided to take back all the equipments they were given by the UPDF, for example the mobile telephones, the vehicle and a few other things they were using at their Pabbo camp. The vehicle was left somewhere in town. The mobile phone was sent back to UPDF through one of the coordinators. (by that time – October 2001 – I had just come so I was visiting UPDF)

The LRA disappeared from Pabbo without informing the military headquarters in Gulu. After they had gone back to Sudan there was nothing much anybody in Uganda could do about it, except that people were worried now that these few numbers of LRA were allowed to come freely into the town then they might have taken the whole plan which may give them courage to come and attack Gulu at any time. People who were co-ordinating this dialogue, for example the LCV chairman Lt Col Walter Ochora and other leaders, lost their chances of talking with the LRA.

When the LRA who were inside Uganda went back and reached Sudan they were told not to come back because Kamdulu was forcing this dialogue without the acceptance of the chairman JK but he never knew what was happening although dialogue could bring peace between LRA and Government of Uganda. Until now they are in Sudan

1st November 2000: 9 military commanders left LRA camp and escaped to Juba with about 35 children whom they had gone with to work in the field at a place called Nisitu (the former camp). These are the ones who came later and stayed in Hotel Roma in Gulu in February 2002.

The Nine Officers who escaped on 1 November 2000

Rank & Name	From
Colonel Sururu Abudhala	West Nile (ex-WNBF. He also worked during Amins' regime and then joined WNBF after which he joined LRA)
Major Mohamed Nasuru	Bombo (Amin's soldiers, joined WNBF then LRA)

Captain Okwera Bruhan	Adjumani (Amin's soldiers, also WNBF, then LRA)
Captain Adam Faisle	Busoga (Jinja area) (ADF, WNBF, LRA)
Captain Okilan Joseph	Teso/Soroti (UPA, LRA)
2 lieutenant Okodel	Teso/Soroti (UPA, LRA)
Lieutenant Mina Mukwas	Kapchorwa (UPA, LRA)

The first group which returned to Sudan was led by Lt Col Odongo. At this time I was planning how to leave the camp. On 23 February 2001 450 LRA soldiers were selected to go and collect food in connection to attack one of the Dinka defences which was in a place called America. This is a place which was settled by the SPLA because the area is materialise and is full of minerals. For example, gold is found there. So LRA fought with them and they overran the camp. And they started mining gold from this area. Two officers lost their lives during this operation. Others returned back with a lot of things, for example cattle, sheep, goats, sorghum and many other things they got in the SPLA camp. When these people who had gone for the operation returned back to the camp at Lubanga Tek they reached the camp on the 25 February. Then the following day was made to be a victory for those who had been for the operation. So a big ceremony was organised.

Section 4: Escape

4.1: Escape to Nisitu

By then I was working as the military adjutant in the headquarters. I was having a lot of work to do until I decided to leave the camp because I found that nothing was happening that could push LRA ahead. We were just getting blocked and people were now returning to village life although we were in a military combat. Also unnecessary arrests had already started amongst high ranking officers and even junior officers, as a result of which some even lost their lives.

Before these officers left there was a meeting which was called and the meeting included all the tribes who were non-Acholi. He tried to politicise these people by saying that 'we really like you in our Movement and we don't have any segregation with you at all because we know you are part of us and we need your assistance to develop our Movement so we can work together', but these people were quiet to such questions. They knew there was something going to be wrong since they had been marginalised and talked of. So they decided to leave the camp without anybody knowing.

After these nine officers who felt they were being victimised for being non-Acholi escaped, JK gave a strict order to the camp saying that whoever is found escaping would be killed straight away, and if anyone is captured attempting to escape only the evidence need to be brought, not the body. As a result many people became afraid.

So, as I was working in the office I did watch what was going on and I decided for myself that I have already served enough for the Movement so I must go home and rest my brain. Alright ... Then I got organised, informed my wife, informed my friends and fellow brothers that I may leave you anytime but they never knew the date.

It was night time after the celebration when I picked my woman and child and I picked another fellow with his two women and five children and we left the camp at around midnight. We had to travel all the night; fifteen kilometres from Lubanga Tek to Nisitu. When we reached there I left my wife and child and the other people hidden in the bush and I entered the Sudanese military defense in the morning at around 6 o'clock in the morning where I was welcomed by the guards. They informed the commanding officer, a major Salah Fadal Mullah (he was a best friend to me, I used to go to his place and repair his TVs and other equipment) in charge of the barracks of Nisitu.

When he heard I had already arrived he picked his vehicle, a Toyota Landcruiser and rushed to check on where I was. Immediately he got me he was very happy to see me. So he asked me whether I had come alone but I told him there were some people somewhere. Then we went and collected the children and women and the other fellow whom I had left to look after them from where they were hiding in the bush. We picked them and all our luggages and we got into the car and we were taken to the defense in Nisitu.

4.2: Transfer to Juba

From there we had our breakfast and were then put into another lorry which was going up to Juba. We were escorted until up to Juba bridge where the Sudan security lies. We were taken to live with the security for some two days. We were cooked food, we ate and everybody enjoyed. Then on the third day we were then taken to the security office handled by the military police for investigation. When we arrived there we were pushed to jail direct, leaving the women and the children outside. From here all of us were again confused because we had no idea what might happen. Either the Sudan security would take us back or they would give us chance to stay in Juba or continue with our journey up to Khartoum.

We stayed in jail from 8.30 in the morning until we were released again at 8 in the evening. This was because they wanted to know whether our escape was really from the bush and what we were talking about was true. So the Sudan security officers whom we knew came and met with us and they emphasised that if these people had left JK's camp in this way in this great number then it means there might be something wrong down in the camp. So the following day the investigating officers were sent and they came to us. Both of us who were men were then investigated and we told them we were tired of suffering in the bush and that what we wanted was to be connected so that we come home rather than being enslaved in the bush.

After the investigation was finished and the vehicle was ready our things were checked and anything connected to military combat like chargeable batteries, uniforms, shoes, books and other documents was removed from us. We were then taken right to the airport and we entered the office of the security where we were again checked to find that there was nothing. We met with the Acholi chief of Pajok (Mr Okumu Charles) who is working hard in connection with the Sudanese security to connect children who escape their way from the bush to find their way home.

We were then handed over to a certain organisation in Juba which is working in connection with UNICEF Toto Chan [Total Child?] Centre for Trauma (*centre me lit wic*). *(tel Juba 20606)*. We found also a Japanese woman who is the coordinator of this camp called Mrs Tetseku Karuanagi. We also stayed with other people who helped us within the camp, people like the director of this camp called Mr Jimmy Long. The camp had a cook called Mary Kamala, a driver called Mr Wilson Anthony, an assistant called Mr Michael, and a senior Acholi woman called Esther who was very interested to see that all the Acholi children who were taken to Sudan were repatriated back to their homes. Then you have some other people like Soro Jatoma and Enineio Soro and these were the workers we got there in Toto Chan. We stayed there for nine days. We enjoyed the camp, it was well furnished with two storeyed houses and all the facilities to welcome the escapees who are brought to this centre. They also have things like television and radios which they are using all these things to change the minds of the traumatised children who come from the bush at any recent time. They were showing films of how a woman can stay with a man and again may decide to refuse a man, for example the most interesting tape we had was about a Nigerian lady called Ama of Nigeria.

4.3: Transfer to Khartoum

We stayed comfortably in this camp until on the 10th March when early in the morning three vehicles were brought. One for our transport, two for the Sudan security, the third vehicle was for the co-ordinator of Toto Chan. We entered the vehicles with all our luggage and were then escorted to Juba airport. We were then taken inside, everything we had was checked and packed properly. We had to wait for one and a half hours, before the plane which we were booked on, Sudan airlines flight 313 Juba-Khartoum, landed. That is when I knew everything was changing and I can reach home now safe from any pursuit by the LRA.

After our tickets were brought to us (the amount per person was 26,039 Sudanese Dinar) we entered into the plane and the plane took off thirty minutes later. It took us two and a half hours until we landed safely in Khartoum airport where we were then welcomed and taken into a transit vehicle which was already informed and waiting for us. From here we went to check offices in the airport then we were transported up to Soba Camp where we were received nicely. We met some of our friends who had escaped earlier. We even had information about some of our friends who had already been repatriated down to Uganda.

We started staying there, we met different people, different decisions and many other interesting places. So we get used to Khartoum. Three days later on 12 March 2001 ambassadors from different embassies, including the British, German, Egyptian, Danish and Canadian Embassies, came to meet and witness our presence within the centre. Carter Center was also present. They started bringing us new clothing, shoes, bags, and any other essential items to meet our basic needs. On the 13th March men and women were separated into different camps. Children and women were handed over to the organisation called Save the Children while men were to be kept by the IOM International Organisation for Migration headed by the programme manager called Salah in the head office in Khartoum.

4.4: *Seven months in Khartoum*

We met many different people in Khartoum. We were taken to places of interest. For example, we went to the Zoo where we saw different types of animals and many other things. We went to Omdurman to see how the place is developed. On Sundays they always hired buses to take us for Sunday services. While I was in Khartoum I never thought of staying without any job. I started to do my handiwork within the camp. I also decided to open my workshop in a place called Engazi where I was moving to every morning to repair radios, TVs, and other electronic equipment. I made a lot of friends and even went to visit other places like Jebel Awuliya, Kassala, and Souk Libya, the biggest market situated on the western side of Sudan.

By this time many of the children who were coming from the bush were re-patriated down to Uganda. We had not yet got enough information about what was happening in Uganda. We could only hear things from people who came to Uganda, or read them from newspapers or hear them when listening to Radio Uganda during news hours (from 6 o'clock until 9 o'clock in the evening). So we sent one of the representatives from the Carter Center concerned with conflict resolution to go down to Uganda and come back to inform us about the current situation. When he returned back to Sudan he told us Uganda at the moment is a peaceful country. So you can go back without any fear, although there was some news of ambushes which can be heard through radios being operated between Gulu and Kitgum.

We then decided that if the current situation in Uganda cannot cool down then we would decide to go and resettle ourselves outside to places like Canada and United States. We continued staying for some months until some delegates from Nairobi headquarters of the IOM came to our camp (Soba) to check our condition, how we were surviving in the camp. We met, talked with them and we made our decision that we feel we should go back home in Uganda. So from there they took our photographs, they went with them up to Nairobi where they said they will go and find what is happening in Uganda and then afterwards they will inform us and arrange for our repatriation back to Uganda. Immediately they left a group of three people came from Uganda sent by the Uganda Government to go and check on those of us who were still living in Khartoum. If at all we were ready to respond to the Amnesty Act no 2 which states that any person 'referred to under subsection (1) shall not be prosecuted or subjected to any form of punishment for the participation in the war or rebellion for any crime committed in the cause of the war or armed rebellion'

But, although we were convinced by the delegates which includes Justice Onega, chairman of the Amnesty Commission, Commissioner Lutara, Rafael Makoa, we accepted their appeal but we had no trust on the amnesty because we had an example of a man who was called Goan who returned to Uganda through Zaire after 29 years in exile and was then prosecuted for the alleged killing of the Gombolola chief in Mbarara. And we also feared that if we were to come down to Uganda we might be abducted again because those people who escape and go back to Uganda are all known by the rebel LRA who are still in the bush.

4.5: Repatriation

However, on October 14th we had a report from the office of the Manager of IOM calling on us to get ready for repatriation because the headquarters in Nairobi had arranged for our tickets to fly us back to Uganda. We finished making all the possible arrangements for the journey until on the 19th of October we were celebrated well until midnight by both Save the Children and IOM staff. They then brought two mini-buses, two land-cruisers. We greeted our friends who were remaining in the camps, everybody was joyous, and at 12 midnight we entered the mini-buses. We took photographs for the memories until we had to wave to our brothers who were remaining in Soba camp.

Then we were taken to the airport in Khartoum. We were directed to the reception in the airport where all the checkings on our luggages and tickets were done until the plane we were boarding came from Cairo. At 4 o'clock in the morning we then boarded the plane from Khartoum to Nairobi. It took us three and a half hours to reach Nairobi. We arrived at Nairobi at 7.15am. Then we went to the reception where again we were checked then after one and a half hours we had to board the same plane, Kenya Airways, from Kenyatta Airport in Nairobi. We flew to Entebbe which took us two hours 50 minutes to reach. At around five minutes to midday we then landed at Entebbe airport.

When I reached Entebbe I could not believe I was already at home because when I reached I found everything was quite different from where I had come from. As soon as we landed and came out of the plane it was raining but the rain stopped immediately. When we came out we thought we were the prisoners of war brought from elsewhere because there was nothing that showed to us that we were fully welcome as had happened to some of our friends who came for the first time. We never knew who received us in the airport until I saw journalists with their cameras just taking photos. Except we were then guided by one of the white men to the reception where we took some sodas and bread.

At this point the programme which had been agreed to in Khartoum was changed without consulting us. Although we were brought as families we were once again split up and the programme told us each and every one should go to his own district. We then had to divide ourselves from our families. My wife and my child were flown to Kitgum. Those going to Gulu then boarded a mini-bus (kamwunye) which then carried us from 2 o'clock up to 6.30pm. When we arrived in Gulu we were taken to the centre called World Vision and received a nice welcome.

From there again we were divided into two groups. Others were then taken to GUSCO centre. That was on the 20th October in the evening. We had to stay in World Vision for one month. After five days I decided with one of my brothers to go and visit our family in the KICWA centre in Kitgum. We went there and we got them and others were already counselled to go home. So I accompanied my family down to the village in Namukora at a place called Omiyanyima, where I left my wife and child. IRC would not allow me to sleep there because I only had permission to go to KICWA, but I met several people who had come to see their daughter which I had brought to them. I was then thanked for the endeavours I had made to bring the girl back home together with the child. Then I had to come back up to KICWA where I spent three days before returning World Vision.

I continued staying for a little number of days and I decided to leave for home. When I went home I found that my name was already cancelled and everybody knew I was already dead, so when I met my brothers and sisters they started crying and I gave them courage that it was God's plan for me to be captured and since he has brought me back nobody should worry. When I reached my home I found that all my parents were already dead and one of my brothers had also died and there was nothing I could do except pray for their souls to be in eternal life. Then they had to make a party for me and everybody was happy to see me back home. Until now I am staying a peaceful life with my fellow countrymen.

Section 5: Treatment of Stragglers

When people are moving in a convoy and you get tired you are not left behind because they know the UPDF could pick information from you. When a convoy is moving, five or six people known as 'blocking forces' are left about one mile behind to find any stragglers and deal with them. They carry radio and com-municate with headquarters.

If they feel you are somebody important, somebody whom they think has a particular job to do, such as a teacher or nurse, they can send back some soldiers to carry you along on the stretcher. If you are not important, they take a small axe known as Lukile and they strike you at the base of the skull from behind. If you do not die immediately, you are just left behind on the ground. These 'Blocking Forces' carrying Chinese rifles with bayonets on them can spear you to finish you off or else you can be thrown in the bush to rot there without anybody knowing about you. While waiting to die, blood comes from the nose. That is why when you talk of the atrocities committed by LRA, the UPDF were collecting true information.

When adapting to that life of marching 80km every day, I had a problem with my feet. When you don't have shoes to protect your leg, you cannot move such long distances. You need a sandal or if somebody has an extra pair of gum boots then you can walk freely. People end up walking on their heels because the wounds on the soles of their feet do not allow them to walk fully on the whole foot. I was not killed because they knew I was a technician. I took some remaining slippers which were of different sizes. One side of the slippers gave me a pair. All my nails came off during that first journey and only grew back when I reached Sudan. All the skin was removed from the soles of my feet. They used to give us shea nut oil to rub on. After some time they got cured".

Section 6: Control exercised over people's sex lives

Cases of **bwoc** (impotence) included both people who were already **bwoc** at home, and others who became **bwoc** after abduction. Some people stayed a long time without having sex and don't have the appetite. It is the chairman who decides if you are ready for a woman; even if you don't want you are given. In this process you will find that complaints are brought forward by women that so and so is impotent. Many cases of such were there. Joseph Kony tried very hard to help these people, even some of the high officers who had these cases were also cured. If you are given a lady and she fails to get pregnant people will start to ask 'what is wrong with this fellow?' If they find that you have this problem with you, then they will process these herbs and they start giving to you until when you feel better and you resume your normal way of life.

It happened once that a lieutenant called Obedi who was in Gilver brigade was killed in a firing squad having committed anal sex (**butu ki dud latin**) with a 14 year old boy. Moreover, he had two women. His neighbours had discovered him when he was already behind the young boy. He was discovered because officers don't share their rooms with women. In case they want them they just call the woman for a night or two after which the women go back to their houses. So one of his neighbours had come across to his house at night to inform him about the work programme which was going to happen the next day, but he came across them and found the man was already on the bed with the young boy. When the young boy was asked he revealed that he was having sexual relations with commander. The young boy was then taken to the authorities concerned with handling cases within the defense, after which the military committee decided according to the standing orders that whoever has committed such an offense is liable to firing squad. The lieutenant was then tied to a tree and executed.

Nothing was ever done to the boy but he was given some herbs to swallow and prayers were conducted to relieve him from thinking too much of what happened to him (he was still too young to have a wife of his own). The wives of the man who was shot were taken to other positions and given to other men who could look after them.

Immediately after the firing squad everybody was called to the assembly to be informed of such happenings and the chairman and his commanders revealed to all the LRAs by revising the standing orders that whoever was found committing offenses against the standing orders will be killed or dealt with according to the law. This made many people to be threatened about their lives because in case you are caught you would think yourself dead".

Section 7: LRA Sick Bays

A sick bay is a safe place where wounded casualties are taken to seek treatment. This one is always a place where no-one can find the position where the sick people are kept. There are very many such sick bays. People are taken in small numbers in each so that it is easy to care for them. These places are co-ordinated by civilians who will look for food, drugs, and other necessary items ... Also some well armed soldiers are left there to guard the sick. We also have some of the medical assistants who were captured sometime back and taken to the bush (these included 'Dr' Onen Griffiths, 'Dr' Elia, 'Dr' Acito, 'Dr' Otim, Alice, Okwera, Gama, 'Dr' Ochol, 'Dr' Saidi, 'Dr' Oloya [died 2000 on operation in Uganda] and many others). These are the people who were giving assistance to the wounded from battle, and were mostly people chosen by the Holy Spirit of the LRA to go and participate in looking after people in the bay.

Pregnant women and children are also kept there, and other people to keep the bay we have them [there are other people there who look after the place]. They always come to neighbouring villages to collect food from the civilians by attacking them and looting their food and properties. The strength of the Holy Spirit protects the sick bay; whenever the UPDF is to go and look for the LRA in the bay they will just get lost.

The people in the sick bay also have radio for communication which they normally use to inform the LRA base in southern Sudan about the situation inside Uganda and the programme of the UPDF against LRA. Also some of the civilians who help them carrying the food to the bay are not allowed to reach the exact position ...

Regulations in the bay:

While you are in the bay you are not allowed to go anywhere until you are fully cured. Prayers are conducted at all times. Fasting for up to 40 days at a time (people can eat and drink at night. Also small children and mothers with very small children are allowed to eat and drink) until when the Holy Spirit reveals that everyone should now stop fasting and prayers are conducted to everybody and they are told other things that may come or regulations to be followed while in the bay.

Fasting can be done 1) when there is war 2) when there is expectation of epidemic 3) to prevent a happening such as an attack. After a long fast the Holy Spirit may reveal to Joseph Kony that from now onwards such a happening will not be. Then people will continue eating and chewing 4) if there is a message from the Holy Spirit about any fighting which may come 5) when there is a complete lack of assistance from external sources such as Sudanese Govt 6) when people are going for war they are made to fast for a few days.

Sometimes, when the malaika (Holy Spirit) reveals that nothing bad is going to happen, then he may cancel the fasting for the soldiers going for war but they are not allowed to meet with their women. They call this Agaba. Sometimes you stay outside the camp defences, you don't come home when you are going for the battle. Except when you fall sick or there is another change of command in which case you are allowed to come back.

When the wounded are completely cured they are allowed to join the convoy for another battle. Others who were (more) seriously wounded or have broken legs continue staying in the bay until they get cured. So for many years LRA had been very strict in keeping many people in the sick bay. For example, women who get pregnant always have the advantage of delivering their children without any effect from military offensives.

Some women may be taken to the neighbouring village (some of the wounded also may be left with people in the village; the healthy go to the village, look for somebody known to them, give some money to keep that patient for a certain period of time until they get well). It was not difficult because this is a war which was supported by the community. The community would just assist because they know that these are our children so we need to keep/look after them. There were also some cases where people informed the UPDF about sick people being kept within the village, and they were then surrounded and taken to the barracks. For example, we have a boy who was called Oloya who was found by UPDF in one of the villages in Atiak and was taken back to UPDF HQ in Gulu and was then ferried to World Vision to be counselled ..."

Section 8: Herbal Remedies used in the LRA

The major drug or herb in both Sudan and Uganda that LRA uses for people who have deadly wounds and broken legs is what we call fungi from rotten trees (Obwol Yat). They grind this fungi to make it soft and they tie or bandage it with the broken leg and the deadly wounds are also dressed with this and many people get cured

- Animal furs such as that of emekemek, an animal which crawls and is found in mountains
- Fat from python is drunk for TB (moo nyalo)
- cassava is fermented and mixed with other ingredients like yeast from millet or sorghum, bark of ogali, olilimo, ocayo and many others
- soda lime from ash is used to generate quality, makes the drug taste a little bit bitter
- for people who are eunuchs (Labwoc) [impotent] drugs like the bark of Ok-weyo, banana roots/suckers, Latubetube – a plant growing in a dry area like Atiak: this one is even collected from Atiak, carried up to the camps in Juba where it is dried and pounded and sold to Arab traders in Juba who take it up

to Saudi Arabia and sell it. Even a very small amount will make you hungry for sex immediately.

- Mad people are given Oketodede; this is made out of barks of trees and other ingredients like paraffin. **Kinds of madness (lapoya)**: when people die in battles you will see blood coming out of dead people, you will be moving over dead people, so the souls can catch you so you find other people became mad. People can start shouting, moving like a soldier, seeing things others can't see, having nightmares. There were very many cases because the area where people were camping had once been SPLA camps and many had people died there and the remains of the skulls and bones of their bodies were left there. The remains of their huts can be got there until now, along with grinding stones, animal bones and mango plantation.
- skin diseases: Agaba (a climbing plant), shea nut oil, burnt banana leave ash mixed with shea nut oil were also used
- infertile women (Lalur): take banana roots, roots (te) of a tree called te kworo, te akere, and many other herbs that can make them reproduce
- They also distil drugs to make injections. E.g. the bark of Opok, Ogali, Olilimo, and grasses like Ajan, Obiya (spear grass), Ogada (elephant grass), are distilled and injected for syphillis and many other diseases.

Section 9: LRA Organisational Chart for the Year 1999–2000

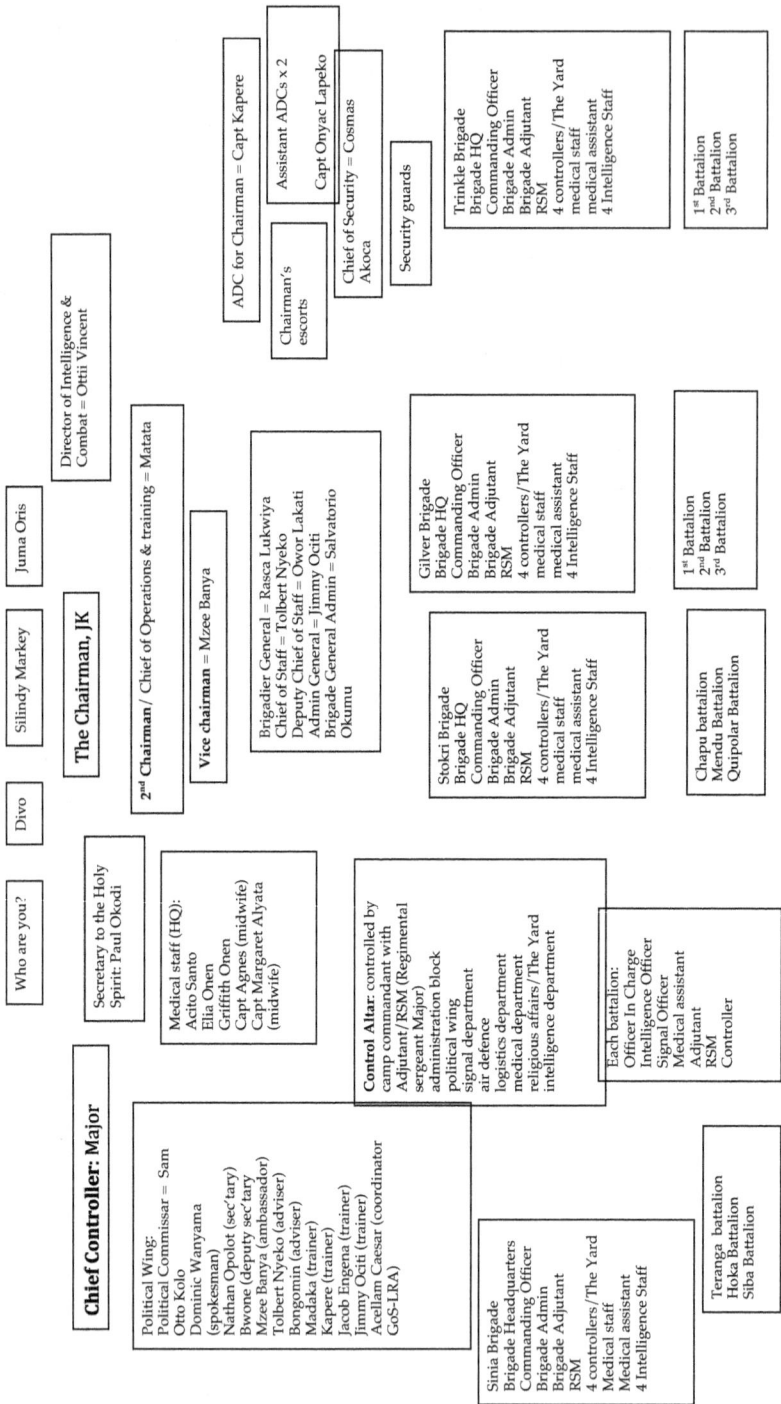

Who are you?

Divo

Silindy Markey

Juma Oris

Director of Intelligence & Combat = Ottii Vincent

The Chairman, JK

ADC for Chairman = Capt Kapere

Assistant ADCs x 2

Capt Onyac Lapeko

Chairman's escorts

Chief of Security = Cosmas Akoca

Security guards

Trinkle Brigade
Brigade HQ
Commanding Officer
Brigade Admin
Brigade Adjutant
RSM
4 controllers/The Yard
medical staff
medical assistant
4 Intelligence Staff

1st Battalion
2nd Battalion
3rd Battalion

2nd **Chairman** / Chief of Operations & training = Matata

Vice chairman = Mzee Banya

Brigadier General = Rasca Lukwiya
Chief of Staff = Tolbert Nyeko
Deputy Chief of Staff = Owor Lakati
Admin General = Jimmy Ociti
Brigade General Admin = Salvatorio Okumu

Gilver Brigade
Brigade HQ
Commanding Officer
Brigade Admin
Brigade Adjutant
RSM
4 controllers/The Yard
medical staff
medical assistant
4 Intelligence Staff

1st Battalion
2nd Battalion
3rd Battalion

Stokri Brigade
Brigade HQ
Commanding Officer
Brigade Admin
Brigade Adjutant
RSM
4 controllers/The Yard
medical staff
medical assistant
4 Intelligence Staff

Chapu battalion
Mendu Battalion
Quipolar Battalion

Chief Controller: Major

Secretary to the Holy Spirit: Paul Okodi

Medical staff (HQ):
Acito Santo
Elia Onen
Griffith Onen
Capt Agnes (midwife)
Capt Margaret Alyata (midwife)

Political Wing:
Political Commissar = Sam Otto Kolo
Dominic Wanyama (spokesman)
Nathan Opolot (sec'tary)
Bwone (deputy sec'tary)
Mzee Banya (ambassador)
Tolbert Nyeko (adviser)
Bongomin (adviser)
Madaka (trainer)
Kapere (trainer)
Jacob Engena (trainer)
Jimmy Ociti (trainer)
Acellam Caesar (coordinator GoS-LRA)

Control Altar: controlled by camp commandant with Adjutant/RSM (Regimental sergeant Major)
administration block
political wing
signal department
air defence
logistics department
medical department
religious affairs/The Yard
intelligence department

Each battalion:
Officer In Charge
Intelligence Officer
Signal Officer
Medical assistant
Adjutant
RSM
Controller

Sinia Brigade
Brigade Headquarters
Commanding Officer
Brigade Admin
Brigade Adjutant
RSM
4 controllers/The Yard
Medical staff
Medical assistant
4 Intelligence Staff

Teranga battalion
Hoka Battalion
Siba Battalion

Section 10: The Four Holy Spirits Guiding Joseph Kony

Juma Oris: is the malaika (angel/spirit) which controls peace within LRA. He makes sure there is complete health within the camp. If there is any epidemic he informs Joseph Kony to improvise a local drug which should be used – this might include stopping people from eating a particular type of food or fruits. Spear grass may be woven and tied around the wrist and last for three days after which when he says it is already enough then these things are removed and that expectation of the epidemic will have gone and only a few people will suffer from it.

Silindy Makay: This is a female spirit, the one who called LRA to go and stay in Sudan. She said 'come and stay in my place, nothing will happen to you, you will be assisted properly in all ways by the country you are going to live in'. She first appeared in Bethlehem (in alero, Gulu district). So when people got in problems they would say 'wa lego Silindy maleng' (let us pray to the virgin Silindy), and some parents have named their daughters after her.

Who are you? Is the malaika or holy spirit which is a commander and controls wars and commands wars whenever LRA is going to face any battle he is the one to reveal all the information through JK

Divo is the malaika which receives all the information about what is going to happen to LRA. Whenever advice is brought forward by this spirit immediate action is always taken ... For example, if there is any visitor coming to LRA with any progressive ideas then the spirit reveals it earlier before the visitor can come. The spirit may propose or say that 'such and such a lady will give birth at this time' – it does happen exactly. 'Children who are born at this period of time must be baptized exactly' – people respond. 'Ladies who are without children must go to the yard and take some herbs' – everybody takes time [to go to the yard]. When there is any good information or bad information the spirit informs all the people in the camp to undergo fasting for a particular period and people do respond positively.

So these were the few important jobs done by the Holy spirits which is up to now controlling and maintaining LRA at a full stand, and the motto of LRA is to resist until they succeed.

Section 11: The Yards

The Yards are circular spaces with an altar in the middle and a thatched hut where clean water and shea nut oil is kept for anointing people. The men who work in the yards are known as controllers. Their duties are to control the war and divert the enemy plans by sprinkling clean water and other witchcraft ideologies which may tend to break the enemy plans. The controllers are said to be 'clean' people who don't quarrel, they are ready to teach other people who fell into mistakes. Their work is to anoint people, for example women who lose their former husbands and need to be engaged to other men. Women who lose their husband take six months or less without meeting with another man until the process from the yard (Wire) is finished and they come to swear in the yard. Then they will be allowed to go and continue with their living. If wire is not done, you may find that the soul of the deceased husband could come and disturb his children.

In Lubanga Tek the main yard (Gang Twer) was right next to the Head Quarters. ... we normally pray on Friday and after prayers nobody is allowed to go and do any work. People sit fully and rest the whole day. And when going to the prayers, all officers put on white gowns (kanjji). People sit according to status. Women sit separately. The whole yard is surrounded by guards.

Prayers started at about 7.30 and could go on until about 11.00. When we went to the Yard we normally entered the yard with high respect. When you go in you put your clothing or mat to sit down on where you are supposed to sit. You sit with your legs underneath to one side or straight out in front of you and holding your rosary. You clasp your hands across your chest and pray for yourself. Then you open your eyes. Then one of the ladies may start the chorus so people start clapping and singing. You sing and finish, then the chairman comes in to preach. He may take a verse in the bible and preach about it to people, comparing what happened in the past with what is happening at present within the LRA and also in the world. Then people are told to stand up. When you stand up, you stand putting your hands on your chest. You sing songs. After singing, people sit down.

The chairman (Kony), after his preaching, will comment on the issues that have been happening during the week. He will tell people some of the messages revealed to him by the Holy Spirit. He may give orders to certain conditions which are not favourable to behaviours, health, way of living and of course going to dig and give assistance to disabled people within the camp. Officers may come with issues which are happening within their brigade and these messages are always put to the chairman to go and decide with the committee what is to be done.

For example, somebody may be very ill in the brigade and needs to be taken to the hospital, then the committee has to see what is to be done and after that the person is driven in a car and taken to hospital in Juba. Another one is when a woman is about to give birth they have to bring the information before the congregation to know what is happening. Also when somebody died, all this information is taken to let the committee officers and other people to be well aware. Also when new-born babies are brought to the yard, then JK has to decide a day on which these children are to be baptised in the yard. He also informs women who have children to take the young ones to the yard to be given local drugs which protects them against certain diseases.

He may also talk about maintaining better types of food, proper utilisation of whatever one may be having in his home. Then people are asked to kneel down and touch their heads to the floor and people pray say for 15 minutes; throughout this time he is praying. After which people answer amen and resume sitting position. Then people can break off and go outside the Yard, meet your friends from different brigades, discuss, chat. Everybody goes to their respective homes. People can visit each other on such days after prayers".

Map 2. Map of a Yard. The circle was indicated using white stones.

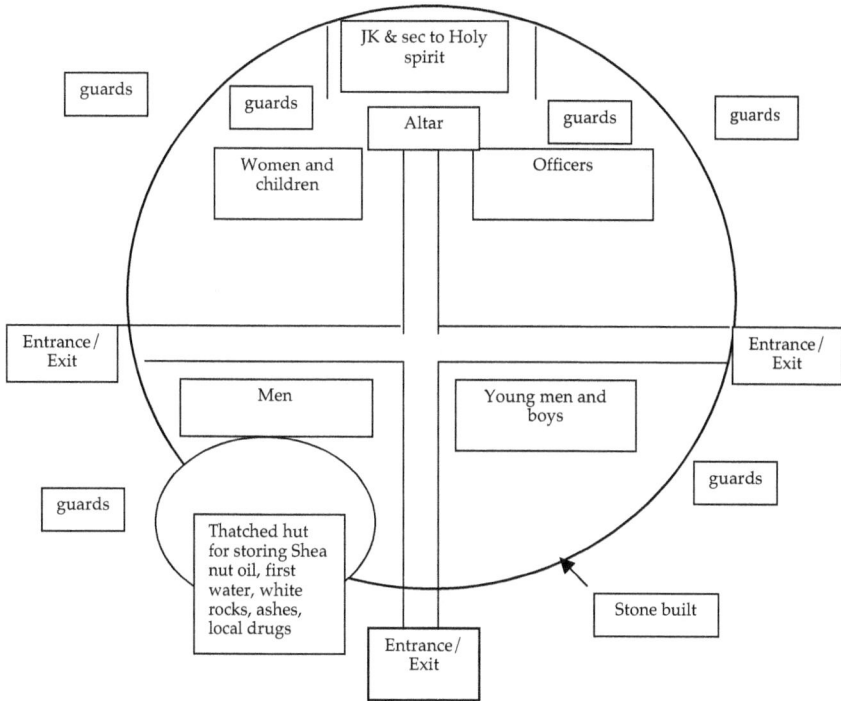

Section 12: The Controllers (*Lunyut Twer*)

The Lunyut Twer are used by JK for many purposes. He instructs them on specific medicines they must give to people, he sends them out into the bush to divert attacking soldiers. For example, if the chairman tells you that 'soldiers are coming to attack the defense and we need to send soldiers to defend but none of them will get killed if you perform the right things' then they go and perform the duties, and it happens as the Chairman said.

These people are chosen by the Holy Spirit. They are always men. They are the ones who have dreadlocks (Wic anginya). There is a tree called Opobo which they remove the barks and after removing the barks they pound it. After pounding it they wash their hair with it. After washing the hair begins to twist. After twisting they weave it into dreadlocks.

To enter the yard they have first to wash completely and come when they are clean. (A menstruating woman can never enter the Yard[10]). There are other control measures performed in the Yard while the battle is being carried on; this is where they can detect the strength of the war and they apply their magicianship by using stoves (sigri) and some of the man made models of human beings out of clay. These are put on the stove and they curse them (e.g. 'shoot him, shoot him' 'who are you, you are the master of the battle, don't let your people be overrun! Make sure the enemies are defeated!', 'sprinkle water!'. When they see that the war is going to be tougher, they also improvise other means to make sure our people can overrun the enemies). This is the work of the controllers. The controllers handle the cross, the calabash with water inside. They go to the front when people are fighting and sprinkle water in the middle of the fighting as others are firing weapons. Also singing songs of praise.

In headquarters we had about twelve controllers. Each brigade had its own yard, and at times Joseph Kony would order that the people go and pray in their brigade yard rather than the main yard in Headquarters.

Each brigade might have four controllers who move with the brigade. This is because there are some instances where the headquarters cannot rush immediately to rescue somebody who is sick, so the controllers are instructed from JK by radio on what to do. Some of the commanders can also be given that strength of the spirit when they are going for battles and they can perform twer themselves in connection with the controllers.

In the Yards the controllers are responsible for keeping the area clean, checking the things in the yard, giving the reports of the work they were told to do. Giving drugs to people with different sicknesses. Guarding the yard so that nobody comes and enters the yard without authority from the yard commander. The following few people I know were the recommended controllers working in the yard in Lubanga Tek in 1999:

- the Yard commander was a Major called Onen Unita
- Captain Ogila
- 2nd Lieutenant Omony
- Lieutenant Okwera (now deceased; hit by a bomb shelled by the enemies to the camp. When the bomb fell on him he was blasted and torn into pieces)
- Captain Murefu died on his job while he was in Uganda when he went for an operation
- Lieutenant Ojok is still continuing with his work with the Yard
- 2nd Lieutenant Okello still performs his duties up to now
- Lieutenant Opira died in a battle inside Uganda.
- Lieutenant Oryem is still continuing with his work
- Lieutenant Oyat is a hard worker in the Yard

Section 13: List of items kept in the Yard Store (*Ot Twer*)

Shea nut oil (Moo Ya): This is called a holy tree of which the oil was picked and used for anointing Jesus. So they use that oil for all purposes such as when somebody has a muscle dislocation, on open wounds, anointments when a lady is going to be married to somebody. It is put on the eyes, the face, the arms, legs etc. When somebody has eye disease they put shea nut oil in the eye. When somebody is poisoned they give shea nut oil mixed with other drugs to drink and the poisons come out. We used to smear pimples with it. When there is epidemic they may look for a water pool, mix other drugs with shea nut oil and then drop [the mixture] into the pool. So people go there, swim and cross the water pool and you come out. Meaning that noone will be attacked by any of these diseases. And shea nut oil is not eaten by the LRA (but it is eaten in Gulu and other places).

First Water (Pi Kot Maleng): This is the water collected during the first rainfall of the new year. For this occasion new jerrycans are used in which to collect the rainwater. These jerrycans are not touched by any women or other people except the controllers. First water is used when people are ready to go for war and it is filled into small bottles for everyone to keep on their own as an emblem of faith in LRA/M. You really believe in the Holy Spirit of the Lakwena. You don't drink that one, just carry it in a small bottle around the neck. It is also used to sprinkle as a sign of cleanness.

White rocks (got matar/got twer): this one is pure white, and its location is indicated by the Holy Spirit. These are the same type of rock as was used by Alice Lakwena as stone bombs. When given to people in small pieces to be worn on bracelets or around the neck, it stops the enemies from identifying who you are. Instead they will just get confused and will not look at you. During operations these stones can be placed around the place where the soldiers are resting and enemies cannot find them. Joseph Kony and the controllers tell people to place stones in certain locations near where they are coming to rest, cook etc and he will set the hour for departure, and even if the enemy come very near they will not see the LRA. When leaving, the rocks are often left behind.

Ashes/camouflage (buru matar): this is a white soil smeared on people as a traditional drug to change your feelings about past events and to indicate that you are now a new person in LRA. You take three days after using it and then you can go and wash yourself. Then now, you belong to this society in all ways possible. The controllers are the people who know where all these ashes (buru matar/camouflage) are extracted from. But no-one else knows where these things are got and nobody is allowed to use this anyhow. When you first arrive you can stay for two days, then the report form the Holy Spirit will tell Joseph Kony that all the abductees who are brought must be taken to the Yard and smeared with Ashes, shea nut oil, and sprinkled with First Water. Then after this you are given all the regulations that you have to follow while you are in the camp [see Section A].

Notes

1. This is the title given by Jacob himself
2. Jacob noted that the amount of sympathy people received depended on whose authority they fell under. Some of the LRA had been trained in the UNLA, WNBF etc and had some sympathy, others had been abducted themselves from deep in the villages and did not know any other way.
3. According to Jacob there was no intermarriage with Sudanese women as a result.

4. A man who once worked together with Mama Alice Lakwena fled with her to Nairobi where they were taken to a place called Thika to camp. After four years he decided to rejoin LRA movement.

5. This section exemplifies the narrator's occasional tendency to try to distance himself from responsibility when describing actions which will be viewed negatively, but equally the difficulty of sustaining this distanced narrative position. Thus 'they' sent people to raid, but 'when they reached the village I was among them'.

6. He later died in Khartoum on 9 March and was also buried there.

7. According to Jacob, Ottii Lagony & Okello Can Odonga were assassinated on 6 December 1998, following allegations that they had sold a radio to the Sudanese. Lagony's ten wives were then distributed to other commanders, as were two of Can Odonga's three wives. The third committed suicide by swallowing Ambush, a pesticide, when she heard that her husband had been killed. This differs from Temmerman's account that Lagony was killed after having been accused by Kony of plotting to surrender with all the children under the terms of the Amnesty Act in the wake of the 1999 Nairobi agreement (2001: 158).

8. Another reason given is that 'drinking alcohol and smoking may cause difficulty to soldiers and it may be difficult for them to get these things because all these you need to walk to look for them and also the problem of money, whereby if everybody were engaged in drinking and smoking then it would be difficult to keep the defense and to stick to orders'.

9. This account differs from that given by De Temmerman, in that he describes meetings with both Lagira and Kony, neither of whom were available according to Temmerman (2001: 132). It confirms however, Temmerman's account that one of the girls who did talk to Sister Raquele was killed following the visit (2001; 148).

10. This appears to confirm the account given by a returned abductee to the Monitor: '"If someone has their menstruation," said Josephine, "she must report it. You are not to cook, to touch anybody, not to work, only sit and wait for food. You don't go for any activities. It's believed a girl who is menstruating, if you accept her service or touch her, you will be killed during the war" (The Monitor, 15 April 1998, *Kony kids survive on urine*).

ANNEX B

AN ACCOUNT OF THE 1994 PEACE TALKS

The account given below seeks to give a sense of some of the dynamics at play in the various meetings. It is drawn from two principal sources. Firstly a series of lengthy key informant interviews with one of the elders who was present at the meeting of 10 January and at the Atoo Hills meeting of 22 January,[1] secondly a transcript of a significant portion of the meeting of 22 January 1994 which was made from a video-tape and subsequently translated into English. There are some discrepancies between details of the story recounted by the elder, that which emerges from the transcript, and that of given by a journalist who attended the 1993–4 meetings (O'Kadameri, 2002),[2] but the overall convergence between the different accounts is strong.

Meeting of 10th January 1994 (summarised from elder's account)

In the run up to the January meeting, Mrs Betty Bigombe, then Minister of State for Pacification of the North, called over 45 elders from Kitgum and Gulu to a meeting at the Medical school in Gulu Hospital. During four days discussion of possible causes of the war there was some tension between the two districts as those from Kitgum blamed Gulu for hosting the rebels. When it came to selecting twenty people for the delegation, eighteen came from Kitgum, and only three from Gulu. The Gulu people said *'since you [people in Kitgum] are blaming us you should go and talk with them'*.[3] [4] The delegates were identified by giving priority to those whose fathers and grandfathers had been *Rwodi* (chiefs/ elders), and also included people known within the district but not connected to Government, such as Reverend Ochola, later to become Bishop of Kitgum and a prominent peace activist. The chairman for the Acholi elders was Mr Akera Anania from Gulu District, and the vice chairman was *Rwot* (Chief) Opoko Labogoloro from Kitgum District. They were led by Colonel Wasswa (Muganda) of Gulu 4th Division and Mrs Bigombe (Acholi).

They left Gulu at 8.30, in army vehicles and with eleven guards to escort the Divisional Commander, and reached Pagik, a venue chosen by the LRA, before 10.00am. At the barracks they were stopped and received a message from Kony to proceed without guns. After much discussion the whole delegation decided that if the Minister was willing to die so were they and all guns were left behind. The Divisional Commander eventually agreed.[5]

They left Pagik at ten, on foot, and after about 1km they found the first rebel road-block. Over twenty rebels started sprinkling water on their bodies and checking them for weapons. They were allowed to pass. The Vice chairman (Okot Ogony) was leading because Pagik was his home area. After another 1km they found a second road-block, with the same checks and sprinkling with water, which the rebels described as their greeting. The third road-block was the same.

At Okot Ogony's home they found more rebels and were checked a fourth time. The home had been a collection centre for cotton production, and the LRA were using it to store foodstuffs like simsim (sesame). Okot Ogony's sons were transporting simsim for the rebels, selling it in town and bringing the proceeds to the rebels, and some of Ogony's family members were also staying there.

At the fifth road-block the sprinkling of water was done by young soldiers, but older ones were also present. Men outnumbered women, though all wore the same combat uniform and proper gum boots – the same as the UPDF (see Chapter 5 for further discussion). Passing the sixth road-block they found a clearing prepared under a big tree, with some logs for seats. The rebels saluted the fourth Division Commander and the Minister. Kony's representative and 2nd in Command, Odego, talking in English, outlined for them the LRA's structure and described the training he had received under Obote in Israel, America and Germany. He welcomed Bigombe's delegation, saying she was a trusted woman who loved Uganda and Acholiland, and that even though he himself was a Lugbara from West Nile he was convinced that the elders who accompanied her were true Acholis because otherwise they would fear being killed. As young people the LRA were ready to reach a compromise with Government representatives and elders which would enable them to come out of the bush (By this time there were very many soldiers there).

He then introduced some of the other LRA leaders, and proceeded to make a number of points. He reminded the elders that he had heard of their 1991 resolution that the whole population should take up bows and spears to fight the LRA. He also raised two questions to be addressed by the Government delegation: Firstly, what had happened to Kilama (a member of the UPDA who was killed after the peace agreement in 1988)? Secondly, how would they be treated if they came out of the bush?

Colonel Wasswa responded, saying they were good questions, that the purpose of the peace talks was to address such issues, and that in their company they had church leaders, *rwodis* and other elders who had agreed to go with Bigombe to witness the peace talks. Bigombe said she had nothing to add at that moment, and was not yet willing to go into any depth [i.e. neither question was answered]. As Kony himself had not yet been seen up to this point, she asked them to call Kony to explain to them what they were doing as they said they were God's agents doing what the Bible said. Kony was in fact already there, sitting among the rebels, dressed like an ordinary soldier.

Kony greeted people in fluent English, translated into Luo by one of his people, and then began a long speech, beginning by stating that he was aware of all the blame being put onto him for his soldiers killing people, abducting young women, and raping married women. He said he was an agent of God doing God's work, that he was led by the Holy Spirit in all things, and could predict what successes and failures would befall his troops.

He said they knew the elders blamed them for having fought the bush war, but they also knew as rebels that when Museveni took over it was the elders who had urged them to resist, arguing that a Munyankole (a member of the Banyankole ethnic group) could not lead the Acholi. He claimed that it was this initial blessing of the elders which had brought the LRA this far. He then pointed out that according to tradition the Rwodi Moo (the anointed chiefs) were not supposed to go to where the fight was (because they were 'clean people'), and that by going to peace talks in the battle zone they had already failed in their traditional mandate. He also said that for him, as a member of the Catholic church who was doing what was stated in the Bible, he was really ashamed to have seen elders who had blessed his fighting then telling him to stop doing so. He said he was contented that the initial blessing the elders had given him was still valid and so there was nothing that would shake him from his power.

Returning to the two questions posed by his deputy, he reiterated that they were reluctant to come out if the Government could not answer the questions about Kilama and their safety. He said he had asked many friends both in and outside the country what he should do: some had encouraged him to stop, others to continue. He pointed out that their success in getting connected with the Government of Sudan was a result of the Government of Uganda agreeing to host the SPLA in Uganda. He also said it was from observing the SPLA-GOU relationship that they learned the value of friendship. For all those reasons he would be content to come out of the bush, but not because of being defeated. How they would come out of the bush was not yet clear (i.e. they might come out fighting).

He closed by saying that Bigombe had a good feeling for a mother who should be looking after her children at home.[6] He said he should be forgiven for the two and a half hours he had talked because he was talking on behalf of the Holy Spirit. He suggested that the next peace talks be held at Te Got Atoo (at the base of Mount Atoo on the way to Cwero), and concluded by saying that he was aware that the Government was not in a position to give answers to the questions, so there was nothing further to discuss.

According to the respondent there was complete silence as he spoke, and the delegates were all asking themselves whether they would leave the place alive. When at about 5pm Bigombe and the Divisional Commander said *'let's have some lunch of tinned meat and biscuits'*, the rebels said *'no, we cannot eat something from the Government'*. When the rebels refused to eat (Acholi tradition says that once someone has eaten with another person they cannot kill that person (see also Finnström, 2003: 234, 297)) some of the elders wet themselves and others developed acute diarrhoea. But they had to persevere, so after Kony had wished them a good journey and shaken hands with Bigombe and Wasswa they set off back to Pagik at 5.30pm. Some were so affected by fear that they could not walk properly, and it took them until 8.00pm to reach Pagik. On the way they all talked of other things.

At the barracks they boarded the lorry the same night and went back to Gulu. Those from Kitgum spent the night in the medical school. Those from Gulu were taken home. They were informed to report at 9am to the medical school and receive some allowances, 10,000/= each for those from Gulu, 17,000/= each for the delegation from Kitgum. After receiving the allowances a discussion was held. Minister Bigombe started by saying 'you have now seen what is involved in talking with Joseph Kony'. Some of the elders reacted that if that was the way then it was their last time and that what the rebels did was not good because at the end when Joseph Kony spoke some developed diarrhoea and others were also very afraid. Opoka Laphokoloro and Akera Anania, leaders of the approximately nine *Rwodi Moo* (anointed chiefs), said that the other elders had let them down and should be released, and indeed they eventually resolved that they could not go because of the shameful treatment they had received.

The meeting of 22 January 1994 (summarised from video transcript and elder's narrative)

When the date for the Atoo hills talks came, the elders from Kitgum failed to come back. The much reduced delegation left Gulu at nine thirty in the morning, following the Moroto Road using a Landrover, three Isuzu trucks, a Toyota pickup and uniformed soldiers with fully loaded Light Machine Guns.[7] After seven kilometers they turned left towards Ato primary school where they found the first and only road-block less than one kilometre from the venue where they were received. The footage shows the LRA delegation of around fifty people arriving led by a man talking out loud as he cleanses the 'conference centre' by sprinkling holy water all around. Three of the delegation were dressed in religious clothing. Joseph Kony himself was not among them.

Odego, the LRA representative who had talked to them at the previous meeting, introduced the key commanders and controllers, all of whom he referred to as *Lapwony*, meaning 'teacher'.[8] He then stated the LRA's purpose as being '*to sign an agreement which will show that there are no more hostilities between us and the NRA. Most of the talking will come after finishing this. Praise be to the almighty God*'.

Bigombe expressed the fear that Kony's absence showed a lack of commitment. She also stressed the need to come out of the meeting with an agreement, arguing that '*what delays becomes stale*'. She pointed out that;

There are many who do not want peace to prevail. There are those people who are benefiting from the war. There are others who think that if this thing ends, they will have nothing to lean on. There are some people who do not feel that being happy is good, who believe that development shouldn't take place and peace shouldn't be there. Such people can also come to you to discourage you, and to us the Government to discourage us. This will bring doubts. We will find ourselves reaching a point where we shall say that if it's like this let the talks stop, if it's like then we still have no answers. So I want to say that we should come up with something and that it should materialise quickly so that it may bring shame on those who do not have interest in peace prevailing.

Colonel Waswa also expressed disappointment at Kony's absence before handing over to Colonel Fred Tolit, Director of Military Intelligence and himself an Acholi from Omia Anyima village in Kitgum. Tolit rapidly de-railed proceedings by questioning the sincerity of Joseph Kony:

We as human beings try to measure the level of seriousness by what those people who are directly involved in an issue say about it [i.e. Kony is not serious because he is not here to tell us what he has to say]. Myself, as a government representative, as someone who was sent from Kampala to add weight by joining the Minister and the Division Commander to see what we were discussing, I feel as if we are turning these talks into a joke ...

... I would pray that you analyse critically, use the power of God (most of you talk about God), so use the power of God to enable sincerity and truth to come amongst you...

... we should know that the Government, as a body that sees what is in this country and beyond, has its own programmes, which are many. In these programmes people are assigned different duties, that such and such a person do this, such a person do this. Once they have completed their duties they meet and will be asked to report back.

Having made the point that dealing with the LRA is only one amongst many concerns of the Government, he goes on to suggest that the LRA's concerns for their own safety are unfounded, arguing that the Government would have no interest in killing people who come out of the bush as this would defeat the purpose of their own overthrow of the previous Government, which was to stop it from killing at will. He then states that

From the government side, we took the issue of ceasefire as a mutual understanding between you and us, as a local arrangement ... that affects us as Ugandans. Because the war that has been going on in Acholi since 1986 is causing problems in all other areas of Uganda, because there are many things which we as Acholi could have cultivated and sold, the proceeds of which would have been collected and submitted to the Government to assist it in buying drugs for our hospital. But because there is no cultivation or any other meaningful activity being done here you find that money that is collected from other people is sent to the treasury, part of which is sent to us here for making roads, buying drugs and helping schools.

He then requested the LRA to show them the document they had drawn up so that they could discuss it and amend it appropriately, reminding them however that

Government has policies which must be followed. Whatever we do we should do it on condition that we are respecting government, because even God put it clearly in the Bible that Government should be respected. This is found in Paul's letter to the Romans, Chapter 13. Reverend, please read for us Chapter 13 from verse 1 to about the 10th which talks about respect to God, no no, respect to Government'.[9]

Commander Omona Komakech responds by saying:

We ... the LRA ... even if everybody abuses us and say this is a curse and not a holy spirit, we know that it is the Holy Spirit.. Now, I have come to respond to what Lt. Col. Tolit, who is a son of Acholi, has said. Son of Acholi and my brother, let me respond. I will start answering in the following way; that one thing we must all focus our feelings on is the truth. Because if we do not have the feeling of truth in our hearts ... then whatever we do, even if we collect ourselves and say let us go together [i.e. join the Government], there will still be bloodshed - the way Tolit wants it. For us to have truth in our hearts, let us stop despising one another ... Secondly, my brother Tolit, you should note that if we [the officers] were not there or the young soldiers were not there ... Kony would not be in the bush.'

He also reacts to the pressure from Tolit to reach a signed agreement by drawing parallels with the 1988 peace agreement with the UPDA:

Did it bring peace? Why not? Isn't it because of shallow thinking? They separated from us and they rejected us and started shooting at us, yet we had been telling them let us unite together so that we all come out of the bush together and join the Government. So what happened? Have you weeded the banana trees? [i.e. have you destroyed us?] eh ... Acholi have a proverb that 'doing things in a hurry made the hyena spotted – like an army uniform'.. is that what you want to do to us? [i.e. as you did with the UPDA].... if there is no hidden agenda, we are very serious on this issue and the talks will not fail, and I want to repeat that you will not hear that LRA have picked guns to go and fire at NRA. Never, unless you people start shooting at us with a plan of your own, then we defend ourselves.

He goes on to draw out the divisions within the Government delegation, particularly between Bigombe and Wasswa on the one hand, and Tolit on the other:

I am just praying Mama [i.e. Bigombe]. You are the key, you and Wasswa. You know very well that you are the key for this peace negotiation ... we do not want to deal with individual interests.... Because there are people who want to push us the way they think best suits their interests, so that others think they are the ones who worked very hard to bring us out of the bush ...

I used to think you were not taking us locally, but today I have heard from Tolit that this is 'local' peace talk. Today I have understood. I have thoroughly understood. But this will not stop us and should not prevent you from going ahead: you [Bigombe] don't give up, you and Wasswa. The total destruction which has occurred in Acholi makes me feel sad and also makes you feel sad. It also makes Wasswa feel sad even though he is not an Acholi. That is why the two of you tried your level best, who else apart from the two of you has tried to look for us so that we can talk peace face to face? There is no-one. [long pause] I feel very annoyed and very sad to hear this. [long pause]. Because if people pursue worldly or personal interests then this is going to spoil the talks. Because you want things to be done your way, but not in the interests of everybody. This issue must not end when it only meets Government interests, or only the interests of the LRA; it must meet the interests of all the parties, including our elders who have suffered.

In a dramatic shift of the discussion, he starts telling a story of how one of the rebels had been caught defiling an eight year old girl the previous night. Both the man and the girl were brought forwards. Omona goes on as follows:

> *Some of the crimes that have been happening are done by people whom we have sent to be arrested today so that you may know them; if we have ten children there are bound to be wizards amongst them; later we are going to show you, we the followers of Kony, that we do not want bad things. We are going to show you now a soldier of ours, a wrong-doer whom we arrested and who is here. We are going to show you here, we are going to shoot him by firing squad in front of everybody here. You should note that such wrong-doers are not working in the interests of Joseph Kony to rape girls, abduct people in the villages or to do bad things. You should note that even among God's servants, be it a reverend or whoever, there are those who, even if they have a white collar, could be witch-doctors. In the same way among us there could be such people. Among us we do not say we are all holy. There are always people who do bad things. You see, they will always be there. So you have to pardon us if bad things are done. You should pardon us and we pray that you pardon us. Such people are the ones we shall start working on. Even on your side, there are some NRA [who do bad things], you see?*

Omona ends with a direct attack on Tolit:

> *... Lieutenant Colonel Tolit..., it looks as though what you have been talking about is basically telling us to put down our arms and surrender the way you want it. But let me tell you that <u>we are not surrendering</u>. For us, we are not people who have come here to surrender. We have come to negotiate for peace ... We are not saying that you have been defeated in fighting us or scattering us, neither are we saying that we can no longer fight. So you must know that the way you want us to come out is not what we want. Because much of what you say, if people listen to you carefully, and if people follow, it will bring a lot of sadness to them. So I still want to repeat and as I wind up I still say that we do not want any more bloodshed; what will not happen again is that Holy has started fighting against the NRA. You should know that those of us who are present here, we are fighting against the Devil. If we were to be given the freedom to spread the word (of God) then we would not be fighting now. We are not here fighting to be rulers or leaders of the country, and Kony does not want to become a President. Kony has already been given his office, the Holy Spirit has anointed him to be the preacher, to go and spread the word of God. Praise be to our Lord Jesus Christ. [ends and sits down]*

Tolit responded to this by trying to explain his use of 'local':

> *... most of the times at home where we grew up if someone says you are 'local' then we think that that person thinks you are hopeless or simply somebody who has nothing. (In this case) 'Local' means something that has been made from home to help people in that area.*

He also further provokes the LRA by saying '*I do not see that we should start unbuttoning shirts to see who has the bigger chest*'.

After an intervention by the LRA spokesperson the Reverend Ochola from Kitgum urges that the soldier be spared:

> *Earlier on one of our brothers said that people who have done bad things should be killed by firing squad, even Museveni said 'if a soldier does something wrong then he should be taken for firing squad', but this does not solve problems. Death is not a solution for bad deeds, and killing does not solve problems.*

He also draws on the parable of the prodigal son, implying that the Government delegation should behave as the father towards the LRA as the prodigal son, and he draws on ethnic and national patriotism when he says:

> *I will be grateful if you respect Mother Bigombe, if you respect our country Uganda and more especially Acholiland. So that our name, which has been tarnished for a long time, should be clean again. So that we know that we are all God's children. Just like other children of God in other countries.*

Bigombe sought to move the negotiations on by saying that the LRA had done well in arresting the soldier:

> *I even heard with great delight that you are not happy when some children under your command commit atrocities and you will always want to punish them in order to teach them not to repeat such atrocities. We have heard about this, but we want to request you to put aside this issue of the firing squad. We should look for other ways of teaching them.*

She then called on the meeting to move on to discuss the main points of the ceasefire. Seven soldiers and seven LRA were chosen to discuss the details and went away from the main meeting for about two hours to discuss and write. While waiting, Bigombe's team took soda and biscuits. The LRA again refused these, saying that once talks were concluded they could sit together.

When the fourteen came to report back, the LRA representative reported that they had met resistance. They had asked how much money the government would give, and also wanted a guarantee from the Government that they wouldn't be killed in the same way as Kilama was. They said the Government soldiers had refused these requests and that they knew it was Tolit who had instructed them not to accept what the rebels would say.

Unfortunately, the video recording ends at this point. According to the key informant, the man charged with defiling a girl was taken and beaten to death in front of the Government delegation's eyes, using sticks. When Bigombe protested, they replied *'we have been annoyed by Tolit, he said we have been defeated so we want to show that we still have power'*. He goes on to report that the LRA spokesman had said *'we shall conclude another time'*, after which the Government delegation boarded their vehicles with a lot of fear. Over the next six miles or so they found seven road-blocks, at which they were checked but no arms or ammunition were removed and they were not sprinkled with water. People were not happy with Tolit for trying to interpret the Bible, saying this should have been done by the religious leaders.

It appears that a further meeting did take place, as the text of a written ceasefire agreement was later signed in Lacekocot on 2nd February 1994 between Col Samuel Wasswa, and George Komakech Omona (see ACCORD 2002: 82).

Notes

1. Interviews held on 4, 7 and 11 August 1998, Gulu.

2. E.g. events which O'Kadameri places on 2 February are covered in the video footage as being on the 22nd January.
3. These included: Okot Ogony (muslim representative), Okot Payera (muslim representative), Erico Ogulu Odong (Omoro), Yonacana Latigo (Odek – now stays near Pece stadium), Okidi Angol (Son of Rwot Angol in Kitgum district, Patongo county), Nicolas Opoka, Arweny.
4. Under British rule Kitgum and Gulu formed the Acholi region, and were subsequently divided into two and have since been further split with the creation of Pader district in 2000 and Amuru district in 2005. There are some minor linguistic differences which broadly correspond to the Kitgum/Gulu division, with people in Kitgum talking '*Acholi mamalo'*, and those in Gulu talking '*Acholi mapiny*'.
5. In O'Kadameri's account Kony's demand delayed the whole process by a day as the army members were not initially permitted to leave their weapons behind (2002: 39).
6. This could be interpreted to mean that her involvement was regarded in a positive way – or a veiled suggestion that she would be better off fulfilling traditional roles.
7. The delegation included Mrs Bigombe, Colonel Wasswa, Colonel Tolit, Rev'd Ochola, Rev'd Olwedo Laker, Islamic representative from Pabbo called Juma (who was not in the first delegation), Kot Ogoni (elder from Paicho Pagik whose home was being used and who was later killed by rebels), Akera Anania (Bobbi Division and secretary General of the UPC Gulu district), Captain Kibula (District Administrator), Yusuf Adek and Erico Ogulu.
8. Commanders included George William Omona Komakech, Alex Otii Lagony, Sunday Arop, Matata, Jackson Achana, Tolbert Nyeko, Kato Kizito, Onen, Okello Kega, Simon Okot. Controllers included Ginaro Bongomin Abonga, Amos Lagen and Vincent Makamoi.
9. Book of Romans, Chapter 13, Verse 1 'Let every person be in subjection to the governing authorities. For there is no authority except from God, and those which exist are established by God'.

BIBLIOGRAPHY

Internet resources I have consulted include www.allafrica.com, IRIN (Integrated Regional Information Network (www.irinnews.org), FEWSNET (Famine Early Warning Systems NET) Monthly Newsletter (http://www.fews.net/current/monthlies/), the Norwegian Refugee Council/Global IDP Project (http://www.idpproject.org), Kacokke Madit's excellent e-newsletter (www.km-net.org), Justice and Peace News on the ARLPI website (www.acholipeace.org).

Abrahamsen, R. (2000). Disciplining Democracy: Development Discourse and Good Governance in Africa. London, Zed Books.

ACORD (2001). Research Report on Internally Displaced Persons (IDPs), Gulu District. Gulu, ACORD: 29.

ACORD (2002). Gender-Sensitive Programme Design and Planning in Conflict-Affected Situations. London, ACORD.

ACCORD (2002). Protracted Conflict, Elusive Peace: Initiatives to End the Violence in Northern Uganda. London, Conciliation Resources and Kacokke Madit.

Afako, B. (2002). Operation Iron Fist: What Price for Peace in Northern Uganda? Kampala, African Rights: 9.

Allen, T. (1987). 'Kwete and Kweri: Acholi Farm Work Groups in Southern Sudan'. *Manchester Papers on Development* III(2): 60–92.

———.(1991). 'Histories and Contexts: Using Pasts in the Present on the Sudan/Uganda Border.' *Bulletin of the John Rylands University Library of Manchester* 73(3): 63–91.

———. (1991). 'Understanding Alice: Uganda's Holy Spirit Movement in Context.' *Africa* 61(3): 370–399.

———. (1994). 'Ethnicity and Tribalism on the Sudan-Uganda Border', in K. Fukui (ed.), *Ethnicity and Conflict in the Horn of Africa*. London, James Currey Ltd: 112–139.

———. (1995). *The Violence of Healing*, unpublished manuscript.

———. (1998). 'Internal Wars and Humanitarian Intervention', in M. Last (ed.), *Healing the Social Wounds of War*. Edinburgh, Edinburgh University Press.

———. (2005a). War and Justice in Northern Uganda: A Risk Assessment of the International Criminal Court's Intervention. London, Crisis States Programme, London School of Economics and Political Science: 89.

———. (2005b). *Sudan/Uganda Border Study D3*, Open University: 24.

Amnesty International (1997). 'Breaking God's Commands': The Destruction of Childhood by the Lord's Resistance Army. London, Amnesty International: 45.

———. (1999). Breaking the Circle: Protecting Human Rights in the Northern War Zone. London, Amnesty International: 75.

Anywar, R. S. (1948). 'The Life of Rwot Iburaim Awich.' *Uganda Journal* 12: 72–81.

ARLPI (2001). Let My People Go: The Forgotten Plight of the People in the Displaced Camps in Acholi. Gulu, ARLPI and Justice and Peace Commission of Gulu Diocese: 36.

———. (2002). Report on Acholi-Jie Peace Dialogue and Reconciliation, 26 February–1 March 2002. Gulu, ARLPI.

———. (2002). Seventy Times Seven: The Impact of the Amnesty Law in Acholi. Gulu, ARLPI.

———. (undated). Guidelines for Sub-Counties Peace Animation Programme. Gulu, ARLPI.

Asowa-Okwe, C. (1996). Insurgency and the Challenges of Social Reconstruction in North and North-Eastern Uganda, 1986–1996. Centre for Development Research, Copenhagen.

Atkinson, R. R. (1989). 'The Evolution of Ethnicity among the Acholi of Uganda: The Pre-colonial Phase.' *Ethnohistory* 36(1): 19–43.

———. (1999). The Roots of Ethnicity: The Origins of the Acholi of Uganda before 1800. Kampala, Fountain Publishers Ltd.

Azar, E. (1986). 'Ten Propositions on Protracted Social Conflict', in E. A. J. W. Burton (ed.), *International Conflict Resolution: Theory and Practice*. Wheatsheaf: 28-39.

Bayart, J.-F., S. Ellis, and B. Hibou (1999). *The Criminalization of the State in Africa*. Oxford, James Currey.

Behrend, H. (1998). 'War in Northern Uganda', in C. Clapham (ed.), *African Guerillas*. Oxford, James Currey: 107–118.

———. (1999). Alice Lakwena and the Holy Spirits: War in Northern Uganda 1985–97. Oxford, James Currey.

Berdal, M. and D. Keen (1997). 'Violence and Economic Agendas in Civil Wars: Considerations for Policymakers.' *Millennium* 26(3).

Berdal, M. and D. Malone (eds) (2000), *Greed versus Grievance*. IPA.

Bere, R. M. (1946). 'An Outline of Acholi History.' *Uganda Journal* 11(1): 1–8.

Bere, R. M. (1947). 'An Outline of Acholi History.' *Uganda Journal* 11(1): 1–8.

———. (1955). 'Land and Chieftainship among the Acholi.' *Uganda Journal* 19(1): 49–56.

Boccassino, R. (1939). 'The Nature and Characteristics of the Supreme Being Worshipped among the Acholi of Uganda.' *Uganda Journal* 7: 195–201.

Bramucci, G. L. (2001). *Unearthed Grace: Stories from Northern Uganda*. Kampala, Fountain Publishers Ltd.

Browning, C. R. (1992). *The Path to Genocide*. Cambridge, Cambridge University Press.

Bruderlein, C. (2000). The Role of Non-State Actors in Building Human Security – The Case of Armed Groups in Intra-State Wars. Geneva, Centre for Humanitarian Dialogue: 18.

Carnegie (1997). Report of Commission on Preventing Deadly Conflict. New York, Carnegie Corporation.

Castells, M. (2000). *End of Millennium,* Blackwell.

Church Missionary Society (undated). *Northern Uganda: Break the Silence*. London, Church Missionary Society: 19.

Cohen, S. (2001). States of Denial: Knowing About Atrocities and Suffering. Cambridge, Polity Press.

Collier, P. (2000). Economic Causes of Civil Conflict and Their Implications for Policy. Washington DC, World Bank: 23.

Colson, E. and C. P. Kottak (1996). 'Linkages: Methodologies for the Study of Socio-cultural Transformations', in E. F. Moran (ed.), *Transforming Societies, Transforming Anthropology*. Ann Arbor, University of Michigan: 103–134.

COPA (1996). One Day Sensitisation Workshop in Gulu (Northern Uganda). Nairobi, Kenya.

———. (1996). Second Africa Consultation of Coalition for Peace in Africa (COPA). Nairobi, Kenya.

———. (1999a). Northern Uganda Reconstruction Programme (NURP II) District Profile Study, Final Report, Volume I. Kampala, Office of the Prime Minister: 219.

———. (1999b). Northern Uganda Reconstruction Programme (NURP II) District Profile Study Volume II, part 1, Acholi Region. Kampala, Office of the Prime Minister: 140.

Crazzolara, F. J. P. (1961). 'Lwoo Migrations.' *Uganda Journal* 25: 136–148.

Crelinsten, R. D. and A. P. Schmid, (eds) (1995). The Politics of Pain: Torturers and Their Masters. State Violence, State Terrorism, and Human Rights. Boulder, Westview Press, Inc.

Crocker, C., F. Hampson, et al. (2001). 'A Crowded Stage: Liabilities and Benefits of Multiparty Mediation', in C. Crocker, F. Hampson and P. Aall (eds), *Turbulent Peace*. United States Institute for Peace.

Ddumba-Sentamu, John, G. D., and Jan Kees van Donge (1999). *What Does the Showcase Show? Programme Aid to Uganda*. Stockholm, SIDA: 153.

Dolan, C. (1992). 'British Development NGOs and Advocacy in the 1990s', in M. Edwards and D. Hulme (eds), *Making a Difference – NGOs and Development in a Changing World*. London, Earthscan.

———. (1993). 'Communities in Transition: Representation and Accountability.' *Critical Health* (Johannesburg) (42).

———. (1997). 'The Changing Status of Mozambicans in South Africa and Its Impact on Their Repatriation to and Reintegration in Mozambique', in R. Black and K. Khoser (eds), *Voluntary Repatriation: The End of the Refugee Cycle?* Berghahn.

———. (1998). 'Principled Aid in an Unprincipled World.' *Development in Practice*, 8(3).

———. (1998). 'The Emergence of Complexity: Issues in the Analysis of Conflicts and Their Associated Interventions at a Local Level'. Unpublished paper presented at COPE Review Workshop, Leeds.

———. (1999). Key Research Findings: An Introduction to the Conference 'Peace Research and the Reconciliation Agenda'. Gulu, ACORD.

———. (2000). What Do You Remember? A Rough Guide to the War in Northern Uganda, 1986–2000. London, ACORD: 28.

———. (2002). 'Which Children Count? The Politics of Children's Rights in Northern Uganda.' *ACCORD* 1(11): 68–71.

———. (2002). 'Collapsing Masculinities and Weak States: A Case Study of Northern Uganda', in F. Cleaver (ed.), *Masculinities Matter! Men, Gender and Development*. London, New York, Cape Town, Zed Books.

———. (2002). 'In Whose Best Interests? The Optional Protocol to the Convention on the Rights of the Child on the Involvement of Children in Armed Conflict.' *Journal of Conflict, Security and Development* 2(2). Kings College, University of London.

———. (2005). 'Understanding War and Its Continuation: The Case of Northern Uganda', PhD thesis, Institute of Development Studies, London School of Economics and Political Science.

———. (2006). *Uganda Strategic Conflict Analysis,* September 2006, Stockholm, SIDA.

Dolan, C. and E. Bagenda (2004). Militarization and its Impacts: Northern Uganda Strategic Conflict Assessment. London, Christian Aid: 36.

Dolan, C. and L. Hovil (2006). *Humanitarian Protection in Uganda: A Trojan Horse?* London, Overseas Development Institute, HPG Background Paper: 30.

Dolan, C. and J. Schafer (1997). The Reintegration of Ex-combatants in Mozambique: Zambezia and Manica Provinces. Maputo, USAID.

Doom, R. and K. Vlassenroot (1999). 'Kony's Message: A New Koine? The 'Lord's Resistance Army' in Northern Uganda.' *African Affairs* 98: 5–36.

Duffield, M. (1994). 'The Political Economy of Internal War: Asset Transfer, Complex Emergencies and International Aid', in J. M. A. Zwi (ed.), *War and Hunger: Rethinking International Responses to Complex Emergencies.* London, Zed Books: 50–69.

———. (2000). 'Global Governance', paper on Globalisation and Conflict, London, CODEP.

———. (2001). Global Governance and the New Wars, Zed Books, London.

Ehrenreich, R. (1997). The Scars of Death: Children Abducted by the Lord's Resistance Army in Uganda. New York, Human Rights Watch: 78.

El Bushra, J. and C. Dolan (2002). 'Don't Touch, Just Listen! Popular Performance from Uganda' *Review of African Political Economy.* 29 (91): 37–52.

Emmanuel, O. (1999). *Awach Baseline Survey Report,* Red Barnet and GUSCO: 18.

Ferme, M. C. (2001). *The Underneath of Things: Violence, History, and the Everyday in Sierra Leone.* Berkeley and Los Angeles, University of California Press.

Finnström, S. (2003). Living with Bad Surroundings: War and Existential Uncertainty in Acholiland, Northern Uganda. Uppsala, Uppsala University.

———. (2005). 'For God and My Life': War and Cosmology in Northern Uganda', in P. Richards (ed.), *No Peace, No War: An Anthropology of Contemporary Armed Conflicts.* Oxford, James Currey: 98–116.

Fisher, R. J. and L. Keashly (1996). 'The Potential Complementarity of Mediation and Consultation Within a Contingency Model of Third Party Intervention', in J. Bercovitch (ed.) *Resolving International Conflicts: The Theory and Practice of Mediation.* Lynne Rienner: 235–259.

Foreman, M. (2002). *Combat AIDS: HIV and the World's Armed Forces.* London, Healthlink Worldwide: 57.

Galtung, J. (1969). 'Violence, Peace, and Peace Research.' *Journal of Peace Research* VI(3): 167–189.

Gersony, R. (1997). The Anguish of Northern Uganda: Results of a Field-Based Assessment of the Civil Conflicts in Northern Uganda. Kampala, USAID: 105.

Gilligan, J (2000). *Violence – Reflections on Our Deadliest Epidemic,* London, Jessica Kingsley Publishers Ltd.

Girling, F. K. (1960). *The Acholi of Uganda.* London, Colonial Office.

Glover, J. (1999). Humanity – A Moral History of the Twentieth Century, Yale University Press.

Goodhand, J. (1997). NGOs and Peace Building in Complex Political Emergencies: An Introduction. Manchester, University of Manchester and INTRAC.

Goodhand, J. (1999). 'From Wars to Complex Political Emergencies.' *Third World Quarterly* 20(1): 13–26.

Gray, S. J. M. (1951). 'Acholi History, 1860–1901 – Part I.' *Uganda Journal* 15(2): 121–143.

———. (1952). 'Acholi History, 1860–1901 – Part II.' *Uganda Journal* 16(1): 32–50.

———. (1952). 'Acholi History, 1860–1901 – Part III.' *Uganda Journal* 16(2): 132–144.

Gray, R. (1961). *A History of the Southern Sudan, 1839–1889.* London, Oxford University Press.

Griffin, J. H. (1964). *Black Like Me.* London, Panther Books Ltd.

Groves, E. B. (1999). 'Peace Lessons Are Only the Beginning – EMU Students Take Learnings Back to Embattled Home'. *The Mennonite.*

Harrell-Bond, B. (1986). *Imposing Aid: Emergency Assistance to Refugees.* Oxford, New York and Nairobi, Oxford University Press.

Harriss, J. (1998). *'Missing Link' or Analytically Missing? The Concept of Social Capital – An Introductory Bibliographic Essay.* London, Institute of Development Studies Institute, London School of Economics and Political Science.

Hayley, T. T. S. (1940). 'The Power Concept in Lango Religion.' *Uganda Journal* 7: 98–122.

Hayner, P. B. (2001). Unspeakable Truths: Confronting State Terror and Atrocity. New York and London, Routledge.

Hilberg, R. (1993). Perpetrators, Victims, Bystanders – The Jewish Catastrophe 1933–1945. Harper Collins.

HRW (1992). Conspicuous Destruction: War, Famine and the Reform Process in Mozambique. New York, Human Rights Watch.

———. (1997). *Uganda – The Scars of Death.* New York, Human Rights Watch.

———. (2003). Stolen Children: Abduction and Recruitment in Northern Uganda. New York, Human Rights Watch: 24.

———. (2004). *State of Pain: Torture in Uganda.* London, Human Rights Watch: 76.

HURIFO (2002). Between Two Fires: The Human Rights Situation in 'Protected Camps' in Gulu District. Gulu, Human Rights Focus (HURIFO): 86.

ICG (2004). *Northern Uganda: Understanding and Solving the Conflict.* Nairobi/Brussels, International Crisis Group: 42.

ICRC (2000). A Household Economy Study by the International Committee of the Red Cross in Five IDP Camps in Acholi Land, Kampala. Kampala, ICRC.

IDC (2001). Evaluation of EC Country Strategy, 1996–2000. European Commission: 88.

IDEA, I. (2003). *Reconciliation after Violent Conflict: Policy Summary.* Stockholm, International Institute for Democracy and Electoral Assistance: 29.

IOM (2001). *Needs Assessment.* Kampala, IOM and UNICEF.

ISIS-WICCE (2000). Women's Experiences of Armed Conflict in Uganda, Gulu District 1986–1999, Part 1. Kampala, ISIS-WICCE.

Jabri, V. (1996). *Discourses on Violence: Conflict Analysis Reconsidered.* Manchester and New York, Manchester University Press.

Jackson, T. (1998). *Assessment Report for USAID.* E. Masters. Kampala, Northern Uganda Emergency Reconstruction Program, USAID.

Jefferys, A. (2002). Giving Voice to Silent Emergencies. ODI: 5.

Jones, A. (2004). *Genocide, War Crimes and the West.* London, Zed Books Ltd.

Kaiser, T. (1999). Experiences and Consequences of Insecurity in a Refugee Populated Area in Northern Uganda. Oxford, Institute of Social and Cultural Anthropology.

Kaldor, M. (2001). New and Old Wars: Organized Violence in a Global Era. Cambridge, Polity Press.

Kaplan, R. D. (1994). 'The Coming Anarchy: How Scarcity, Crime, Overpopulation and

Disease Are Rapidly Destroying the Social Fabric of Our Planet.' *Atlantic Monthly:* 44–76.

Kapuscinski, R. (1998). *The Soccer War.* London, Granta Books.

Keegan, J. (1998). War and Our World: The Reith Lectures 1998. London, Hutchison.

———. (1994). The Benefits of Famine: A Political Economy of Famine and Relief in South-western Sudan, 1983–1989. Princeton, Princeton University Press.

Keen, D. (2000). 'Incentives and Disincentives for Violence', in M. Berdal and D. Malone (eds), *Greed versus Grievance.* Boulder, Lynne Rienner: 19–41.

———. (2005). Conflict and Collusion in Sierra Leone. Oxford, James Currey.

Keen, D. and J. Ryle (1996). 'The Fate of Information in the Disaster Zone.' *Disasters* 20(3): 169–172.

Kelly, C. H. H. (1913). *Sudan-Uganda Boundary Rectification,* Sudan Archive, University of Durham.

Kelman, H. C. (1992). 'Informal Mediation by the Scholar/Practitioner', J. Bercovitch and J. Rubin (eds), in *Mediation in International Relations.* Macmillan: 65–95.

———. (1995). 'The Social Context of Torture: Policy Process and Authority Structure', in R. D. Crelinsten and A. P. Schmid (eds), *The Politics of Pain: Torturers and Their Masters.* Boulder, Westview Press: 19–34.

Khadiagala, G. M. (2001). The Role of the Acholi Religious Leaders Peace Initiative (ARLPI) in Peace Building in Northern Uganda. Washington, USAID/MSI: 24.

Kottak, E. C. C. (1996). 'Linkages, Methodologies for the Study of Socio-cultural Transformations' in E. F. Moran (ed.), *Transforming Societies, Transforming Anthropology.* Ann Arbor, University of Michigan Press: 103–134.

Lake, D. A. and D. Rothchild (1996). 'Containing Fear: The Origins and Management of Ethnic Conflict.' *International Security* 21(2): 41–75.

Lan, D. (1985). *Guns and Rain.* Harare, Zimbabwe Publishing House (Pvt) Ltd.

Large, J. (1997). 'Disintegration Conflicts and the Restructuring of Masculinity.' *Gender and Development* 5(2).

Levi, P. (1989). Sommersi e Salvati (The Drowned and the Saved). London, Abacus.

Liu (2002). *A Call for Action in Northern Uganda.* Vancouver, Liu Institute for Global Issues, University of British Columbia: 8.

LRM (1998). 'The Strength for Peace: Building for the Future.' London, *Lord's Resistance Movement:* 29.

LRM/A (1998). 'Uganda: 'A Nation Under Siege' – Response to the Amnesty International and Robert Gersony Reports.' *Lord's Resistance Movement/Army:* 35.

Luttwak, E. N. (1999). 'Give War a Chance.' *Foreign Affairs* 78(4).

Mamdani, M. (1988). 'Uganda in Transition.' *Third World Quarterly* 10(3): 1155–81.

———. (1997). 'From Truth to Transformation: The Truth and Reconciliation Commission in South Africa' in C. Leys and M. Mamdani (eds), *Crisis and Reconstruction: African Perspectives.* Uppsala, Nordisk Afrikainstitutet: 17–25.

———. (1997). 'From Justice to Reconciliation: Making Sense of the African Experience', in C. Leys and M. Mamdani (eds), *Crisis and Reconstruction: African Perspectives.* Uppsala, Nordisk Afrikainstitutet: 17–26.

Melamed, B. G., J. L. Melamed, et al. (1990). 'Psychological Consequences of Torture: A Need to Formulate New Strategies for Research', in P. Suedfeld (ed.), *Psychology and Torture.* New York, Hemisphere Publishing Corporation: 13-30.

Mendes, A.M. d. R. (1998). Nutritional Survey: Children Under 5 Years Old and Female Adults Living in Displaced Camps in Gulu District, Uganda. ACF-USA Uganda.

Middleton, J. (1970). The Study of the Lugbara: Expectation and Paradox in Anthropological Research. New York, Holt, Rinehart and Winston.

Millwood, D. (1996). *The International Response to Conflict and Genocide: Lessons from the Rwanda Experience*. Synthesis Report, Steering Committee of the Joint Evaluation of Emergency Assistance to Rwanda.

Minear, L., C. Scott and T. Weiss (1996). *The News Media, Civil War and Humanitarian Action*. London, Lynne Rienner Publishers.

Mitchell, C. (1981). *The Structure of International Conflict*. London, MacMillan Press Ltd.

Moorehead, A. (1973). *The White Nile*. Harmondsworth, Penguin Books Ltd.

Murru, M. (1998). 'Uganda: Between a Tragic Past and an Uncertain Future.' International Edition of *Cuamm Notizie*, Supplement to n.2/98: 4–12.

Museveni, Y. K. (1970). 'Fanon's Theory on Violence: Its Verification in Liberated Mozambique.' in N. M. N. Shamuyarera (ed.), *Essays on Liberation of Southern Africa*.

Museveni, Y. K. (1997). Sowing the Mustard Seed: The Struggle for Freedom and Democracy in Uganda. London, MacMillan.

Mutibwa, P. (1992). Uganda Since Independence: A Story of Unfulfilled Hopes. London, Hurst and Company.

Mwenda, A. (1996 August 26–28). 'Pulkol Draws Lessons from Karamoja, Calls for Talks with Acholi Folk on War.' *The Monitor*. Kampala: 1.

Nader, L. (1992). Coercive Harmony – The Political Economy of Legal Models, University of California Press.

Nagele, D. S. (2000). Dr Matthew Lukwiya; An Advent Reflection. *Africa (St Patrick's Mission)*: 14–15.

Nevins, J. (2003). 'Restitution Over Coffee: Truth, Reconciliation, and Environmental Violence in East Timor.' *Political Geography* (22): 677–701.

Ninh, B. (1994). *The Sorrow of War*. London, Minerva Paperbacks.

Nyekorach-Matsanga, D. R. (1998). '"Origin and Objectives" – Presentation of Its Case to International Community in London 27 June 1998', *Lord's Resistance Movement/Army*: 21.

O'Brien, N. (1998). The Fragmented Pearl: An Exploration of Conflict as Process – Why Is War in Uganda Not a Complex Political Emergency? London, ACORD.

O'Kadameri, B. (2002). 'LRA/Government Negotiations 1993–94.' *ACORD: An International Review of Peace Initiatives* 1(11): 34–41.

OCHA (2002). Affected Populations in the Great Lakes Region. OCHA.

Ocheng, D. O. (1955). 'Land Tenure in Acholi.' *Uganda Journal* 19(1): 57–61.

Odong, M. (2003). 'From the Desk of Msgr. Matthew Odong – Rector.' *News from Sacred Heart Seminary Archdiocese of Gulu, Uganda* 1(13): 4.

Ogot, B. A. (1961). 'The Concept of Jok.' *African Studies* 20(2): 123–130.

OHCHR (2001). Statement of The High Commissioner for Human Rights Pursuant to Resolution 2000/60, on the Abduction of Children from Northern Uganda (Internet).

Okeny, K. (Undated). *Royal Drums and State Formation in Acholi, C. 1679–1802: A Reconsideration*. Department of History. Nairobi, University of Nairobi.

Oranje, J. (2001). Uganda en Conflict. Concept Verslag van het gesprek van het desk-overleg met genodigden. Den Haag.

p'Bitek, O. (1971). *Religion of the Central Luo*. Nairobi, East African Literature Bureau.

———. (1985). *Song of Lawino, Song of Ocol*. London, Heineman Educational Books Ltd.

Papadopoulous, R. K. (2002). *Therapeutic Care for Refugees: No Place Like Home.* London, New York, Karnac.

Parkhurst, J. O. (2002). 'The Uganda Success Story? Evidence and Claims of HIV-1 Prevention.' *The Lancet* 360: 78–80.

Prunier, G. (1995). The Rwanda Crisis, 1959–1994: History of a Genocide. London, Hurst and Company.

Ramsbotham, O. and T. Woodhouse (1996). *Humanitarian Intervention in Contemporary Conflict: A Reconceptualization.* Cambridge UK, Cambridge MA, Polity Press.

Richards, P. (1996). Fighting for the Rainforest: War, Youth and Resources in Sierra Leone. Oxford, James Currey.

———. (2005). No Peace, No War: An Anthropology of Contemporary Armed Conflict. Oxford, James Currey.

Schaffer, B. (1984). 'Towards Responsibility: Public Policy in Concept and Practice', in C. Schaffer (ed.), *Room for Manoeuvre*, 142–190.

Seaton, T. A. J. (1999). The Media of Conflict: War Reporting and Representations of Ethnic Violence. London, Zed Books.

Staub, E. (1990). 'The Psychology and Culture of Torture and Torturers.' in P. Suedfeld (ed.), *Psychology and Torture*. New York, Hemisphere Publishing Corporation: 49–73.

———. (1995). 'Torture: Psychological and Cultural Origins', in R. D. Crelinsten and A. P. Schmid (eds), *The Politics of Pain*. Boulder, Westview Press: 99–111.

Stewart, F. (2002). 'Horizontal Inequalities as a Source of Conflict', in F. O. Hampson and D. Malone (eds), *From Reaction to Conflict Prevention: Opportunities for the UN System*. Lynne Rienner: 104–136.

Suedfeld, P. (ed.) (1990). *Psychology and Torture: Clinical and Community Psychology.* New York, Hemisphere Publishing Corporation.

Summerfield, D. (1990). 'The Psycho-Social Effects of Conflict in the Third World.' *Development in Practice* 1(3): 159–73.

Temmerman, E. D. (2001). *Aboke Girls: Children Abducted in Northern Uganda.* Kampala, Fountain Publishers.

The Sphere Project (2004). The Sphere Project: Humanitarian Charter and Minimum Standards in Disaster Response. Geneva, The Sphere Project: 3–344

Turton, D. (1997). 'Introduction: War and Ethnicity', in D. Turton (ed.), *War and Ethnicity: Global Connections and Local Violence*. New York, University of Rochester Press: 1–45.

UN (2001). Report of the Panel of Experts on the Illegal Exploitation of Natural Resources and Other Forms of Wealth of the Democratic Republic of the Congo. UN Security Council.

UNAIDS/WHO (2000). Epidemiological Fact Sheet on HIV/AIDS and Sexually Transmitted Infections: Uganda. Geneva: 12.

UNICEF (2001). Abductions in Northern and South-western Uganda 1986–2001: Result of the Update and Verification Exercise. Kampala, UNICEF: 8.

UNOCHA (2001). Uganda Case Study: Conference on Internally Displaced Persons: Lessons Learned and Future Mechanisms. Oslo, UNOCHA: 14.

———. (2004). 'When the Sun Sets We Start To Worry' – An Account of Life in Northern Uganda. Nairobi, UNOCHA/IRIN.

USDS (2002). *Patterns of Global Terrorism, 2001.* Washington, United States Department of State: 204.

Voutira, E. (1995). Conflict Resolution: A Review of Some Non-Governmental Practices – 'A Cautionary Tale. Uppsala, Nordiska Afrikainstitutet.

————. (1998). 'The Language of Complex Humanitarian Emergencies and the Idioms of Intervention', in S. F. Nafziger W, and R. Vaeyrynen (eds), *War, Hunger and Displacement: The Origins of Humanitarian Emergencies*. Oxford, Oxford University Press.

De Waal, A. (1997). Famine Crimes: Politics and the Disaster Relief Industry in Africa. Oxford, James Currey.

Weeks, W. (2002). Pushing the Envelope: Moving Beyond 'Protected Villages' in Northern Uganda. New York, UNOCHA: 49.

Weiss, T. and C. Collins (1996). Humanitarian Challenges and Interventions: World Politics and the Dilemmas of Help. London, Westview Press.

Westbrook, D. (2000). 'The Torment of Northern Uganda: A Legacy of Missed Opportunities.' *The Online Journal of Peace and Conflict Resolution* (3.2): 15.

WFP (1999). WFP Assistance to Internally Displaced Persons: Country Case Study of Internal Displacement. Uganda: Displacement in the Northern and Western Districts. Rome, World Food Programme: 42.

————. (2002). WFP Operations in Gulu District, Northern Uganda. Kampala, World Food Programme.

Williams, G., C. A. Obonyo, et al. (2001). Resilience in Conflict: A Community-based Approach to Psycho-Social Support in Northern Uganda. Kampala, AVSI/UNICEF: 68.

Wright, A. C. A. (1940). 'The Supreme Being among the Acholi of Uganda – Another Viewpoint.' *Uganda Journal* 7: 130–137.

Wrong, M. (2001). *In the Footsteps of Mr Kurtz*. London, Fourth Estate, Harper Collins Publishers.

Zur, J. (1993). 'The Psycho-Social Effects of "La Violencia" on Widows of El-Quiche, Guatemala.' *Focus on Gender* 1(2): 27–30.

————. (1998). Violent Memories: Mayan War Widows in Guatemala. Boulder, Westview Press.

INDEX

www.ingramcontent.com/pod-product-compliance
Lightning Source LLC
Chambersburg PA
CBHW072048020426
42334CB00017B/1432